MOON

W9-BZP-818

ROUTE 66

Road Trip

CANDACY TAYLOR

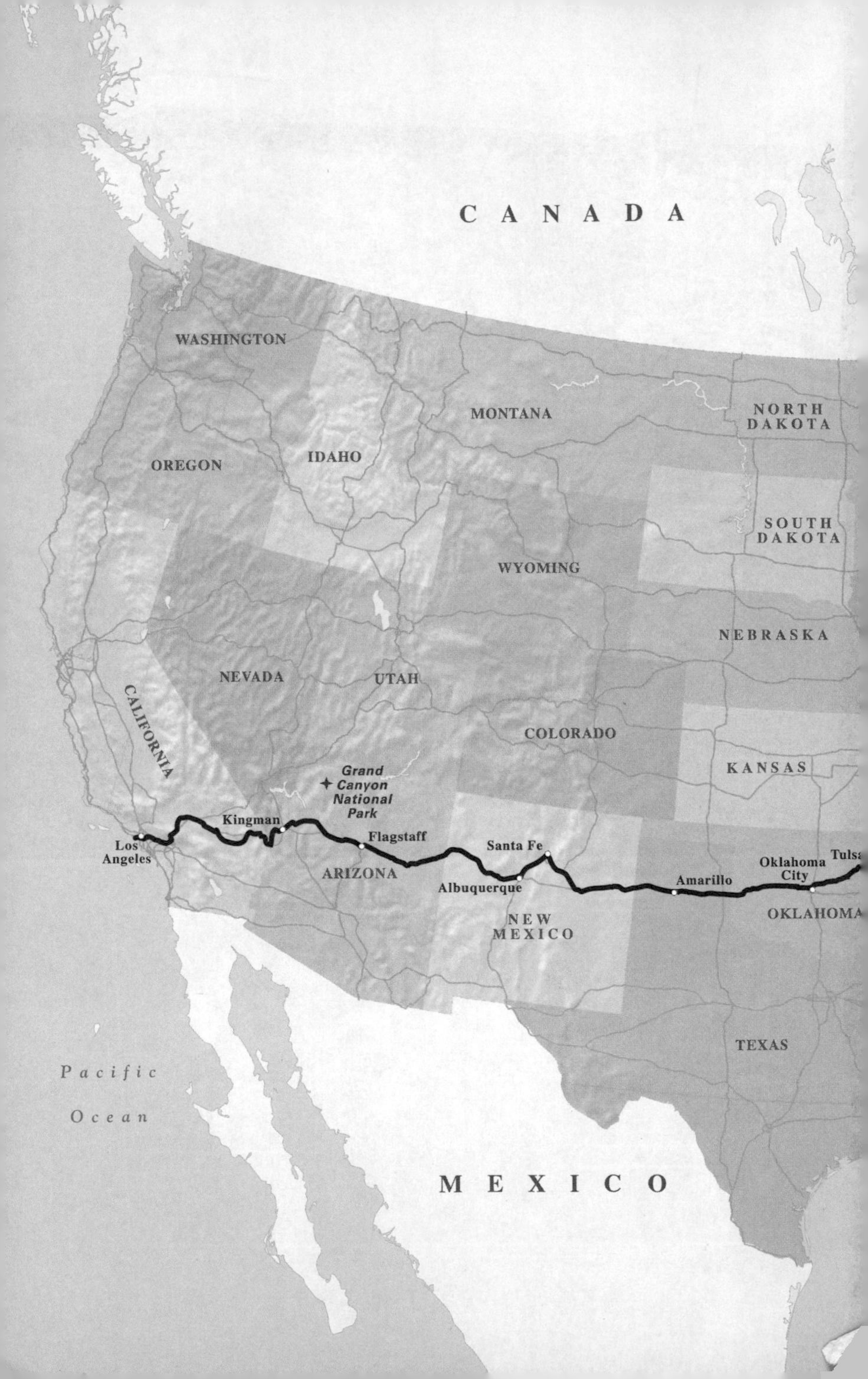
CANADA
WASHINGTON
MONTANA
NORTH DAKOTA
OREGON
IDAHO
SOUTH DAKOTA
WYOMING
NEBRASKA
NEVADA
UTAH
CALIFORNIA
COLORADO
KANSAS
Grand Canyon National Park
Kingman
Los Angeles
Flagstaff
Santa Fe
ARIZONA
Albuquerque
Amarillo
Oklahoma City
Tulsa
OKLAHOMA
NEW MEXICO
TEXAS
Pacific Ocean
MEXICO

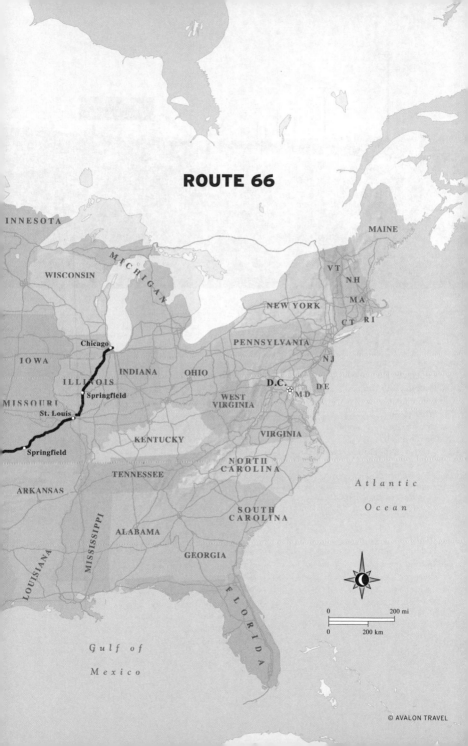

CONTENTS

DISCOVER
Route 66

Route 66 is the quintessential road trip—an artery stretching more than 2,400 miles, connecting urban and rural communities from Chicago, Illinois to Los Angeles, California.

During its heyday, gas stations, motor courts, and diners dished out hospitality to thousands, from Great Depression and Dust Bowl escapees to postwar suburbanites in Airstream trailers. Though much of the myth surrounding Route 66 has been an ideation of the past, underneath this nostalgia the Mother Road's asphalt curves have been shaped by progress, gender, and race. Carved within the grooves of this fabled highway is a troubled social history lined with abandoned buildings, dusty trailer parks, and rusted oil refineries that bear witness to the legacy of the Interstate as it bypassed towns and people. Threaded throughout are the stories of the earlier times of the route—of the Trail of Tears and of the Green Book properties during the Jim Crow era.

These bumps, bruises, and battle scars shape the Mother Road's cycle of triumph, redemption, and survival. Laid out around every bend of this beloved and timeworn trip are sights and experiences that speak to the spirit and stamina of Route 66. Historic Harvey Houses still service road-weary travelers, diners that have been run by the same family for generations open their doors, and art deco buildings sit restored to their vintage shine. This layered patina of roadside history retains the tenor of a bygone era—it's visible on paint-chipped signs, weather-beaten barn-side advertisements, and cracked neon bulbs. As Leonard Cohen sings "There's a crack in everything, that's how the light gets in."

Crack open the pages, hit the road, and let the light in. You'll rediscover America like never before.

PLANNING YOUR TRIP

Where to Go

Route 66 crosses eight states and three time zones. Some of its best-preserved sections include the stretch between Springfield, Missouri and Tulsa, Oklahoma; the road west of Seligman, Arizona; and the Oatman Highway through the Black Hills of Arizona.

Illinois
Chicago: Where it all begins. The Mother Road starts in the Windy City and stretches through Illinois to St. Louis, Missouri. Though much of the route has been replaced by I-55, there's still plenty of two-lane blacktop left to explore. Starting in Chicago, Route 66 heads southwest to **Pontiac.** Visit the **Route 66 Hall of Fame** and stretch your legs over the historic **Swinging Foot Bridges.** In **Springfield** you'll learn about the **1908 Race Riots,** and in **Staunton** stop to pet some furry friends at **Henry's Rabbit Ranch.**

Missouri and Kansas
In **Missouri,** the Mother Road enters Ozark country passing through lush rolling hills, quaint historic towns, and pristine farmland. This leg of the trip starts in St. Louis, where you'll walk across the **Chain of Rocks Bridge,** play in the artistic wonderland of **City Museum,** and treat yourself to frozen custard at **Ted Drewes.** Cross another signature bridge in **Devils Elbow,** visit landmarks from the **Trail of Tears** in **Waynesville,** and spend a day in **Springfield,** the official birthplace of the Mother Road.

Route 66 only covers 13 miles through **Kansas,** but there are several places worth a stop, like **Cars on the Route** in **Galena**

for souvenirs and **Angel's on the Route** in **Baxter Springs.**

Oklahoma
Oklahoma has more drivable miles of Route 66 than any other state. You'll cross some of the **earliest roadbeds** and one of the **longest bridges** on the Mother Road. Start in **Catoosa** with a visit to the iconic **Blue Whale** then stop for a soda at **Pop's** in **Arcadia,** where you'll choose from more than 600 varieties. Head to **Tulsa** and explore the stunning **Art Deco downtown.** Learn about the Tulsa Race Riots at the **Greenwood Cultural Center** and the devastating Dust Bowl at the **Woody Guthrie Center.**

Texas
Route 66 bisects the Texas panhandle, running parallel to I-40. The drive offers that middle-of-nowhere feeling with rusting grain silos and abandoned motor courts. Don't miss **Shamrock**'s **Tower Station and U-Drop Inn,** a Depression-era Art Deco marvel. Stop in **McLean,** a ghost town preserved in time, and head west to **Amarillo** with a quick detour to the **Cadillac Ranch,** where 10 tail-finned Cadillacs sit buried-nose deep in a Texas wheat field. The **MidPoint Café** in **Adrian** marks the halfway point of this road trip.

New Mexico
After entering the state near **Tucumcari,** we'll follow the **pre-1937 alignment** and leave I-40 behind. Head north to **Santa Fe,** stopping to enjoy some of the best chile at **Tia Sophia's.** Route 66 then dips south to **Albuquerque,** home of the opulent Pueblo Deco **KiMo Theatre.** Learn about American Indian culture at the **Acoma Pueblo** and then head west to the **El Rancho Hotel** in **Gallup.**

Arizona
Parts of the original Route 66 are not passible in the east side of the state, making I-40 the most practical driving option.

clockwise from top left: Fair Oaks Pharmacy, Pasadena; burros, Oatman; Mojave ruins

Lunch at **Joe & Aggie's** in **Holbrook** and then spend an afternoon browsing downtown **Williams.** The best overnight option on Route 66 is **La Posada Harvey House** in **Winslow.** After reaching the iconic **Delgadillo's Snow Cap Drive-In** in **Seligman,** Route 66 opens up to 159 miles of a pristine two-lane black top all the way to **Kingman.** Brave the hairpin curves through the Black Mountains on the way to the mining town of **Oatman.**

California

California here we come! On the home stretch, Route 66 passes by desert towns, an ancient volcano, and contorted Joshua Trees. After crossing the **Mojave,** stop in **Oro Grande** to gaze at the eclectic **Elmer's Bottle Tree Ranch** and order a Brian burger at **Emma Jean's Holland Burger** in **Victorville.** This stretch of the route includes *two* **Harvey Houses** plus the **Fair Oaks Pharmacy,** a 1915 soda fountain in **Pasadena.**

The suburban slab leads to the historic district in downtown **Los Angeles,** the original terminus of Route 66. But the *official* end of the Mother Road is actually in **Santa Monica** at the **Santa Monica Pier** overlooking the magnificent Pacific Ocean.

When to Go

The best time to attempt a Route 66 road trip is from **late spring to early summer** and in the **early fall.** The weather is usually temperate and roads are open, as are most Route 66 businesses.

Avoid travel during **August,** when the temperatures can reach more than 100 degrees in Texas, Arizona, New Mexico, and the California desert. Though it's a dry heat in those states, Illinois, Missouri, and Kansas can be oppressively muggy.

July through early September is the monsoon season in New Mexico, Arizona, and California. Every afternoon the sky opens up and pours rain—then just as quickly, the storm disappears. Some storms can be quite spectacular with thunder and lightning, but flash flooding can be deadly and some roads can become flooded and impassable. You may have to modify your schedule if you plan to hike or be outdoors.

Winter should be avoided altogether. This Route 66 road trip starts in Chicago, which is notorious for cold and brutal winters. Even the western leg of Route 66 is still subject to inclement weather. (Driving this trip in late October, I found Oklahoma windier and colder than Chicago.) From **November to March,** mountain passes through New Mexico and Arizona (near Flagstaff) may be closed due to snow and ice. Many Route 66 businesses close for the season from **October to April.**

Driving Tips

When Route 66 began in 1926, it was one of the few highways that cut diagonally across the country. Today, approximately 15 percent of Route 66 is completely gone. It is no longer possible to follow the route uninterrupted from Chicago to Los Angeles. Since its inception, Route 66 has also been realigned at least three times. Some re-alignments were major, such as in New Mexico when the road changed direction, while others shifted the asphalt less than one-eighth of a mile.

This road trip outlines the best way to experience Route 66 today, with detailed navigation notes that generally follow the **pre-1930s alignment.** There will be times when freeway driving is unavoidable and other options explore later alignments that offer the best variety of sights and attractions. Regardless which alignment you take, avoid following "Historic Route 66" signs if they divert away from the suggested route. These can refer to older alignments that lead down rutted dirt paths, dead-ends, or disappointing detours.

HIT THE ROAD

14 Days on the Mother Road

This two-week itinerary hits the key highlights on the Mother Road and honors the places that have stood the test of time. However, things change quickly on Route 66, so consider prioritizing the mom-and-pop, off-the-wall places—every year more of them are forced to shut their doors due to lack of business. Approaching each major town or city, there are usually Route 66 alignments that bypass the most congested areas; since much of Route 66 was realigned along the interstate, it's easy to jump on the freeway to get to the next destination quicker. But there are many factors you can't control: road closures due to weather and construction, businesses that don't stick to their posted hours, and time to chat with locals and fellow tourists.

Day 1: Chicago
CHICAGO TO PONTIAC: 100 MILES
Day one starts in Chicago (see details and suggestions on page 26). Have lunch at **Lou Mitchell's**, then head to **Pontiac** to see the **Route 66 Hall of Fame** and walk over one or three of the swinging footbridges. Have dinner at the **Old Log Cabin Inn & Restaurant** and stay the **Three Roses B&B** in Pontiac.

Day 2: Illinois
PONTIAC TO ST. LOUIS: 200-225 MILES
Start the day early and drive southwest about 50 miles along Route 66 to **Funk's Grove** to pick up some "sirup." Have lunch at **Ariston's** in **Litchfield** about 1.5 hours away (102 miles). Head to **Staunton,** about 15 miles away, to say hello to **Rich Henry** and his loveable

rabbits. In another 20 miles, enjoy dinner at **Cleveland-Heath** in Edwardsville. From there it's only 23 miles to St. Louis. Check into the **Magnolia Hotel** for the night.

Day 3: Missouri
ST. LOUIS TO SPRINGFIELD: 215 MILES
Have breakfast (or dinner) at the all-night **Eat Rite Diner** in **St. Louis.** Spend a couple of hours exploring **Union Station** or the **City Museum**. In the afternoon, drive about 80 miles to **Cuba**, check out the murals, the **Wagon Wheel Motel** and the **World's Largest Rocking Chair.** Head to **Springfield,** the birthplace of Route 66, spend the night at Springfield's, **Best Western Route 66 Rail Haven** (call ahead to book the Elvis Suite).

Day 4: Missouri
SPRINGFIELD THROUGH KANSAS TO TULSA: 180 MILES
Start the day with red-velvet pancakes at **Gailey's Breakfast Café** before driving about 75 miles to the Missouri state line at **Joplin.** Continue for a brief 13-mile jaunt through **Kansas** before checking out **Cars on the Route** in **Galena** and having a quick bite at **Angels on the Route** in **Baxter Springs.** From there you cross into Oklahoma, home to some of the best Route 66 attractions. The **Coleman Theater** in **Miami** is 10 miles from the Oklahoma border. Plan to drive the **"Sidewalk Highway"** between Miami and **Afton.** This 3-mile, 9-foot wide stretch of 1922 roadbed actually pre-dates Route 66. From Afton, it's 40 miles to see the **Andy Payne statue** in **Foyil** and then another 30 miles to **Tulsa,** where you'll spend the night at **The Mayo** or **The Campbell.**

Day 5: OKLAHOMA
TULSA TO OKLAHOMA CITY: 100 MILES
Have breakfast at **Maxxwells,** before visiting the **Greenwood Cultural Center** and **John Hope Franklin Reconciliation Park,** where you'll learn the history of one of the worst race riots in U.S. history.

The Green Book

During Route 66's peak, the segregated south was notorious for shutting blacks out, but it was even more challenging for blacks to travel in the Western United States. Forty-four out of 89 counties along Route 66 were "Sundown Towns," all-white communities with signs posted at the county line warning blacks to be out of town before sundown. While most black travelers aimed to stay in larger towns, options were still limited.

The Negro Motorist Green Book was a travel guide published in 1936-1966 to help black people navigate the Jim Crow era. Victor H. Green, a black postal worker from Harlem created the book, which featured restaurants, hotels, barbershops, beauty parlors, taverns, garages, and gas stations that were willing to serve blacks. Below are some of the key businesses that were listed in black traveler guides during the Jim Crow era on Route 66.

* **Warren Hotel,** Tulsa, OK (page 140)

* **The DuBeau,** Flagstaff, AZ (page 251)

1956 edition of the Green Book

* **DeAnza Motor Lodge,** Albuquerque, NM (page 217)

* **Clifton's,** Los Angeles, CA (page 323)

For more information and a short video about the Green Book, visit www.taylor-madeculture.com.

Afterwards, head west for 106 miles to Oklahoma City and stop at **Pops,** a neo-modern gas station and soda nirvana. In Oklahoma City, check out the **Gold Dome Building** inspired by Buckminster Fuller's design and spend the night at **Skirvin Hilton Hotel** or the **Aloft.** Relax with a blood-orange margarita at the **Iguana Mexican Grill** then prepare your arteries for onslaught at **Ann's Chicken Fry Steakhouse.**

Day 6: Oklahoma
OKLAHOMA CITY TO
AMARILLO: 250-300 MILES
Head out early and check out the **Pony Bridge** and drive about 115 miles to the Texas state line. The beautifully restored **Tower Station and U-Drop Inn Cafe** in **Shamrock** should be your first stop.

Drive about 20 miles to **McLean** and tour the **Devil's Rope Museum.** Have lunch at the **Red River Steakhouse.** Head 70 miles to **Amarillo** and stay overnight at the **Courtyard Marriott** downtown. Have dinner at the **Golden Light Cantina.**

Day 7: Texas
AMARILLO TO TUCUMCARI: 115 MILES
The next morning, have breakfast at the **Stockyard Café** and tour **Amarillo's historic district.** Don't miss **Cadillac Ranch,** about 6 miles west as you leave **Amarillo.** Drive about 40 miles and stop at the **MidPoint Café** for a photo op, marking the halfway point on Route 66. Cross the state border in 22 miles as you enter **New Mexico.** Drive 40 miles to **Tucumcari** and tour the **murals.** Stay

The Women of 66

Many women contributed greatly to the story and success of Route 66. Following are some women who have (or should) become icons of the Mother Road.

* Hazel Funk, **Funk's Pure Maple Sirup**, Funks Grove, IL (page 56)

* Sharon Hanson, **Three Roses Bed & Breakfast,** Pontiac, IL (page 53)

* Molly Schuyler, **Big Texan Steak Ranch,** Amarillo, TX (page 183)

* Lucille Hamons, **Lucille's Service Station,** Hydro, OK (page 163)

* Zelta Davis, **Blue Whale,** Catoosa, OK (page 137)

* Dawn Welch, **Rock Cafe,** Stroud, OK (page 149)

* Annabelle Russell, **Sandhills Curiosity Shop,** Erick, OK (page 170)

* Lillian Redman, **Blue Swallow Motel,** Tucumcari, NM (page 196)

Madonna of the Trail in Upland

* Mary Colter, **La Fonda,** Santa Fe, NM and **La Posada,** Winslow, AZ (pages 204 and 242)

* Olive Oatman, **Oatman,** AZ (page 281)

* **Madonna of the Trail,** Albuquerque, NM and Upland, CA (page 219)

the night in the iconic **Blue Swallow Motel.**

Day 8: New Mexico
TUCUMCARI TO SANTA FE: 120 MILES
The next day, eat breakfast at the **Comet II Drive-In** in **Santa Rosa,** which is about an hour away from Tucumcari. Take the pre-1937 alignment and drive 120 miles to **Santa Fe.** Tour the historic **La Fonda,** a former Harvey House and have lunch at **Santa Fe Bite.** After lunch, stroll the shops on **The Plaza,** and step way back into the past at the **Palace of the Governors,** the oldest public building in the U.S. Have dinner at **Tomasita's** and see a flamenco performance at **El Farol's** and call it a night at **Hotel Chimayo.**

Day 9: New Mexico
SIDE TRIP TO TAOS: 80 MILES
Have breakfast at **Tia Sophia's** and detour north on the High Road that winds through historic villages for 80 miles to Taos. On the way, have lunch at **Sugar Nymphs Bistro,** near **Peñasco.** Stop at the **Rio Grand Gorge Bridge** and then head to **Earthship Biotecture** to tour the world's largest off-the-grid community. Eat dinner at **La Cueva** and stay in an Earthship overnight; if they're full, spend the night at the **El Pueblo Lodge** in Taos.

Day 10: New Mexico
TAOS TO ALBUQUERQUE: 150 MILES
Drive 150 miles south to **Albuquerque** and have lunch at **Duran Central Pharmacy.** Tour **Old Town,** catch a

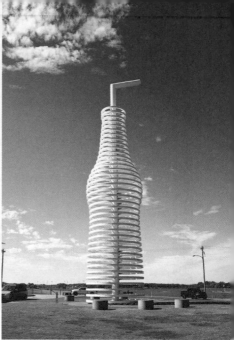

clockwise from top left: pre-1937 sign on Route 66, Santa Fe; Pops, Arcadia; Henry's Rabbit Ranch, Staunton.

Harvey Houses

Casa del Desierto Harvey House, Barstow

In the late 1800s, most people traveled west by rail, but there were few places to buy food. Enter Fred Harvey, who built a restaurant every 100 miles along the Santa Fe rail line. These Harvey Houses were the first chain restaurants in the U.S. Most Harvey Houses were built in train stations, and there are some stunning examples near and on Route 66 (the El Tovar at the Grand Canyon is not located on Route 66 and others are close to but not officially on Route 66).

+ **Station Grille,** St. Louis, MO (page 86)

+ **Santa Fe Depot and Hotel,** Amarillo, TX (page 183)

+ **La Fonda,** Santa Fe, NM (page 204)

+ **Gallup Cultural Center,** Gallup, NM (page 229)

+ **Painted Desert Inn,** Petrified Forest National Park, AZ (page 238)

+ **La Posada Hotel & Gardens,** Winslow, AZ (page 242)

+ **El Tovar,** Grand Canyon, AZ (page 257)

+ **Williams Depot,** Williams, AZ (page 268)

+ **El Garces Harvey House,** Needles, CA (page 292)

+ **Casa del Desierto Harvey House,** Barstow, CA (page 308)

movie at the historic **KiMo Theatre** and have dinner at the **Standard Diner.** Spend the night at the lovely **Los Poblanos Inn** or sleep in an Airstream trailer at **Enchanted Trails RV Park.**

Day 11: Arizona
ALBUQUERQUE TO WINSLOW: 270 MILES
This day, visit the **Acoma Pueblo,** about 70 miles west of Albuquerque. Stop in **Gallup** to shop the trading posts and see the historic **El Rancho Hotel** before crossing the border into Arizona. About 45 miles from the border, drive through the **Painted Desert** then stop for lunch in **Holbrook** at Joe & Aggie's **Café.** Spend the evening at **La Posada** in **Winslow,** about 30 miles west. For an upscale experience, dine at the **Turquoise Room;** for something more casual, but just as delicious, eat at the **E & O Kitchen.**

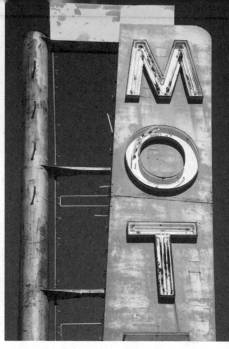

clockwise from top left: Roy's Motel and Café, Amboy, CA; Route 66 near Bagdad Café, Newberry Springs; Lucille's Gas Station, Hydro.

Vintage 66 Landmarks

Cadillac Ranch In Amarillo

Route 66 sights include everything from wacky roadside vernacular, such as Cadillac Ranch, to the ancient Palace of the Governors in Santa Fe.

* **Chicago Architecture Foundation Tour,** Chicago, IL (page 29)

* **Pullman District,** Forrestville, IL (page 32)

* **Frank Lloyd Wright Home and Studio,** Oak Park, IL (page 40)

* **Riverside Architectural District**, Riverside, IL (page 41)

* **Rialto Square Theater,** Joilet, IL (page 43)

* **Normal Theater,** Normal, IL (page 55)

* **Dana-Thomas House,** Springfield, IL (page 62)

* **Coleman Theater,** Miami, OK (page 131)

* **Hogue House,** Chelsea, OK (page 135)

* **Downtown Tulsa Art Deco**, Tulsa, OK (page 141)

* **Tower Station and U-Drop Inn Café**, Shamrock, TX (page 176)

* **Cadillac Ranch,** Amarillo, TX (page 184)

* **Vega Motel,** Vega, TX (page 185)

* **Odeon Theatre,** Tucumcari, NM (page 195)

* **The Palace of the Governors,** Santa Fe, NM (page 203)

* **KiMo Theatre,** Albuquerque, NM (page 219)

* **Tewa Motor Lodge,** Albuquerque, NM (page 219)

* **El Vado Auto Court Motel,** Albuquerque, NM (page 221)

* **Aztec Hotel,** Monrovia, CA (page 313)

Day 12: Arizona
WINSLOW TO KINGMAN: 200 MILES
Today, drive 60 miles toward **Flagstaff.** Tour the historic downtown, have breakfast at **Miz Zips;** if you're looking for something different, **Satchmos** is a good choice. Drive 30 miles to **Williams.** Spend an hour roaming through downtown and then head to **Seligman** for lunch at **Angel's Delgadillo's Snow Cap Drive-In**. Chat with locals and tourists and then set out to take the pristine two-lane drive to **Kingman,** passing through **Peach Springs** and **Hackberry.** Spend the night in **Kingman** at the **El Trovatore** or for more modern accommodations try the **Springhill Suites.**

Day 13: California
KINGMAN TO BARSTOW: 210 MILES
Leave Kingman driving the 1926 alignment via the **Oatman Highway,** a scenic winding road through the Black Mountains. But take your time—the road has hairpin turns, steep mountain grades, and 15-mph switchbacks. In Oatman, stop at the **General Store,** feed the town burros, and have lunch at the **Oatman Hotel & Restaurant,** where the walls are papered with more than 100,000 one-dollar bills. As you cross the border into **California,** gas up in **Needles** because you'll soon be driving through the Mojave Desert. From Needles, it's 140 miles west to Barstow. If you're up for a very cool side trip, drive about 60 miles south to the town of **Joshua Tree** (passing the iconic **Roy's Motel** in Amboy). Joshua Tree has beautiful accommodations, like **Joshua Tree Mountain Vista.**

Day 14: California
BARSTOW TO LOS ANGELES: 130 MILES
In Joshua Tree, have breakfast at **Crossroads Café** and take a driving tour of **Joshua Tree National Park** before hitting the road for the final stretch to Los Angeles. From **Barstow,** it's 75 miles to the **Fair Oaks Pharmacy** in **Pasadena,** a good place to have a vintage sweet treat or just browse the 1915 soda fountain.

Time your arrival into downtown LA before 3pm to avoid traffic. The **original Route 66 terminus** is at **7th and Broadway**. This historic downtown area is undergoing a revitalization, so there's a lot to see and do. Tour the galleries, grab a bite at the **Grand Central Market,** and stay at the **Ace Hotel** or **Hotel Figueroa.** If you head to **Santa Monica** and it's a weekday, try not leave downtown after 2pm; the 15-mile drive to Santa Monica can take 1.5 hours during rush hour. In Santa Monica, meet the end of the Mother Road at the edge of the glorious Pacific Ocean at the **Santa Monica Pier.**

Car Culture

Red's Old School Hydraulics in Albuquerque

The following Route 66 sights are dedicated to the age of the automobile, including museums, restored gas stations, racing tracks, and classic car storerooms. Many of the gas stations have been placed on the National Historic Registry.

- **Ogden Top and Trim,** Berwyn, IL (page 39)

- **Ambler's Texaco Gas Station,** Dwight, IL (page 48)

- **Pontiac Oakland Automobile Museum,** Pontiac, IL (page 53)

- **Sprague's Super Service Station and Café,** Normal, IL (page 55)

- **Soulsby Shell Service Station,** Mt. Olive, IL (page 67)

- **Route 66 Visitor Center**, Baxter Springs, KS (page 121)

- **Conoco Hole in the Wall,** Commerce, OK (page 130)

- **Vickery Phillips Station,** Tulsa, OK (page 143)

- **Chandler Phillips 66 Station,** Chandler, OK (page 151)

- **Magnolia Gas Station,** Vega, TX (page 177)

- **Route 66 Auto Museum,** Santa Rosa, NM (page 199)

- **Red's Old School Hydraulics,** Albuquerque, NM (page 221)

- **Budville Gas Station,** Budville, NM (page 227)

- **Roy's Garage,** Grants, NM (page 229)

- **Pete's Gas Station Museum,** Williams, AZ (page 268)

- **Petersen Automotive Museum,** Los Angeles, CA (page 318)

Evanston
Skokie
Oak Park
Berwyn   Chicag
eaton   Cicero   INDI

ILLINOIS

US

66

HISTORIC ROUTE
BEGINS

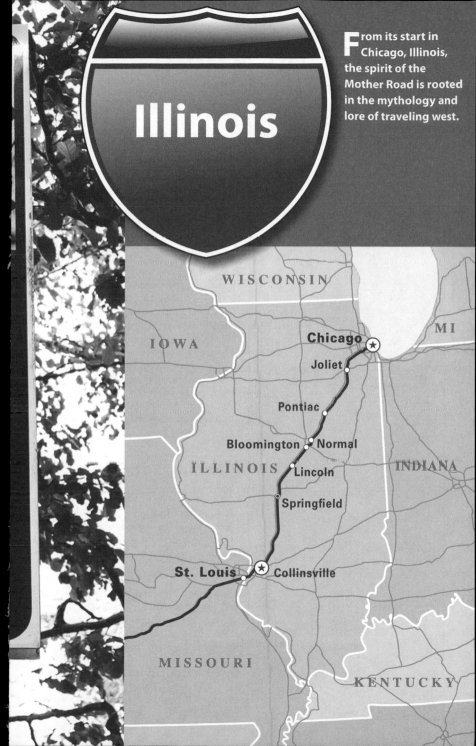

Illinois

From its start in Chicago, Illinois, the spirit of the Mother Road is rooted in the mythology and lore of traveling west.

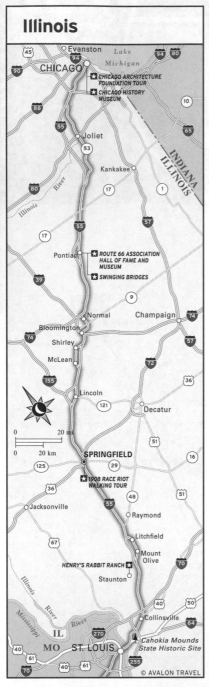

Illinois

Evanston · *Lake Michigan* · CHICAGO · 45 · 90 · 94 · 94 · 80 · 88 · CHICAGO ARCHITECTURE FOUNDATION TOUR · CHICAGO HISTORY MUSEUM · 10 · 55 · 65 · Joliet · 53 · Kankakee · 17 · 1 · 80 · *Illinois River* · 57 · 17 · 55 · Pontiac · ROUTE 66 ASSOCIATION HALL OF FAME AND MUSEUM · SWINGING BRIDGES · 39 · 9 · Normal · Champaign · 74 · Bloomington · 74 · Shirley · 57 · McLean · 72 · 155 · 36 · Lincoln · 121 · Decatur · 0 20 mi · 0 20 km · 51 · SPRINGFIELD · 16 · 125 · 29 · 1908 RACE RIOT WALKING TOUR · 36 · 48 · 51 · Jacksonville · 55 · Raymond · 67 · Litchfield · Mount Olive · 70 · HENRY'S RABBIT RANCH · Staunton · *Illinois River* · 40 · 50 · IL · *Mississippi River* · Collinsville · 64 · MO · ST. LOUIS · Cahokia Mounds State Historic Site · 270 · 255 · 40 · 61 · 61 · 70 · © AVALON TRAVEL · INDIANA / ILLINOIS

Chicago: Where it all begins. It was November 11, 1926 when the Mother Road was born here, and the Windy City marks the starting point of this epic road trip.

When first built, Route 66 originally followed Illinois Route 4, also called the Pontiac Trail, the first numbered highway in Illinois and the quickest path from Chicago to East St. Louis, Missouri. Today, Route 66 runs 300 miles through the urban, gritty metropolis of Chicago to the wide-open farming fields, factory towns, and coal-mining centers of Joliet, Wilmington, Braidwood, Dwight, Atlanta, Springfield, and Mt. Olive.

Much of Route 66 was replaced with I-55—in some instances, the freeway was built right on top of the Mother Road. For the purposes of this trip, a little freeway driving is unavoidable. Fortunately, there are still more than 200 miles of two-lane highways ahead.

Planning Your Time

Start your trip on Route 66 by spending the night in **Chicago.** Plan **two days** to travel diagonally across the state, driving 105 miles (3 hours) from Chicago to overnight in Pontiac. The second day, you'll cruise around 200 miles south past Litchfield and Staunton and across the border into Missouri, where you'll bed down in St. Louis. If you can swing it, four days will allow extra time to explore Chicago, Pontiac, and Atlanta before zooming across the state line.

Driving Considerations

Traffic may be a factor when leaving Chicago. If time is a concern, take I-55 instead. Plenty of gas stations and auto

above: the *Crown Fountain* in Millennium Park, designed by Jaume Plensa

Highlights

★ **Chicago Architecture Foundation Tour:** Choose from more than 85 tours where you can ride, walk, boat, or bike to view some of the most diverse and stunning architecture in the United States (page 29).

★ **Chicago History Museum:** This comprehensive museum exhibits more than 20 million photographs, drawings, letters, costumes, textiles, films, books, furniture, and music about the Windy City (page 31).

★ **Route 66 Association Hall of Fame and Museum, Pontiac:** One of the best Route 66 museums on the road (page 51).

★ **Swinging Bridges, Pontiac:** These late-19th and early-20th-century suspension bridges have carried a tremendous amount of history over the years (page 53).

★ **1908 Race Riot Walking Tour, Springfield:** Explore Springfield on foot and learn about the events that led to the founding of the NAACP in 1909 (page 62).

★ **Henry's Rabbit Ranch, Staunton:** Listen to Rich Henry tell stories about Route 66 and his adventures with his adorable four-legged friends (page 67).

services line the road until Joilet; gas up here before continuing on to Pontiac.

Chicago is infamous for brutal winters. The best time to travel this section of Route 66 is from **late spring to early fall.** If you must drive during winter, or happen to run into a blizzard, it's best to take the interstate over smaller roads since the larger thoroughfares are generally de-iced first.

Getting There

Starting Points
Car
The **1926 alignment** of Route 66 started at Jackson Boulevard and Michigan Avenue; then in 1933, the start of the route was moved a couple of blocks east to Jackson Boulevard and Lake Shore Drive. Leaving Chicago, head west on Ogden Avenue to join Joilet Road. Drive south on Highway 53 through Joilet, Wilmington, and Gardner. West of Gardner, Historic U.S. 66 branches off Highway 53 to head south alongside I-55 through Pontiac, Bloomington, Funks Grove, and Atlanta into Springfield. The 1926-1930 alignment (also Route 4), heads west of Springfield; however, our route follows the **post-1930s alignment** to head south from Springfield toward Litchfield and Mt. Olive. We rejoin the **pre-1930s alignment** in Staunton. From there, Highway 157 heads southwest through Edwardsville then enters the busy metropolis of St. Louis.

Car Rentals
Most car rental companies are located at **Chicago O'Hare Airport** (1,000 W O'Hare Ave., 800/832-6352, www.flychicago. com) and **Midway International Airport** (5700 Cicero Ave., 800/832-6352, www. flychicago.com). Midway has fewer rental companies, but is easier to navigate than O'Hare. At Midway, **Hertz** (5150 West 55th St., www.hertz.com, 773/735-7272, 6am-1:30am daily) and **National** (5150 West 55th St., www.nationalcar.com, 877/222-9058, 5am-1am daily) are good options.

At O'Hare, a rental car shuttle service is at the arrival curbside area (located on the lower level outside of baggage claim). O'Hare has 12 rental car companies including Ace, Advantage, Alamo, Avis, Budget, Dollar, Enterprise, Firefly, Hertz, National, Payless and Thrifty. **Enterprise** (847/928-3320, www.enterrpise.com, 5am-midnight daily) has good rates, but only serves deplaning airport customers; make sure you have your boarding pass. **Avis** (10000 Bessie Coleman Dr., 888/849-0277, www.avis.com) offers exclusive

Best Accommodations

★ **Kinzie Hotel, Chicago:** It's the perfect place to stay on your Route 66 road trip since "Chicago Starts Here" (page 34).

★ **Palmer House, Chicago:** Spend the night at the longest continually operating hotel in the United States (page 35).

★ **Acme Hotel, Chicago:** This hotel caters to Route 66 travelers with $0.66 treats and Spotify playlists for your road trip (page 34).

★ **Three Roses B&B, Pontiac:** One of the best B&B's on Route 66 also serves one of the best breakfasts (page 53).

★ **Colaw Rooming House, Atlanta:** This Victorian "rooming house" embraces the spirit of Route 66 (page 58).

deals for AARP members and has a signature class series with Maserati's, BMW's and Corvette Coupes. This road trip crosses eight states, so be sure to select a national rental company in case you need roadside assistance.

To reach downtown Chicago from O'Hare, take I-190, which turns into I-90 and goes directly into downtown. From Midway Airport, drive north on Cicero Avenue to I-55 north.

Air

Chicago O'Hare Airport (ORD, 1,000 W. O'Hare Ave., 800/832-6352, www.flychicago.com) is one of the world's busiest airports, with more than 880,000 flights annually. **Chicago Midway International Airport** (MDW, 5700 Cicero Ave., 800/832-6352, www.flychicago.com) is a medium-size airport about eight miles from Chicago's downtown Loop, served by Delta and Southwest Airlines.

Airport Transportation

Since it's difficult and expensive to park downtown (hotels charge $40-85 per night), if you're staying for more than one night, you might want to take a taxi or public transportation from the airport to your hotel and use public transit and cabs for sightseeing in Chicago. When you're ready to hit the road, you can rent a car downtown.

To reach downtown Chicago from O'Hare Airport, take the **L,** Chicago's elevated train system; the Blue Line to downtown takes about 45 minutes. Trains depart from the airport at Terminal 3 (Jet Blue, Virgin, American, and international airlines), which is accessible via the pedestrian tunnels at Terminal 1 (United and Lufthansa) and Terminal 2 (Delta and Air Canada). From Terminal 5 (international airlines), take the ATS (Airport Transit System) to Terminal 3 and follow the signs.

To reach downtown from Midway Airport on the L, take the Orange Line, which arrives downtown in about 25 minutes. As you exit the airport, follow the "Trains to City" signs.

A **taxi** from O'Hare Airport to downtown can take 25-75 minutes, depending on traffic, and costs about $40. A taxi from Midway Airport to downtown can take 15-40 minutes for about $25.

Train and Bus

Union Station (210 S. Canal St., 800/872-7245, www.amtrak.com, 5am-1am daily) is the third-busiest rail station in the United States and operates as a major hub for Amtrak, with service around the country. The *Texas Eagle* follows Route 66 in Illinois passing through Joliet, Pontiac, Bloomington, Lincoln, Springfield, and St. Louis.

Best Restaurants

★ **Lou Mitchell's, Chicago:** This time honored whistle-stop has been a Chicago institution for more than 90 years (page 35).

★ **Green Door Tavern, Chicago:** The Windy City's oldest tavern is a must-stop (page 35).

★ **Dell Rhea's Chicken Basket, Willowbrook:** Since 1938, Dell Rhea's has been serving crispy fried chicken to hungry Route 66 travelers (page 42).

★ **Palms Grill Cafe, Atlanta:** Dining here is a step back in time to 1934 (page 58).

★ **Ariston Cafe, Litchfield:** It's one of the longest operating restaurants on Route 66 (page 65).

★ **Cleveland-Heath, Edwardsville:** This handsome restaurant in a historic building serves gourmet comfort food (page 69).

One Day in Chicago

Have an early breakfast at **Lou Mitchell's,** and if the weather permits, take an **Architecture Foundation Tour** or walk through **Grant Park.** If it's so cold it hurts to breathe, which happens in Chicago, spend the day inside at the **Chicago History Museum** or the **Art Institute of Chicago.** Have lunch at **The Billy Goat Tavern,** then check out the **Money Museum,** gaze at the beautiful lobby at the **Palmer House,** and then pick up snacks for the road at **Garrett's Popcorn.** For dinner, have some deep-dish pizza at **The Exchequer,** and if you're up for a night out, go hear some classic Chicago blues at the **Green Mill.**

The Chicago **Greyhound Bus Station** (630 W. Harrison St., 800/231-2222 or 312/408-5821, www.greyhound.com) is a few blocks south of Union Station and offers service to all major U.S. cities.

The **Chicago Transit Authority** (CTA, 800/968-7282, www.transitchicago.com) operates the local subway system, or elevated **L train** ($2.25 adults) with bus and train service to 35 suburbs. Most buses ($2 adults) arrive every 10-20 minutes. An owl symbol indicates all-night service; these buses run every 30 minutes. Subway train lines run every 10-15 minutes and are color-coded; most trains run daily, except the Purple Line, an express train to downtown.

Chicago

Chicago has everything you'd expect in a great American city—soaring skyscrapers, the best museums, turn-of-the-20th-century subway platforms with trains that rumble overhead, the sweet scent of deep-dish pizza and steamed hot dogs dressed to the nines.

When Route 66 started in 1926, Chicago was considered the City of Industry; it was the birthplace of the Spiegel, Montgomery Ward, and Sears and Roebuck mail-order catalogs. Business was booming—but just a few years later, when the stock market crashed in 1929, the huge workforce that relied on the manufacturing industry took a devastating hit. Chicago was one of the hardest hit cities in the country. By 1933, the unemployment rate for manufacturing workers, African Americans, and Latinos skyrocketed to 50 percent. Just six years after the start of Route 66, Chicago couldn't afford to meet its payroll, and the emergency relief funds were gone.

It was a dark time in the Windy City, and regardless of race or privilege, no one escaped poverty. In Studs Terkel's *Hard Times,* Louis Banks said, "I'd see 'em floatin' on the river where they would commit suicide because they didn't have anything. They'd steal and kill each other for fifty cents. Black and white, it didn't make any difference because everyone was poor." People stood in breadlines that wrapped around churches and watched as protesters demanded government intervention. By 1940, one-third of the workers in the manufacturing industry had unionized. When President Roosevelt's New Deal funds came through, Lake Shore Drive, the starting point of Route 66, was built as part of a work relief program. Works Progress Administration (WPA) workers earned $27.50 a month for digging a ditch, which was great money at the time. Although much of Route 66 in Illinois was paved in 1926, the New Deal put thousands to work building, improving, and maintaining roads. The entire length of Route 66 was paved by 1938.

Today, Chicago is home to more than 70 diverse neighborhoods. Bronzeville is a historic African American neighborhood with pubic art and

Downtown Chicago

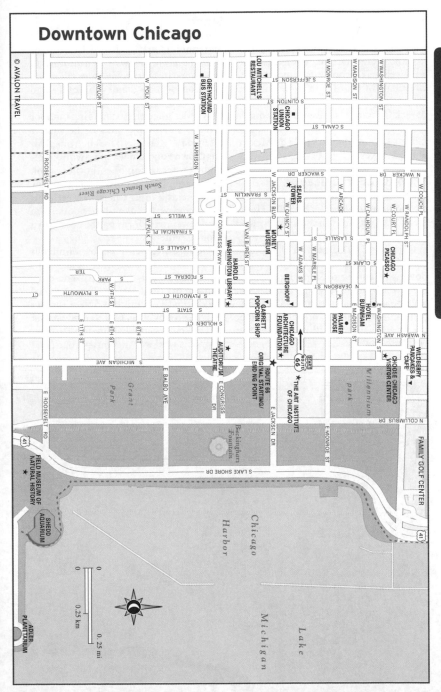

© AVALON TRAVEL

LOU MITCHELL'S RESTAURANT

GREYHOUND BUS STATION

CHICAGO UNION STATION

SEARS TOWER

MONEY MUSEUM

CHICAGO PICASSO ★

HAROLD WASHINGTON LIBRARY ★

BERGHOFF

HOTEL BURNHAM

PALMER HOUSE

CHOOSE CHICAGO VISITOR CENTER

WILDBERRY PANCAKES & CAFÉ ▼

GARRETT POPCORN SHOP ★

CHICAGO ARCHITECTURE FOUNDATION ★

ROUTE 66 START

ORIGINAL STARTING/ENDING POINT ★

AUDITORIUM THEATRE ★

★ **THE ART INSTITUTE OF CHICAGO**

W TAYLOR ST

W POLK ST

W ROOSEVELT RD

W HARRISON ST

S Branch Chicago River

South Branch Chicago River

W POLK ST

W WELLS ST

S WELLS ST

S FINANCIAL PL

W CONGRESS PKWY

S LASALLE ST

S FEDERAL ST

S PLYMOUTH CT

S PARK TER

W 9TH ST

S PLYMOUTH CT

E 11TH ST

E 9TH ST

E 8TH ST

STATE ST

S HOLDEN CT

S MICHIGAN AVE

E BALBO AVE

E CONGRESS DR

W JEFFERSON ST

S CLINTON ST

S CANAL ST

W MONROE ST

W MADISON ST

W WASHINGTON ST

W JACKSON BLVD

W QUINCY ST

W ARCADE

W ADAMS ST

W MARBLE PL

W VAN BUREN ST

S FRANKLIN ST

S WACKER DR

N WACKER DR

W COUCH PL

W RANDOLPH ST

W COURT PL

W CALHOUN AVE

W CALHOUN PL

S LASALLE

N CLARK ST

N DEARBORN PL

E MADISON ST

E WASHINGTON ST

N WABASH AVE

N COLUMBUS DR

E MONROE ST

E JACKSON DR

S LAKE SHORE DR

E ROOSEVELT RD

41

41

FAMILY GOLF CENTER

Millennium Park

Grant Park

Buckingham Fountain

FIELD MUSEUM OF NATURAL HISTORY ★

SHEDD AQUARIUM

ADLER PLANETARIUM

Chicago Harbor

Lake Michigan

0 0.25 km
0 0.25 mi

beautiful buildings by Mies van der Rohe; Lakeview/Boystown is a thriving gay community; Lincoln Square, traditionally a German neighborhood, has quaint shops on cobblestone streets. The University of Chicago in Hyde Park is a vibrant neighborhood that was home to Barack Obama. The Pilsen area is one of the largest Latino neighborhoods, and Little Village is dubbed as "The Mexico of the Midwest."

◆ Route 66 in Chicago

The starting point for Route 66 has moved several times. The 1926 alignment was at Jackson Boulevard and Michigan Avenue, near the Art Institute of Chicago. In 1933, the start of Route 66 moved a couple of blocks east to Jackson Boulevard and Lake Shore Drive, near the World's Fair. Then, in 1955, Jackson became a one-way street heading eastbound; Adams Street, one block north, became the new westbound starting point for Route 66.

Sights
Millennium Park

Millennium Park (55 N. Michigan Ave., 312/742-1168, www.millenniumpark. org, 6am-11pm daily, free) tops Chicago's lakefront when it comes to beauty and inspiration. Renowned architect Frank Gehry designed the astounding outdoor **Pritzker Pavilion** as well as the subtler **BP Bridge,** Gehry's first. The conspicuous **Crown Fountain** features two 50-foot-high towers facing one another, upon which are projected images of everyday Chicagoans. Linger when the weather is warm and watch as water shoots from each tower, transforming the area into a cooling center.

Cloud Gate, sculpted by Bombay's Anish Kapoor, looks like a giant polished-chrome jellybean, but that description doesn't do it justice. The curves of the distinctive sculpture reflect the sky and the groups of people gathered around it. The images are distorted in surprisingly beautiful ways as you approach and

Millennium Park

pass through the gate. *Cloud Gate* has become one of the city's most reliable photo opportunities.

Art Institute of Chicago

Located in the heart of Millennium Park, the **Art Institute of Chicago** (111 S. Michigan Ave., 312/443-3600, 10:30am-5pm daily, $23) is one of the best museums in the country. More than 300,000 pieces of ancient and contemporary art are housed in eight buildings totaling nearly 1 million square feet. You don't need a degree in art to recognize and appreciate the work on offer.

★ Chicago Architecture Foundation Tour

Chicago is the birthplace of the skyscraper and has some of the most innovative and magnificent architecture in the world. A **Chicago Architecture Foundation** (224 S. Michigan Ave., 312/922-3432, www.architecture. org, 9am-6pm daily, $15-85) tour explores art deco masterpieces, turn-of-the-20th-century skyscrapers, America's most iconic buildings by Frank Lloyd Wright, and Mies van der Rohe's Farnsworth House. With more than 85 tours via trolley, bus, boat, bike, subway, and even Segway, vacationers and locals agree this is the best way to see Chicago. Check the website for the schedules and book early; some of the popular tours, like the Frank Lloyd Wright, Riverfront, and Downtown Deco tours, can sell out quickly.

The Chicago Architecture Foundation also has 90-minute architecture tours on **The Chicago First Lady Cruises** (112 E. Upper Wacker Dr., 847/358-1330, www. cruisechicago.com, 10am-7:30pm daily Apr.-Nov., $50). Learn about the design and creation of 50 buildings on a 92-ton steel ship that holds about 300 passengers. The boat has an open-air upper deck, a climate-controlled main deck, and bistro seating with aluminum mesh armchairs, that harks back to the 1920s cruising yachts.

Money Museum

The "bottom line" is pretty much how this country is run, so go learn about how the Federal Reserve System works at the **Money Museum** (230 S. LaSalle St., 312/322-2400, www.chicagofed. org, 8:30am-5pm Mon.-Fri., free). This small but mighty museum teaches visitors about the history of the U.S. monetary system. There's a short video about the Chicago federal system, and huge $100 and $2 bills that you can put your head into for a fun photo op. If you ever wanted to know what a million dollars looks like, the cube in the middle of the room made of one million one-dollar bills put things into perspective.

Sears Tower

Sears Tower (aka Willis Tower, 233 S. Wacker Dr., 312/875-9447, www.thesearstower.com) is the reigning champion

of the Chicago skyline. Designed by the firm Skidmore, Owings & Merrill and completed in 1973, the Sears Tower scratches the stratosphere with its awe-inspiring 1,450 feet. It is so tall that on certain days the weather at the 110th floor is different from the weather on the ground. Staring up at the structure is simply not enough: Everyone save the severely acrophobic should ascend to the **Skydeck** (103rd Fl., 9am-10pm daily Apr.-Sept., 10am-8pm daily Oct.-Mar., $20 adults, $13 children) on one of the fast elevators. On a clear day, the observation deck allows you to peer over 50 miles of land, taking in all of Chicago's other, suddenly small-looking buildings, much of massive Lake Michigan, and sometimes parts of other states.

Grant Park

Grant Park (bounded by E. Randolph St. Michigan Ave., Roosevelt Rd., and Lake Michigan St.) is one of the oldest parks in Chicago, home to several attractions, world-class museums, and some of the best public art in the country. In 1893, Grant Park hosted the World Exposition, and fairgoers were introduced to diet soda, Aunt Jemima's syrup, Cracker Jacks, and Pabst Blue Ribbon.

Buckingham Fountain (301 S. Columbus Dr.) sits in the middle of Grant Park. The Chicago landmark was built in 1927 and is one of the largest fountains in the world, with an ornate, baroque-style design modeled after a fountain at the Palace of Versailles. The fountain contains about 1.5 million gallons of water. At the top of each hour (Apr.-Oct.) there's a 20-minute choreographed water show; after dusk, the water dances to music and 820 lights.

top to bottom: downtown Chicago; *Jaume Plensa: 1004 Portraits* exhibition in Grant Park; Art Institute of Chicago

Field Museum of Natural History

The **Field Museum of Natural History** (1400 S. Lake Shore Dr., 312/922-9410, www.fieldmuseum.org, 9am-5pm daily, $31 adults, $21 children) may be one of the few attractions known as much for what's not on display as for what is. The museum's library holds 250,000 volumes on the history of the earth and upward of 20 million curios from around the world, each catalogued and set aside for study when not out for all to see.

Like that of many Chicago museums and landmarks, the Field Museum's inception coincided with the 1893 Columbian Exposition. In 2000, the museum garnered international attention when it debuted Sue, the largest, most complete, and best-preserved *Tyrannosaurus rex* fossil ever discovered. Several other permanent exhibits exploring Africa and Asia trace the culture and environment of those continents with life-size dioramas. The museum regularly unveils new items and collections, and special events bring regular visitors back for another helping.

John G. Shedd Aquarium

Part of the trinity of Museum Campus institutions that explore the natural world, the **Shedd Aquarium** (1200 S. Lake Shore Dr., 312/939-2438, www.sheddaquarium. org, 9am-6pm daily June-Aug., 9am-5pm Mon.-Fri., 9am-6pm Sat.-Sun. Sept.-June, $38 adults, $29 children), the world's largest indoor aquarium, offers an amazing escape from city life, submerging visitors in aquatic environments stocked with exotic fish and animals.

Built using a $3 million bequest from the second president of Marshall Field and Company, John G. Shedd, the aquarium opened its doors just two months after the 1929 stock market crash. At the opening, some of the exhibits still lacked their aquatic residents, but the Shedd has been steadily improving its offerings ever since.

The aquarium's most striking attribute might be its dolphin and beluga whale exhibits, in the Oceanarium downstairs. A wide, curving window that looks out over the lake borders the simulated Pacific Coast environment that includes a large open tank. When the weather cooperates, the lake makes the tank look like it extends out for miles, an inspiring illusion, especially as a backdrop to the regular gravity-defying dolphin shows.

Museum of Science and Industry

Tucked down in Hyde Park, the **Museum of Science and Industry** (5700 S. Lake Shore Dr., 773/684-1414, www.msichicago.org, 9:30am-4pm daily, $18 adults, $11 children) has long been one of Chicago's most popular destinations, drawing some two million visitors annually. A playground for adults and children alike, the museum is full of surprises that range from detailed exhibits on genetics to an actual Boeing 727.

The MSI, opened in 1933 in the 1893 Columbian Exposition's Palace of Fine Arts building, explores the links between science and society. In one of its permanent displays dedicated to farming and coal mining, visitors are taken on a ride that simulates a 600-foot descent into a mine. Several temporary exhibits make their way to the museum each year, and have included 500 timepieces from the collection of Seth G. Atwood (founder of the Time Museum in Rockford, Illinois); a 110-million-year-old, 40-foot-long crocodile skeleton; and a room investigating the roots of rap music and hip-hop culture.

★ Chicago History Museum

It would be a shame to visit Chicago and not learn about its history. For more than 150 years, the **Chicago History Museum** (1601 N. Clark St., 312/642-4600, www. chicagohistory.org, 9:30am-4:30pm Mon.-Sat., noon-5pm Sun., $14) has been collecting thousands of manuscripts, paintings, costumes, and artifacts, such as the bed Abraham Lincoln died on, along with a wide range of exhibits on

Historic Pullman District

Architecture and railroad history buffs should visit the **Historic Pullman District** (11111 S. Forrestville Ave., 773/660-2341, www.pullmanil.org, free). It was a planned model company town built in the 1880s for the Pullman Palace Car Company about 13 miles south of downtown Chicago. Nearly 1,000 of the original row houses are still there, and the buildings range from modest homes for factory workers to elegant mansions for the executives. There is also a large mural of Pullman ironworkers, an herb garden, and a beehive with honey for sale near the **Visitors Center** (773/785-8901, 11am-3pm Tues.-Sun., $5). Make this your first stop to learn more about the town's history. View the exhibits on rail travel service and pick up a brochure for a self-guided walking tour. Ninety-minute guided tours (1:30pm Tues.-Sun., $10) are also available, beginning at the Visitors Center. If you're staying downtown and don't feel like driving, the Metra Electric subway line from Millennium Park takes you right there. However, if you do want to drive, it's a good excuse to stop for breakfast at **Daley's** (809 E. 63rd St., 773/643-6670, www.daleysrestaurant.com) because it's on the way.

labor, culture, fashion, and photography. The permanent exhibit, "Chicago: Crossroads of America," has several galleries that highlight Chicago's retail, manufacturing, architecture, social activism, diverse communities, and jazz history. The information you learn here will make what you see in the next few days on Route 66 in Illinois much more meaningful.

Once you're on the road or even just walking through the city, visit the Chicago History Museum's website, which has **Studs Terkel's Radio Archive**

Dana Hotel

(http://studsterkel.org). It's a comprehensive collection of interviews with America's most famous oral historian and broadcaster. He joined the WPA's Federal Writers' Project, and his radio program aired in Chicago between 1952 and 1997. He interviewed everyone from Bob Dylan to Martin Luther King Jr. and Langston Hughes. What made him famous was that he believed that every person's story was valuable, whether it was from a world leader or a waitress. The website has more than 7,000 recordings of Terkel's interviews to choose from.

Entertainment

The Green Mill (4802 N. Broadway, 773/878-5552, www.greenmilljazz.com, noon-4am Mon.-Fri., noon-5am Sat., 11am-4am Sun., cover $10-15) has been hosting jazz greats since 1907. In the 1920s, the venue was a mob hangout—Al Capone's booth was near the curve of the bar—and the tunnels underneath the building came in handy when the

cops raided the joint during prohibition. Today, the Green Mill still has a sophisticated speakeasy vibe with a stylish art deco decor and one of the longest running poetry slams in the country. Located in Chicago's Uptown neighborhood, about 20 minutes from Route 66, it's worth the detour. A free parking lot is reserved for customers (6pm-6am daily) one block west at Lawrence and Magnolia Streets.

When the owners of the Green Door Tavern bought the building in the 1980s, they broke through a wall in the basement and discovered a 1920s time capsule: a secret speakeasy stocked with early-20th-century bottles, a circus tapestry, and the original cash register. The space is now a separate bar called **The Drifter** (676 N. Orleans St., 312/631-3887, 5pm-2am Wed.-Sat., cover $5), a hidden alcove that seats 40 people and serves clandestine libations printed on Tarot cards. You have to knock on the door to get in.

Thalia Hall (1807 S. Allport St., 312/526-3851, shows at 8pm daily) was founded at the turn of the 20th century as a multipurpose property with commercial storefronts and a public hall for the community. After closing in the 1960s, it sat empty until 2013, when it was restored by Bruce Finkelman and Craig Golden. Today, it is one of the best music venues in Chicago. Thalia Hall is located near public transit, five blocks east of the 18th Street Pink Line L stop. The number 18 bus stops at the corner of 18th Street and Racine Avenue; Thalia Hall is half a block away.

The Betty (839 W. Fulton Market, 312/733-2222, 4pm-2am daily) is a bar in love with the past, with an antique cash register, tufted leather seating, dark wood-paneled walls, and bookshelves stocked with vinyl records and vintage glassware. Handcrafted cocktails are served with green-tea syrup, fennel bitters, and orange-chili oil. If you're hungry, the kitchen serves croquettes, pierogis, and flatbreads until 1am.

A "temple of satire," **Second City** (1616 N. Wells St., 312/337-3992, www.secondcity.com) sparked the careers of several *Saturday Night Live* stars. Enjoy a performance on the scripted Mainstage or the lightning-fast e.t.c. improv stage, Second City's claim to fame.

Accommodations

The ★ **Kinzie Hotel** (20 W. Kinzie St., 312/395-9000, www.kinziehotel.com, $175-365) was inspired by John Kinzie, a silversmith, Indian trader, and businessman extraordinaire from the late 1700s. The modern and sleek guest rooms clock in at more than 300 square feet with views of stunning skyscrapers. A historic map of Chicago covers the wall behind the comfy beds, fitted with sheets that make you wonder why your bed at home can't be more like this. A complimentary breakfast buffet is set up on each floor; all you have to do is wake up, walk down the hall in your robe, pick up breakfast, and go back to your room. It's genius.

A perfect place to stay is the ★ **Acme Hotel** (15 E. Ohio St., 312/894-0800, www.acmehotelcompany.com, $199-329), an intimate, cool, and fashionable boutique hotel in a historic building. The decor is fun and full of character, with elevators covered in vinyl records and red lip-print lights on the bathroom mirrors. Rooms feature king, queen, or two double beds, with 40-inch flat-screen TVs (with Apple plug-and-play) and free Wi-Fi; the size can be a little tight, but the unusual decor and quality service make up for it—there's nothing like staying in a place where the staff really cares. The hotel sometimes offers special deals for Route 66 travelers: an extra $0.66 gets you treats from West Town Bakery and a $10 Spotify card to build your own playlist for the road.

If you want to feel how the 1 percent lives, you should stay at **The Langham Hotel** (330 N. Wabash Ave., 312/923-9988, www.langhamhotels.com, $400-680). It's a five-star property that sits right on the Chicago River. If you're wondering what that extra star is all about, the Langham will show you. They have 316 impeccably appointed rooms with about 300 staff members to provide the ultimate in personalized service. The wall between the bathroom and the living area has an automatic privacy feature that frosts at the touch of a button. If you pay an additional fee and join the Langham Club, you receive personalized butler service, valet assistance to iron, pack, and unpack your bags, complimentary in-town car service within two miles of the hotel, and free access to the 4,000-square-foot club lounge, with city views, champagne, and a gourmet buffet station. The room decor is elegant and understated and yet extravagant, kind of like an Yves Saint Laurent suit—it may look like a regular suit until you try it on, and then you understand why it costs so much more.

For something more modern, the **Dana Hotel** (660 N. State St., 312/202-6000, www.danahotelandspa.com, $249-287) encourages you to "come as you are." It has a youthful and supercool vibe that feels friendly and welcoming, not that alienating involuntary-eye-roll hipster scene you see in some places that look this trendy. They use natural, sustainable materials, the ceilings are concrete, and the walls are glass, with floor to ceiling views of downtown. Oh, and the bathroom wall has that cool frosting feature that the Langham has, but for a fraction of the price.

If you want a reprieve from the hustle and bustle of downtown, try **Hotel Lincoln** (1816 N. Clark St., 312/254-4700, www.jdvhotels.com, $150-320). You'll feel right at home as you see the Hotel Lincoln sign behind font desk—it looks like a huge license plate—and the mosaic of dresser drawers all along the front of the counter. The rooms have a stylish vintage vibe with bedside tables that look like 19th-century trunks trimmed in rivets. The chairs are upholstered in old advertising, original works from local artists hang on the walls, and the rooms have views of Lake Michigan and Lincoln Park.

The **Talbott Hotel** (20 E. Delaware Pl., 800/825-2688, www.talbotthotel.com, $350-525) exudes the charm of a bygone era. The lobby has dark wood walls, posh indigo velvet chairs, chocolate-colored tufted couches, and crisp marble floors. The rooms are more than 350-square feet with pillow-top bedding, down pillows, and an Apple Mac mini with more than 50 HD channels and a DVR. They also have a Pampered Pooch package, where you and your four-legged family member can get a one-hour massage by a certified animal therapist—a great way to get those muscles primed for the next 2,400 miles of driving.

The ★ **Palmer House** (17 E. Monroe St., 312/726-7500, www.palmerhouse-hiltonhotel.com, $149-349) is an exquisite, opulent, historic property with 24-karat gold Tiffany chandeliers, gilded sculptures that weigh more than a ton each, and a spectacular frescoed ceiling. Charles Dickens, Oscar Wilde, Mark Twain, Sinatra, and Liberace have been here. The pastry chef who worked here invented the brownie, and the Palmer was one of the first properties to use the Edison light bulb and the telephone. They also had the city's first elevators, which were advertised as "a perpendicular railroad that connects floor to floor, rendering passage by the stairs unnecessary." The Palmer House has undergone a $170 million renovation to incorporate historic elegance with modern convenience and comfort. The rooms are spacious for an old building and decorated with plush fabrics in jewel-tone accents. If you book months in advance, you could land a special "early bird" rate. Even if you don't stay here, come just to see the lobby. This is one of the last grand hotels left in America.

Food
Breakfast

Though it's only open for breakfast and lunch, ★ **Lou Mitchell's** (565 W. Jackson Blvd., 312/939-3111, www.loumitchell-srestaurant.com, 5:30am-3pm Mon.-Fri., 7am-3pm Sat.-Sun., $8-15) has been a time-honored whistle-stop and Chicago institution for more than 90 years. Travelers and locals alike love the generous portions, friendly service, and fantastic food. Stop in for fresh-squeezed orange juice, light and fluffy pancakes, and thinly sliced fried potatoes that are both crunchy and creamy. Don't let the line to get in thwart you—they hand out sugar-dusted doughnut holes while you wait. Once inside, a free box of Milk Duds awaits you at tables surrounded by Route 66 memorabilia on the walls.

For a more contemporary breakfast, **Wildberry Pancakes & Café** (130 E. Randolph St., 312/938-9779, www.wildberrycafe.com, 6:30am-2:30pm daily, $8-15) has won awards for the best pancakes in Chicago. They feature homemade breads and food made with local farm-fresh ingredients, and the coffee is from Intelligentsia. Some of the favorites are red-velvet French toast, perfectly crisp hash browns, and the Denver skillet with eggs, veggies, meat, and potatoes. This place is very popular, so be prepared to wait.

Lunch and Dinner

In operation since 1921, the ★ **Green Door Tavern** (678 N. Orleans St., 312/664-5496, 11:30am-2am daily, $8-13) is Chicago's oldest tavern. The building it's housed in was built in 1872, one year after the Great Chicago Fire. The front door (warped because it has been in use for 137 years) was painted green during prohibition as code for a speakeasy. The tavern interior has a lived-in feel with a dark wood, memorabilia on the walls, a good beer selection, and delicious yet reasonably priced pub grub like corned beef and gooey grilled triple-cheese sandwiches.

Or opt for the Bootlegger Burger, with applewood bacon, whiskey ketchup, cheese, and an egg over-easy alongside crunchy and well-seasoned fries.

John Daley opened **Daley's Restaurant** (809 E. 63rd St., 773/643-6670, www.daleysrestaurant.com, 6am-7pm Mon.-Thurs., 6am-9pm Fri.-Sun., $4-14) in 1892. In the 1920s, Daley's was run by Greeks before becoming a soul food mecca in the mid-1960s. Sam Cooke, comedian Moms Mabley, and Route 66 crooner Nat King Cole all ate here. Today, they serve the best chicken and waffles, collard greens, and buttery corn muffins that are little gifts from heaven. It's a little out of the way, but worth the trip.

Chicago has so many good restaurants, but what makes them special is the history behind them. For more than 40 years, the staff at **The Billy Goat Tavern** (430 N. Michigan Ave., 312/222-1525, 6am-2am Mon.-Fri., 10am-3am Sat., 10am-2am Sun., $3-8) has entertained customers by yelling out, "Try the double cheese! It's the best!" In 1978, *Saturday Night Live* made the Billy Goat Tavern's burgers famous with its "Cheezeborger! Cheezeborger!" skit that starred John Belushi, Dan Aykroyd, Bill Murray, and Laraine Newman. If for some reason you don't order the cheezeborger (you have to say it like that), they also have good breakfast specials and other sandwiches. There are several locations throughout the city, but this one, on Michigan Avenue near the Wrigley Building, is the original.

Formento's (925 W. Randolph St., 312/690-7295, www.formentos.com, 11:30am-2pm and 5pm-10pm Mon.-Thurs., 11:20am-2pm and 5pm-11pm Fri., 10am-2pm and 5pm-11pm Sat., 10am-2pm and 5pm-9pm Sun., $14-49) is an inspired 1950s supper club with sprawling brick-red leather booths, crisp white tablecloths, and authentic Italian-American cuisine. Full of Old World charm, the dining experience offers a contemporary take on the classics—roasted heirloom

Lou Mitchell's

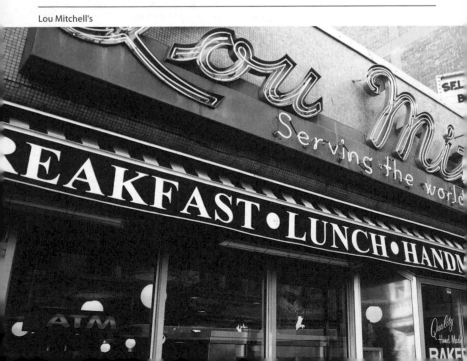

beet salad with blood oranges, ricotta, and pistachios—as well as a more familiar spaghetti and meatballs.

For Chicago deep-dish pizza, opt for **The Exchequer** (226 S. Wabash Ave., 312/939-5633, www.exchequerpub.com, 11am-11pm Mon.-Thurs., 11am-midnight Fri.-Sat., noon-10pm Sun., $11-28), which serves some atmosphere and history to go with your pie. Al Capone hung out in this classic Chicago pub; inside, a moody old-school gangster vibe is enhanced by historic pictures of Chicago all over the walls. The deep-dish pizza is baked in a buttery crust and topped with a tangy, sweet tomato sauce and a thick, gooey, too-good-to-be-true layer of cheese. For those who are not fans of deep dish, they also serve steaks, ribs, burgers, and salads. Wash it all down with a beer-of-the-month special, usually a local or German brew.

When the **Berghoff** (17 West Adams, 312/427-3170, www.theberghoff.com, 11am-9pm Mon.-Sat., $7-26) opened in 1898, it was a men-only saloon; customers were served a free sandwich with purchase of their "nickel" beer. Today, they serve old-world German dishes like sauerbraten and apple strudel as well as contemporary dishes, gluten-free options, wine, and beer to anyone who walks in the door. The decor is as old-school as they come, with dark wood and stained-glass in a landmark setting.

Road Snacks

No road trip is complete without snacks, so don't leave Chicago without stopping at **Garrett's Popcorn** (27 W. Jackson Blvd., 312/360-1108, www.garrettpopcorn.com, 10am-8pm Mon.-Sat., 11am-7pm Sun., $5-15). They've been serving up creative sweet and salty mash-ups since 1949. The "Garrett Mix" is the perfect marriage of sugary caramel and sharp cheesy goodness. It's an Oprah fave, so give yourself extra time in case there's a line, and grab a few wet naps on your way out. It's messy and worth every calorie.

Information and Services

The Choose Chicago visitor information center is located at the **Chicago Cultural Center** (77 E. Randolph St., 312/744-6630, www.choosechicago. com, 10am-5pm Mon.-Sat., 11am-4pm Sun.), which has free brochures, multilingual maps, and complimentary concierge service. They can plan customized itineraries and help you make the most of your time in the Windy City. To see Chicago through the eyes of a local, contact **Chicago InstaGreeter** (chgogreeter@ choosechicago.com) for a free one-hour walk through Chicago's downtown.

◈ Getting on Route 66

As you leave Chicago, you'll need to take the 1955 alignment from West Adams Street and Michigan Avenue. Drive west for about two miles, then take a left (southwest) on Ogden Avenue. In 5 miles you'll reach Cicero.

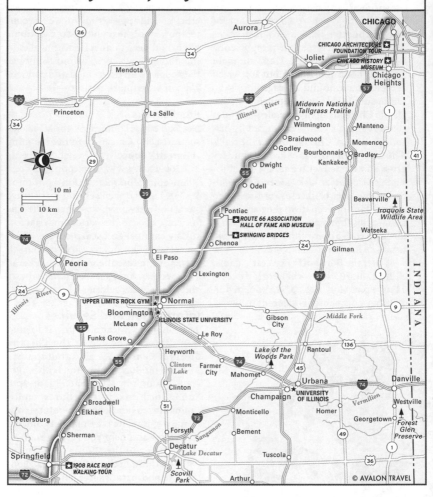

Chicago to Springfield

Cicero

According to sociologist James Loewen's *Sundown Towns*, there were more than 450 "sundown" counties in Illinois. Sundown towns were all-white communities with signs posted at their borders warning African Americans to leave town before sundown. Cicero was a sundown town. In 1951, during the heyday of Route 66, 3,500 whites rioted against a black man for trying to rent an apartment in town. Four hundred and fifty National guardsmen and 200 Cook County police offers were called in to mitigate the violence.

Capone came to Chicago in 1921 to manage the Four Deuces Club, casino, and bordello. During the 1924 municipal elections, Capone turned the town of Cicero into a war zone: He bullied voters, kidnapped pollsters, and threatened news reporters into voting for the people who supported his criminal behavior. It's hard to believe that Al Capone spent less than 10 years ripping and running through Chicago streets, but Capone's brazen, ruthless, and outrageously violent behavior left such an indelible mark on the city that many people believe it lasted longer than it did.

Sights
Castle Car Wash
The 1925 **Castle Car Wash** (3801 W. Ogden Ave. at S. Hamlin Ave.) is a castle-shaped building with a brick-laced turret that was built by Louis Ehrenberer. Over the years, it has housed several businesses, but it's most famous for doubling as a hideout for Al Capone.

It's rumored that Al Capone lobbied to pave Route 66 for the faster delivery and transport of his bootlegged liquor. To confuse cops, Capone painted his bullet-proof 1928 Cadillac V8 the same green-and-black pattern of the police cars at the time; it even had a siren and searchlight mounted on the roof. Holes were installed at the bottom of the window for rifles barrels to slip through in order to shoot from the sides of the car.

Hawthorne Works Factory
The cops opened fire on Capone and his crew right across the street from the **Hawthorne Works Factory** (southeast corner of Cermack Ave. and Cicero Ave.). From 1905 to 1986, this 200-acre complex manufactured 14,000 consumer projects—everything from telephone equipment to microphones, refrigerators, and film projectors. Hawthorne was one of the largest manufacturing sites in the country; it employed about 40,000 people in more than 100 buildings and had its own hospital, fire department, sports team, rail yard, and savings and loan.

Hawthorne Works conducted trailblazing studies on worker motivation and efficiency, offering loyal lifelong employees (many of whom were immigrants from central Europe) pensions, paid vacations, disability pay, and home loans.

The complex has since been replaced by a shopping mall, but the original water tower remains. To learn more about the factory, private and group tours are available at **The Hawthorne Works Museum and Archives** (3801 S. Central Ave., 708/656-8000, ext. 2321, call ahead for a tour of the archives).

To get there: From West Ogden Avenue, head west. Past South Hamlin Avenue, take a soft right onto West Cermak Road. Cross the railroad tracks; the next block is Cicero Avenue (SR-50). Turn left into the shopping mall and look for the tower looming behind Foot Locker.

To reach the Hawthorne Works Museum and Archives from the Hawthorne Factory site: Exit the shopping mall parking lot and turn south (left) onto Cicero Avenue (SR-50). Take a right (southwest) onto West Ogden Avenue, then take a left (south) onto South Central Avenue.

◆ Back on 66
Keep heading west on Ogden Avenue for a couple of miles to the neighboring suburb of Berwyn.

Berwyn

Sights
Ogden Top and Trim
During Route 66's heyday, Ogden Avenue, from the west side of Chicago to the town of Berwyn, was known as "Automobile Row," with 14 gas stations and numerous garages and car dealerships. The **Ogden Top and Trim** (6031 W. Ogden Ave., Berwyn, 708/484-5422, www.ogdentopandtrim.com) is the only

Local Eats

The **Chicago-style hot dog** was born at the 1893 Worlds Fair's Columbian Exposition. It's a steamed (never grilled) all-beef frankfurter with diced onion, tomato wedges, relish, mustard, pickled serrano peppers, a dill pickle spear, and dash of celery salt, all crammed into a poppy-seed bun. With all those layers of flavors and textures, there's no need for ketchup; in fact, according to Chicagoans, putting ketchup on a hot dog is the ultimate sin.

One of the best places to have a classic Chicago hotdog is at **Henry's Drive-In** (6031 W. Ogden Ave., Cicero, 708/656-9344, 10am-9pm Mon.-Sat., 11am-8pm Sun., $7-10). When Henry's opened in the 1950s they advertised their dogs as "A meal in itself." At the time, they had no indoor seating and served hotdogs out of a walk-up window. Today you can sit inside, and they also have sandwiches, pizza puffs (similar to a deep-fried calzone), and French bread dipped in Italian beef gravy.

remaining auto business from that time still in operation. The three-generation family-owned shop started in 1919; today, they specialize in innovative restorations and custom interiors for everything from classic Packards to street rods and muscle cars. There's nothing to see on-site, but their website includes photos of their impressive restoration work.

Berwyn Route 66 Museum

Berwyn Route 66 Museum (7003 W. Ogden Ave., Berwyn, 708/484-9349, www.berwynrt66museum.org, 9am-5pm Mon.-Fri., free) is a small museum with Route 66 memorabilia, a gallery, a display of classic hubcaps, and large aerial photographs that show how much the Ogden Street portion of Route 66 has changed over time. Also on-site is a miniature of the popular Spindle Sculpture, a former Berwyn public art landmark by Dustin Shuler that once appeared in Cermak Plaza. The sculpture had eight real cars stacked on a 40-foot-tall spike. The museum is in the process of recreating the original Spindle sculpture that was torn down in 2008, replaced with a Walgreens.

⬥ Back on 66

Oak Park is 4.5 miles north of Route 66. Drive west on Ogden Avenue (Route 66) and turn right (north) on S. Oak Park Avenue.

⬥ Side Trip: Oak Park

Sights
Ernest Hemingway Birthplace and Museum

About five miles north of Route 66, you can get a dose of literary history and pick up some roadside reading material at the **Ernest Hemingway Birthplace and Museum** (339 N. Oak Park Ave., 708/366-3981, www.ehfop.org, 1pm-5pm Sun.-Fri., 10am-5pm Sat., $15). On July 21, 1899, literary history was made when baby Ernest was delivered by his father, Dr. Ed Hemingway, upstairs in his mother's bedroom. The Queen Anne home offers a glimpse into early 1900s Victorian life.

Before visiting the house, you may want to brush up on the history and legacy of Hemingway at the nearby museum in the **Oak Park Arts Center** (200 N. Oak Park Ave., 708/848-2222, www.ehfop. org). They have more than 800 photographs, printed materials, clothing, art, furniture, and rare artifacts, including Hemingway's childhood diary. The gift shop sells books, DVDs, posters, and literary tchotchkes like secret boxes made to look like real books.

Frank Lloyd Wright Home and Studio

Oak Park has the world's largest collection of Wright-designed buildings, set in a designated Historic District. Just a few blocks from Ernest Hemingway's birthplace is **Frank Lloyd Wright's Home and Studio** (951 Chicago Ave., Oak Park, 312/994-4000, www.cal.flwright.org, 9am-4:15pm daily). Guided 60-minute tours ($17) available from trained interpreters offer insight into Wright's career and family life. Forty-minute walking tours are also available ($15). Tickets can be purchased online, and advance reservations are highly recommended.

◈ Back on 66
To return to Route 66, head south on S. Oak Park Avenue for 4.5 miles and turn right (west) on Ogden Avenue. To continue on to Riverside, drive west on W. Ogden Avenue, passing Highway 43, and make a right (north) on Lionel Road, which curves into Riverside Road.

Riverside

As Route 66 passes through the suburb of Berwyn, there's not much to see other than aging strip malls. However, in Riverside, just west of Berwyn, there's a hidden gem for architecture buffs.

Sights
Riverside Architectural District
The historic **Riverside Architectural District** (bounded by Ogden Ave., 26th St., and Harlem Ave./SR-43, Riverside) features one of the first suburban communities in the United States. Frederick Law Olmstead, who designed Central Park in New York City, threw out the grid layout and developed this neighborhood with curved roads, parkland, and gas street lighting. The neighborhood also features many homes designed by Frank Lloyd Wright.

To learn more about the area and its history, visit the **Riverside Museum**

top to bottom: Castle Car Wash, Cicero; Dell Rhea Chicken Basket; Union Station, Chicago.

(10 Pine Ave., 708/447-2542, www.riversidemuseum.net, 10am-2pm Sat.). Since it is only open on Saturday, check the website for self-guided and online driving tours.

◈ Back on 66:
Riverside to Joliet

The 1926 Route 66 alignment went through Joliet. In 1940, Route 66 moved west to go through Plainfield, Shorewood, and Channahon before rejoining the route at Braidwood. To drive to Joliet, return to Ogden Avenue heading west. Turn left (south) on Lawndale Avenue in Lyons, then turn right (southwest) onto Joliet Road. Joliet Road curves west to turn into West 55th Street. Take a left (south) on East Avenue, then pick up Joliet Road again by turning right (southwest) after about 0.5 miles. Joliet Road travels through Countryside to merge onto I-55 south.

Willowbrook

Food
Dell Rhea Chicken Basket

One of the best places to eat on Route 66 is ★ **Dell Rhea Chicken Basket** (645 Joilet Rd., Willowbrook, www.chicken-basket.com, 630/325-0780, 11am-9pm Sun.-Thurs., 11am-10pm Fri.-Sat., $8-20). It's a little tricky to get here, but the cool neon sign and delicious food make it worth a stop. In 1938, Dell Rhea's served meals to Route 66 travelers in baskets for easy transport on the road. Diners worship their succulent crispy fried chicken and fried mac-and-cheese balls with extra cheese sauce on the side. While the owner could skimp on the quality of the ingredients and make more money, that's not what this place is about.

To get here from I-55: Take Exit 274 onto Kingery Highway (SR-83) north. Drive 0.3 miles, then take a right (east) onto Midway Drive, which dead-ends at South Quincy Street. Take a right (south)

and drive to North Frontage Road. Dell Rhea's will be on the left (southeast) side of the street.

◈ Back on 66:
Willowbrook to Joliet

To rejoin I-55, turn left (southwest) out of the parking lot and take the first right (west) on 79th Street, which will turn into Frontage Road. At the dead-end, take a left (west) on Midway Drive and then the next left on Kingery Highway south (SR-83). Follow signs for I-55 west.

Heading west on I-55, about six miles from Kingery Highway (SR-83), you'll pass through Darien, Woodridge, and Bolingbrook. After the I-355 interchange, Route 66 splits off into pre- and post-1940s alignments. The post-1940s alignment bypassed Joliet and went through Plainfield. But I recommend taking the **pre-1940s alignment** through Joliet. From I-55 near Bolingbrook, take Exit 267 and turn left (south) onto SR-53. When the road comes to a T-junction at Joliet Road, turn right (southwest) and continue south for 8 miles on SR-53 into Joliet.

Joliet

Joliet became an official part of Route 66 in November 1926, and the Mother Road ran through the town for decades before it was rerouted through Plainfield in 1940. But Joliet is the preferred route due to a rich labor and manufacturing history that reflects America's resilient and enduring immigrant history.

In the 1870s, southeastern Europeans and Irish immigrants arrived in Joliet to work at the Elgin, Joliet, and Eastern Railway and the second-largest steel mill in the country. By 1960, more than one-third of the population of Joliet was employed in the manufacturing sector. With such a large labor force, Joliet became a mecca for manufacturing companies and foundries that produced stoves, beer, horseshoes, windmills, and pianos. Even inmates from the penitentiary mined the bluish-white limestone from the local quarry, giving Joliet the nickname "City of Stone." The town appeared unbreakable, but with major changes in the manufacturing industry in the 1970s, Joliet started to decline and the unemployment rate rose to 26 percent. By 1983, Joliet had the highest unemployment rate in the nation. Since the 1980s, the town has diversified its employment base, and the economy has revitalized with retail trade, casinos, NASCAR, and the heavy machinery company Caterpillar.

◈ Route 66 through Joliet

As you head toward downtown, turn left (east) after Granite Street to follow SR-53. Make an immediate right (south) after crossing the Des Plaines River.

Sights
Route 66 Park

If you want to stretch your legs, as you enter Joliet on SR-53 (Broadway St.), stop for an ice-cream cone at the **Rich & Creamy** (920 N. Broadway St., 815/740-2899, 11am-10pm Mon.-Sat., noon-10pm Sun.) and then walk next door to the **Route 66 Park** (920 N. Broadway St., 217/525-9308). There are informational kiosks on Route 66 and a great view of the Collins Street Prison.

Joliet Area Historical Museum

A good place to stop and get a full introduction of the area and learn more about Route 66 is at the **Joliet Area Historical Museum** (204 N. Ottawa St., 815/723-5201, www.jolietmuseum.org, 10am-5pm Tues.-Sat., noon-5pm Sun., also 10am-2pm Mon. summer, $6), 0.5 miles south of Route 66 Park on SR-53. Exhibits include a 500-square-foot moon-landing simulator with interactive panels, diagrams, and maps. The museum gift shop sells local history books and Route 66 gifts, books, and collectibles. If you're interested in

seeing the industrial ruins of the Joliet Iron Works Historic Site, be sure to pick up an Iron Works brochure.

Rialto Square Theater

Don't miss the historic **Rialto Square Theater** (102 N. Chicago St., 815/726-6600, www.rialtosquare.com, tours 11am-1pm Mon.-Fri. summer, 1:30pm Tues. winter, $5), right around the corner from the Route 66 Diner. The theater opened in 1926—the year Route 66 began—as a vaudeville movie palace. In its time, the remarkable neo-baroque and Byzantine architecture rivaled the motion picture palaces of Chicago and New York. The lobby was inspired by The Hall of Mirrors in the Palace of Versailles; the rotunda featured 18 Corinthian-style columns and an eight-arm crystal chandelier with 200 fixtures and 250 lights. The arch between the rotunda and the esplanade was copied from the Arc de Triomphe in Paris. The Rialto closed as a movie theater in the 1970s, but was saved from demolition in 1980. Today, the theater hosts a broad range of entertainers, including the likes of Buddy Guy, Sinbad, Craig Ferguson, and Sesame Street Live. Afternoon tours with limited hours are available, so you don't have to attend a live show to see the interior.

Note that North Chicago Street dead-ends one block past the Rialto Square Theater.

Jacob Henry Mansion

A fine example of Renaissance Revival architecture, the **Jacob Henry Mansion** (20 S. Eastern Ave., 815/722-1420, www.jacobhenrymansion.com, call to schedule a tour) is a 16,800-square-foot Victorian built in 1873 by Jacob Henry, a wealthy railroad magnate. The National Historical Landmark took three years to complete; the house is made of limestone, red Illinois sandstone, and deep-red brick with a large Byzantine dome. Inside are several ornate fireplaces with hand-rubbed black walnut and oak carvings, and a solid walnut staircase with 119 hand-carved spindles.

To get there from Route 66 (SR-53): Drive one block south of the Rialto Theater and take a left (east) on U.S. 6. Continue east for three blocks, then turn right (south) onto South Eastern Street. The mansion will be on the left at the corner at 1st Avenue.

Joliet Iron Works Historic Site

The second-largest steel mill in the country once stood at the **Joliet Iron Works Historic Site** (927 Collins St., 815/727-8700, 8am-sunset daily, free). The factory was dismantled in the 1930s, and although the buildings are gone, the remnants of the foundation are still here. Before you walk the one-mile self-guided paved trail, get a copy of the Iron Works brochures at the nearby Joliet Area Historical Museum (204 Ottawa St., www.jolietmuseum.org) to appreciate the magnitude of what was once standing here. What's left today are the abandoned ruins of the stock house, casting beds, gas washers, engine houses, blast stoves, and furnaces.

To get here from downtown Joliet: Take I-53 east on Jackson Street or Route 30. Turn left (north) on SR-171, and the Iron Works will be less than one mile on the left (west) side of the street.

Old Joliet Prison Park

A few blocks north of the Iron Works ruins is the **Joliet Prison** (1125 Collins St.). Although it's no longer open, the prison housed inmates from 1858 to 2002, including the infamous Leopold and Loeb, two wealthy University of Chicago students who kidnapped and murdered a 14-year-old boy. The murder inspired the Alfred Hitchcock film *Rope*. Leopold and Loeb were initially held at the Joliet Prison, then transferred to Statesville Penitentiary. Joliet was also the prison where Jake was released at the beginning of the film *The Blues Brothers*.

The prison is on private property and is closed. The parking lot on the south side of the prison walls has been transformed into the **Old Joliet Prison Park** (1125 Collins St., www.cityofjoliet.info, dawn-dusk daily, free). There are eight informational kiosks on the inmates and history of the facility on-site.

Route 66 Raceway

The **Route 66 Raceway** (500 Speedway Blvd., 815/722-5500, tickets 888/629-7223, www.route66raceway.com, $5-25) hosts NASCAR events and pays homage to early drag racing and hot rod culture. A Route 66 Classic ($20) event is held in August, where you can see custom dragsters pop wheelies and burn rubber. The rest of the year, the raceway features concerts, motorsports, demolition derbies, drag racing, and a swap meet (Oct., $5) for racers, restorers, and collectors.

The raceway is located south of downtown Joliet, about 2.5 miles south of I-80. From downtown Joliet, drive south on Highway 53 and turn left (east) on E. Laraway Road. The Raceway is less than one mile on the right (south).

Food

The **Joliet Route 66 Diner** (22 W. Clinton St., 815/723-3865, 6am-3pm Mon.-Sat., 6am-2pm Sun., $6-12) has good prices, friendly service, and a Monte Cristo sandwich that locals love. The authentic old-school interior includes wood-paneled tables and walls and the original counter—it looks like the place hasn't changed in decades. The diner is located one block south of Route 30 and two blocks south of the Historical Museum.

✦ Back on 66

As you leave Joliet, North Chicago Street dead-ends one block past the Rialto Square Theater. From the intersection of West Clinton Street and SR-53, head south through downtown. Keep following signs for SR-53 until you pass I-80. Continue south on SR-53 for 12 miles to Midewin National Tall Grass Prairie Preserve.

Midewin National Tallgrass Prairie Preserve

As you continue south on Route 66 (SR-53), the road opens up to 19,000 acres of prairie farmland, and the landscape looks much like it did in the 1800s. The **Midewin National Tallgrass Prairie Preserve** (30239 SR-53, 815/423-6370, www.fs.usda.gov/main/midewin, trails 4am-10pm daily, free) was once the Joliet Army Ammunition Plant and is now returning back to nature. This is the largest tallgrass prairie restoration project in the United States and it's a quintessential snapshot of the heartland of America. You can stretch your legs, take a hike, or do some bird-watching.

The **Welcome Center** (8am-4:30pm Mon.-Fri. Nov.-Mar., 8am-4:30pm Mon.-Sat. Apr.-Oct.) has trail maps, exhibits, and information about the cultural and natural history of the area. Picnic tables and portable toilets are available at all trailheads. With the exception of the Welcome Center, there are no sources of water available in the preserve.

The **River Road Seedbed** walk features Midewin's largest native seed production area. You will see rows of native plants in bloom from spring to fall. To access the trailhead from the Welcome Center, turn left on SR-53 and drive one mile to River Road. Turn right and continue for 2.2 miles to Boathouse Road; turn right again onto gravel Boathouse Road. A parking area will be on the right and the seedbeds will be on the left. The **Explosives Road Trail** is a 1.5-mile loop hike with access to about 20 bunkers at the 811 Bunker Field. To reach the trailhead from the Welcome Center, turn right onto SR-53 and after 1.7 miles, turn left onto Explosives Road.

Follow the signs to the trailhead and parking area.

❖ Back on 66

Continue south on Route 66 (SR-53) for 2.5 miles to the town of Wilmington.

Wilmington

As you approach Wilmington, SR-53 curves to the right (southwest) and turns into East Baltimore Street.

Look for the **Gemini Giant Muffler Man** (810 E. Baltimore St. at Daniel St.) on the right (northwest) side of East Baltimore Street. These quirky fiberglass roadside statues were popular in the 1960s as part of a nationwide advertising campaign. Standing more than 20 feet tall, each statue has its own special theme—Wilmington's celebrates our love affair with space travel. This muffler man was named after the Gemini Space program, though his space helmet looks more like a welding mask. In his hands is a silver rocket with the American Flag on the tail, a reference to the now-closed Launching Pad Drive-In restaurant. The diner may be closed, but the Muffler Man lives on.

As you continue west through downtown Wilmington, look for the **Sinclair Dinosaur** (Main St. and E. Baltimore St.), a small, green dinosaur located on top of auto body shop with a Route 66 sign immediately below.

❖ Back on 66

Keep cruising southwest on Route 66 via SR-53, and you'll come to the town of Braidwood in about 4.5 miles.

Braidwood and Godley

Soon after its inception in 1873, Braidwood had a population of about 2,000 people, consisting mostly of European immigrants and transients

with a slew of political, cultural, and religious differences. Fights were common, and riots broke out during elections.

Braidwood had a coal-mining boom when farmer Thomas Byron struck "black diamonds" in 1864. In 1877, after several pay cuts and years of mistreatment, the miners went on strike. The coal mining companies brought in black miners, called "black legs," from the Chicago, Wilmington, and Vermillion mines, and the strikebreakers formed groups with plans to kill them. The Governor called in 1,300 militiamen to restore the peace, but the "black legs" didn't feel safe. Most were eventually run out of town.

By 1890, the United Mine Workers Union was formed to demand fair pay and better working conditions. Mining was dangerous work—a snowmelt in February of 1883 flooded the mine, killing 74 men and boys. The Braidwood mines were closed in 1900; strip-mining began in 1927, one year after Route 66 began, and lasted until 1974.

Sights
Polk a Dot Drive In
If you want a sweet treat, the **Polk a Dot Drive In** (222 N. Front St., Braidwood, 815/458-3377, 11am-8pm daily, $7-13) has been around since 1962. Today it's been "Disney-fied" into a slick 1950s recreation of a diner with jukeboxes at the tables and fiberglass sculptures of Marilyn Monroe, Elvis Presley, and Betty Boop. Be sure to check out the wall of vintage photographs of Hollywood icons like James Dean, Joan Crawford, and Lucille Ball. They serve the usual diner fare of sandwiches, burgers, and chili-cheese fries, but their ice cream milk shakes, floats, and banana splits are the highlights on the menu.

top to bottom: Gemini Giant Muffler Man, Wilmington; Standard Oil Gas Station, and old Mobil station, Odell

Burma Shave

Heading west on SR-53 toward Godley, keep an eye out for red and white Burma Shave signs. Burma Shave was a brand of shaving cream with a clever advertising campaign from the 1920s to the 1960s. Typical jingles were divided among six evenly spaced signs and posted along the edge of the highway.

This sign near **Godley** was posted in 1930.

DOES YOUR HUSBAND
MISBEHAVE
GRUNT AND GRUMBLE
RANT AND RAVE
BURMA SHAVE

Route 66 Godley Red Carpet Cruise

If you love muscle cars, lowriders, and motorcycles and happen to be in Godley in early May, check for the annual **Route 66 Godley Red Carpet Cruise** (150 S. Kankakee Rd., Godley, 815/458-2222, www.classiccars.com, free). The two-day family event celebrates the people, history, and cars that cruise the Mother Road with food, music, a raffle, a craft fair, and a flea market.

✪ Back on 66

Drive southwest on Highway 53 for 2.5 miles to Godley, and then continue on Highway 53 for 5 miles to Gardner.

Gardner

As you approach the town of Gardner along SR-53, turn right (west) onto East Washington Street. After a few blocks, turn left (south) onto North Center Street and look for the **Streetcar Diner** (5650 SR-53 at E. Mazon St.). This streetcar was moved to Gardner as a diner in 1932. In 1937, the diner became a playhouse and cottage. After the diner closed in 1939, it was an unofficial Greyhound Bus stop.

The **Route 66 Association of Illinois** (www.il66assoc.org) restored the diner and dedicated the building to the late Bob and Peggy Craft. The Crafts owned the Riviera Roadhouse in Gardner, a popular supper club and speakeasy frequented by Al Capone in the 1920s. After

a suspicious fire destroyed the Riviera in June 2010, the Streetcar Diner (housed on the premises of the Riviera) was moved to this location. The diner was inducted into the Route 66 Hall of Fame in 2001. You can't go inside, but you can peer through the windows and see the wooden benches and stools that line chrome counter.

Next to the diner is the **Gardner Jail,** which was built in 1906 and operated through the 1950s. With only two jail cells, however, it was really more of a drunk tank than anything else.

✪ Back on 66

Follow SR-53 through Gardner. SR-53 makes a sharp right (west) after East Odell Street as you head out of town. Turn left (southwest) onto Route 66. This stretch of Route 66 runs south through seven miles of green pastures alongside I-55 before it branches off into the town of Dwight.

Dwight

✪ Route 66 through Dwight

There are two Route 66 alignments that go through Dwight.

1926 Alignment

As you approach Dwight on Historic U.S. 66, a left (southeast) turn onto South Brewster Road (aka Dwight Rd.) is the 1926 alignment and will take you through downtown Dwight.

Post-1940s Alignment

If you're short on time, the post-1940s alignment continues straight on U.S. 66 and bypasses downtown.

Sights

Ambler's Texaco Gas Station and Dwight Welcome Center

If you want to explore Dwight, you can see one of the longest operating gas stations on Route 66. **Ambler's Texaco Gas Station** (417 W. Waupansie St.) was run by Basil "Tubby" Ambler from 1938 to 1966. It was built in 1933 in the domestic, quaint cottage-style with an A-frame roof, multipaned windows, and asphalt shingles to appear more residential and fit in with the nearby suburban architecture. Over the years, the large wide-legged brick columns and tall Texaco gas pumps were replaced with straight columns and shorter, squatter Sky Chief gas pumps. It operated as a gas station for 66 years (good number!) and then from 1999 to 2002 it was an auto repair shop. The

National Park Service Route 66 Corridor program provided matching funds to restore the station and painted it to match the 1940s color scheme.

Today, it's the **Dwight Welcome Center** (815/548-3077, 10am-4pm daily May-Oct., free) with an outdoor display of a map of the town, a replica of the station inside, and maps and tourist information about local and statewide attractions. There are also oddities like old fan belts and a collection of vintage S&H green stamps from the 1960s.

Keeley Institute

From 1879 to 1965, the famous and controversial **Keeley Institute** (134 W. Main St., 815/584-1652) was one of the leading drug and alcohol rehab facilities in the country. Dr. Leslie Keeley claimed a 95 percent cure rate for those suffering from alcohol, opium, and tobacco addiction. Patients received four daily injections of a cocktail of chemicals dissolved in red, white, and blue solution. While Keeley's

Ambler's Texaco Gas Station, Dwight

medical industry peers considered these concoctions everything from mysterious to miraculous to pure quackery, the more than 200 centers had a 50 percent success rate and became wildly popular.

The Keeley Institute attracted more than 800 addicts each week and treated more than 400,000 patients. To keep up with the steady stream of new arrivals, roads were paved, electric lights replaced gas lamps, and sewage systems were updated. The Keeley Institute put Dwight on the map, and the town became known as the most famous village of its size in America.

Today the Keeley Institute is housed in the William W. Fox Development Center, which serves people with developmental disabilities. Some of the buildings throughout town that formerly housed Keeley patients include the Livingston Hotel (corner of W. Main St. and Mazon Ave.), the Keeley Building (310 S. Prairie Ave.), and the John R. Oughton House (101 W. South St.).

Railroad Depot

Dwight's **Railroad Depot** (119 W. Main St., 800/872-7245, 7:45am-10:25am and 5:15pm-7pm daily) is a gothic Romanesque stone structure that dates from 1891. It was designed by Chicago architect Henry Ives Cobb, who also designed the buildings at the University of Chicago. This is one of the few remaining Amtrak stations along Route 66 that feature the original architecture from the late 1800s. The foundation is made of stone from Joliet and the cathedral ceilings are made from oak wainscoting.

To get here from Route 66, take SR-17 east to S. Prairie Avenue and turn right (south). After three blocks, take a left onto West Main Street.

First National Bank

The 1906 **First National Bank** (122 W. Main St., 815/584-1212, 9am-3pm Mon.-Thurs., 9am-5pm Fri., 9am-noon Sat., free), across the street from the railroad depot, was designed by Frank Lloyd Wright. The building is an early example of Wright's Prairie style, with limestone block and deeply recessed horizontal windows. One of the most distinctive architectural features is the interior fireplace, which was uncommon in an office building.

Food

The John R. Oughton House was a 20-room Victorian mansion that formerly housed Keeley patients. Now it's the **Country Mansion Restaurant** (101 W. South St., 815/548-2345, www.thecountrymansion.com, 11am-8pm Tues.-Thurs., 11am-3pm and 4pm-9pm Fri.-Sat., 8:30am-6pm Sun., $8-25). The dining room is original and the oak wood interior is beautiful. Most dishes are made from scratch, and the prime rib and bacon-wrapped pork chops are extremely popular. And despite its history, they do serve alcohol.

The restaurant is located south of downtown Dwight. From Route 66, drive east on SR-17, turn right (south) onto South Franklin Street, and then make another right (west) onto South Street.

The **Old Route 66 Family Restaurant** (105 S. Old Route 66, 815/548-2920, www. route66restaurant.com, 5am-9pm Sun.-Thurs., 5am-10pm Fri.-Sat., $8-12) is located across the street from Ambler's gas station, right on the corner of SR-17 and Route 66. The restaurant serves a cheap and tasty breakfast and their famous "broasted" chicken by the bucket. If you've never heard of broasted chicken, you're not alone. After slowly marinating the chicken, it is lightly breaded and then broasted—a special high-pressure cooking fryer seals in the natural juices while blocking the cooking oil. So you get the taste and texture of fried chicken without all the grease.

◈ Back on 66

Heading south out of Dwight, Historic U.S. 66 parallels I-55 for about seven miles. As I-55 veers right (west), stay on Route 66 south. In one mile, turn left onto Odell Road (N. West. St.) to follow the 1926 alignment to the town of Odell.

Odell

Upon entering Odell, the road branches off into the post-1940s route and bypasses the town. If time allows, I recommend taking the pre-1940's alignment, Turn left (southeast) onto Odell Road. In less than one mile, Odell Road becomes Prairie Street. In in two blocks, take a left (southwest) on North West Street.

Odell was once a railroad town and a major resource for grain collection. In the 1870s, more than 1.5 million bushels of grain were shipped out of Odell.

Keep an eye out for an **old Mobil station** (102 S. West St.) on the right (west) side of the road, with a classic logo of the red-winged Mustang on the front of the garage. It has long been closed and thankfully hasn't been restored.

(Restorations can make things look too polished and erase the etched patina that took decades to make.) This mobile station is one of those roadside relics that look like it has stood the test of time.

The road through Odell was paved in 1922, just four years before Route 66 was born. By 1933, locals were so frustrated with Route 66 traffic that they built a **Pedestrian Tunnel** beneath Route 66 in order to cross it. The tunnel is closed now, but you can see entryway across the street from Saint Paul's Church at the corner of South West Street (Route 66) and West Hamilton Street.

As you head south (west) on Route 66, the road curves left, and on the west side is the perfectly restored **Standard Oil Gas Station** (400 S. West St.). Unlike the Mobil station, this 1932 refurbished classic looks frozen in time. The station was in service through the mid-1960s and operated as a body shop until 1975. The Illinois Route 66 Association spearheaded a grassroots effort to raise the necessary funds to restore it to its former glory; it won the National Historic Route 66 Cyrus Avery Award for its meticulous preservation. Today, the property is a **Welcome Center** (815/998-2133, 10am-4pm daily) and souvenir shop.

◈ Back on 66

As you head south out of Odell, South West Street rejoins Route 66. I-55 parallels Route 66 for about three miles until Route 66 veers south of I-55 near the town of Cayuga. From Cayuga, it is 6 miles south to Pontiac.

The original 1920s pavement was 18 feet wide and six inches deep. In the 1940s, the 18-mile segment that started in Cayuga and ended in Chenoa could not handle the excess weight and volume of military traffic during World War II. In 1943-1944, the road was modernized into 24-foot-wide, 10-inch-thick concrete with 11-foot driving lanes, two feet wider than the previous ones. The northbound lanes have been repaved, but the southbound lanes, for the most part, still have the original concrete surface.

Pontiac

Pontiac is one of those places that makes you feel like you've stepped into a Norman Rockwell painting—it's what nostalgia lovers live for. For the rest of us, it's fascinating to think that life could be this simple.

Pontiac was named after Chief Pontiac (1720-1769) of the Ottawa Indians. He was a fierce warrior who fought the British military occupation that was invading the Great Lakes area. Chief Pontiac was unusual because he unified other nations such as the Ojibwa and Potawatomi to fight with him. He realized that not all Europeans were bad and joined forces with the French, who appeared to hate the Brits as much as he did. He saw the value in adopting some of their customs but realized it was a detriment because his people would become dependent on them and lose their traditions and independence. Ultimately, they lost, and the French eventually turned on them, but legend has it that as a result of Pontiac's strategic efforts, the British decided it would be a mistake to underestimate the intelligence and power of tribal nations.

◈ Route 66 through Pontiac

To explore Pontiac's charming tree-lined streets, 24 murals, beautiful parks along the Vermillion River, and 18th-century brick buildings, you have to leave Route 66 temporarily. From Route 66, turn left (south) onto Pontiac Road. At the corner near the **Old Log Cabin Restaurant** (N. 1600 E Rd.), the road splits. Stay to the right to remain on Pontiac Road. Traveling southwest on Pontiac Road, turn left (south) onto North Main Street and drive less than one mile to SR-116. A right turn will take you to the Route 66 Association Hall of Fame and Museum.

Sights

If you happen to visit Pontiac from May through August, don't miss the annual **Pontiac Cruise Night** (815/882-8037, www. pontiaccruisenight.com, 5pm-8pm 3rd Sat. May-Aug.). It's a major community event held in downtown Pontiac around the square. There are classic cars, a DJ, racing hot wheels, raffles, face painting, food, and just an all-around good time.

For more information about Pontiac, visit the **Pontiac City Hall and Visitors Center** (115 W. Howard St., 815/844-3396, www.pontiac.org).

Old Log Cabin Inn & Restaurant

As you approach Pontiac, you'll see the **Old Log Cabin Inn & Restaurant** (18700 Old Rte. 66, 815/842-2908, 5am-8pm Mon.-Sat., $5-13) on the south side of the highway, right before the turnoff for Pontiac Road. Even if you're not hungry, stop to check this place out. The restaurant opened in 1926 as a lunchroom and gas station. Made of cedar telephone poles and knotty pine walls, which are still here today, the restaurant attracted customers with the smoke coming off the beef and pork barbecue from the small building in the back. After Route 66 became a four-lane highway and literally moved one block to the west side of the Log Cabin, they picked up the building and turned it around to face the new road. Hundreds of people from town came to watch this major event. If you walk behind the restaurant today, you can see the original Route 66 alignment along the railroad tracks.

★ Route 66 Association Hall of Fame and Museum

One of your first stops in Pontiac should be the **Route 66 Association Hall of Fame and Museum** (110 W. Howard St., 815/844-4566, 9am-5pm daily Apr.-Oct., 10am-4pm daily Nov.-Mar., free). It's one of the best Route 66 museums on the route, so be sure to set aside at least an hour to see the museum and the street

Burma Shave

Soon after the split in **Pontiac**, keep an eye out for another set of Burma Shave signs. A couple of them are missing, so they don't make sense today, but this is what they said in 1942:

IF HUGGING
ON HIGHWAYS (missing)
IS YOUR SPORT (missing)
TRADE IN
YOUR CAR
FOR A DAVENPORT (missing)
BURMA SHAVE

murals outside. The museum is located in a historic firehouse with reportedly the world's largest mural of the Route 66 road sign on the building. Inside there are thousands of pieces of noteworthy Illinois artifacts and Route 66 memorabilia, including a piece of the original Route 66 pavement. This museum is great because it celebrates the people and business owners who made Route 66 one of the most memorable and important highways in the world. One featured tribute is to the late great Route 66 artist Bob Waldmire. His Volkswagen van, rocking chair, and record and rock collections are on display. Legend has it that Waldmire stashed his marijuana under his van in two boxes, which are still there. When the cops inquired about the contents of the boxes, Waldmire said the nests for his snakes were inside and shouldn't be disturbed. He died in 2009, but his spirit lives on in the whimsical artwork printed on his postcards sold along Route 66.

International Walldog Mural & Sign Art Museum

The **International Walldog Mural & Sign Art Museum** (217 N. Mill St., 815/842-1848, http://muralmuseum.com, 9am-5pm Mon.-Sat., 9am-4pm Sun., free) section features "Walldogs," artists that painted murals and advertisements on buildings and barns throughout the United States. It was originally a derogatory name for mural painters who worked "like dogs" in all kinds of weather from the 1890s through the mid-1900s. The aged murals are fading cultural keepsakes of the story of American advertising and a reminder of a time when ads were painted by hand.

Mural Walking Tour

There's plenty of free parking in Pontiac, so if the weather is nice and you want to ditch the car, take a walk and see the murals throughout the town. Across from the Route 66 Museum is the **Bob Waldmire Memorial Mural** (E. Howard St.). Waldmire designed the mural, but he died before finishing it, so 500 of his friends stepped in to complete it. The 66-foot-long mural tells the story of Route 66, a stunning testament to Bob's dedication and contribution to the Mother Road.

One block south is the **Chautauqua Movement Mural** (southeast corner of W. Madison St. and Main St.). The Chautauqua Movement was a Christian-based educational movement popular in rural America from the late 1800s to the early 1930s. Musicians, entertainers, speakers, and preachers traveled throughout the country to promote small-town values, an early form of mass entertainment and culture. At its peak in 1924, about 40 million people attended their events. President Theodore Roosevelt called the Chautauqua Movement "One of the most American things in America." Critics, however, such as author Sinclair Lewis, considered the movement provincial and claimed that it didn't accurately reflect the reality of American life.

The **Chief Pontiac Mural** is about one block west on Madison Street, at the corner of North Mill Street. Since there were no photographs of Chief Pontiac, the image is a composite based on descriptions from Ottawa tribe members.

Pontiac Oakland Automobile Museum

Car lovers will enjoy the **Pontiac Oakland Automobile Museum** (205 N. Mill St., 815/842-2345, www.pontiacoakland-museum.org, 9am-5pm daily Apr.-Oct., 10am-4pm daily Nov.-Mar., free). The museum is home to about 15 gorgeous vintage Pontiacs and a comprehensive library of brochures, designs, drawings, maps, and service manuals. It's not the biggest auto museum on Route 66, but it's beautiful and it's free.

The Automobile Museum is located one block south of the Chief Pontiac mural on North Mill Street.

★ Swinging Bridges

There is so much to do in Pontiac that you'll want to have more time to explore the historical bridges that cross the Vermillion River. There are three swinging pedestrian bridges. The oldest bridge is the **1898 Pedestrian Bridge,** which was built by the Joliet Bridge Company to help shoe factory workers get to factories on the north side of town. It's 190 feet long and 4 feet wide.

If you walk across the bridge, on the other side of the river is **Play Park.** From here, you can easily access the **1926 Swinging Footbridge** by turning left and walking southeast about 500 feet along the riverbank to the footbridge. This bridge was built for the Pontiac Chautauqua Assembly and led folks from Play Park to Chautauqua Park.

The newest pedestrian bridge is about 0.5 miles west at the **Humiston-Riverside Park** (W. Water St. and Oak St.). This bridge was built in 1978 mainly for aesthetic purposes. If you're limited on time, the 1898 and 1926 bridges are recommended, as they are close in proximity and have the most interesting history.

To get here from the auto museum, head south Mill St. and then east on Washington Street and turn right (south) onto Riverview Drive. Riverview Drive curves east after Timber Street; the 1898 Pedestrian Bridge is straight ahead before the curve.

Accommodations and Food

Pontiac lodging options are limited, with the exception of the usual chain motels. Reserve a room in advance at the Three Roses B&B. If Three Roses is booked, consider the Chateau Hotel in Bloomington, about 30 miles away.

One of the best B&Bs on Route 66 is ★ **Three Roses Bed & Breakfast** (209 E Howard St., 815/844-3404, www.three-roses.us, $100-160), a beautiful 1890 Victorian with a lovely front porch, charming rooms, comfy beds, and warm hospitality. Owner Sharon Hanson has two mottoes: "Do unto others as you would have them do unto you" and "Always give the customer more than they pay for." Sharon lives by this, with a big homemade breakfast (pancakes, eggs Benedict, homemade granola, fresh cinnamon rolls, sausage, biscuits, hash browns, and scones) cooked from scratch that is absolutely delicious.

If you decide to eat at the **Old Log Cabin Inn & Restaurant** (18700 Old Rte. 66, 815/842-2908, 5am-8pm Mon.-Sat., $5-13), you're in luck. The bacon is so crispy it crackles, the pork chops are good and tender, and the pies are homemade.

From the front, **Edinger's Filling Station** (423 W. Madison St., 815/419-2255, 5:30am-4pm Mon.-Fri., 5:30am-2pm Sat., $8-13) looks like a classic gas station, but inside great homemade pies are made. While coconut crème is a favorite, there are also plenty of savory options such as crispy cheese balls, fluffy homemade biscuits, meatball soup, and fried mac-and-cheese.

Locals love **Pontiac Family Kitchen** (904 W. Custer Ave., 815/844-3155, 5am-9pm Sun.-Thurs., 5am-10pm

Fri.-Sat., $7-$12), where the Friday night fish fry and hot turkey sandwiches with cranberry sauce are comfort food favorites.

⊕ Back on 66

To return to Route 66 from downtown Pontiac, take Howard Street west to South Ladd Street (old Route 66) and turn left. Turn right (west) onto W. Reynolds Street and the next left (south) will put you onto Route 66 for about nine miles south to the town of Chenoa.

Chenoa

As you approach Chenoa on Route 66, take a left (south) on N. Division Street. Stay to the right and in less than a mile merge onto North Veto Street. The Chenoa Pharmacy, on Green Street, is three blocks south.

Chenoa was born as a railroad town that developed into an agricultural center because it has some of the richest, most fertile soil in the world. Today it's a sleepy town with beautiful old buildings like the **Chenoa Pharmacy** (209 S. Green St., 815/945-4211, 9am-5pm Mon.-Fri., 9am-noon Sat.), which has been open since 1889. One of the longest-running businesses in the area, the pharmacy's wood floors and antique cabinetry are original.

A few doors down across the street, look for the **Selz Royal Blue Shoes Mural** (224 Green St.), a cool re-creation of a vintage advertisement that was discovered when the adjoining building was torn down.

⊕ Back on 66

To rejoin Route 66 from the Selz Royal Blue Shoes Mural, head south on Green Street for two blocks to U.S. 24. Turn right (west) and then left (south) onto Route 66. The next town, Lexington, is about seven miles south.

Lexington

Lexington was started in 1836, and its survival was in question until the railroad came to town in 1854. Once Route 66 was underway, Lexington became a railroad stop between Chicago and St. Louis—a key factor in its success. Once rail traffic declined and was replaced by auto traffic, Lexington became a popular stopping point on Route 66 from the 1950s through 1978, when I-55 became the preferred, faster route.

Lexington has repurposed and preserved an old section of Route 66 as a walkway and a park, aptly named **Memory Lane** (102 Morris Ave.). It's the perfect place to get out, stretch your legs, and look at the 1940s vintage billboards and Burma Shave signs. Memory Lane is located right off Route 66 near West Main Street.

Along Route 66 near Main Street, keep an eye out for a recently restored 1940s red-and-white **Lexington Neon Sign** with an arrow pointing eastward.

⊕ Back on 66

Heading south on Route 66, you'll be in the town of Towanda in about seven miles.

Towanda

Train travel was essential to the development of Towanda. Most towns in the area, such as Pontiac, Lexington, and Bloomington, were laid out around a town square, but Towanda's Main Street was laid out diagonally and parallel to the railroad tracks. Passenger service stopped in the 1940s; in 1955, Route 66 was widened to four lanes and partially divided with a grass median. The former southbound lanes are no longer used, and the northbound lanes are now the two-lane highway. In 1977, when I-55 was developed, Route 66 traffic was rerouted to the northwest side of Towanda, and a 3.25-mile section of the southbound lane was closed.

A 2.5-mile stretch of this abandoned roadway has been developed into the **Towanda Route 66 Park and Restoration Project,** a geographic tour and scenic walkway with murals, flower gardens, shrubs, trees, benches, picnic tables, Burma Shave signs, bridges, and flagpoles. There is a large interactive map with historical plaques on Route 66 that originated as a class project for the Normal Community High School. The students and the town have also petitioned to save an old Route 66 bridge that was slated for destruction. (It warms the heart to know that the next generation wants to preserve and protect the Mother Road.) The walkway begins near SR-29 and runs south parallel Route 66.

⊕ Back on 66

Heading south on Route 66 toward Normal, the 1926 alignment breaks up as it enters from the northeast. Route 66 used to follow the railroad tracks, but was rerouted in 1940.

To follow as much of the early route as possible, stay on Old U.S. Route 66 as it heads south out of Towanda. In about 4 miles, Old U.S. Route 66 runs alongside I-55 (Veterans Pkwy.). Route 66 becomes Shelbourne Drive in Normal. Turn left (south) onto Henry Street and then right on Pine Street (southwest) as it veers right (west).

Normal

Normal was named after what is now Illinois State University, but in the 1850s, "normal" schools were institutions that trained high school graduates to become teachers. Many state universities, including UCLA, were once "normal" schools.

Sights
Sprague's Super Service Station and Café

On the left (south) side of Pine Street is **Sprague's Super Service Station and Café** (305 E. Pine St. at N. Walnut St.), a Tudor Revival-style station that was built in 1931 and is one of the largest two-story gas stations on Route 66. Similar to Ambler's Texaco Station in Dwight, Sprague's was built in a cottage-style design to fit in with its suburban surroundings. The gas pumps were removed in the late 1970s, and the building was then used as a storefront for manufacturing companies, Yellow Cab, and Avis Rent-a-Car. It's been listed on the National Register of Historic Places, and efforts are underway to restore it.

Head west on Pine Street, then turn left (south) on Linden Street. Turn right (west) onto East Willow Street and then follow Business U.S. 51 (Center St.) south.

Normal Theater

The **Normal Theater** (209 W. North St., 309/454-9720, www.normaltheater.com, shows 7pm, $7) is a very cool restored theater dating from 1937. Its Streamline Moderne art deco architecture is incredible, and it was the first theater wired for sound for the "talkies" in the Twin Cities. For Depression-era moviegoers, this $0.25 and $0.10 theater was a welcome escape to temporarily forget about their problems and get lost in the art of film. The week of its opening, The Normal featured films with Bing Crosby, Jack Benny, Ida Lupito, and the Barbara Stanwyck comedy *Breakfast for Two.* Today, the theater still plays "oldies but goodies" and host live music and theater performances.

From Business U.S. 51, turn left (east) on West College Avenue. Take a right (south) on South School Street and then turn left (east) on West North Street. The theater is one block down on the right (south) side.

⬥ Back on 66

Heading south on Center Street (Business U.S. 51) you'll approach the town of Bloomington. To stay on Route 66, pass East Locust Street then merge right to keep following Business U.S. 51, which turns into North Madison Street. A newer alignment runs parallel and carries the eastbound traffic (N. East St.).

Bloomington

From North Madison Street (Business U.S. 51), turn left (east) onto West Washington Street and then make another left (north) onto North Main Street.

Sights
David Davis Mansion

Lincoln history buffs will enjoy the **David Davis Mansion** (1000 Monroe Dr., 309/828-1084, www.daviddavismansion. org, 9am-4pm Wed.-Sat., free, $4 suggested donation) where docents share the cultural history of the mid-to-late 1800s outlining servant, domestic, and family life in a Victorian mansion built in 1872. When Lincoln was president, judge David Davis helped the President's political and legal career. The gardens outside of the property are patterned after 17th century Italian and 18th century English gardens. Eighty-nine gardeners volunteered 5,300 hours of labor to keep them looking beautiful.

McLean County Museum of History

In Bloomington you can learn how to beat a rug and push a steel plow at the **McLean County Museum of History** (200 N. Main St., 309/827-0428, www.mchistory.org, 9am-5pm Mon. and Wed.-Sat., 9am-9pm Tues., $5, Tues. free), located in the former 1901 courthouse. There are seven exhibition galleries with 19,000 objects, more than 11,500 rare books, and 1,700 feet of historical papers. The exhibits examine prairie life for different cultures, from Irish immigrants to South Asians living in McLean County.

Accommodations

Chateau Hotel (1621 Jumer Dr., 309/662-2020, www.bloomingtonchateau.com, $50-120) is a large, smoke-free property with 180 rooms and suites. Rooms feature modern furnishings with flat-screen televisions, a desk, and ergonomic chair. A full-size heated indoor swimming pool, sauna, and whirlpool spa are on the property; washer and dryers are available on every floor (guest laundry comes in handy for long road trips).

Food

If you're in the mood for pizza, a meatball sub, or fettuccini Alfredo, the **Lucca Grill** (116 E. Market St., Bloomington, 309/828-7521, www.luccagrill.com, 11am-midnight Mon.-Wed., 11am-1am Thurs.-Sat., 3pm-9pm Sun., $7-14) is worth a stop. A Route 66 tradition since 1936, Lucca's has some of the best thin-crust pizza in the area. Try to get a seat downstairs where the dark, old-school atmosphere will remind you that this place has been around forever.

From Business U.S. 51 south, turn left (east) on East Market Street then and left (north) onto Business U.S. 51, which carries the eastbound Route 66 traffic. Lucca's is on the left (west) side of the road.

⬥ Back on 66

U.S. 51 south becomes Center Street as it leaves Bloomington. To stay on Route 66, turn right (west) on I-55/Veterans Parkway. Continue west on South Beich Road, which is the frontage road for I-55 for about seven miles to Funks Grove.

Funks Grove

Sights
Funks Grove Pure Maple Sirup

Since the late 1800s, three generations

of the Funk family have been making **Funks Grove Pure Maple Sirup** (5257 Old Route 66, 309/874-3360, www.funksmaplesirup.com, 9am-5pm Mon.-Fri., 10am-5pm Sat., 1pm-5pm Sun. Mar.-Aug.). In 1948, they attached 600 buckets at the trees and made up to 240 gallons of "sirup" priced at $7 per gallon; by 2001, there were 6,400 taps producing an average 2,000 gallons of sirup each season. During the early years of Route 66, Hazel Funk owned the property. In her will she made sure the farmland would be protected by a trust for future generations, and she also wanted "sirup" spelled with an "I," which was the *Webster's Dictionary* spelling referring to a product made from boiling sap with no added sugar. Today, it remains a Route 66 landmark, and they've maintained the traditional spelling in honor of Hazel. The gift shop sells their legendary sirup, maple candy, T-shirts, hats, and gift boxes.

Sugar Grove Nature Center

About one mile west of Funks sirup is the **Sugar Grove Nature Center** (4532 N. 725 East Rd., 309/874-2174, www.sugar-grovenaturecenter.org, 9am-5pm Tues.-Fri., 10am-3pm Sat., noon-4pm Sun. Apr.-Oct., 10am-3pm Tues.-Sat. Nov.-Mar., trails dawn to dusk daily, free), with more than 1,000 acres of pristine prairieland and woods for hiking and wildlife viewing. It's located in Funks Grove, with four nature preserves and the largest remaining intact prairie in Illinois.

There are seven miles of well-maintained trails. Consider hiking the **Orange Trail,** a 0.5-mile walk along Timber Creek. At just under two miles, the **Blue Trail** starts at the nature center and goes to the Funks Grove Church and the Chapel of Temple Trees, which was built by the Funk family, who started the sirup company. Also on-site are plant, butterfly, and herb gardens.

◆ Back on 66

The next stop on Route 66 is the small railroad town of McLean. From Funks Grove, follow Route 66 three miles west as it curves left (south) onto Steward Road. Stay on Steward Road south for two blocks and take a right (west) on Carlisle Street. Turn left (south) on Main Street to the junction with U.S. 136 in McLean.

McLean

In the 1920s, businesses sprang up to accommodate Route 66 traffic. The most significant business was **Dixie Trucker's Home** (598 Main St.), which started as a mechanic's garage and sold sandwiches at a counter with six stools. By the 1930s, it was a fully functioning restaurant open 24 hours a day, 365 days a year; the only day it closed was due to a fire in 1965. The Beeler family owned and operated the business from 1928 through 2001, when they declared bankruptcy. Since then, it has changed ownership several times. In 2009 it was completely remodeled and is now a "Travel Plaza" with a more commercial feel, and has lost the essence of that roadside character Route 66 aficionados live for.

◆ Back on 66

As you leave McLean, head west on U.S. 136 then turn left onto Historic U.S. 66 (before the railroad tracks). In about five miles, you'll approach Atlanta. There is a later alignment that bypasses the town, but you don't want to miss Atlanta's historic downtown.

Atlanta

As Historic U.S. 66 veers southeast from the railroad tracks, turn right onto Sycamore Street. Sycamore Street becomes Arch Street, which will take you into downtown Atlanta.

Sights

Atlanta was the commercial center and hotspot for central Illinois in the mid-1800s. There were more than 40 wood buildings, but fires destroyed many of them. In 1867, the **Downey Building** was the first brick building in Atlanta. It's a beautiful two-story building in a classic Italianate style with arched windows. Over the years it has been a bank, law office, grocery, millenary shop, and hardware store.

Paul Bunyon Muffler Man

The **Paul Bunyon Muffler Man**, across the street from the Palms Grill, holds a gigantic hot dog in place of an ax. The 19-foot-tall fiberglass sculpture was moved from Bunyon's Hot Dog stand in Cicero to its current location Atlanta in 2003, when the town won a bid for this larger-than-life piece of Americana.

Atlanta Route 66 Arcade Museum

For fun, you can battle space invaders at **Atlanta Route 66 Arcade Museum** (114 SW Arch St., 309/289-1725, 9am-4pm Mon.-Sat., admission free, games $0.25). They have vintage pinball and video games from 1934 to 1982, including *Dog Fight, Monster Gun, Pac-Man, Asteroids, Frenzy, Battlezone, Space Encounters,* and *Card Whiz.*

Seth Thomas Clock

Walking around downtown Atlanta, you'll pass the 1908 library with the 1901 **Seth Thomas Clock** (100 Race St.). The 40-foot tower and eight-sided clock is still wound by hand.

J. H. Hawes Grain Elevator Museum

Until 1975, the **J. H. Hawes Grain Elevator Museum** (301 SW 2nd St., 217/648-2056, www.haweselevator.org, dawn-dusk daily, tours 1pm-3pm Sun. June-Aug., free) was used to store grain before the railroad shipped it out to nearby states.

It's the only restored vertical wooden grain elevator on the National Register of Historic places in Illinois. Where else are you going to see a real grain elevator from 1903?

From Arch Street, walk southwest one block to Race Street and turn right (northwest). Head two blocks north to 2nd Street and take a left (southwest).

Accommodations and Food

The ★ **Colaw Rooming House** (204 NW Vine St., 217/671-1219, www.the-colawhouse.com, $150) is set in a 1947 Victorian just two blocks from Route 66. The three-bedroom, two-bath house features rooms with lots of natural light, beautiful hardwood floors, and antique queen beds. Although breakfast isn't served, coffee and tea are available in the kitchen, and you'll receive a complimentary breakfast for two at the Palms Grill Café, which is even better!

The ★ **Palms Grill Cafe** (110 SW Arch St., 217/648-2233, www.thepalmsgrillcafe.com, 7am-7pm Tues.-Sat., $5-12) opened in 1934, and with the help of a grant from the National Park Service Route 66 Corridor Preservation Program, is still there today. The café has been lovingly restored to its roots—the tables, booths, bar, lighting fixtures, flooring, and even the antique cash register ring back to a time when food and life seemed less complicated. Waitresses wear 1940s uniforms and dish out blueplate specials, beef noodle soup, and grilled-cheese sandwiches. Don't miss the amazing and award-winning pies. If you're too full, take a slice to go for the road.

⏚ Back on 66

As you leave Atlanta, head southwest on Arch Street, which will rejoin the post-1940s alignment of Route 66. Take Route 66 west for about eight miles toward Lincoln.

Lincoln

◈ Route 66 through Lincoln
The 1926 Route 66 alignment goes through downtown Lincoln, while the 1940s alignment bypasses most of the town.

1926 Alignment
To drive the 1926 alignment, turn left (southeast) on Kickapoo Street just before reaching Lincoln. Make a quick right (southwest) onto Business I-55 (which is still Kickapoo St.). After about one mile, turn right (northwest) onto Keokuk Street.

About two miles after Kickapoo Street, the road makes a sharp turn to the left (south). This was one of the deadliest spots on Route 66—according to locals there was a car crash every few hours, earning it the name "killer curve."

Post-1930s Alignment
If your time is limited, stay on Route 66 (aka Lincoln Parkway) as you approach Lincoln to follow the newer alignment, a four-lane bypass that was built in 1944.

Sights
Lincoln Heritage Museum
The town of Lincoln was named after Abraham Lincoln before he was president. If you love Lincoln, American politics, and Civil War history, stop at the **Lincoln Heritage Museum** (300 Keokuk St., 217/735-7399, www.museum.lincoln-college.edu, 9am-4pm Mon.-Fri., 1pm-4pm Sat., $5), which features remnants of Lincoln's life and legacy. The museum exhibits campaign banners from 1860, Lincoln's desk, furnishings from his home, and even a lock of his hair.

The museum is located on Keokuk Street, about 0.5 miles north of Kickapoo Street. To stay on the **1926 alignment**, from Keokuk Street head southwest on North Sangamon Street. Sangamon Street curves right (west) as it turns into 3rd Street. In less than one mile, turn left (south) onto South Washington Street.

Mill Restaurant
At the corner of 2nd and South Washington Streets, you'll see the now-closed **Mill Restaurant** (738 S. Washington St.), a 1929 Dutch-themed restaurant with a large windmill out front. In the 1940s a barroom and dance-hall were added. The Mill was famous for fried schnitzel until it closed in 1996. The building was slated for demolition in 2005, but since then there has been a formidable, community-wide effort to save the historic structure. To learn more, visit www.savethemill.org.

World's Largest Covered Wagon
For a cheesy photo-op, drive five blocks north to 5th Street and turn left (west). After crossing Lincoln Parkway, look for the **World's Largest Covered Wagon** (1750 5th St.), with Abraham Lincoln in the driver's seat. The 25-foot wagon is made of oak and steel with a 12-foot tall Abraham Lincoln in the driver's seat. The covered wagon was created in 2001 by David Bentley and finished in time to celebrate the 75th anniversary of the Mother Road.

Food
Hallie's On the Square (111 S. Kickapoo St., 217/732-6923, 11am-8pm Mon.-Fri., $5-10) has been using the original schnitzel recipe from the historic Mill Restaurant (now closed) since 1945. In addition to schnitzel, Hallie's serves burgers, hot sandwiches, and unusual menu items such as frog legs, gizzards, and "Horseshoes" (sandwiches topped with French fries and swimming in cheese sauce). Hallie's is located a few blocks east of Sangamon Street via Broadway Street.

◈ Back on 66
Heading out of Lincoln, continue south on Washington Street as it turns into Stringer Avenue and turn left (south) on

Lincoln Parkway (BUS-55). Drive 2 miles and turn left (southeast) on Historic U.S. 66. Within one mile, the road parallels I-55. In 2.5 miles, Route 66 curves left into Logan County 22 (near exit 119). Drive southwest on Route 66 for 3.5 miles into Elkhart.

Elkhart

Entering Elkhart on Route 66, turn left onto Governor Oglesby Street and drive east for two blocks to North Bogardus Street.

Elkhart had a thriving downtown in 1938. At the height of her career, the child actress Shirley Temple stopped here to eat lunch at The House by the Side of the Road restaurant on her way to a premier of her film *Little Miss Broadway* in Springfield. It meant so much to the owner of the restaurant that they roped off the area where she ate and no one ever sat there again. The metal **Shirley Temple Silhouette Statue** (209 Governor Oglesby St.) commemorates her visit with a silhouette depicting Temple drinking a soda and being served by a waitress. The statue is located a couple of blocks east of Route 66.

◆ Back on 66
As you leave Elkhart on Route 66, it's a straight shot about five miles south to Williamsville. As the pre-1930s alignment enters **Williamsville** (on Oak St.), turn left (northwest) on Highway 123 to join I-55 west. In less than three miles, take Exit 105 and turn right (south) on Business I-55/Sherman Boulevard.

Sherman

From Business Route 55, turn right onto Cabin Smoke Trail. The 1926 segment is on the left (south) side of the road.

Carpenter Park in Sherman has a short **abandoned segment** of Route 66. The two-lane, 16-foot-wide road was paved in 1922 with a mixture of gravel and cement with expansion joints placed every 30 yards. Though this segment has been closed since 1936, you can still see parts of the road with its original four-foot gravel shoulders and four-inch curbs. The post-1930s four-lane alignment bypassed this segment a few yards east.

The abandoned segment starts at the **Cabin Smoke Trail** and travels about 0.25 miles south to the Sangamon River and the site of the former Old Iron Bridge (now only concrete abutments remain). Though you can't drive on this section of the road, you can walk along it, which is actually better. Look down to see the forest creeping up through the cracks in the road and slowly reclaiming it.

◆ Back on 66
As Business I-55 curves west, Sherman Road becomes North Peoria Road. To stay on Business I-55, turn left at the Veteran's Parkway stoplight. In about three miles, you'll reach Springfield.

Springfield

If you love Lincoln, you're in luck. The only home he ever owned is in Springfield, the state capitol. Abraham Lincoln practiced law here from 1843 to about 1852, and he is buried at the Oak Ridge Cemetery.

Sights
Many of the Lincoln sites are within walking distance of each other. If you'd like to do a walking tour, visit the **Springfield Visitor's Bureau** (109 N. 7th St., 800/545-7300, www.visitspringfieldil-linois.com, 8:30am-5pm Mon.-Fri., free) to pick up a brochure and maps.

Abraham Lincoln Presidential Library and Museum
The **Abraham Lincoln Presidential Library and Museum** (212 N. 6th St.,

217/557-4588, www.illinois.gov, 9am-5pm daily, last admission 4pm, $15) is one of the most popular presidential libraries. It's a 200,000-square-foot complex with 40,000 square feet of galleries, theater presentations, historical artifacts, and interactive exhibits.

Lincoln Home National Historic Site

The **Lincoln Home National Historic Site** (426 S. 7th St., 217/492-4241, www.nps.

gov, 8:30am-5pm daily, free) is the two-story Greek Revival home that Lincoln lived in from 1844 to 1861. Built in 1839, the property has been restored to look as it did when Lincoln lived here, and several pieces of furniture on display are originals. Summer is the busy season, so it's best to arrive as early as possible.

Lincoln's Tomb State Historic Site

Lincoln's final resting place is north of

downtown at the **Oak Ridge Cemetery** (1500 Monument Ave., 217/782-2717, www.lincolntomb.org, 9am-5pm daily Apr.-Aug., 9am-4:30pm Wed. Sept.-Mar.), the second-most popular cemetery in America after Arlington National Cemetery in Washington DC. After Lincoln was assassinated, his body was interred here in 1874. His three youngest sons and Mrs. Lincoln are also buried here. The granite tomb sits on a rectangular base located on a 12.5-acre plot in a semicircular entranceway with a 117-foot tall obelisk. A bronze reproduction of Lincoln's head sits on a pedestal at the entrance.

Old State Capitol

The **Old State Capitol** (1 Old State Capitol Plaza, 217/785-9363, www.illinoishistory.gov, 9am-5pm Wed.-Sat., free) is where Lincoln's body lay in state after his assassination in 1865. It is also where Lincoln delivered his famous "House Divided" speech. In the speech Lincoln said he believed "A house divided against itself cannot stand. I believe this government cannot endure, permanently half slave and half free." The speech was a major turning point in Lincoln's career and inspired senatorial debates regarding the moral issue of slavery, whether slavery should be legal in the North, and if slaves are human beings.

Also at the Old State Capitol, a kiosk in the plaza marks the departure point for the **Donner Party**'s ill-fated trip in April 1846. Look for the kiosk just south of the building between 5th and 6th Streets. Nine covered wagons and 87 emigrants set out on a 2,500-mile journey to California that was supposed to take four months. After trying to take a shortcut, an early snowfall trapped them in the Sierra Nevada Mountains. They ran out of food, and almost half the party died, mostly of starvation, and some resorted to cannibalism to stay alive.

★ 1908 Race Riot Walking Tour

Two blocks east of the state capitol marks a dark chapter in Springfield's history. In 1908, Springfield had a population of 47,000 people; approximately 5.5 percent were black, the highest percentage of black residents of any city of comparable size in Illinois. A limited job market heightened racial tensions as industry owners used black laborers as strikebreakers during labor strikes. Two black men were accused of rape and assault, which triggered a white lynch mob of about 150 people. The mob lynched black citizens and looted and destroyed black-owned businesses and homes. It was a shocking embarrassment that this could happen in Lincoln's hometown. It took about 5,000 national guardsmen to end the two-day riot. The event made national news and led to the founding of the National Association for the Advancement of Colored People (NAACP).

The **1908 Race Riot Walking Tour** is a self-guided eight-marker tour that leads from the county jail where the mob formed to key sites where the riot ensued. The tour begins at the corner of 7th and Jefferson Streets, but your first stop should be the **Springfield Convention and Visitors Bureau** (109 N. 7th St., 800/545-7300, www.visitspringfieldillinois.com, 8:30am-5pm Mon.-Fri., free) to pick up brochures and maps. There are also other historical walking tours at the visitors center.

Dana-Thomas House

There is some great architecture in Springfield, including Frank Lloyd Wright's **Dana-Thomas House** (301 E. Lawrence Ave., 217/782-6776, www.dana-thomas.org, 9am-4pm Thurs.-Sun., suggested donation $10). Take a one-hour tour to explore one of the best examples of Wright's famed Prairie architecture. The Dana-Thomas House was built in 1902; the home is 12,000-square feet with 35 rooms, 100 pieces of furniture, 250 art-glass windows, 3 main levels, and 16 varying levels.

About four blocks west of the Dana-Thomas House is a **John Kearney sculpture** (425 S. College St.) of a white-tailed deer made from chrome car bumpers. Look for it in front of the Capitol Complex Visitors Center.

Cozy Dog Drive In
The **Cozy Dog Drive In** (2935 S. 6th St., 217/525-1922, www.cozydogdrivein. com, 8am-8pm daily, $5-10) lies south of Springfield, after Route 66 merges with 6th Street. Ed and Virginia Waldmire (parents of Route 66 artist Bob Waldmire) opened the Cozy Dog in 1949. It's still run by the Waldmire family and the place is packed with souvenirs, Route 66 memorabilia, and throngs of travelers eating cornbread-coated wieners on a stick. The drive in is located on a busy highway, but you can't miss it. Just keep an eye out for a huge yellow sign with two giant red hotdogs in a sweet, warm embrace.

Route 66 Twin Drive-In
For a fun night out retro-style, check out the **Route 66 Twin Drive-In** (1700 Recreation Dr., 217/698-0066, www. route66-drivein.com, movies start at dusk Apr.-Oct., $8), a restored drive-in that screens double features.

Accommodations and Food
If you want to stay the night in Springfield, **The State House Inn** (101 E. Adams St., 217/528-5100, www.ascend-collection.com, $100-150) is across from the State Capitol and Presidential Library. Rooms feature 1960s modern furnishings with pillow-top mattresses and baths with granite counters and cast-iron tubs.

Another option is the **Route 66 Hotel**

top to bottom: Lincoln family statue by Larry Anderson, Springfield; Cozy Dog Drive-In, Springfield; resident of Henry's Rabbit Ranch, Staunton

Local Eats

The **horseshoe sandwich** has been Springfield's signature dish since 1928. It's a platter-size open-faced sandwich with two thick slices of bread, meat, a pile of french fries, and a thick Welsh rarebit cheese sauce smothering the entire plate. In the original sandwich, the ham was made into the shape of a horseshoe, and the potato wedges on top resembled nails. In the 1970s, the horseshoe became the preferred workday lunch meal for laborers. Hamburger and processed yellow cheese sauce were substituted for the ham and the Welsh rarebit. It was the perfect meal for laborers because it was so much food, they didn't even need to eat dinner after working all day.

Today restaurants like **Maldaner's Restaurant** (222 S. 6th St., 217/522-4313, www.maldaners.com) offer smaller "pony shoes," which is a better idea for your waistline.

& Conference Center (625 E. St. Joseph St., 888/707-8366, www.rt66hotel.com, $60-80). It was originally a Holiday Inn and now has been revamped as a Route 66 conference center with a restaurant and comedy club. The rooms are spacious with basic amenities. The lobby has a 1941 Model T Ford, an old phone booth, and a vintage Shell gas pump.

Fast food history was made at the **Maid Rite Sandwich Shop** (118 N. Pasfield St., 217/523-0723, www.maid-rite.com, 10am-4pm Mon.-Fri., 11am-3pm Sat., $5-10). It opened in 1926 and claims to have the first drive-thru window in the country. It's a Midwestern staple that the locals love. They sell loose-meat burgers and homemade root beer. If you've never had a loose-meat burger, it's kind of like a sloppy Joe without the sauce. Locals like them with extra mustard and onions. It's worth checking out. Where else are you ever going to have a loose-meat sandwich and eat at a restaurant that still serves the same food they did more than 70 years ago?

If you're in the mood for a sit down meal, try **Saputo's** (801 E. Monroe St., 217/544-2523, 10:30am-10:30pm Mon.-Fri., 5pm-10:30pm Sat., 5pm-9:30pm Sun., $8-30). It's a family-owned restaurant that has been serving celebrities, dignitaries, and politicians since 1948. This southern-Italian supper club has good standbys like baked lasagna and chicken parmesan. When you walk in this place,

the decor makes you feel like you stepped back into the late 1960s.

A restaurant that oozes history is **Maldaner's Restaurant** (222 S. 6th St., 217/522-4313, www.maldaners.com, 11am-2:30pm Mon.-Fri., 5pm-9pm Tues.-Thurs., 5pm-10pm Fri.-Sat., $7-32). It's been open since 1884 and was a political watering hole back in the day. It's right on Route 66, making it one of the oldest restaurants on the route. When they tried to take the horseshoe sandwich off the menu, the locals protested until it was put back on. They serve classic dishes like quail stuffed with sausage, and beef Wellington with truffle sauce and mashed potatoes. This place is all about tradition.

⏏ Back on 66

As you head south out of Springfield, 6th Street turns into I-55 south, and you'll cross **Lake Springfield,** an artificial lake that formed 1931-1935. When the water level is low, sometimes the submerged 1926 Route 66 alignment can be seen.

Post-1930s Alignment

From Springfield to the Illinois-Missouri state line, you have two Route 66 alignments to choose from. The 1926 alignment follows historic Route 4, which predates Route 66 and goes through Chatham, Auburn, Carlinville, Thayer, and Girard. Route 4 has many twists and turns through farmland and old country towns. Since Route 66 only followed this route for four years, there are not many surviving businesses. I recommend the post-1930 Route 66, which parallels I-55 and travels through the towns of Litchfield and Mount Olive.

Glenarm

Traveling south on I-55, take the first exit south of Lake Springfield (Exit 88 Chatham) and turn right (southwest) on Palm Road, which curves left (south) to parallel I-55. The road becomes Douglas Street and then Frazee Road.

The **Sugar Creek Covered Bridge** (1 Covered Bridge Rd., Glenarm, 217/483-2451) looks like it should be on a calendar of picturesque bridges of Vermont. The Sugar Creek Bridge is believed to be one of the oldest surviving covered bridges in Illinois. It's 110 feet long and was constructed in 1880 using the Burr Arch wooden truss design, a combination of a wooden arch with multiple triangle-shaped supports. To get there, follow signs off Frazee Road.

✈ Back on 66

Continue south on Frazee Road. Take I-55 south to Exit 80 at **Divernon.** Turn right (west) onto East Brown Street and then the next left (south) on Reichert Road. In 11 miles you will enter Farmersville.

Farmersville

The classic sign in front of **Art's Motel** (101 Main St.) was restored in 2007, but unfortunately has closed for business.

✈ Back on 66

Return to I-55 and drive south for 19 miles to Exit 52 in Litchfield. Turn left (east) onto Highway 16 and in less than one mile, turn right (south) onto Old Route 66. (Do not follow E.

Frontage Road/Historic Route 66, which dead-ends.)

Litchfield

Sights
Litchfield Museum
Route 66 Welcome Center

Unlike most Route 66 museums, the **Litchfield Museum Route 66 Welcome Center** (334 Old Route 66 N., 217/324-3510, www.litchfieldmuseum.org, 10am-4pm Tues.-Sat., free) exhibits local memorabilia and historical information about the impact Route 66 had on the small Midwestern town of Litchfield.

Sky-View Drive-In

For a fun night under the stars, take in a flick at the **Sky-View Drive-In** (1500 Old Route 66 N., 217/324-4451, www.litchfieldskyview.com, shows start at dusk Apr.-Oct.), a few blocks north on Route 66. The venue has been in continuous operation since 1950 (they had a patio and a dance floor back in the day) and currently screens modern films. Although they don't have the old drive-in speakers that used to hang inside your car door (today the sound is tuned via your radio), they still have lots of goodies at the snack bar.

Food

Dining at the legendary ★ **Ariston Cafe** (413 Old Route 66 N., 217/324-2023, www.ariston-cafe.com, 11am-9pm Tues.-Thurs., 11am-10pm Fri., 4pm-10pm Sat., 11am-8pm Sun., $7-24) is an absolute must. The Ariston Cafe has been run by the Adam family for more than 90 years; it is one of the longest operating restaurants on Route 66. The cafe was originally located on Route 4 in Carlinville two years before Route 66 began. In 1935, the Ariston moved to this spot in Litchfield because this segment of Route 66 was the heaviest-traveled road in the state. The cafe cost $3,625 to build, and two gas pumps were installed in front to attract customers. When it opened, a porterhouse steak cost $0.85 and a BLT was $0.25.

Today, the gas pumps are gone and a banquet wing has been added, but the counter inside still takes you back to 1935. This is one of the finest classic eateries on Route 66, with a wide-ranging menu of home-cooked food, from prime rib to patty-melts. Dessert is nonnegotiable, even if you're on a diet (though there may be sugar-free options)—Ariston has the best red velvet cake in the world. Not hungry? Get something to go.

And go now, because time is of the essence: At time of publication, the Ariston Cafe was for sale, but the owners are taking their time to find the right buyer who will provide the same quality food and service.

◆ Back on 66
From Litchfield, head south on Old Route 66 for 8 miles (the railroad tracks will be on the east, or left, side of the highway). At the town of Mt. Olive, turn left onto Mt. Olive Road.

Mt. Olive

As you enter Mt. Olive, the post-1940s alignment splits off to the right just after St. John Road. If time is a factor, take this route to continue on Route 66. To enter the town, turn left (south) after St. John Road on Old Route 66 and follow the post-1930s alignment as it curves west into the Mt. Olive.

Sights
Union Miners Cemetery
Mt. Olive is a small mining town that opened its first coal shaft in 1875. The **Union Miners Cemetery** (Mt. Olive Rd. and Old Reservoir Rd., www.illinoislaborhistory.org) is the only union-owned cemetery in the country. In 1898, four miners were killed in the Virden

Ariston Café, Farmersville

Massacre, a shootout that started when mine operators brought in 180 black strikebreakers. Labor activist Mary Harris Jones, also known as Mother Jones, asked to be buried here next to the coal miners she referred to as "her boys." A granite column memorializes her life and dedication to the cause.

From Old Route 66, turn right (north) on Lake Street. The cemetery is five blocks on the left (west).

Soulsby Shell Service Station
On the west side of Old Route 66, look for the **Soulsby Shell Service Station** (710 W. 1st St.). Built in in 1926—the year Route 66 opened—the station stopped pumping gas in 1991, but continued to serve soda pop and snacks and check the oil for Route 66 travelers until closing its doors in 1993. The station has been beautifully restored with the help of the Route 66 Corridor Preservation Program. Though it is no longer open, the original gas pumps remain outside.

◆ Back on 66
Route 66 continues south from Mt. Olive, curving left to become East Frontage Road. Continue 3 miles south toward the town of Staunton.

Staunton

At the intersection of East Frontage Road and Old Route 66, continue south on East Frontage Road for Country Classic Cars, located on the west side of the road.

After looking at so many classic car props on Route 66, it's refreshing to find that **Country Classic Cars** (2149 E. Frontage Rd., 618/635-7056, www.countryclassiccars.com, 9am-5pm Mon.-Fri., 9am-3pm Sat.) actually has some cars for sale. Browse their inventory of more than 600 classic cars—everything from a 1927 Ford Model T to a 1957 Cadillac and a 1969 Chevy Impala. Country Classic also ships cars and trades vehicles; if you just want to gaze at their beauties, they have several storage sheds full of cars. There are also some older cars rusting away outside. The sheer volume and variety is impressive.

◆ Back on 66
From East Frontage Road, return to the junction with Old Route 66 and head southwest. Cross Staunton Road (Main St.) and follow the signs for Old Route 66 as it heads south. Old Route 66 merges with Bentrup Road, briefly becomes Henry Street, and then dips south onto Historic Old Route 66. Henry's Rabbit Ranch is about 0.5 miles along on the right (west) south of Henry Street.

★ Henry's Rabbit Ranch
Henry's Rabbit Ranch (1107 Old Route 66, 618/635-5655, 9am-4pm Mon.-Fri., 9am-1pm Sat., www.henrysroute66.com, free) is one of those special places on the side of the road that you never forget. The ranch is like a Route 66 information center and gift store—with rabbits—inside

Springfield to St. Louis

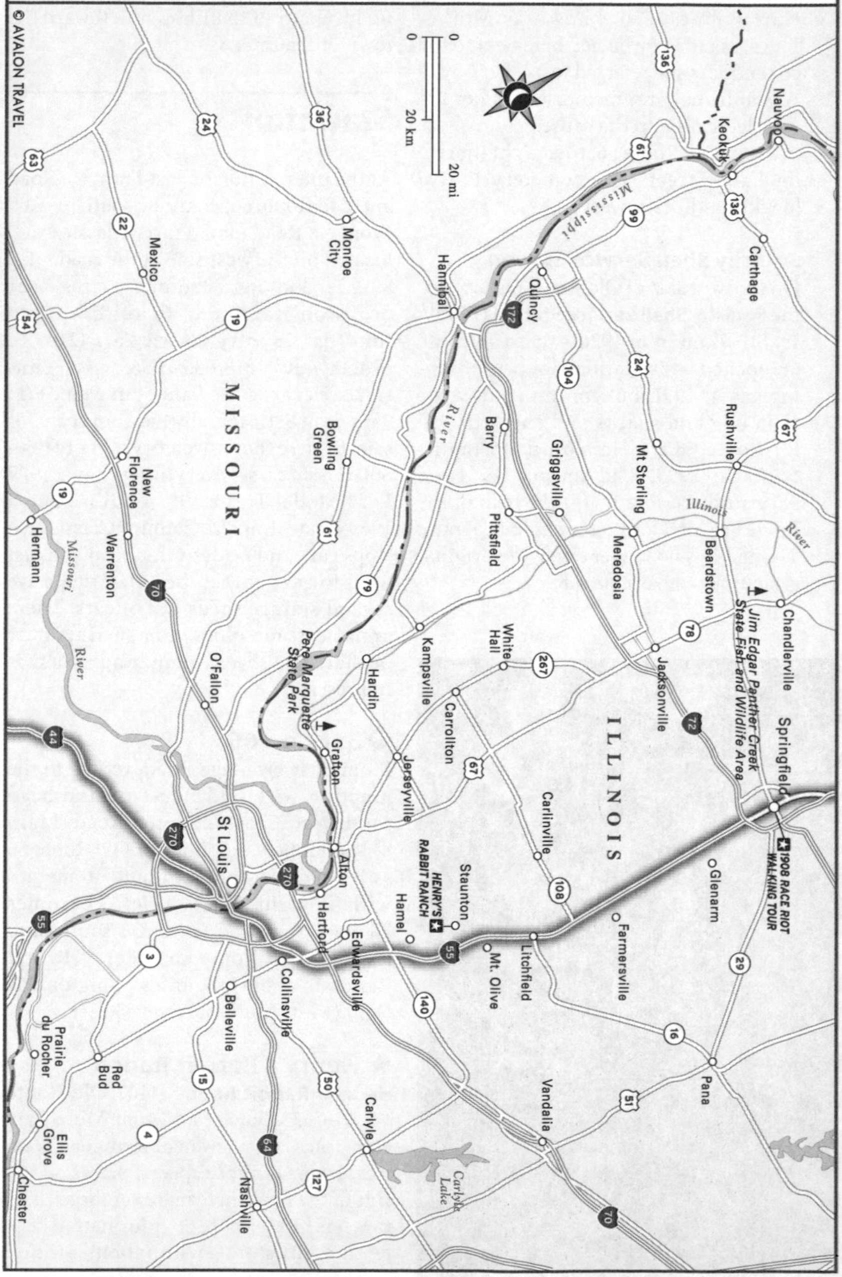

what appears to be an old filling station. Owner Rich Henry will bring out a rabbit, set him or her on the counter, and let you pet his furry friend and just feel good about life for a while. Make sure to chat with Rich; he can tell you some stories about Route 66 and his furry, four-legged soul mates. He even campaigned for one of his rabbits, Montana, to run for president, and he has the campaign posters to prove it. This place won't be around forever, so make sure you appreciate it while it's still here.

◆ Back on 66
Leaving Staunton, head south on Historic Old Route 66. The road will join South Madison Street, which then turns into Sievers Road. Turn right (west) onto Williamson Road (not Williamson Ave.) and then turn left (south) onto Route 4. Now we're back on the 1926 alignment.

Hamel

As Route 66 (Rte. 4) approaches I-55, turn right (southwest) on Possum Hill Road and take the next left (southeast) onto Old U.S. Route 66 (W. Frontage Rd.) After about 2.5 miles, the road will veer west from I-55 toward Hamel. Follow Old U.S. Route 66 into Hamel.

Food
Weezy's Route 66 Bar & Grill (108 S. Old Route 66, Hamel, 618/633-2228, 6am-9pm Mon.-Thurs., 6am-10pm Fri.-Sat., 7am-7pm Sun., bar until midnight or 1am daily, $5-10) is a 1930s roadhouse and regulars' hot spot. The joint is decorated with a black-and-white checkered floor, red vinyl booths, and chrome tables and chairs, and there's an outdoor patio. The furniture is actually from Johnny Rockets, so it looks a little "processed," but the authenticity comes from the vintage signs, the homemade pies, and the hearty breakfasts, like biscuits and gravy served with fresh sausage from local hogs.

◆ Back on 66
From Hamel, continue south on Old U.S. Route 66 (SR-157) for eight miles to Edwardsville.

Edwardsville

From Old U.S. Route 66 (SR-157), turn right (west) onto East Vandalia Street (SR-143) and head to the northeast corner of Main Street (SR-159).

Sights
Edwardsville is the third-oldest city in Illinois and has about 40 historic buildings. Built in 1911, the **Bohm Building** (100 N. Main St., 618/692-1211, www.bohmbuilding.com) served a steady stream of Route 66 travelers. The first floor contained seven or eight retail outlets, including restaurants, a beauty and barbershop, and a pharmacy; the second floor housed 18 office spaces. Over the years, businesses came and went (there are none from that time still operating today), but the character, history, and some recent renovations definitely make it worth a stop. The original front doors, found in the basement, have been restored, and a Frank Lloyd Wright statue was installed in the alley. The gate door is made from flooring planks that were used in the Bohm barn, while a courtyard wall was designed from barn scrap wood. Restorations are still underway, but there are a few businesses operating, such as a tattoo shop, a consulting firm, and an Internet and graphic design company.

Food
A wonderful restaurant you won't want to miss, the ★ **Cleveland-Heath** (106 N. Main St., 618/307-4830, www.cleveland-heath.com, 11am-10pm Mon.-Thurs., 11am-11pm Fri., 10am-11pm Sat., $9-28) serves gourmet comfort food without a whiff of pretention. While foie gras and marinated octopus might feel a little stuffy for a road trip, familiar dishes like

deviled eggs, pulled-pork sandwiches, BLTs, and cheddar-ham sliders (served on buttery biscuits that are both crumbly and moist) manage to be high-brow and down-to earth at the same time. Housed in the beautiful, historic Bohm building, the low-key vibe is enhanced with a handsome wood bar, exposed brick walls, and tin ceilings.

✿ Back on 66

Leaving Edwardsville, head west on Old U.S. Route 66 (SR-157). In five miles, continue through the stoplight at South University Drive and follow the curve west onto Chain of Rocks Road.

✿ Side Trip: Collinsville

A post-1940s alignment of Route 66 travels through Collinsville. From Chain of Rocks Road, head south on Highway 111 for almost 8 miles. Turn left (east) onto

Collinsville Road, and in less than two miles turn right (south) onto Ramey Street.

Sights
World's Largest Catsup Bottle

At the former Brooks Foods plant sits a 170-foot tall replica of a catsup bottle. The **World's Largest Catsup Bottle** (800 S. Morrison Ave.) was built in 1949 by W. E. Caldwell Company for the G. S. Suppiger catsup bottling plant. The big water tower with an idiosyncratic twist can be seen south of downtown Collinsville on the east side of Highway 159.

Cahokia Mounds State Historic Site

Cahokia Mounds State Historic Site (30 Ramey St., 618/346-5160, www.cahokiamounds.org, 9am-5pm Wed.-Sun., donation) is the largest pre-Columbian settlement north of Mexico. The site was inhabited from about AD 700 to 1400 with a population of up to 20,000 people.

Luna Café, Mitchell

Cahokia was one of the most sophisticated prehistoric cities, with more than 120 mounds, plazas, and agricultural fields. It's unknown what actually happened to the Cahokian Indians and their city, but by 1400 the site had been abandoned. Some believe that climate change and social unrest may have affected crop production and forced them to leave. Not much physical evidence remains of their existence except the mounds, which include the 100-foot Monk's Mound—the largest prehistoric earthwork in North America.

Visit the **Interpretive Center** to pick up a guidebook ($1), which includes three 30- to 45-minute hiking trails, for a better understanding of the site. There are also self-guided iPod tours ($3) that take you to the Grand Plaza, Monks Mound, and Woodhenge, the ancient sun calendar. A gift shop sells books, games, and handmade Native American textiles, ceramics, artwork, and jewelry.

◈ Back on 66

To return to Route 66, drive west on Collinsville Road about one mile to Highway 111 North (right). Drive 5 miles to Chain of Rocks Road and turn left (west) to enter the town of Mitchell.

Mitchell

Chain of Rocks Road is dotted with old motels and classic signs but none hold a candle to the **Luna Café** (201 E. Chain of Rocks Rd., 618/931-3152, 10am-2am daily), a 1924 roadhouse that was popular with prohibition gangsters like Al Capone. There was gambling in the basement and a brothel upstairs, but what really makes this place special is the restored neon sign of a huge cocktail glass with a cherry in the bottom. Legend has it that when the red cherry was lit, the women in the then-brothel were working. Today it's a quiet locals bar with prohibition memorabilia inside.

◈ Back on 66

Several Route 66 alignments splinter off into a tangled web of roadways here, so the easiest way to get to St. Louis, Missouri from Mitchell is to follow I-270 West.

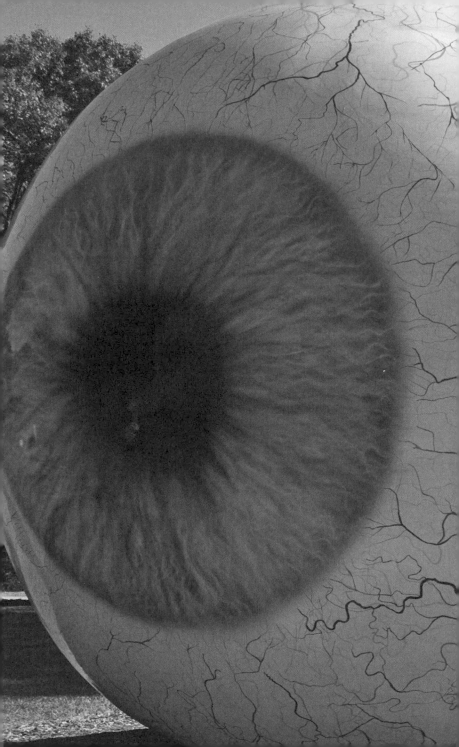

Missouri and Kansas

Route 66 continues on to St. Louis and through Ozark Country. Pass through this gateway to enter the American West.

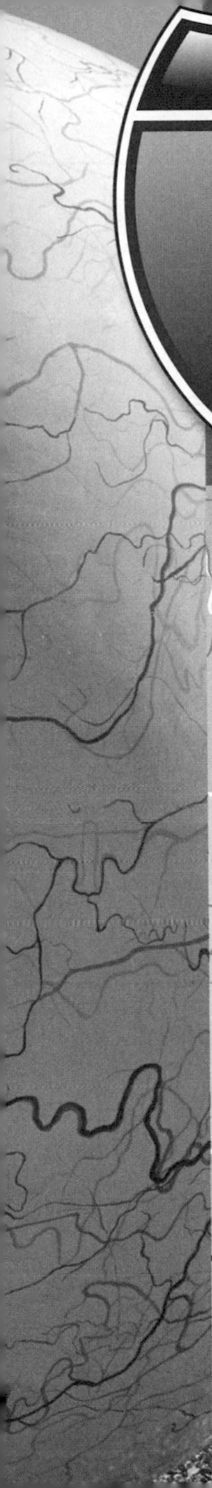

IOWA

ILLINOIS

Springfield

MISSOURI

St. Louis

KANSAS

Cuba

Lebanon

Baxter Springs

Springfield

Joplin

OK

ARKANSAS

TN

Tony Tasset, *Eye*, 2007, Laumeier Sculpture Park Collection, St. Louis

MS

Missouri

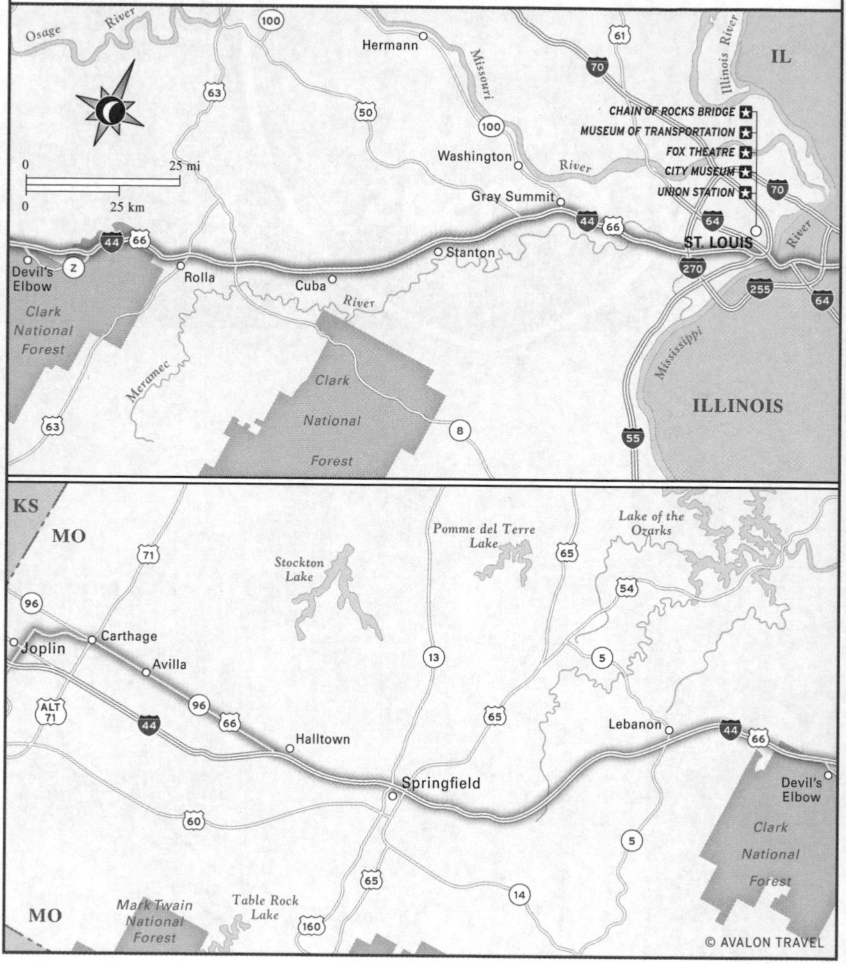

CHAIN OF ROCKS BRIDGE
MUSEUM OF TRANSPORTATION
FOX THEATRE
CITY MUSEUM
UNION STATION

© AVALON TRAVEL

Route 66 was patched together through Missouri from rutted roads, farm to market routes, and Osage Indian migratory paths.

In 1803, the Louisiana Purchase opened Missouri to western settlement and the Lewis and Clark expedition, which started here, symbolized the entrance to the New Frontier. Other seminal trails that originated here were the Overland, Oregon, and Santa Fe. Missouri also has a rich Civil War history. In 1858, the U.S. government installed telegraph lines along the Osage Indian trail and called it the "Old Wire Road." This critical route was used for communication and the delivery of

Highlights

★ **Chain of Rocks Bridge, St. Louis:** This is one of the best examples of early 20th century bridge construction with a 30-degree kink in the middle (page 78).

★ **City Museum, St. Louis:** This 600,000-square foot industrial jungle gym is a creative wonderland for adults and kids. It's made from repurposed building

materials, salvaged bridges, and abandoned airplanes (page 82).

★ **Union Station, St. Louis:** This national landmark was once the busiest passenger rail terminal in the world (page 82).

★ **Fox Theatre, St. Louis:** This opulent movie and

entertainment palace has a fascinating history (page 83).

★ **Museum of Transportation, Kirkwood:** Explore one of the best and largest collections of planes, trains and automobiles on Route 66 (page 90).

supplies during the Civil War and eventually paved the way for Route 66.

The path was laid, but the roads were made of wooden planks that quickly rotted and made travel a miserable experience. The first automobiles appeared in Missouri in 1891, and within 20 years there were more than 16,000 cars on its rickety roads. In 1920, the "Get Missouri Out of the Mud" campaign allocated $60 million to improve the roads. By 1931, the entire Route 66 stretch through Missouri was paved; it was the third state (proceeded by Illinois and Kansas) along the Mother Road to turn to smooth asphalt.

During the Depression, federal funds were used to re-route Route 66 along major thruways in an effort to boost tourism and commerce. Even though Route 66 had become one of the busiest highways in the nation, the Federal government considered it obsolete because it didn't meet the road building standards issued under the Federal-Aid Highway Act. Compared to the success of the Pennsylvania and New Jersey Turnpikes, Route 66 fell short. Denser concrete was added to handle the heavy traffic, but once I-44 was underway in 1956, Route 66 quickly became a distant memory. In fact, the original Route 66 signs between St. Louis and Joplin were removed as early as 1977, eight years before the official decommissioning of the road.

For approximately 300 miles, large segments of Route 66 remain intact through 11 Missouri counties. This road trip drives over lush rolling hills and past roadside churches, quaint towns, and pristine farmland to historic landmarks restored with the help of the National Park Service Route 66 Corridor Program, including the Wagon Wheel Motel in Cuba and the Boots Motel in Carthage.

Planning Your Time

If you use your time wisely, you can make it across Missouri in **two days**—but there is a lot to do and see. Start the first day in St. Louis and head west about 216 miles to spend the night in Springfield, a drive of about 4-5 hours. The second day will eventually see you cross three states off your Route 66 bucket list as you exit through Missouri through Joplin, zip along the 13-mile stretch in Kansas, and end in Tulsa, Oklahoma.

Driving Considerations

In Missouri, Route 66 was re-routed more times than in any other state. After the Depression, Springfield, Joplin, and Rolla added alternate routes, but the most convoluted changes were in the St. Louis area, where Route 66 branches off into six different roadways west of the Mississippi River.

If you're pressed for time, I-44 offers an alternate option for speedy transport between towns. It's best to drive this

Best Accommodations

★ **Magnolia Hotel, St. Louis:** Sleep with the stars at this elegant, renovated hotel with a cinematic history (page 86).

★ **Wagon Wheel Motel, Cuba:** This classic mom-and-pop motor court features cabins with attached garages (page 95).

★ **Munger Moss, Lebanon:** This iconic roadside motel offers a classic vintage vibe (page 102).

★ **Dickey House Bed & Breakfast, Marshfield:** This bed-and-breakfast is a Greek Revival mansion (page 103).

★ **Boots Motel, Carthage:** This Streamline Moderne classic is being restored to its former glory (page 114).

portion of Route 66 during the **spring** or the **fall,** since winter roads can be icy and the summers can be muggy. Although you'll be driving through the some remote areas of the Ozarks, there are several towns with **gas** stations en route, so keep the tank at least half-full and you'll be fine.

Getting There

Starting Points
Car
Route 66 has two starting points in Missouri: the **north route** bypasses the city of St. Louis via the McKinley Bridge, while the **post-1930s route** crosses the Mississippi River on the Martin Luther King Bridge.

This road trip starts in St. Louis, then either follows Vandeventer Avenue south or Olive Street and Chouteau Avenue (Hwy. 100), both of which travel west out of downtown. If you're short on time and want to **bypass the city,** enter St. Louis via the McKinley Bridge, north of downtown.

Car Rental
The **Enterprise** Corporate Headquarters is in St. Louis. Their airport branch (9305 Natural Bridge Rd., 314/427-7757, www.enterprise.com, 6am-10:30pm daily)

is usually at the top of their game, and there's also an Enterprise branch downtown (2233 Washington Ave., 314/241-0073, www.enterprise.com, 7:30am-6pm Mon.-Fri., 8am-3pm Sat., 11am-3pm Sun.). Another option would be **National Car Rental** (10124 Natural Bridge Rd., 877/222-9058, 24 hours); if you're an Emerald Club member you can bypass the counter and pick any car you want from the Emerald Club Aisle.

Air
St. Louis Lambert International Airport (STL, 10701 Lambert International, 314/426-8000, www.flystl.com) is the largest airport in the state of Missouri, with non-stop service to more than 50 US and Canadian airports and five international destinations such as Cancun, Puerto Vallarta, and Jamaica. The airlines include Air Canada, Air Choice One, Alaska Airlines, American Airlines, Cape Air, Delta, Frontier, Southwest, United, and US Airways. The airport is about 12 miles northwest of downtown St. Louis.

The smaller **Springfield-Branson Airport** (SGF, 2300 N. Airport Blvd., 417/868-0500, www.sgf-branson-airport.com) is about 11 miles northwest of Springfield, located in the southwest area of the state. SGF offers limited service to Atlanta, Denver, Detroit,

---

Best Restaurants

★ **Eat Rite Diner, St. Louis:** How many greasy spoons qualify as iconic? This one does (page 87).

★ **Ted Drewes Frozen Custard, St. Louis:** The custard is so thick they call it "concrete" (page 87).

★ **Spencer's Grill, Kirkwood:** This St. Louis landmark has been around since 1947 (page 91).

★ **Slice of Pie, Rolla:** Choose from more than 25 different award-winning pies for a slice to go (page 97).

★ **Cookin' From Scratch, Doolittle:** Opt for slow-cooked, pan-fried chicken at this family-friendly diner (page 98).

★ **Gailey's Breakfast Cafe, Springfield:** Enjoy red-velvet pancakes in an old pharmacy and soda fountain established in 1942 (page 109).

Chicago-O'Hare, Los Angeles (LAX), Phoenix, Memphis, Minneapolis, Orlando, and Tampa. Airlines include: American, Delta, Allegiant, Northwest, and United Airlines.

Train and Bus

Amtrak (430 S. 15th St., 800/872-7245, www.amtrak.com, 24 hours) is located right downtown and is served by three routes: the Texas Eagle, which goes from Chicago through St. Louis, Dallas, San Antonio, and Los Angeles; the Missouri River Runner, which travels daily to Kansas City, MO; and the Illinois service, which goes to Chicago, Quincy, and Carbondale. Ticket sales end 10 minutes before departure times, and boarding gates close five minutes before the train leaves. At the Amtrak station you also can catch a **Greyhound Bus** (430 S. 15th St., www.greyhound.com, 314/231-4485, 24 hours) with both Network and Express service throughout the United States.

St. Louis

St. Louis played a critical role in shaping U.S. history. The city was settled by Native Americans, who built the Cahoika Mounds on the east side of the Mississippi River. The French arrived in the late 1600s, and St. Louis was later established in 1764. The Mississippi River was a key factor in making the city a major fur trading post for beaver and buffalo hide. In 1803, the French sold the land west of the Mississippi River to the United States as part of the Louisiana Purchase. By the mid-1840s, there was a massive immigration of Irish fleeing the Great Potato Famine, and Germans arrived after the 1848 Revolution. On top of all that, Missouri was a border slave state, which made it the center for filing freedom lawsuits, including the famous *Dred Scott v. Sanford* case. In the early 1900s, a large number of African Americans migrated from the South to work in the industrial jobs available in St. Louis.

The brewing industry also originated here. Anheuser-Busch was the first company to bottle and market pasteurized beer and transport it in refrigerated railroad cars across the country. St. Louis has had other notable firsts: Most historians agree that the ice cream cone was invented here at the 1904 World's Fair, when Syrian immigrant Ernest Hamwi ran out of ice cream dishes and curled a waffle cookie as a makeshift receptacle. St. Louis also recorded the first auto theft in 1905 and had the first chain gasoline station, the American Gasoline Company in 1907.

Sights
★ Chain of Rocks Bridge

Route 66 originally entered Missouri via the McKinley Bridge, but it was rerouted in 1936 to the **Chain of Rocks Bridge** (Chain of Rocks Rd. near Schillinger Rd., 314/416-9930, free). The bridge was built from 1927 to 1929 to bypass downtown and alleviate traffic in heart of St. Louis; this became the preferred road for Route 66 travelers because it was faster than driving through downtown. The Illinois side was lined with 400 elm trees, and the Chain of Rocks Amusement Park was alongside the river. The steel long-span truss bridge stands 60 feet above the Mississippi River with a sharp turn in the middle. The Chain of Rocks Bridge is named after a 17-mile granite rocky outcrop that formed treacherous rapids and caused huge problems for boaters navigating the river. The bridge was originally designed to be straight, but boatmen protested because the placement of the bridge was going to make river travel even more difficult. The other issue was that the bedrock was not sufficient to support the 10-span bridge that cantilevered over massive concrete piers. The only solution was to incorporate a 30-degree bend. The designer

One Day in St. Louis

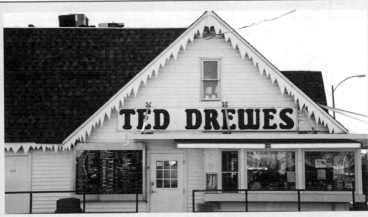

Ted Drewes Frozen Custard

Enter St. Louis via the Chain of Rocks Road and take a nice stroll over the **Chain of Rocks Bridge.** Head south to the **Mary Meachum Freedom Crossing** and then have a bite to eat at the **Eat-Rite Diner.** Take a tram to the top of the **Gateway Arch** and then burn off some energy at the **City Museum.** Go to the Riverfront and browse the historic building along the cobblestone streets of Laclede's Landing. Have sushi at Drunks Fish or Bailey's Range before heading to the Union Station Hotel for the night. The next day on your way out of town, stop by **Ted Drewes Frozen Custard** and then visit Laumiere Park and the abandoned town of Times Beach, where the **Route 66 State Park** sits along the Meramec River.

assured officials that the turn wouldn't be a problem, but it caused a bottleneck that frustrated Route 66 travelers well into the 1960s. As cars got longer and bigger and the interstate systems called for new wider roads, a new Chain of Rocks Bridge opened less than 2,000 feet upstream in 1967.

Fewer people drove the 1929 bridge, and the city could no longer afford to maintain it, so it closed in 1968 and was slated for demolition in 1975. When the value of steel fell in 1976, it became too expensive to tear it down, so it sat for another 20 years. It was filmed in "Escape from New York," but the bridge otherwise sat abandoned until a nonprofit decided to turn it into a bicycle and pedestrian bridge in 1989. Now spared from the wrecking ball, this is one of the best-preserved remnants of large-scale bridge construction from the 1920s.

Getting There

It's best to see the bridge on your way into St. Louis, because there's no safe parking on the west side. To get there from Route 66, head west on Chain of Rocks Rd. As it curves south, enter I-270 westbound. You're taking 270 just to cross the railroad tracks, so stay in the right-hand lane and immediately exit on Old Alton Rd. Turn right (southwest), cross under 270, and then turn right (northwest) onto West Chain of Rocks Rd. Drive west for about 2 miles to the Chain of Rocks bridge. Once you arrive, park in the Illinois Parking Area on Chain of Rocks

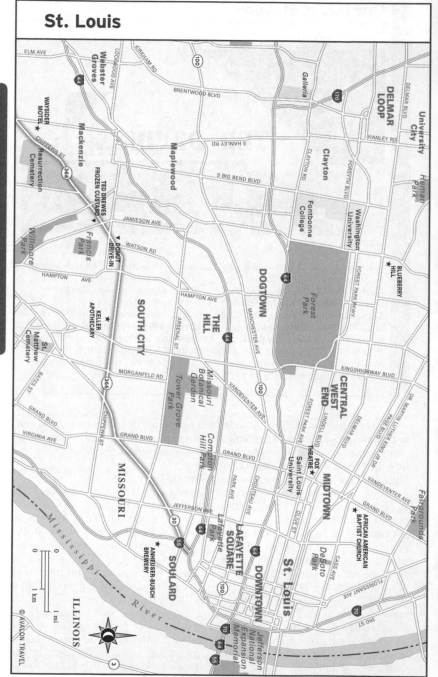

St. Louis

Road. If you don't have time to walk across and just want a great view of the bridge, turn left (south) on West Chain of Rocks Rd. to the Chouteau Island Fishing Area. If you do park and walk across the bridge, don't leave any valuables visible in the car and bring your wallet and cell phone with you.

◈ Back on 66

To leave the Chain of Rocks, drive east on West Chain of Rocks Road to Highway 3 (Lewis and Clark Blvd.) and turn right (south). Drive about 7 miles, and then when Highway 3 splits off onto 4th Street, follow Cedar Street instead, which will take you to the McKinley Bridge heading west across the Mississippi River. Take Exit 34 and turn left (south) on Riverview Drive.

Mary Meachum Freedom Crossing

After crossing the McKinley Bridge, about a mile north along the Mississippi River is the spot where Mary Meachum, wife of John Berry Meachum, helped people cross the Mississippi to escape slavery in 1855. To see the exact spot, go to the **Mary Meachum Freedom Crossing** (Prairie Ave. and St. Louis Riverfront Trail, 314/584-6703, www.visitmo.com, dawn-dusk daily, free). This marks the first Missouri site on the National Park Service's National Underground Railroad Network. The park is a work in progress, but there are a few murals and historic signs marking this inconceivable time in American history.

◈ Back on 66

To reach the Mary Meachum Freedom Crossing from the McKinley Bridge, travel west on McKinley Street and turn right (north) onto North Broadway. Drive about three-quarters of a mile and turn right (northeast) on East Grand. Take a left on Hall Street (northwest) and then turn right on East Prairie Avenue and continue to the end. The historic markers

and murals are south of Prairie Avenue, along the Riverfront Trail.

Gateway Arch

The **Gateway Arch** (11 N. 4th St., 877/982-1410, www.gatewayarch.com, 8am-10pm daily in summer, 9am-6pm daily in winter, $10 tram to the top) is a 630-foot stainless steel monument that points westward, symbolizing the path to prosperity, opportunity, and freedom. The arch was completed in 1965 and is the tallest manufactured monument in the United States. A pair of elevators takes visitors on a four-minute ride to the top, where you'll find an observation deck and panoramic views. Summer is the high season, so tram tickets sell out fast. To order in advance, visit the website or call. The last tram leaves one-hour before closing.

The **Gateway Arch Ticketing and Visitor Center** is located two blocks west in the **Old Courthouse** (11 N. 4th St., 7:30am-8pm daily Memorial Day-Labor Day, 8am-5pm daily Labor Day-Memorial Day, www.gatewayarch.com), which is worth a stop. In 1847, it was here that two slaves, Dred and Harriet Scott, tried to sue for their freedom. The case made national news and was one of the catalysts of the American Civil War. This was also the court where Virginia Minor fought for women's right to vote. Displays include newspaper articles and court records, as well as exhibits about St. Louis' role in the early settlers' westward migration. The gift shop has a large collection of books, videos, clothing, and educational toys related to St. Louis history.

Claymorgan Home

Laclede's Landing is a bustling area with cobblestone-lined streets and businesses housed in old warehouses along the riverfront. Once the seat of operations for the steamboat industry and fur trade, these historic warehouses were owned by wealthy residents like **Jaques Clamorgan**, a West Indian fur trader.

Clamorgan was a lifelong bachelor who fathered three children with mixed-race women at a time when most African Americans were slaves. He signed his property over to his former slave and mistress, Esther, who became one of the earliest female property owners in St. Louis. His **home** was at 701 North First Street. The house is no longer there, but "Clamorgan Alley" has a sidewalk engraving on the ground commemorating his legacy. It's located off Morgan Street between 1st and 2nd Streets.

★ City Museum

What can talented, innovative artists do with scrapped pieces of America's infrastructure? See for yourself at the **City Museum** (750 N. 15th St., 314/231-2489, www.citymuseum.org, 9am-5pm Mon.-Thurs., 9am-midnight Fri.-Sat., 11am-5pm Sun., $12), where the 600,000-square-foot former International Shoe Company has been transformed into a surreal labyrinth of steel and concrete artworks made from salvaged bridges, construction cranes, chimneys, and two abandoned airplanes. The City Museum is the brainchild of the late sculptor Bob Cassilly, who died in 2011. Cassilly said, "The point is not to learn every fact, but to say, 'wow, that's wonderful.' And if it's wonderful, it's worth preserving." These powerful words are alive in huge wire-mesh walkways, tile-encrusted floors and columns, a 10-story circular slide, and a human-sized slinky. An entire wall is made from industrial kitchen food pans. This is much more than a museum—it's an industrial playground that will bring out the kid in you.

During spring and summer, a **Ferris Wheel** ($5) operates on the roof, where there are more tunnels and slides. Also on-site is a **shoelace factory** that shows how bootstraps were made for U.S. soldiers during WWII and a **gift shop** (until 11pm Fri.-Sat.) selling unique handmade gifts by local artists. There are five **food venues** serving sandwiches, pastries, pizza, tacos, hotdogs, floats, cotton candy, and more. There is also a full bar in the **Cabin Inn;** for entertainment, DJs spin dope beats on the weekend.

The City Museum is open until midnight on weekends. If you'd rather not compete with the kids for turf, plan your visit after 5pm on Friday or Saturday. The sharp metal objects are large with lots of rough edges, so bring kneepads and a flashlight and wear long pants and closed-toe shoes. There are no lockers—leave your flip-flops, sandals, skirts, and purses in the car. All limbs must be free and clear to play with ease! The museum is located about a mile west of the Gateway Arch.

★ Union Station

The iconic **Union Station** (1820 Market St., 314/421-6655, www.stlouisunionstation.com, 10am-9pm Mon.-Sat., 10am-6pm Sun., Mar.-Oct.; 11am-7:30pm Mon.-Sat., 11am-6pm Sun. Nov.-Feb., free) sits on 11 acres in downtown St. Louis. When it opened in 1894, it was reportedly the largest, most beautiful train station in the United States. Modeled after a medieval city in southern France, it has sweeping Roman archways, fresco and gold leaf detailing, mosaics, stunning stained-glass windows, and a 65-foot, barrel-vaulted ceiling. The midway area features a light steel-trussed roof of glass and iron. The train shed was one of the largest single platforms ever built—at 140-feet tall, 700-feet long, and 600-feet wide, it spans 42 tracks over 11.5 acres. Each night (hourly 5pm-10pm) in the Grand Hall Lounge, there's a dynamic 3D light show that looks like it came straight out of Vegas, with vibrant video animations of flying birds, sea creatures, flowers, and trains that move across the 65-foot ceiling.

In the 1940s, Union Station served more than 100,000 people, but after World War II, train travel dwindled. In 1976, the station was designated a National Historical Landmark; two years later, the last train pulled out of the station. It was eventually purchased for $5.5 million and given a $150 million dollar restoration, making it the largest adaptive re-use project in America.

The **Whispering Arch** (in the grand entrance on the north side of the building) is an architectural sonic phenomenon. Stand facing the wall at the base of the arch and speak in a normal volume; your voice will be carried along the arch to a person on the other side—they can hear you perfectly. (Make sure to speak directly at the wall, and don't look up at the arch as you talk.)

Inside Union Station, the **Memories Museum** (second level, 314/421-6655, 10am-9pm Mon.-Sat., 10am-6pm Sun., free) celebrates the history of Union Station and the romance of train travel.

Although there are about 20 specialty shops, restaurants, and a hotel operating in Union Station today, it's not the lively place it once was. Today it feels more like a tarnished relic compared to its glamorous, illustrious history, but it's still worth strolling through this cavernous monument, which will transport you back in time. Union Station is about a mile west of the Gateway Arch and less than mile southwest of the City Museum.

African American Baptist Church

Unsung American hero John Berry Meachum was born to slave parents. Meachum learned carpentry and cabinetmaking, which allowed him to earn enough money to purchase his family's freedom. After he moved to Missouri, he founded the first **African American Baptist Church** (3100 Bell Ave. 314/533-8003, free) in St. Louis and became part of a group of local African American aristocrats.

Meachum owned two Mississippi steamers and a barrel factory; he purchased slaves in order to teach them a trade working in his barrel factory until they could make a living on their own. When St. Louis enacted a law banning the education of black people, Meachum was forced to shut down his school.

In 1847, Meachum circumvented the law by anchoring his steamboat in the middle of the Mississippi River and taught classes on the boat. Since it was no longer on Missouri land, it was not subject to state law. He called it the Floating Freedom School.

The African American Baptist Church is less than two miles northwest of Union Station. From Market Street near Union Station, turn right (north) on North Jefferson Avenue and then left (west) on Delmar. Drive five blocks and turn right (north) on North Cardinal Avenue. The church is on the left (west) side.

★ Fox Theatre

When the **Fox Theatre** (527 N. Grand Blvd., 314/534-1678, tours 10:30am Tues., Thurs., and Sat. $8-10; performances $25-70) opened in 1929 it was the second-largest theater in the United States. This opulent performance arts center is decorated in a Byzantine style inspired by East Indian design; the entrance features bronze and glass doors with a terracotta facade that references Thailand's Vat Anong Temple and India's Adina Mosque. The Fox was the first theater in the United States to be built with full "talkie" equipment and attracted people from all walks of life. For the price of a ticket, folks of modest means could rub elbows with the elite and forget about their troubles for the evening.

The Fox went bankrupt in 1936; one year later, shares were given away as souvenirs because the stockholders believed the Fox had no value. From the late 1930s until 1978, it was leased by Harry Arthur and featured performances by Benny Goodman, Mae West, and Frank Zappa. Today, the Fox hosts a wide range of acts—from Broadway plays like *Wicked* to music acts like the Alabama Shakes and Beck.

The Fox Theatre is located less than a mile west of Meachum's church. From

Harvey Houses

In the late 1800s, **Fred Harvey** revolutionized train travel and railroad dining by opening fine-dining restaurants in railway stations throughout the United States. Until then, railway passengers had limited food options on the road; the further west one traveled, the less reliable the quality and safety of food became. That was until Fred Harvey.

Fred Harvey's **"Harvey House"** restaurants featured chefs wearing big stovepipe hats, and his signature "Harvey Girls" were impeccably dressed "good girls" from the Midwest. They wore starched uniforms, hair bows, nylons, and pinafores while serving quality food on fine china, and their manners and morals matched their sanitized uniforms. Former Harvey Girl Charlotte Solberg said, "We had to walk a certain way, we had to carry the food a certain way, our uniforms had to be pressed and spotless, the silverware and glasses had to be set correctly, and those plates had better come out perfect. No hair on the face, very little make-up, no gum chewing." Every move was monitored for professionalism and efficiency. Harvey Girls had to seat and serve about 130 customers immediately after a train pulled in, so timing was critical. Travelers would place their orders on the train, which was then wired to the restaurant; when passengers arrived, everything would be ready and waiting.

Market Street, head west to turn right (north) on South Jefferson Avenue. Take a left (west) on Olive Street and turn right (north) on North Grand Boulevard.

Forest Park

At 500 acres larger than New York's Central Park, **Forest Park** (5595 Grand Dr., 314/367-7275, www.forestparkforever.org, 24 hours, free) is one of the largest urban parks in the United States. It was also the site of the 1904 World's Fair. Located within the park is the **Missouri History Museum** (5700 Lindell Blvd., 314/746-4599, 10am-5pm Mon. and Wed.-Sun., 10am-8pm Tues., www.mohistory.org, free), with exhibits about the fair, the Lewis and Clark expedition, and Missouri immigrant history.

South of the museum is the **Jewel Box** (Wells and McKinley Dr., 314/531-0080, 9am-4pm, Mon.-Fri. 9am-11am Sat., 9am-2pm Sun., $1), an art deco greenhouse with 50-foot walls and 17 acres of tropical trees, floral displays, and exotic plants. Seasonal shows include a chrysanthemum exhibit in the fall. Other cultural attractions in the park include the Saint Louis Art Museum, a zoo, a science center, a boathouse, and a community golf course.

Forest Park is located two miles west of the Fox Theatre. From Market Street, head west and turn right (north) on South Jefferson Avenue. Turn left (west) on Olive Street, which turns into Lindell Boulevard. Follow Lindell Boulevard to Kings Highway Boulevard and turn left (south). Turn right (west) on Forest Park Avenue to enter the park.

Blueberry Hill

Find your thrill at **Blueberry Hill** (6504 Delmar, 314/727-4444, tickets 800/745-3000, www.blueberryhill.com, 11:30am-1:30am daily, $5-33), a landmark restaurant and music club that has been serving locals and tourists since 1972. Music acts range from indie rock to blues, hip-hop, reggae, and folk artists (Chuck Berry played here weekly for years). A full-service restaurant spans the entire block in front of the St. Louis Walk of Fame, where bronze stars and biographical plaques feature St. Louis natives such as Miles Davis, Chuck Berry, Tina Turner, Redd Foxx, and Josephine Baker.

Blueberry Hill also hosts the largest annual dart tournament in the United

States, with about 500 participants. Their dart room is lined with pop culture memorabilia and features seven boards, video games, and pinball machines. With calorie-dense comfort food, a dart room, live music, and a wrap-around bar, it's a popular hangout for students.

Blueberry Hill is located less than 2 miles north of Forest Park. From Market Street, head west and turn right (north) on South Jefferson Avenue. Turn left (west) on Olive Street, which turns into Lindell Boulevard. Follow Lindell Boulevard to Kings Highway Boulevard and turn right (north). Take a left (west) onto Delmar Boulevard.

St. Louis Car Museum & Sales

Car lovers should check out the **St. Louis Car Museum & Sales** (1575 Woodson Rd., 800/957-5707, www.stlouiscarmuseum. com, 9am-6pm Mon.-Fri., 10am-2pm Sat., free), with more than 80,000-square feet of classic muscle cars, vintage motorcycles, and airplanes. The carpeted showroom is climate-controlled and includes everything from Bugattis to Bentleys to Caddys from 1914 to the 1970s.

The car museum is located about five miles northwest of Forest Park and 13 miles west of the Gateway Arch. From Market Street, head west to turn right (north) on South Jefferson Avenue. Turn left (west) on Olive Street, which turns into Lindell Boulevard. Follow Lindell Boulevard to Kings Highway Boulevard. Turn right (north) and then left (west) onto Delmar Boulevard. Turn right (north) on North McKnight Road, which turns into Woodson Road.

Anheuser-Busch Brewery

The **Anheuser-Busch Brewery** (12th and Lynch Sts., 314/577-2626, www.budweisertours.com, 9am-5pm Mon.-Wed., 9am-7pm Thurs.-Sat., 11:30am-7pm Sun., June-Aug.; 10am-4pm Mon.-Sat 11:30am-4pm Sun., Sept.-May; tours vary) offers several tours and tasting options. The 45-minute complimentary tour takes visitors to the Clydesdale stables and demonstrates the entire seven-step brewing process. The Day Fresh Tour ($10) shows guests how beer is produced from "Seed to Sip." The 75-minute tour starts at the Clydesdale stables and continues to the beechwood aging cellar, brewhouse, and packaging facility. The History Tour ($25) is held in the Old Lyon Schoolhouse and showcases nearly 400 items from the Anheuser-Busch archives. The Beermaster Tour ($35) offers guests a behind-the-scenes look at the brewing process, along with a comprehensive two-hour tour of the stables, fermentation cellar, packaging facility, and finishing cellar. Finally, Beer School ($15) is an interactive beer-tasting and food-pairing class that highlights a variety of beers, ingredients, and proper pouring techniques.

Wayside Motel

In its heyday, Route 66 was a commercial windfall for most business in this area, as evidenced by its string of vintage hotels. Built in 1940, the **Wayside Motel** (7800 Watson Rd.) sits across the street from where art deco classic the Coral Court Motel stood before it was razed. Its cottage-style brick construction and decorative stone walls offer a good example of the type of accommodations popular in the 1940s. The Wayside has also retained the original carports Route 66 travelers loved so much.

Keller Apothecary

If you need to pick up any drugstore items, skip the popular chains and check out **Keller Apothecary** (5346 Devonshire Ave., 314/352-5201, www.kellerrx.com, 9am-6pm Mon.-Fri., 9am-1pm Sat.). Keller's has been serving St. Louis since 1933, and their pharmacists have years of experience. Inside are antique mortar and pestles, pillboxes, bandages, and beakers on display. The apothecary is located south of Highway 366 near Macklind Avenue.

Accommodations

The ★ **Magnolia Hotel** (421 N. 8th St., 314/436-9000, www.magnoliahotels.com, $173-276) is an upscale, 18-story landmark west of Laclede's Landing. In the 1920s, the former Mayfair Hotel served elite movie stars like Cary Grant, John Barrymore, and Douglas Fairbanks. In its heyday, the elegant hotel had a barbershop and beauty parlor, and was the first hotel to put chocolates on guest pillows. (The idea is credited to Cary Grant, who allegedly tried to seduce a female guest by laying a trail of chocolates from the pillow in her bedroom to his penthouse suite.)

The golden patina faded on the Mayfair, and it closed in 2013, re-opening as the Magnolia Hotel after a $15 million dollar renovation. Rooms today blend historic elegance with modern comfort and are decorated in yellow and silver tones with tufted headboards, full-length mirrors, and wooden nightstands with nickel knobs. A chocolate is included with turndown service. The on-site **Robie's Restaurant and Lounge** is an homage to John Robie, the character played by Cary Grant in *To Catch a Thief.*

The lobby of **The Double Tree by Hilton** (1820 Market St. 314/621-5262, www.doubletree3.hilton.com, $130-300, parking $20-27, pets ok) is located right in the middle of Union Station. Guestrooms are sleek and modern with spacious work desks. Executive-level rooms are more traditional, decorated in an early American style with dark wood furnishings. Among several on-site dining options are a food court, Landry's, and the Hard Rock Café. To soak in more ambiance and history, check out the **Station Grille** (1820 Market St., 312/802-3460, 6am-10pm daily, $11-35), a former Harvey House.

A few blocks east of Blueberry Hill is the eco- and pet-friendly, lunar-themed **Moonrise Hotel** (6177 Delmar Blvd., 314/721-1111, www.moonrisehotel.com, $130-250). Spacious rooms are stylish,

Moonrise Hotel

clean, and comfortable. A welcome mat for your four-legged friend (complete with water bowl) is at the check-in desk.

Food

If you're hungry for sushi, **Drunken Fish Sushi** (Laclede's Landing, 612 N. 2nd St., 314/241-9595, www.drunkenfish.com, 11am-10pm Mon., 11am-11pm Tues.-Thurs., 11am-1am Fri., 4pm-1am Sat., 4pm-10pm Sun., $13-30) serves 20 different kinds of fish, with a good selection of creative rolls and 32 signature cocktails in a vibrant modern decor. There are two more locations in St. Louis at the Ballpark Village (601 Clark St., Ste. 104, 314/899-0500) and in the central west end (1 Maryland Plaza, 314/367-4222).

A few blocks from the Magnolia Hotel is the upscale modern burger joint **Bailey's Range** (920 Olive St. 314/241-8121, www.baileysrange.com, 11am-1am Mon.-Sat., 11am-11:30pm Sun., $6-12), where burgers are made from grass-fed bison, lamb, and beef. The Ozark burger has mushrooms, caramelized onions, and black-peppered goat cheese, while vegetarians get a chickpea, lemon, basil, and arugula burger. The shakes are made with homemade ice cream.

For something less hipster and more old school, head to the ★ **Eat Rite Diner** (622 Chouteau Ave., 314/621-9621, open 24 hours, $5-10), a no-frills, down-to-earth greasy spoon where junkers and Jaguars sit side by side in the parking lot. Everything is cooked to order, and the waitresses are just as iconic as this institution.

For tried and true donuts—no trendy cronut concoctions—this place is the real deal: **Donut Drive-In** (6525 Chippewa St., 314/645-7714, 5am-2pm Sun.-Mon., 5am-9pm Tues., 5am-10pm Wed.-Thurs., 5am-midnight Fri.-Sat.) offers a great selection of raised, old-fashioned, jelly, custard, blueberry cake, cinnamon twist, chocolate iced, and buttermilk-glazed pillows of heaven. Don't eat too many, though, because you need to leave room for ★ **Ted Drewes Frozen Custard** (6726 Chippewa, 314/481-2652, www.teddrewes.com, 11am-11pm daily). Ted's custard is so thick and rich they call it "concrete," because it doesn't move—to prove its density, it's served upside down. My favorite is the "All Shook Up," a peanut butter and banana masterpiece in honor of the king himself, Elvis Presley.

◆ Back on 66

The 1926-1932 alignment in St. Louis followed Market Street and Manchester Road (Route 100), which traveled from downtown St. Louis to Gray Summit. This road trip takes the **post-1932 alignment** via Highway 366 (Chippewa St.). To get to Highway 366 from Market Street (near the Arch), turn left (south) on Tucker Boulevard. As the road passes under I-44 and over I-55, Route 66 turns into Highway 30 (Gravois Ave.). In less than 3 miles, turn right (west) on Highway 366 (Chippewa St.). As you drive west on Highway 366, Chippewa

St. Louis to Springfield

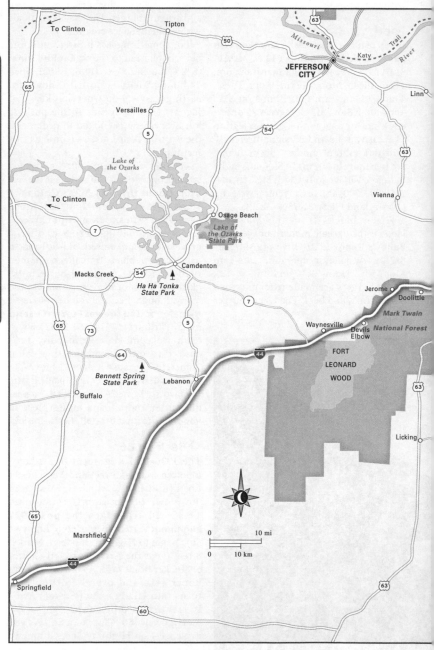

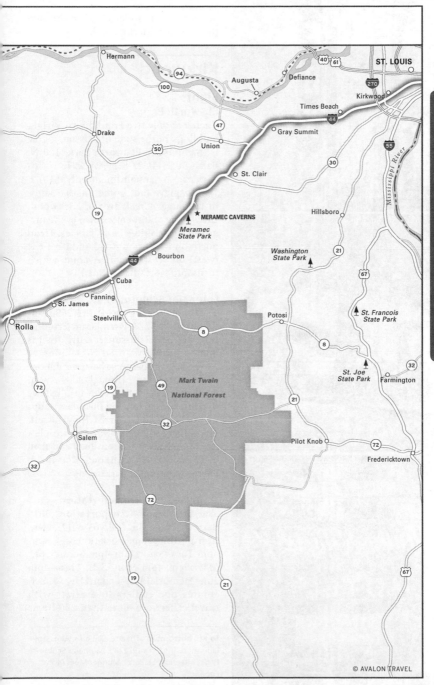

Street turns into Watson Road through the suburb of Marlborough.

Kirkwood

Sights
Ebsworth Park

There are only five Frank Lloyd Wright buildings in the state of Missouri. One is the house in **Ebsworth Park** (120 N. Ballas Rd., 314/822-8359, www.ebsworth-park.org, by appointment only, $10), a 1,900-square foot home on 10.5 acres in the Sugar Creek area of Kirkwood. Everything is authentic down to the furniture, furnishings, and fabrics. Head north on Kirkwood Road and turn left (west) on West Adams Avenue, which turns into North Ballas Road.

Laumeier Sculpture Park

The **Laumeier Sculpture Park** (12580 Rott Rd., 314/615-5278, www.laumeiersculpturepark.org, 8am-sunset daily, free) is home to more than 80 contemporary sculptures. The park also hosts exhibitions and cultural events throughout the year. It's the perfect place to take a walk, have a picnic, and gaze a giant fiberglass sculpture of an eyeball by artist Tony Tassett. To get there from Highway 366, turn left (south) onto South Geyer Road and then make another left (east) onto Rott Road. Follow signs for the parking lot.

★ Museum of Transportation

The **Museum of Transportation** (3015 Barrett Station Rd., 314/965-6212, www.transportmuseumassociation.org, 9am-4pm Tues.-Sat., 11am-4pm Sun., Sept.-May; 9am-4pm Mon.-Sat., 11am-4pm Sun. Memorial Day-Labor Day, $8) celebrates our endless love affair with travel. There are more than 200 items

top to bottom: Fox Theatre, St. Louis; Alexander Liberman, *The Way,* 1972–80, Laumeier Sculpture Park Collection, St. Louis; Munger Moss Motel, Lebanon

on display—including the last steam engine train to operate in Missouri and the world's largest steam locomotive—as well as a comprehensive history of railroad travel. A car pavilion houses a 1963 Chrysler Turbine and Bobby Darin's Dream Car. For military buffs, there's a C-47 military transport from World War II and a Depression-era clunker the Joad family might have driven west in *The Grapes of Wrath*.

The crown jewel for Route 66 lovers is a facade of the beloved 1940s **Coral Court Motel**. When located on Watson Road, it was a large complex of 30 buildings. Their hollow, honey-glazed ceramic tiles and glass blocks curved into a sublime and seamless streamline modern style that rivaled any motor court of its day. The popularity of chain motels and the I-44 bypass of Route 66 eventually led to the Coral Court's demise. Thankfully, we can at least see a piece of it and glimpse just how special it was.

The museum is 3.5 miles north of Route 66. From Highway 366, drive north on I-270 to Exit 8 (Dougherty Ferry Rd). Drive west (left) on Dougherty Ferry Road to Barrett Station Road. Turn left (south) on Barrett Station Road and follow the signs to the museum. The entrance is on the right (west) side of the road.

Food

★ **Spencer's Grill** (223 S. Kirkwood Rd., 314/821-2601, 6am-2pm daily, $6-12) serves delicious pancakes, with a thin yet crispy and buttery edge that just melts in your mouth. It's a small diner with a counter, so you may have to wait, but it's worth it. To get there from Watson Road (Route 66), drive 1.5 miles north on Kirkwood Road.

✚ Back on 66

Heading west on Highway 366 (Watson Road), join I-44 West toward Tulsa to reach Times Beach in about 10 miles.

Times Beach

Times Beach was once the site of a resort community founded in 1925. After the Depression hit, the town fell on hard times and never recovered. By the 1970s, the residents couldn't afford to pave the roads, so they hired a company to come in and "oil" them to control the dust. Little did they know, this oil contained dioxin, a dangerous toxin. By 1985, the entire town of more than 2,000 people was forced to evacuate. In 1997 the Federal government purchased and decontaminated the site, removing 265,000 tons of earth—the cleanup took 33 million dollars and 15 years.

Today the 419-acre **Route 66 State Park** (97 N. Outer Rd., 636/938-7198, www.mostateparks.com, 7am-30 minutes before sunset daily, free) has a picnic area and hiking, biking, and horseback riding trails. Also on-site is the incinerator where contaminated materials were burned and the mound where all the dirt was moved. The **visitor center** (9am-4:30pm daily, Apr.-Nov.) is in the former Bridgehead Inn, a 1935 roadhouse that displays photos and local Route 66 memorabilia.

To access the visitor center take Exit 266 off I-44, east of the Meramec River. Turn right (northeast) and then a quick left (west) on North Outer Road. The visitor center is about one-third of a mile on the left (south) side of the road. Once a bridge crossed the Meramec River, but it is now condemned. To visit the park, you have to get back onto I-44, head west, cross the river, and get off the next exit. Follow signs to hop onto I-44 East, then immediately take Exit 265. The road will curve to the right and turn left (southeast) onto South Outer Road. The park is less than a mile on the right (south) side of the highway.

◆ Back on 66

Drive west on South Outer Road E and turn south on Williams Road. In one block, turn right on Augustine Road. Drive 0.5 mile, curve left, then turn right on Autumn Way. Turn right on Highway 109, drive under I-44, and then take the first left on 5th Street. Follow 5th Street, which parallels I-44 for less than 3 miles, then turn left (south) on Allenton Road.

Food

If you love BBQ, try **Super Smokers** (601 Stockell Dr., 636/938-9742, www.super-smokers.com, 10:45am-8pm Sun.-Thurs., 10:45am-9pm Fri.-Sat., $12-18). They use an applewood rotisserie to make tender, fall-off-the-bone baby back ribs, pulled pork, and beef brisket. The sides are nothing to sing about, but the jalapeno cornbread is a must.

To get here from 5th Street near Exit 264 on I-44, take a right and then an immediate left (west) on 5th Street, and then turn right (north) on North Central Avenue. The restaurant is one block up on the right (east) side.

◆ Back on 66

From I-44 Exit 261, take a left (south) on Allenton Road and drive under the freeway. Turn right (west) on Business Loop 44 (East Osage Street) as it passes through the town of Pacific.

Pacific

The town of Pacific started as a railroad and silica mining center. (The fine silica sand in the nearby bluffs was used to make glassware.) When Route 66 was realigned through Pacific in 1932, it exposed the mining tunnels and on the western edge of town; you can see the **sandstone bluffs** and **silica mine caves** along the highway. Pacific is where Route 66 becomes that quiet two-lane highway dotted highway with old motels and rusted signs that road-trippers love.

◆ Back on 66

Continue heading west on Osage Street. After about 3.5 miles the road joins the pre-1930s alignment in the town of Gray Summit.

Gray Summit

Sights
Purina Farms

Animal lovers won't want to miss **Purina Farms** (200 Checkerboard Dr., 314/982-3232, www.purinafarms.com, 9:30am-3pm Wed.-Fri., 9:30am-4pm Sat.-Sun., mid-Mar.-mid-Nov., free). The visitor center features an animal petting area, wagons rides, an animal barn, a hayloft, educational exhibits, and a snack and gift shop. A dog arena, adjacent to the visitor center, hosts daily canine performances (11am-1pm) such as dog agility, flying disc, and diving by dogs that have been adopted from shelters around the country. There are also cow-milking demonstrations at the visitor center (10:30am, 12:30pm). Pets are welcome.

To get there from Osage Street (Business I-44), turn right (north) on Highway 100 (Historic Route 66), go under the freeway and after about 0.5 mile, turn left (northwest) on Highway MM. The Purina Farms entrance is on the left-hand side of the road.

Shaw Nature Reserve

Stretch your legs and enjoy the natural beauty of the Ozark landscape at the **Shaw Nature Reserve** (Hwy. 100 and I-44, 636/451-3512, www.missouribotanicalgarden.org, 7am-sunset daily, $5). The glacial erosion of the Ozark Plateau formed this area right on the Meramec River, which has more than 2,500 acres of tall grass prairie, woodlands, and wetlands. Today the park sits on an ancient mountain range with 350 acres of abandoned farm fields that have been replanted with prairie grass; invasive honeysuckle has been thinned out to restore the open woodlands. The **visitor center** (9am-5pm Mon.-Fri., 10am-4pm Sat.-Sun.) has trail guides and maps.

Visitors can explore 14 miles of hiking trails, including the **Brush Creek Trail**. This 0.75-mile trail starts at the visitor center and passes 18 native trees as it meanders through the **Whitmire Wildflower Garden**. The **Wetland Trail** is a one-mile loop with a 300-foot boardwalk and elevated observation area of wetlands, plants, and animals.

✪ Back on 66

Leaving Gray Summit, Route 66 (Hwy. 100) dips south and heads west, but to stay on Route 66 continue straight (near I-44 Exit 251). After about 5 miles you will cross Highway 50, and the road joins North Outer Road and parallels I-44. Follow North Outer Road for 5 miles to Exit 242; turn left (southeast) to cross under I-44 and turn right (west) onto South Outer Road (North Commercial Ave.) and continue on to St. Clair.

St. Clair

In 1849, St. Clair was established as a railroad community; then it developed into a zinc and lead mining area.

Food

The **Lewis Café** (145 S. Main St., 636/629-9975, 5am-8pm daily, $7-12) is a local's place that makes you feel right at home. The patty melts are excellent (they raise their own beef), and the hand-battered onion rings are crunchy and delicious. The café is popular for their strawberry-rhubarb, lemon meringue, and apple crumb pies. To get to Lewis Cafe from Route 66, turn left onto Highway 47 (south); it's about 0.5 mile down the road.

✪ Back on 66

Heading west on Commercial Avenue, turn right (northwest) on Highway 30, then take I-44 West. You could drive on the North Service Road, but you'll have to cross over the highway a few times, and there's really not much to see. In the interest of saving time, take I-44 for 10 miles and then Exit 230 into Stanton.

Stanton

Sights
Meramec Caverns

One of the most widely advertised sites on Route 66 is **Meramec Caverns** (Exit 230 off I-44, 573/468-3166, www.americascave.com, 9am-7pm daily May-June, 8:30am-7:30pm daily July-early Sept., 9am-6pm daily Sept. and Apr., 9am-5pm daily Oct. and Mar., 9am-4pm daily Nov.-Feb.; $21 adults, $11 children 5-11, children under 4 free). Discovered in 1720, the limestone cave was opened to the public in the mid-1930s by Lester B. Dill. Today visitors can see a wonderland of stalactites and stalagmites. Guided 80-minute tours depart every 20-30 minutes and are conducted on well-lit walkways in a seven-story amphitheater of colorful mineral formations. In honor of 9/11, a computerized LED light show accompanies the song *God Bless America*. The interior temperature is a constant 58 degrees; bring a jacket and wear sturdy shoes.

From I-44, take Exit 230 in Stanton. Turn left (south) and pass over the railroad tracks. The caverns are about 3 miles away.

✪ Back on 66

If you're tired of the interstate, you can get off at Exit 230 (Meramec Caverns) and take the pre-1930s alignment instead. After exiting I-44, turn left (east) on Highway W and take your first right (south) onto North Service Road. After about 2.5 miles, the road becomes East Springfield Road and enters the town of **Sullivan**.

Sullivan was once a mining town rich in lead, iron, zinc, and copper, and it's

The Barns of Meramec Caverns

Meramec Caverns was launched as a tourist attraction by Lester B. Dill during the Great Depression, so Dill had to be creative about bringing in business. Dill was one of the first people to use bumper stickers as a promotional tool, and he also painted huge ads on barns. No one knows for sure how many barn ads remain, but Dill, together with Jim Gauer, painted hundreds of barns in about 40 states.

For 45 years, the duo traveled the country offering to paint barns for free as long as they could paint the Meramec Caverns logo on the roof. Sometimes they offered watches, whiskey, and cave tour tickets in exchange for prime roadside real estate. In 1968 barn rooftop advertising was banned, but the older Meramec ads were grandfathered in under the law.

also the place where William Randolph Hearst's father was born. Today, however, there's no reason to stop in Sullivan, so keep following Springfield Road until it rejoins the service road alongside I-44. After about 5 miles, you'll reach the town of Bourbon.

Bourbon

Bourbon got its name from railroad workers who liked to drink whiskey from the general store in the 1850s. They called it the "Bourbon Store," and the name stuck. For a fun photo op, there's a Bourbon **water tower** as you head into town.

Food

For a quick bite, **The Circle Inn Malt Shop** (171 Old Hwy. 66, 573/732-4470, 8am-9pm Mon.-Sat., 9am-7pm Sun., $5-10) serves made-to-order grilled-cheese sandwiches, meatloaf dinners, malts, floats, and soft-serve ice cream.

◈ Back on 66

Old Highway 66 dips south and heads west, rejoining the service road for another 10 miles into the town of Cuba.

Cuba

There are eight towns in the United States named Cuba. Cuba, Missouri, was named

after the island country in sympathy for Cubans who were fighting for their independence from Spain. From the late 1800s to the 1930s, Cuba was the largest producer and distributer of apples; its barrel-making industry earned it the nickname "The Land of the Big Red Apple." The iron-ore and farming industry employed most residents until the railroad arrived in 1860, after which Cuba became a major shipping center. Shoe manufacturers also set up shop and became a vital part of the economy until they went out of business. By the 1980s, many citizens were living below the poverty line.

Sights
Murals

Cuba was revitalized with a **mural project** (http://cubamomurals.com) that attracted Route 66 travelers. Twelve outdoor murals line Route 66 and depict the town's heritage, including Route 66 businesses, a series of Civil War Murals, paintings of Amelia Earhart when she landed outside Cuba in 1928, and Bette Davis's 1948 visit to the town in her Packard station wagon. A brochure and mural map is available at the **Visitor's Center** (71 State Hwy. P, 573/885-2531, www.cubamochamber.com, 8am-6pm Mon.-Sat., 11am-5pm Sun.), located at the junction of I-44 (Exit 208) and North Service Road.

Carr Service Station

The **Carr Service Station** (125 Hwy. ZZ)

is an early 1930s Phillips 66 gas station located at the corner of Route 66 and Franklin Street. Over time it has been a Pontiac dealership, a Mobil service station, and a bakery. A fast-food franchise once wanted to buy it, but the owners, Lynn and Bill Wallis, knew it would be torn down so they refused to sell. Thankfully, in 2005 it was restored with a cost-share grant from the National Park Service Route 66 Corridor Preservation Program.

Hayes Family Shoe Store
Shoes played a big part in Cuba's economic history. The **Hayes Family Shoe Store** (103 S. Smith St., 573/885-7312, 8:30am-5:30pm Mon.-Fri., 8:30am-3pm Sat., free) has two shoes that belonged to Robert Wadlow (1918-1940), the tallest man in the world at 8 feet 11.1 inches tall. Wadlow traveled the country as a spokesman for a shoe company, and sometimes he would leave a shoe as a novelty item. Two of his shoes, one size 37 and the other size 35, are on display. The store also sells fitness shoes and hunting and work boots and has an on-site repair shop. The store is located about five blocks west of the Carr Service station.

Accommodations
The historic ★ **Wagon Wheel Motel** (901 E. Washington, 573/885-3411, www.wagonwheel66cuba.com, $60-115) is a classic mom-and-pop motor court featuring cabins with attached garages. (The 1936 motel was unusual for its time—most tourist courts in the 1930s were freestanding without multiple connected units.) The cabins were built from Ozark sandstone, also known as slab rock or giraffe rock. Each unit has a pitched roof, arched doorway, and stone-trimmed windows and doors. Rooms today retain their original glass knobs, wood floors, windows, and doors, but have been updated with pillow-top mattresses, flatscreen televisions, and free Wi-Fi. Shaded outdoor seating areas and decks, fire pits,

and a guest laundry make it a great place to rest up before you hit the road. Pets are welcome.

Food
Have breakfast at **Shelly's Route 66** (402 E. Washington St., 573/885-6000, 6am-6pm Tues.-Thurs., 6am-7pm Fri.-Sat., 7am-2pm Sun., $7-12), conveniently located 0.25 mile west of the Wagon Wheel—it's nice to walk in and see a sign that says "Where friends gather and strangers are made to feel welcome." Order tasty blueberry pancakes and homemade biscuits, or lighter options like a spinach artichoke omelet if your pants are getting tight from too much road food.

For barbeque, try **Missouri Hick Barbeque** (913 E. Washington St., 573/885-6791, 11am-8pm Sun.-Thurs., 11am-9pm Fri.-Sat., $8-15). The owner Dennis Meiser smokes his meat for 12 hours and serves it with five sauces, from smoky to spicy to sweet. Meiser, a master woodworker, created the rustic interior's tables, chairs, and cedar stairs that lead to a balcony.

◈ Back on 66
Head west on Route 66 as it dips south, and after a few miles you'll approach two roadside attractions near Fanning.

Fanning

Sights
World's Largest Rocking Chair
Keep an eye out for the World's Largest Rocking Chair at the **Fanning 66 Outpost General Store** (5957 Hwy. ZZ, 573/885-1474, www.fanning66outpost.com, 9am-5pm Mon.-Fri., 9am-3pm Sat.), located on the right (north) side of the highway. The gigantic rocker is made of steel and pipe and stands 42 feet tall and 20 feet wide; the rockers at the base (put there with two cranes) weigh about a ton a piece. The chair used to rock, but

the owner worried that this monstrosity could tip over and kill someone, so now the rockers are welded at the base. An on-site store sells snacks, sodas, and souvenirs, along with fishing, archery, and hunting supplies.

Bob's Gasoline Alley

From Route 66, take Beamer Lane north to **Bob's Gasoline Alley** (822 Beamer Ln., 573/885-3637), which has a large and diverse collection of old gas pumps, advertising signage, die-cast cars, peddle cars, and other highway relics. If you love roadside memorabilia, call ahead to make a reservation with Bob, a gracious host. He and his wife Darlene will show you around. The barns are filled with rare signage in pristine condition; early 20th-century gas pumps make this a popular stop for car enthusiasts. If the barns are closed, there is still a lot to see outside. To get there from Route 66, take a right (north) on Beamer Lane.

⬥ Back on 66

Bob's Gasoline Alley is less than a mile south of I-44; or stay on Highway ZZ (U.S. 66) as it heads west and then north alongside I-44. In about 2 miles you'll be in the unincorporated town of Rosati.

Rosati

Soon after Rosati was originally settled in 1845, Italian immigrants began to arrive. They built two stores, a saloon, a canning plant, a church, a school, and a post office. They also planted Concord grapes to make wine. The **Rosati Winery** (22050 State Route KK, 573/265-3000, www.rosatiwinerymuseum.com, 11am-6pm Thurs.-Tues. May-Oct., $2.50) was built in 1934; it is now a museum dedicated to the Italian Americans who settled in the Ozark Mountains. Historical artifacts, documents, vintage wine-making equipment, and oral histories tell the story of their residents' connection to Welch's

Grape Company. There is an on-site gift shop and wine tasting room.

From Route 66, turn south onto Highway KK. The winery will be 600 feet up on the right.

⬥ Back on 66

The mother road heads west on Highway KK for 6 miles to the town of St. James, as the topography shifts from prairie land to exposed rock outcroppings and the Ozark hills. Continue west and turn right (north) onto Highway 68. As you cross I-44, take your first left (west) after the freeway entrance onto Parker Lane. Make another quick left onto Historic U.S. 66 (North Outer Rd.).

St. James to Rolla

The Murdon Concrete Company has a huge neon sign of a **dripping faucet** (14241 Old Hwy. 66) on the right (north) side of Route 66, three miles west of St. James. In three more miles, turn left (south) to join I-44 West, or stop at the Mule Trading Post before you get on I-44.

In addition to Route 66 maps and books, the **Mule Trading Post** (11160 Dillon Outer Rd., Rolla, 573/364-4711, www.muletradingpostmo.com, 9am-6pm daily) sells unusual antiques, figurines, furniture, kitchenware, knives, moccasins, pottery, local honey, Amish jams and jellies, and mule (yes, mule) T-shirts, hats, pictures, jewelry, and sculptures. The trading post is on the frontage road south of I-44 near Exit 189.

⬥ Back on 66

Head west on I-44 and take Exit 186 into the college town of Rolla.

Rolla

When Route 66 came through Rolla, it was one of the most difficult gravel roads to travel on in Missouri, especially if the weather was bad. The area from Rolla to Lebanon was the last piece of paved road on Route 66 in Missouri; when it was complete, there was a two-mile parade with more than 8,000 people out to celebrate.

To follow Route 66 through Rolla, turn left (south) on Highway 63 (Business 44) and make another left (south) on North Pine Street. In less than one mile, turn right (west) on West 6th Street. After a few blocks, look on the left-hand side of the road for one of the best places for pie in the state.

A stumpy replica of **Stonehenge** (1400 N. Bishop Ave., 573/341-4111, www.rockmech.mst.edu/history/stonehenge, free) is located on the Missouri University of Science and Technology campus. Even though it's a smaller version, this partial reconstruction was made using 160 tons of granite cut by the university's Waterjet equipment. Stonehenge is across from the Great Wall of China restaurant on the east side Route 66 (Bus-44, N. Bishop Ave.).

Food

★ **Slice of Pie** (601 Kings Hwy., 573/364-6203, www.asliceofpie.info, 10am-10pm daily, cash or check only) sells more than 25 different award-winning pies, from fruit and cream to silks and custards. The cakes and cheesecakes are also a hit.

For home-cooked meals, local entertainment, darts, and karaoke, **Joe and Linda's Tater Patch** (103 Bridge School Rd., 573/368-3111, 7am-1:30am Mon.-Sat., 8am-midnight Sun., $8-$20) is worth a stop. Their signature tater patch sampler includes a platter of fried treats; there are also eight versions of baked potato—from the Santa Fe with chicken, salsa, cheese, and ranch to the Cordon Bleu with chicken, ham, and blue cheese. Entertainment includes poker and pool tournaments, dart leagues, and DJs.

Joe and Linda's Tater Patch is on Route 66 (Bus-44) on the way out of town, less than one mile west of Highway 72. Take a left (south) at County Road 251 (Bridge School Rd.). The restaurant is on the left (east) side of the highway.

◈ Back on 66

Leaving Rolla, West 6th Street turns into Kings Highway, which then turns into Business I-44. Head west on Business I-44 to get on I-44 West and drive 5 miles to Doolittle.

Doolittle

Doolittle sits on the edge of the Fort Leonard Wood military base, which was a training center for infantry troops in 1941. Italian and German POWs were also interned here. The Mother Road experienced a boom during this time, because it was the preferred route to shuttle military supplies and transport personnel.

Six cabins, two outhouses, and a broken neon sign are decaying in the forest on a dead-end strip of old Route 66. What remains of **John's Modern Cabins,** once a juke joint in the 1930s called Bill and Bess' Place, has had several owners over the years. During the 1950s-1960s, the owners were John and Lillian Dausch. When improvements were made to Route 66, the Dausch's moved their business north of the original location, abandoning the "shotgun shack" and signing the place John's Modern Cabins. They built three more cabins, a laundry room, and a snack bar where they sold beer on Sunday (which was against the law at the time). The property changed hands two more times, but since the 1970s the cabins have been slowly disintegrating back into the earth. Some have fully collapsed while others retain a few furnishings; the neon sign still has some broken light bulbs.

While not for the faint of heart (keep an eye out for snakes and rusty nails), it's a pretty cool and slightly creepy adventure for those who are up for it. The cabins are parallel to I-44, southeast of Exit 176.

From I-44 take Exit 176, turn left (southeast) onto Road 7300. In 1.3 miles, turn right (south) onto Road 7304; the cabins are about 500 feet up on the left (east).

Food

★ **Cookin' From Scratch** (90 Truman St., 573/762-3111, www.cookinfromscratch. biz, 10:30am-8pm Mon.-Thurs., 7am-8:30pm Fri.-Sat., 7am-3pm Sun., $6-15) is your best option in the area. The family-friendly, down-home diner serves some good pan-fried chicken—so good because they "do it the hard way." The chicken is partially submerged in oil in a cast iron skillet and takes about 45-mintues to cook. From the hand-patted burgers to the slow-roasted prime rib with homemade mashed potatoes, everything takes more time, but you can taste the difference.

◆ Back on 66

Follow I-44 West for 6.5 miles to Exit 172. Turn right (east) onto Highway D (Powellville Outer Rd.) and drive 0.3 mile east. To continue on Route 66 turn left (west).

Jerome

Sights
Trail of Tears Memorial

Segments of Route 66 from Rolla to Springfield follow the 1838 Trail of Tears. This was the northern route onto which U.S. troops forced tens of thousands of Cherokee, Creek, Seminole, Chickasaw, and Choctaw Indians to walk 1,200 miles across the country to reservations in Oklahoma. At least 4,000 died from disease, exposure, and starvation.

A resident of Jerome, Missouri, named Larry Baggett was repeatedly awakened by a loud knocking at his door—but when he answered the door, no one was there. Later he was visited by an old Cherokee man who told him his house was built on the Trail of Tears and that many

Devil's Elbow Bridge

Cherokee had camped near his home. The knocking was from the spirits who were still trying to walk the trail, but Baggett's house was blocking their path.

Baggett built a set of stairs on a stone wall on his property to help the spirits cross and the knocking stopped. Soon after, he built a stone archway, as well as concrete and stone sculptures on his property, to memorialize American Indians and honor their struggle.

Baggett died in 2003, and though the **Trail of Tears Memorial** (21250 Hwy. D, dawn to dusk, free) is now in ruins, this folk-art tribute is still worth seeing. A concrete statue of Baggett out front has been decapitated, but it's still wearing Baggett's boots. There's also a statue of a Native American holding the tail of a buffalo and an elephant emerging from the ground with four trunks. The property was sold after Baggett died, but it now appears to be abandoned.

From I-44, take Exit 172 and turn right (east) at the T-intersection onto Highway D toward Jerome. Baggett's memorial is a few hundred yards up on the left.

❖ Back on 66

Drive west on Powellville Outer Road. In less than 4 miles, turn left (southeast) on Highway J. Cross I-44 and then make an immediate right (southwest) on Highway Z (Route 66). As you pass through Pulaski Country, you're deep in the heart of the Ozarks with dramatic 200-foot rock bluffs, fertile valleys, and rivers cut through limestone rock. In about 2 miles, the road passes through Hooker Cut, once rumored to be the deepest road cut in the United States. To reach Devil's Elbow, turn left on Teardrop Road to take the pre-1930s alignment to Devil's Elbow.

Devil's Elbow

Devil's Elbow got its name from a severe bend in the Big Piney River. A group of lumberjacks lamented over a large boulder and the logjams that occurred in the sharpest part of the bend. It was such a nightmare they figured it must have been put there by the devil.

The 1923 **Devil's Elbow Bridge** is an old steel pony truss bridge that crosses the Big Piney River. The bridge spans 588 feet and is almost 20 feet wide with four concrete deck girder spans. This is one of only two bridges in the state with a curved shape. In 1942, the new four-lane road from Fort Leonard Wood accommodated military transport and bypassed the 1926 alignment. The Devil's Elbow Bridge sat neglected and rusted for years until it was rehabilitated in 2013 into a stronger, sturdier version of itself. Thankfully, it still retains its historic charm and is one of the best examples of what Route 66 must have looked like 80 years ago. The bridge is less than one mile after turning left on Teardrop Road.

Food

The **Elbow Inn Bar and Barbecue Pit** (21050 Teardrop Rd., 573/336-5375, 11am-9pm Wed., 11am-10pm Thurs.-Sat., noon-8pm Sun., $7-14) originally opened as the Munger Moss Sandwich shop in 1929. It became the Elbow in 1946 and has been serving barbecue and cold beer ever since. This all-American roadhouse is usually filled with Route 66 travelers dining under a sea of bras that hang from the ceiling. The staff is friendly and the no-frills food is tasty; the pulled-pork sandwich soaked in barbeque sauce and served on a hoagie bun is popular. There's also smoked chicken wings (not fried) rubbed with barbeque spices. Thursday through Saturday nights often feature entertainment.

✪ Back on 66

From Devil's Elbow, follow Teardrop Road west for 1.5 miles and turn left (southwest) onto Highway Z (Route 66). Highway Z continues west for 6 miles to St. Robert. Keep heading west as Business I-44 joins Route 66. In another 3 miles you'll reach the town of Waynesville.

Waynesville

Named after a revolutionary war hero (General "Mad Anthony" Wayne), Waynesville is the oldest town in Pulaski County. During the 1830s, the town operated as a trading post for settlers and trappers while Native Americans came through on the infamous Trail of Tears. It was also a major training center for troops during the Civil War.

As you enter Waynesville, about a mile after crossing I-44, keep an eye out for a rock emerging from the hill in the shape of a frog. In 1996, tattoo artist Phil Nelson carved **Frog Rock** out of granite, and it has become a roadside mascot of Route 66 in Missouri.

Sights

Waynesville is a pedestrian-friendly town. To explore it further, take the **Waynesville Walking Tour** (www.visitpulaskicounty.org/waynesville, 24 hours, free). The tour starts at the Old Stagecoach Stop (105 N. Lynn St), which operated as a hospital during the war, and continues to Laughlin Park and the Trail of Tears encampment. Stops along the way include a Korean Baptist Church, an early 20th-century courthouse, and a bank building. A scenic spot overlooking the valley commemorates the place where Union troops built a fort to protect telegraph wires during the Civil War.

Trail of Tears National Historic Site

During the Trail of Tears, more than 350 Cherokee Indian camped in the fields along Roubidoux Creek, which is now the **Trail of Tears National Historic Site** (Laughlin Park, Rte. 66 and Olive St., 573/774-6171, www.visitmo.com, dawn-dusk daily). A Cherokee Indian named B. B. Canon kept a journal and wrote the following while in Waynesville:

"Dec. 8, 1837 - Buried Nancy Bigbears Grand Child, marched at 9 o'c. A.M., halted

at Piney a small river, ½ past 3 o'c. P.M., rained all day, encamped and issued corn only, no fodder to be had, 11 miles to day.

December 9, 1937 - Marched at 9 o'c. A.M., Mayfields wagon broke down at about a mile

left him to get it mended and overtake, halted at Waynesville, Mo. 4 o'c. P.M., encamped and issued corn & fodder, beef & corn meal, weather extremely cold, 12 ½ miles to day."

The park has a one-mile path that runs along the Roubidoux River. Restrooms, playground equipment, and a boardwalk that passes above an underwater cave are also on-site.

Shopping

Roubidoux Plaza (115 N. Benton St.) offers a courtyard, fountain, and several specialty stores that Route 66 fans will appreciate. Ursula Lebioda and We Can Development restored the historic plaza with a brick and iron facade that fits right in with the quaint atmosphere of downtown Waynesville. The **Route 66 Candy Shoppe** (115 N. Benton St., 573/201-7455, 10am-6pm Mon.-Fri., 10am-4pm Sat.) sells old-fashioned, hard-to-find sweets like Bubble Tape, Goo Go Clusters, Moon Pies, Wax Lips, and candy cigarettes (scandalous!). The shop is inspired by *Little House on the Prairie* and is decorated with wall-to-wall barrels and farm items that belonged to the co-owner's parents and grandparents.

Cakes, cookies, brownies, and cupcakes with towers of swirled icing that resemble soft-serve ice cream await at The **Sugar Shack...A California Cakery** (115 N. Benton St., 760/885-0782, www.goodiesbyangela.com, 9am-5:30pm Tues.-Thurs., 9am-5pm Fri., 10am-2pm Sat.). **Just Because** (115 N. Benton St., 573/774-4995, www.justbecause.us, 10am-6pm Mon.-Sat.) sells Route 66 memorabilia, home decor, gift baskets, and food items.

If you're due for a haircut or a shave, check out **Roots 66 Barbershop** (115 N. Benton St., 573/201-9467, 10am-6pm Tues.-Fri., 10am-4pm Sat.) for a classic straight razor shave and a haircut. Women and girls are also welcome.

Food

Hoppers (318 Route 66, 573/774-0135, www.hopperspub.com, 4pm-close Mon.-Fri., 11:30am-close Sat.-Sun., $6-13) is a pub and restaurant in downtown Waynesville that pays tribute to Frog Rock. They serve bar food with a dash of international flair—sriracha pepperjack burgers, Thai chili wings, Caribbean steak wraps and taquitos—and have 66 beers on tap.

◈ Back on 66

Leaving Waynesville, head west on Highway 17 (Route 66) and 5 miles

continue to Buckhorn. This area was originally called Pleasant Grove, but was later renamed after the Buckhorn Tavern, a popular stop for stagecoaches on the Wire Road.

Route 66 parallels I-44. At Exit 153, turn left (south) on Highway 17 (Red Oak Rd.) and cross the highway to turn right (west) onto Route 66. In about 1.3 miles, turn right (west) onto Highway P and continue to the town of Laquey (pronounced "Lakeway"). Drive 1 mile and turn left (southwest) onto Highway AA. After about 1.5 miles, turn right (west) on Highway AB. The road winds to the western edge of Fort Leonard Wood and then runs alongside I-44 to become Heartwood Road for about 6 miles. The road turns into Glacier Point Road for almost 4 miles to the town of Sleeper.

Sleeper

If you like puzzles, you are going to love **Ballhagen's Puzzles** (25211 Garden Crest Rd., 417/286-3837, www.missouripuzzle.com, 11am-4pm Mon.-Sat., call for Sun. hours). The shelves are stocked with almost 3,000 puzzles stacked from floor to ceiling with 100 to 24,000—yes, thousand—pieces in almost every theme you can imagine. They also have custom and hand-cut wooden puzzles in a wide selection of shapes, from rectangle to pyramid to a Route 66 puzzle in the shape of an interstate sign.

To get there from I-44, take Exit 135 for Sleeper. Turn right (northeast) onto Garden Crest Drive and continue north for 1 mile. From Glacier Point Road/Route 66, take Highway F north, cross over I-44, and turn right onto Garden Crest Drive.

◈ Back on 66

From Highway F (near I-44 Exit 135), head west on Pecos Drive (Route 66), which leads to the laid-back town of Lebanon in 6 miles.

Lebanon

In the late 1880s, Lebanon was a small yet thriving community with an opera house and the historic Gasconade Hotel (destroyed by fire), which accommodated up to 500 guests. But the town really became popular after Route 66 came through in 1926, because Lebanon was one of the largest towns between Rolla and Springfield.

Sights
Route 66 Museum and Research Center

In 1927, a tent camp called Camp Joy opened at the rate of $0.50 a night. The "Dream Village" had an impressive fountain that tourists lined up for blocks to see. The fountain is no longer around, but a diorama of the "Dream Village" can be seen at the **Route 66 Museum and Research Center** (915 S. Jefferson Ave., 417/532-2148, 8am-8pm Mon.-Thurs., 8am-5pm Fri.-Sat., free), located inside the Lebanon-Laclede County Library. The museum is home to a life-size reproduction of a Phillips 66 gas station (with Texaco gas pumps), a tourist cabin, a diner, a collection of salt and pepper shakers from Route 66 restaurants, and blueprints of the construction of Route 66 as well as rare maps.

To get to the museum from Business I-44, turn left onto South Jefferson Avenue (southeast). It's located about one-third of mile ahead, on the right (southwest) side of the street.

Accommodations

Lebanon is home to one of the most iconic roadside motels, the ★ **Munger Moss** (1336 East Rte. 66, 417/532-3111, www.mungermoss.com, $60). Originally a barbecue joint on the Big Piney River at Devil's Elbow, the Munger Moss was famous for their slow-cooked pork. After Route 66 was re-routed in 1942, new owners moved the venue to Lebanon.

It re-opened in 1946 with 14 cabins and garages next to the rooms. Twenty-six more units were added in 1961.

Bob and Ramona Lehman have run the motel for more than 40 years, offering the upmost in hospitality and cleanliness. Today the well-maintained rooms have a classic vintage vibe with quilted bedspreads, 1970s lampshades, wood-paneled walls, and (depending on what room you get) lots of Route 66 memorabilia on the walls. A tribute room to the Coral Court Motel is dressed up in pink. Thanks to the Neon Heritage Preservation Committee at the Route 66 Association of Missouri and the National Park Service Route 66 Corridor Preservation Program, the Munger Moss was able to restore one of the most impressive neon signs on Route 66.

As Route 66 enters Lebanon on Pecos Drive, it turns into East Seminole Avenue as the road veers away from I-44. The Munger Moss is about 0.5 mile on the left (southeast) side of the road.

Food

Dowd's Catfish and BBQ (1760 W. Elm St., 417/532-1777, www.dowdscatfishbbq. com, 11am-8:30pm Sun.-Thurs., 11am-9pm Fri.-Sat., $7-16) serves Mississippi Delta-style fried catfish and southern favorites like okra, cornbread, and peach cobbler.

◆ Back on 66

Head southwest on East Seminole Avenue until it dead-ends into Business I-44 (Route 66). Turn right (west) and follow Business I-44 for less than a mile as it curves to the left (southwest) on Business I-44.

◆ Side Trip: Camdenton

Ha Ha Tonka State Park (1491 State Rd. D, Camdenton, 573/346-2986, www.mostateparks.com, 7am-sunset daily

Apr.-Oct., 8am-sunset daily Nov.-Mar, free), with breathtaking scenery and the stone ruins of a 100-year old castle overlooking the Lake of the Ozarks, is worth a trip. Robert Snyder, a prominent businessman built this estate at the turn of the 20th century. He spared no expense, using only high-quality materials and the best artisans he could find. After Snyder died suddenly in 1906, his brothers finished the job, adding an 80-foot water tower, greenhouses, and horse stables. When the family fell on hard times, the property became a hotel, then burned down in 1942.

Start your day at the **Visitor's Center,** where you'll find self-guided trail brochures and a large relief map of the park carved in stone. The **Castle Trail** is a moderate trek with scenic overlooks of the Lake of the Ozarks and access to the castle ruins. The trailhead is located at two parking areas along Castle Ruins Road; plan 45 minutes for the round-trip trek. Other trails lead to a natural bridge and the Whispering Dell sink basin.

Ha Ha Tonka State Park is near Camdenton, about 25 miles north of Lebanon. From Lebanon, turn right (northwest) onto South Jefferson Avenue (Hwy. 32). In 1.5 miles turn right (northeast) on East 7th Street (MO 5). Follow MO Highway 5 for 19 miles, turn left (west) on Highway 5-133. After 1.6 miles, turn left (west) to stay on Highway 5-133. Drive 2 miles and then turn right on MO Highway D; the park is about 1,200 feet ahead on the left.

◈ Back on 66

Leave Lebanon via Business I-44. Turn right (west) onto Highway W (Route 66) and head south alongside I-44 for about 9 miles. Cross I-44 via Highway C (I-44 Exit 118) in Phillipsburg. Take your first right (west) on Highway CC (Newport Ave.). In 2.6 miles, stay on Newport Avenue, which will veer away from I-44 and head south through the small community of Conway.

Marshfield

As you follow Highway CC into the town of Marshfield, Route 66 turns into West Hubble Drive. Marshfield has a sleepy main street and a giant train elevator, and it is the birthplace of Dr. Edwin Hubble, the astronomer who inspired the famous telescope. A one-quarter scale **replica of the Hubble Telescope** is displayed at the county courthouse (140 South Clay Street).

To reach the Hubble Telescope replica from Route 66 (West Hubble Dr.) turn left (south) on North Marshall Street and then right (west) on West Jefferson Street and then the next left (south) onto Clay Street. The telescope is on the left side of the street.

Accommodations

A few miles from the Hubble Telescope replica is the ★ **Dickey House Bed & Breakfast** (331 South Clay St., 417/468-3000, www.dickeyhouse.com, $99-169), a Greek Revival mansion built at the turn of the 20th century. The house features three-foot columns, a beveled-glass front entrance with rocking chairs on the porch, and a lawn flanked by oak trees with benches and a garden. Each guestroom has a private modern bathroom with antique accessories. Some rooms have a canopy and four-poster beds, fireplace, Jacuzzi, or screened-in porch. A gourmet breakfast includes bacon-wrapped asparagus with adobo hollandaise sauce and pancakes filled with vanilla cream-cheese and topped with whipped cream and homemade raspberry sauce. Small dogs under 25 pounds are welcome.

From Route 66 (West Hubble Dr.), turn left (south) on North Marshall Street and then turn right (west) onto West Jefferson Street. The next left (south) will be Clay Street. It's a few blocks south of the courthouse, on the right side of the street.

◈ Back on 66

Depart Marshfield heading west on West Jackson Street (Hwy. 38) to merge left (southwest) onto West Washington Street. Route 66 (Hwy. 00) travels south alongside I-44 for about 12 miles into the town of Strafford.

If you skip downtown Marshfield, just continue on West Hubble Drive (Route 66), which turns into West Washington Street (Hwy. 00).

Strafford

Route 66 passed through Strafford, with pavements and improvements completed in 1930. Route 14 (which was Pine Street) was Strafford's original commerce center, but with Route 66 one block away on Main Street, some businesses installed two doors—one on Pine Street, and the other facing Route 66. In 1952, Route 66 was rerouted through the north side of Strafford to divert traffic from downtown, which caused the decline of the town. Historians believe that the **Trail of Tears** passed through downtown Strafford.

◈ Back on 66

Continue west on Route 66 (Highway 00) for 8 miles into Springfield, the "birthplace" of the Mother Road.

Springfield

John Woodruff, an entrepreneur from Springfield, teamed up with Cyrus Avery, the chairman of the Oklahoma Department of Highways (also known as the "The Father of Route 66"), and together they mapped out the Mother Road's diagonal course. In 1925, Congress enacted a law for national highway construction that made Route 66 possible. On April 30, 1926 a telegram was sent from Springfield's Colonial Hotel—demolished in 1997—proposing that the road from Chicago to Los Angeles be named Route 66. It is for this reason that Springfield is recognized as the birthplace of Route 66.

◈ Route 66 through Springfield

1926-1935 Alignment

Route 66 had several realignments through Springfield. The 1926-1935 alignment enters Springfield from the northeast to run west along East Kearny Street (Hwy. 744) and continues south along Glenstone and National Avenues to St. Louis Street, which leads downtown to the Public Square.

If you don't have much time but still want to take the 1926-1935 alignment through Springfield, cross I-65 and follow Kearny Street (Hwy. 744) west for 2 miles and turn left (south) onto Glenstone Avenue (Business 44). Drive two miles south and turn right (west) on St. Louis Street, which turns into Park Central as it wraps around the square. West of the square, the road turns into College Street and joins the West Chestnut Expressway (Business 44). Turn left (west) and keep straight as you leave Springfield. After crossing under I-44, the Chestnut Expressway turns into Highway 266.

Post-1936 Alignment

The post-1936 alignment bypasses downtown Springfield via Highway 744 west and U.S. 160 south. Unless you have a serious time constraint, stop here: Springfield is too rich in Route 66 history to be missed.

Sights

Route 66 Information Visitor Center

Say hello to the friendly folks at the **Route 66 Information Visitor Center** (815 E. St. Louis St., 417/881-5300, 8am-5pm Mon.-Fri.). They have a wealth of information about Route 66, along with fun souvenirs, brochures, maps of Springfield, and

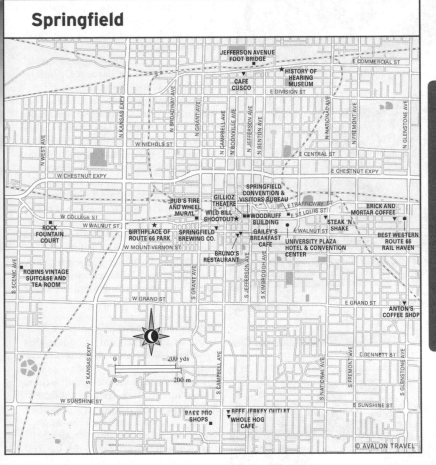

Springfield

a replica of a 1950s diner, gas station fuel pump, and phone booth.

Downtown Springfield is just a few blocks west of the visitor center. There's plenty of parking, so you can get out, stretch your legs and stroll the boutiques, sidewalk cafes, art galleries, nightclubs, restaurants, and theaters.

Woodruff Building

The large building on the northwest corner of Park Central East and Jefferson Avenue is the **Woodruff Building** (E. St. Louis St.). It was owned and named after John Woodruff, the man who established

the U.S. Highway 66 Association in 1926. It was also the area's first skyscraper and received much public acclaim and excitement when it opened in 1911. (Only 10 stories tall, it was a big deal at the time.) Route 66 ran in front of the building. Inside were offices, a pool hall, a barbershop, and two elevators. The building sold for $700,000 a few years after Route 66 began, and an additional 23,000 square feet were added in 1959.

Gillioz Theatre

Next door to the Woodruff Building is the **Gillioz Theatre** (325 Park Central

E., 417/863-7843, www.gillioz.org), which opened in 1926. An enthusiastic audience cherished the lavish Spanish Colonial Revival architecture, with terra cotta tiles, terrazzo flooring, and a grand Wurlitzer. Maurice Earnest Gillioz financed and built the theatre using primarily steel and concrete; wood was only used for the doors and handrails. An arched, stained-glass window, a recessed oculus in the ceiling, decorative urns, plaster friezes, and winged cherubs added to the opulence. As suburban strip malls became more popular in the 1970s, fewer people spent time downtown, and the Gillioz fell into disrepair before closing in 1980. Eventually, a group of locals formed the Springfield Landmarks Preservation Trust and rehabilitated and restored the Gillioz to reopen in 2006. Today, the venue hosts acts ranging from comedian Kathy Griffin to country music singer Dwight Yoakam.

Wild Bill Shootout

It was at 100 Park Central Square that Wild Bill Hickok shot Davis Tutt in the heart over a gambling debt in 1865—the nation's first recorded quick-draw shootout. Tutt drew first, but Wild Bill had a better aim; this incident solidified Hickok's reputation as a serious gunfighter. A small plaque in front of the **Park Central Library** (128 Park Central Square) commemorates the duel, and there are street markers where Hickok and Tutt stood.

Bud's Tire and Wheel

Bud's Tire and Wheel (701 W. College St.) opened in 1958 and was one of the first businesses in the area to supply custom wheels. Today, the shop distributes racing tires and high-performance vehicle parts. Colorful murals (north of Route 66 past Grant Avenue) on the side of the

top to bottom: Springfield Route 66 Visitor Center; Gailey's Breakfast Cafe; Gillioz Theatre

building are inspired by the Mother Road and make for a great photo-op.

Birthplace of Route 66 Roadside Park

In 1947, Red Chaney thought it might be easier for customers to drive up and order his $0.25 burgers through a kitchen window rather than relying on a waitress or carhop. This original idea made **Red's Giant Hamburg** possibly the first drive-through restaurant in America.

The unusual business name was the result of Red's famous sign. The sign was shaped like a cross—the word "Giant" was horizontal, while the word "Hamburger" lay vertical (the two words shared an "A" in the middle). However, Chaney had to saw the "er" off of "Hamburger" once he realized the sign was too tall and would touch the power lines. The unusual spelling didn't affect the business. In fact, it made it almost a religious rite of passage for locals and Route 66 travelers.

Unfortunately, Red's closed in 1984. The building was removed, but a replica of the "Giant Hamburg" sign lives on at the **Birthplace of Route 66 Roadside Park** (1200 Block W. College St., 24 hours, free).

Rock Fountain Court

Heading west from Park Central Square, keep an eye out on the south (left) side of Route 66 for **Rock Fountain Court** (2400 W. College St.). Though it's no longer operating as a motel, it remains a great example of a well-preserved, 1940s-era motor court you can only find in the Ozarks. Nine freestanding cabins are arranged in a semi-circle with a signature Ozark sandstone facade.

History of Hearing Museum

About a mile and a half north of downtown, the **History of Hearing Museum** (628 E. Commercial St., 417/869-6550, www.springfieldmo.org, 9am-4:30pm Mon.-Wed. and Fri., free) is a small, quirky place with historical oddities.

On-site is an early hearing aid in the shape of a hand-held trumpet that collected sound waves and led them to the ear. Compared to the nearly invisible hearing aids we have today, it's miraculous how far we've come in the world of cochlear science.

Jefferson Avenue Footbridge

A few blocks west of the Hearing Museum is one of the longest railroad pedestrian bridges in the country. Historians believe the 1902 **Jefferson Avenue Footbridge** (201 E. Commercial, 417/864-7015, daily 24 hours, free) is the first bridge of its kind to be built in the area. The three-span steel cantilever truss footbridge is 562 feet long with 13 train tracks below and two 50-foot towers. It has been completely restored and is beautifully lit at night.

World's Largest Fork

Almost five miles south of downtown is the **World's Largest Fork** (Noble & Associates building, 2155 W. Chesterfield Blvd., 24 hours). The fork stands 35 feet tall and weighs 11 tons, sticking out of a patch of greenery at a slight angle. Colorado also claims to have the world's largest fork sculpture, but either way this is a fun photo op. From downtown, take Highway 13 south toward U.S. 60.

Fantastic Caverns

About five miles north of Springfield is America's only drive-through cave, **Fantastic Caverns** (4872 North Farm Rd. 125, 417/833-2010, www.fantastic-caverns.com, 8am-4pm daily Nov.-Feb., 8am-6pm daily Feb.-Mar. and Sept.-Oct., 8am-7pm daily Mar.-Apr. and Aug.-Sept., 8am-8pm daily Apr.-Aug., $23.50). You can no longer drive your own car through the cave; instead, a jeep tram with a long wagon takes visitors to see fluted draped stalactites, stalagmites, and flowstones. The creepiest thing about this cave, however, is that the Ku Klux Klan once conducted secret meetings and cross burnings in the cave's "grand ballroom" in the 1920s.

From College Street (Route 66) turn right (north) on Highway 13. Turn left (west) on West Farm Road. 94 and follow it as it turns south and then west to North Farm Road 125. Turn right (north) and drive about a mile.

Shopping

For some vintage shopping and a sweet treat, check out **Robin's Vintage Suitcase and Tea Room** (724 S. Scenic Ave., 417/866-7000, http://robinsvintagesuitcase.com, 11am-3pm Mon., 10am-4pm Tues.-Sat.), less than a mile south of Rock Fountain Court. Robin's sells clothing, antiques, and home decor and furniture from nearby auctions and estate sales. The shop also has new bath products, kitchenware items, and gifts. The desserts at the Tea Room next door (11am-3pm Mon.-Sat.) are devilishly good.

If it's outdoor supplies you need, **Bass Pro Shops Outdoor World** (1935 S. Campbell Ave. 417/887-7334, 7am-10pm Mon.-Sat., 9am-7pm Sun., free) is less than two miles south of downtown. The 300,000-square feet of retail space houses an indoor boat showroom, three restaurants, an indoor waterfall and stream, a barbershop, a firing range, and a fish and wildlife museum with a turtle pond and trout exhibit.

Carnivores will love the **Beef Jerky Outlet** (Sunshine Corners Shopping Center, 228 W. Sunshine St., 417/720-4502, www.mojerky.com, 10am-7pm Mon.-Thurs., 10am-8pm Fri.-Sat., 11am-6pm Sun.). This is nothing like the beef jerky at a 7-Eleven convenience store—this is a meat lover's mecca. The salty treat is stored in wooden barrels and sold in a wide range of varieties, from kangaroo, salmon, and turkey to pheasant and gator. On the right side of the store is the thicker, moist jerky; to the left is the traditional leather-textured chew. They also sell popcorn, trail mix, summer sausages, and cheese from local farms.

Elvis suite at the Best Western Route 66 Rail Haven

Accommodations

The **Best Western Route 66 Rail Haven** (203 S. Glenstone Ave., 417/866-1963, www.bwrailhaven.com, $65-105) has been serving Route 66 roadsters since 1938. Call ahead to book the Elvis suite, which has a Jacuzzi tub and a bed in the shape of a classic car, complete with tail fins that light up. To get there from Kearny Street, head south (left) on North Glenstone Avenue. After two miles, turn right (west) on East St. Louis Street (Route 66).

The **University Plaza Hotel** (333 S. John Q. Hammons Pkwy., 417/864-7333, www.upspringfield.com, $109-149) is a few blocks west of the Steak 'n Shake, with modern accommodations, a fitness center, free breakfast, an indoor and outdoor pool, and a bar and restaurant. Pets are welcome.

Food

If you're lucky enough to land the Elvis room at the Rail Haven, stop at the nearby **Brick and Mortar Coffee** (1666 E. St. Louis St., 417/812-6539, www.brickandmortarcoffee.com, 7am-3pm Mon.-Sat.). They roast and brew artisan, handcrafted, organic coffee from Costa Rica, Kenya, Indonesia, and Papua New Guinea.

Those with a bigger appetite can opt for breakfast at **Anton's Coffee Shop** (937 S. Glenstone Ave., 417/869-7681, 6am-2pm Mon. and Wed.-Sat., 8am-2pm Sun., $7-11), a Springfield tradition for more than 40 years. The biscuits and gravy, buttermilk pancakes, hash browns, and grits are all made from scratch. It's located less than a mile south of St. Louis Street.

For breakfast downtown, the best place is ★ **Gailey's Breakfast Cafe** (220 E. Walnut St., 417/866-5500, 7am-2pm daily, $8-12), located in an old pharmacy and soda fountain that was established in 1942. Red-velvet pancakes and sweet-potato hash browns elevate breakfast to a new level. There may be a wait, but it's worth it. Gailey's has a great atmosphere, delicious food, and it just oozes old-school character. It's one of my favorite breakfast places on Route 66.

The beautiful and original 1962 **Steak 'n Shake** (1158 E. St. Louis St., 417/866-6109, www.steaknshake.com, open 24 hours daily, $5-8) is definitely worth a stop. Many of the mid-century features are still intact, such as the roof, the porcelain exterior wall panels, plate-glass windows, glazed-tile footings, neon signs, kitchen cook line, counter, tile floor, and curb service window and counter. The first Route 66 Steak 'n Shake, which opened in 1934, was in Normal, Illinois, but is now gone, so this one is a classic stop, and on the National Register of Historic Places. It's located west of Glenstone Avenue.

If it happens to be dinnertime, or you want something a little fancy for lunch, **Bruno's** (416 South Ave., 417/866-0007, www.dineatbrunos.com, 11am-10pm Mon.-Thurs., 11am-11pm Fri.-Sat.,

Local Eats

In 1940, David Leong came to the United States from China; Leong opened Springfield's Leong's Tea House in 1963. Once he saw how much the locals worshipped fried chicken, he decided to modify the already established cashew chicken dish from a stir-fried version to a deep-fried remix slathered with oyster sauce and sprinkled with green onions. It was a hit.

By the 1970s, Leong's **Cashew Chicken** was served throughout the city in every type of restaurant--from diners to school lunch cafeterias. Leong's Tea House closed in 1997 and was replaced by **Leong's Asian Diner** (1540 W. Republic Rd., 417/887-7500, 11am-10pm Mon.-Sat., 11am-8pm Sun., $8-16). Even though you can find Springfield-style cashew chicken throughout the city, Leong's uses the original recipe.

$12-27) serves up savory Sicilian food in a 1905 building with a taste of the old country. Choose from a good selection of pomodoro pastas, gnocchi, brick-oven pizzas, and fresh deserts baked daily.

Stop in for a local craft beer at **Springfield Brewing Company** (305 S. Market Ave., 417/832-8277, www.springfieldbrewingco.com, 11am-11pm Mon.-Tues., 11am-midnight Wed.-Thurs., 11am-1am Fri., 8am-midnight Sat.-Sun., $7-23). The six fresh brews on tap include German, English, and American-style lagers and ales. Pub food is served fresh and uses locally sourced ingredients. The black-bean burger will seduce even the most committed carnivores, while salty sweet-potato fries will keep you sipping a rich and creamy Mudhouse Stout.

The **Whole Hog Café** (224 Sunshine St., 417/868-0042, http://wholehogsgf.com, 11am-9pm Mon.-Sat. 11am-8pm Sun., $5-16) is one of Springfield's best BBQ spots. The Hog has won awards for their

Steak 'n Shake

dry-rubbed meat, and they have six different sauces to choose from. Obviously, this is not the place for vegetarians, but carnivores will feel right at home. It's located right next door to the Bass Pro Shop south of downtown.

If you've never had Peruvian food, try **Cafe Cusco** (234 E. Commercial St., 417/868-8088, www.cafecusco.com, 11am-9pm Mon.-Thurs., 11am-10pm Fri.-Sat., 11am-8pm Sun., $8-12), a couple blocks west of the Jefferson Avenue footbridge. When Chef Joe Gidman hiked the Inca Trails, he loved the food so much he decided to bring it back to the Midwest. Dishes are savory and sweet, tangy and flavorful, with honey, beet sauce, pineapple, and black olives. There are also many gluten-free, vegetarian, and vegan options.

✦ Back on 66

Depart Springfield via West College Street, heading west. When West College Street joins West Chestnut Expressway (Business I-44), turn left (west) and keep straight until you cross I-44 as the road turns into Highway 266. The drive west to Carthage is particularly scenic, with rolling hills and romantic reminders of what Route 66 looked like almost 80 years ago.

Plano

About 10 miles west of Springfield is Plano, a ghost town that was bypassed by Route 66. Look for the abandoned stone ruin of a **1902 store**, so old that trees are growing inside of it. This was once a general store with living quarters that hosted town meetings, dances, and church services.

The ruin is about a mile past Farm Road 55; look for the building at the corner of South Farm Road 45, on the north (right) side of Route 66.

✦ Back on 66

Continue west on Highway 266 for 4 miles to Halltown.

Halltown

Halltown was once known as the "Antique Capital of the World," home to almost 20 businesses, including grocery stores and a blacksmith shop and garage. Today it looks like a forgotten stretch of the Mother Road, with old weathered buildings and woodened planked porches that have been baking in the sun for more than 100 years.

The **Whitehall Mercantile** (Main St. and Hwy. Z, 417/830-4510, www.whitehallmercantile.com, 9am-4pm Mon.-Sat. Mar.-Dec.) is still in business, though, with more than 30,000 collectibles including dishware, cameras, old typewriters, radios, tools, marbles, and more.

◈ Back on 66

Head west on Route 66 (Hwy. 266) and avoid signs to Highway 96, a post-1940s alignment of Route 66. You want to stay on the pre-1930s alignment, so continue driving straight on Highway 266 into Paris Springs.

Paris Springs

Three miles west of Halltown, stop at **Gary's Gay Parita Sinclair** (Hwy. 266 and Lawrence 1210, 417/234-4943, www.garysgayparita.com, open 24 hours, free), a re-creation of a gas station owned by Fred and Gay Mason in the 1930s. The separate cobblestone garage built in 1926 is original, but the rest burned down in 1955. Gary Turner wanted to bring it back to life, and built this homage to roadside travel. There's lots of Route 66 information, including books and maps on the Mother Road. Unfortunately, Gary passed away in early 2015, but the spirit of this place still lives on.

◈ Back on 66

West of Paris Springs, Highway 266 (Route 66) dips south and turns right (west) onto South Highway 96 (a post-1940s alignment). The next 30 miles include a string of sleepy towns with meandering creeks and quaint farmhouses dotting the edge of the Ozark plateau.

Red Oak II

Nostalgia is so powerful it can make us imagine a past that never was. Lowell Davis was so obsessed with the past that he re-created his hometown and moved it 25 miles away to this spot near Carthage, Missouri. Davis left Red Oak, Illinois, and when he returned, it had become a ghost town. He was so heartbroken that in 1987 he decided to move the buildings to Missouri and re-create his hometown,

Red Oak II

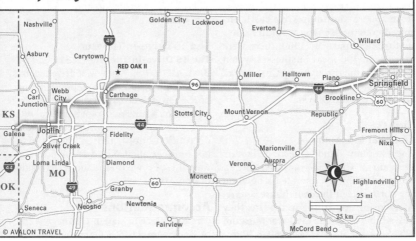

Springfield to Galena

© AVALON TRAVEL

calling it **Red Oak II** (County Loop 122, Kafir Rd., 417/237-0808, 24 hours, free). What remains today is a staged simulation of a time and place, tinged with a hint of desperation. The town is complete with a mock cemetery, a blacksmith shop, a church, a general store, a Phillips 66 station, a feed house, several homes, a one-room schoolhouse, a jail, and a diner.

The house Davis lives in was the former childhood home of the infamous female outlaw Belle Starr, also known as the "Bandit Queen of the Ozarks." Starr was an expert rider and gunslinger, credited for crimes she probably never committed, but she lived and died like an outlaw.

From Route 66 turn right (north) onto County Road 120. Drive about a mile to Kafir Road and turn left (west). The entrance is about 1,100 feet on the south side.

◈ Back on 66
Heading west, Route 66 (Hwy. 96) dips south and joins East Central Avenue into Carthage.

Carthage

Carthage was established in 1842. About 20 years later, most of the city was burned

to the ground by Confederate guerillas during the Civil War. Walking through the town today, with its stately downtown square and impressive castle-inspired courthouse, you wouldn't sense its turbulent past. By 1900, there were more than 100 local businesses; when Route 66 came through, the Chamber of Commerce promoted Carthage as "The Open Gate to the Ozarks."

Sights

Civil War Museum

The notorious "Bandit Queen" Belle Starr grew up in Carthage, and her father, Judge John Shirley, operated a hotel on the north side of the courthouse square. After losing everything in the fire, they moved to Texas. The **Civil War Museum** (205 S. Grant St., 417/237-7060, 8:30am-5pm Tues.-Sat., 1pm-5pm Sun., donations accepted) exhibits a display on Belle Starr, a wall-sized mural of the Battle of Carthage, and numerous artifacts about the Civil War in the Ozarks.

Jasper County Courthouse

After the fire in 1861, Carthage was rebuilt in 1866. It claimed to have more millionaires per capita than any city in the United States due to its robust lead and zinc mines, agricultural trade, marble quarries, and manufacturing business. Today, Carthage has four historic districts and more than 550 buildings listed on the National Registry of Historic Places, including the 1894 **Jasper County Courthouse** (302 S. Main St., 417/358-0421, www.jaspercounty.org, 8:30am-4:30pm Mon.-Fri., free). Built from native Carthage stone, it's an impressive example of Romanesque Revival architecture complete with turrets, towers, and arches that make it resemble a medieval castle.

Powers Museum

The **Powers Museum** (1617 W. Oak St., 417/237-0456, www.powersmuseum.com, 11am-4pm Wed.-Sat., donations accepted) offers rotating exhibits featuring local history with themes on the Civil War, Route 66, and Ozark culture. There's also a gift shop and research library on-site.

The 66 Drive-in Theater

The 66 Drive-in Theater (17321 Old 66 Blvd., 417/359-5959, www.66drivein.com, 8pm-close Fri.-Sun. Apr.-Sept. $7) is one of the few drive-ins left on Route 66. It still sits on a nine-acre plot in a rural setting with a 66-foot-high screen and art deco ticket booth. This is big fun on a hot summer night. The drive-in is on the west side of town on the south (left) side of Route 66.

Accommodations

The best place to stay in Carthage is the ★ **Boots Motel** (107 S. Garrison, 417/310-2989, www.bootsmotel.homestead.com, $66-71), a Streamline Moderne classic built in 1939 by Arthur Boots. The motel was designed with carports, gas pumps, black glass, bullnose (rounded) corners, and a smooth stucco facade. With a radio in every room, tile showers, and a furnace with a private thermostat, it was very modern for its time. (It was so cool, Clark Gable stayed here.) In 2001, the Boots Motel was threatened with demolition; it was to be replaced by a drugstore, but the deal fell through. In 2011, sisters Deborah Harvey and Priscilla Bledsaw purchased the Boots Motel, and they are slowly renovating it to its former glory. The National Park Service's Route 66 Corridor Preservation Program provided a matching grant to replace the pitched roof with its original, Streamline flat roof. The sign has been restored, and today rooms feature hardwood floors, ceramic tile, built-in vanities, and air-conditioning.

Food

Located in an old bank, the **Carthage Deli** (301 S. Main St., 417/358-8820, www.carthagedeli.com, 7am-5pm Mon.-Fri., 7am-4pm Sat., $6-9) is decorated in splashy 1950s decor, complete with a pink Cadillac booth and a view of the stunning courthouse. The BBQ ham and tortilla soup come highly recommended, but the thick, rich, creamy milkshakes shouldn't be missed.

Two miles south of the Carthage Deli is **Iggy's Diner** (2400 Grand Ave., 417/237-0212, www.iggysdiner.com, 6am-9pm Mon.-Sat., $5-8), an 80-seat prefab diner with metal stud walls and a metal roof that gives it a slick, chrome Airstream look. The burgers, Rueben, and thin, crispy onion rings are delicious.

◈ Back on 66

Drive west on East Central Avenue (Route 66) through Carthage. Turn left (south) on Garrison (Hwy. 571) and after two blocks turn right (west) on Oak Boulevard (Route 66). Follow Oak Boulevard to the right (northwest) and cross Highway 171 (SR 49). Take the next left (west) onto Old 66 Boulevard. Turn left (south) on North Pine Street and, after about a mile, turn right (west) on East Main Street. Webb City is less than two miles away.

Webb City

Webb City is a former mining town that once had one of the richest lead and zinc mines in the world.

The National Park Service has designated downtown Webb City a **Historic District.** There are 49 commercial buildings that date from 1883 built in the Italian Renaissance Revival, Romanesque, art deco, and Streamline Moderne styles. Several historic buildings can be seen in the 100 and 200 blocks of North Main Street near Route 66 (Broadway Street). A **mural** (Main and Broadway Sts.) highlighting Route 66 is located at the Bruner Pharmacy. One block west is a small **Route 66 Welcome Center** (Webb and Broadway Sts., 417/673-1154, www.webbcitychamber.

com, 9am-4pm Mon.-Fri., free), located in a former gas station. Inside are vintage vehicles and an 8-foot by 16-foot mural painted by John Biggs portraying 1940s travelers on Route 66 between Carterville and Carthage.

South of Route 66 at Highway 171, **King Jack Park** (555 S. Main St., dawn to dusk, free) is home to a 10-foot tall statue of a kneeling miner sculpted by Jack Dawson. Dawson also has another statue of **praying hands** in the park.

Webb City celebrates Route 66 with a downtown **Route 66 Cruise Night** on the second Saturday of summer months (5pm-8pm Apr.-Sept.). Classic cars compete for trophies as patrons vote for their favorites.

◈ Back on 66

Follow Broadway Street west through Webb City. Turn left (south) on South Madison Street, and after 2.3 miles, turn right (west) on East Zora Street. In less than a mile, turn left (south) on North Florida Avenue. Drive five blocks and turn right (west) on Utica Street. Drive two more blocks to turn left (southwest) on Euclid Avenue. Euclid Avenue dead-ends into North St. Louis Avenue. Turn left (south) and, in less than a mile, turn right (west) on Langston Hughes Street. Turn left (south) on Main Street (Hwy. 43) and enter the town of Joplin.

Joplin

At the turn of the 20th century, Joplin was a boomtown filled with saloons, brothels, and gambling halls. At **City Hall** (602 S. Main St., 800/657-2534, Mon.-Fri. 8am-5pm, free), muralist Thomas Hart Benton's 6-foot by 14-foot mural depicts Joplin's lawless past. The mural is on the right (west) side near East 6th Street.

Sights

Lawlessness continued in Joplin well after Route 66 came through town. In

Drive-Ins

The 66 Drive-in Theater, Carthage

The prosperous post-war years were a golden age for Route 66. This was a time when the Mother Road achieved a new level of popularity inspired by movies, music, and television. Cars were widely advertised and fawned over, and Americans hit the road in unprecedented numbers as World War II rations and travel restrictions were lifted. People loved their cars so much they didn't want leave them—even to eat. Thus carhop restaurants became all the rage.

And if you're going to eat in your car, you may as well be entertained at the same time. Although drive-in movie theaters started in the 1930s, they really took off in the 1950s as cars became the center of American culture. In 1941, there were 52 drive-in theaters; by 1956 there were 4,500.

1933, notorious outlaws **Bonnie Parker** and **Clyde Barrow** robbed several businesses in the area. A neighbor tipped off the cops, which led to a shootout at their apartment. Bonnie and Clyde killed two police officers before fleeing Joplin, leaving behind a camera.

After the film in the camera was developed, authorities finally knew what the devious duo looked like. The **Historical Museum in the Joplin Museum Complex** (504 S. Schifferdecker Ave., 417/623-1180, www.joplinmuseum.org, 10am-7pm Tues., 10am-5pm, Wed.-Sat. free) has some of the photos, along with their clothing, jewelry, and other items left in their apartment. To reach the Joplin Museum Complex, drive west on Route 66 (7th Street) and turn right (north) on South Schifferdecker, then quickly turn left (west) into the park. The complex is on the right (east).

The **house** where the shootout took place is two miles south of Route 66 on 34th Street, between Joplin Avenue and Oak Ridge Drive. It's a sand-colored, square-shaped building on the north side of 34th Street with two garage doors in front. Bonnie and Clyde lived upstairs. Today, it's a private residence.

While you're at the Joplin Museum, stop into the **National Cookie Cutter Historical Museum** (504 S. Schifferdecker Ave., 417/623-1180, www.joplinmuseum. org, 10am-7pm Tues., 10am-5pm Wed.-Sat., free), which has several displays of archive cookie cutters and materials such as advertisements and newsletters. Be sure to ask for a free plastic cookie cutter as a souvenir.

Food

For an old-fashioned American meal, stop at **Granny Shaffer's Family Restaurant** (7th St. and Illinois, 417/624-3700, www.grannyshaffers.com, 6am-8:30pm Mon.-Sat., 7am-3pm Sun., $5-14). The signature country-fried steak is made to order, the hamburgers are ground fresh, and the bread is baked on-site. They also serve great omelets for breakfast. It's on the newer alignment of Route 66 as you approach East 7th Street.

The **Candy House Gourmet** (510 Kentucky Ave., 417/623-7171, www.candyhouse.net, 9:30am-5:30pm Mon.-Sat., 12:30pm-5:30pm Sun.) sells Route 66 snack baskets with Route 66 branded hard candy suckers, cheese popcorn, "Mother Road Munch," Cajun spicy beer brittle, "Fill 'er Up" chocolate bars, and railway ties made from chocolate pecan pretzel rods. It's located a few blocks east off 5th Street as you enter Joplin.

If you want something a little more substantial, **Hackett Hot Wings** (520 S. Main St., 417/625-1333, www.hacketthotwings.com, 11am-8:30pm Mon.-Sat., $5-10) specializes in 13 original flavors of chicken wings. The dry rubs explode with flavor, and the crispy sweet potato puffs and corn nuggets help cool down the heat. It's located a few blocks from the Candy House Gourmet.

✤ Back on 66

As you leave Joplin via Route 66 (West 7th Ave.) it's only 3 miles to the Kansas border.

Kansas

Route 66 is a short jaunt through Kansas—you'll be in Oklahoma before you know it—but the 13-mile journey is loaded with charm and history. Here,

top to bottom: Gary's Gay Parita Sinclair, Paris Springs; Eisler Bros. Old Riverton Store, Riverton; Route 66 Visitor Center, Baxter Springs

Route 66 oozes that small-town feeling as you drive over old roadbeds and across marshes and stop to chat with business operators who have been here for decades.

Kansas was the only state along the Mother Road to be completely bypassed when I-44 replaced Route 66 in the early 1960s. During the heyday of Route 66, Kansas had one of the largest lead mines in the nation; as a result, its roads were finished to facilitate the mining industry. By 1929, Route 66 was paved using waste products from the nearby mines, making Kansas the second state along the Mother Road to be completely paved.

◆ Route 66 through Kansas

Leave Missouri on West 7th Street and take the two-lane **pre-1940s alignment,** just west after Malang Road. As Route 66 curves south, turn right (northwest) on West Old 66 Boulevard. As you cross the state line in 0.5-mile, West Old 66 Boulevard will turn into Front Street and dip south into the sleepy mining town of Galena.

Galena

Galena is one of the oldest and most prosperous mining towns in Kansas; lead sulfite was discovered here in 1876. Within 30 days, 10,000 miners came to cash in on the boom, and by the turn of the 20th-century, there were nearly 30,000 people living here. Galena was quite sophisticated for its time, with paved city streets, water, sewers, and electric streetcars that ran from Baxter Springs, Kansas to Carthage, Missouri. The road that eventually became Route 66 was a critical pathway for the mining industry.

In 1935, a strike occurred at the Eagle-Picher lead smelter mine, the leading processor of lead ore in the country. When the miners banded together to protest their working conditions, violence broke out right on Route 66. Hundreds of strikers threw rocks and threatened to shoot any scabs that attempted to enter or exit

abandoned buildings in downtown Galena

the plant. Traffic stopped and cars were overturned; at one point, the National Guard had to be called in.

◈ Route 66 through Galena

Route 66 enters Galena via East Front Street Turn left (south) on Main Street and then right (west) on 7th Street.

Sights

The former site of the **Eagle Picher plant** is on the north side of the road as you enter Kansas. Once one of the largest smelters in the United States, it was in operation from 1878-2004. Here, workers processed lead, zinc, and cadmium ores to make zinc oxide, sulfuric acid, manganese dioxide, and other noxious materials. By the early 1970s, the mine was pretty much exhausted. Eagle Picher declared Chapter 11 bankruptcy in 2005 when a series of environmental investigations revealed toxic levels of lead, arsenic, mercury and zinc in the surrounding soil, sediments, and surface water. The Environmental Protection Agency (EPA) stepped in, and decontamination efforts are underway.

In the late 1930s through the mid-1940s Works Progress Administration (WPS) writers saw this area covered in man-made mountains of white chert (commonly known as "chat") residue from the mines. They called it a "cinder-covered wasteland." The area has also been called "Hell's half-acre." Today, the contaminated soil has been covered with native grasses. The plant is gone and the only thing left is a single building at 1203 Clark Street, just north of the railroad tracks about 800 feet after Front Street curves south.

As you head south on Main Street, there's a 1952 **Will Rogers Highway plaque** at Howard Litch Memorial Park on the corner of 5th Street.

The **Galena Mining Historical Museum** (319 W. 7th St. 620/783-2192, 9am-11am and 1pm-3:30pm Mon.-Sat. in summer, Mon., Wed., Fri. 1pm-3:30pm rest of the year, free) is located in a railroad depot and has a modest collection of mining artifacts, mineral specimens, mining equipment, and a model of the Grand Central Mine. There is also a collection of Model Ts and Model As in the back garage.

Food

On the corner of Front and Main Streets is a historic service station that was purchased by four women in 2006 and named "Four Women on the Route." Ownership changed hands in 2013 and it's now called **Cars on the Route** (119 N. Main St., 620/783-1366, www.kansastravel.org, 10am-5pm Tues.-Sat.) in homage to the Pixar film *Cars*. Inspired by the film character "Tow Mater," the building features two eyes taped on the station's window with buck teeth on a front grill. Two red and yellow KanOTex gasoline pumps and a 1951 International Boom truck sit outside. Inside, they sell

sandwiches at the snack bar as well as gifts made from local artists.

✛ Back on 66

Head west on East 7th Street for about 3 miles to Riverton.

Riverton

There's not much to see in Riverton, but on the right (north) side of the road, keep an eye out for a little 1925 grocery store nestled amongst the trees. The **Eisler Bros. Old Riverton Store** (7109 Southeast Highway 66, 620/848-3330, www.eislerbros.com, 7:30am-8pm Mon.-Sat., noon-7pm Sun.) still sells groceries, flowers, Route 66 memorabilia, gifts, and local handmade crafts all under an original embossed tin ceiling. The deli counter has traditional cold cuts, cheddar, Swiss, marble jack, Munster, and hot pepper cheeses along with old-fashioned pickle loaf.

✛ Back on 66

Follow the **pre-1930s alignment** from Riverton by heading west on Route 66 to SR-400. At the roundabout, continue straight to Beasley Road. In about 1 mile, Beasley Road (Route 66) will curve south; at the turn, take a quick right (northwest) to follow SE Beasley Road and then make your first left (southeast) onto Old 66 Highway. In about 900 feet you'll cross the Brush Creek Bridge.

Brush Creek Bridge

This is the only remaining example of a "Marsh Arch" bridge on Route 66 in Kansas, named after its designer James Barney Marsh. His signature style featured two arched ribs on either side that look like the top of a wagon wheel. Two other Marsh Arch bridges that crossed Willow Creek and the Spring River on Route 66 were dismantled in the 1990s.

✛ Back on 66

Right after crossing the bridge, turn left (southeast) on SE Beasley Road, which dead-ends into 50th Street. Turn right (south), and the road becomes North Willow Avenue as it enters Baxter Springs.

Baxter Springs

Baxter Springs could have been another Dodge City. Named after resident cowboy John Baxter, who stood 6 feet 7 inches tall and died in a gun battle in 1859, the town was known far and wide for its rough and tumble ways and was a popular spot for ranchers, drifters, and gamblers. Today, however, Baxter Springs is a quiet town with old gas stations, historic buildings, and an important Civil War fort.

Originally the area belonged to Cherokee Indians and was popular for its healing mineral springs, used by the Osage Indians in the 1800s. It was believed the springs could cure illness and rejuvenate the body. The town created a marketing campaign to promote the springs' miraculous healing properties and people flocked to the area in droves. Many stayed at the Planters, a lavish hotel on the edge of the business district. Eventually renamed the Springs Hotel, it was destroyed by fire in 1913. The springs are also long gone (probably due to the mining industry), but they were just south of what is now 7th Street near the Baxter Springs Heritage Center.

✛ Route 66 through Baxter Springs

Turn left (east) on West 3rd Street and then make a left on SR-69 (Route 66/ Military Rd.).

Sights
Baxter Springs Heritage Center

Baxter Springs also saw one of the bloodiest battles in the Civil War. In 1863, Confederate guerrillas ambushed and brutally butchered nearly 100 unarmed Union soldiers in 15 minutes. The notorious William Clarke Quantrill led the massacre that targeted the Second

Car Culture

The Great Depression had a major impact on the gas industry in Baxter Springs, and oil companies had to get creative to rebuild their brands. Many started designing gas stations to resemble cottages, complete with pitched roofs, shuttered windows, and brick-and-stucco walls, inspiring the comfort and security of home. One example of this "automotive cottage" is the **Baxter Springs Independent Oil and Gas Service Station** (940 Military Ave., 620/856-2385, 10am-4pm Mon.-Sat., 1pm-4pm Sun., free). When the station opened in 1930, it was one of the area's finest Tudor cottage-style stations and was popular with the locals. Less than one year after it opened, it merged with Phillips Petroleum Company, which owned the station until 1958. It then passed through many hands until it was converted into an office building in the 1970s. In 2003, the station was placed on the National Register of Historic Places. With the help of community support and a grant from the National Park Service Route 66 Corridor Preservation program, the station has been restored to its 1940s roots, and today operates as the **Route 66 Visitor Center**.

Kansas Colored Infantry division, which had recruited free blacks and former slaves who had fled to Kansas. Most of the dead are buried in the Baxter Springs cemetery two miles west of town. The Fort Blair site of the attack is on Route 66 at 6th Street.

The **Baxter Springs Heritage Center** (740 East Ave., 620/856-2385, www.baxterspringsmuseum.org, 10am-4:30pm Mon.-Sat., 1pm-4pm Sun., free) has more than 20,000 square feet of exhibits and self-guided driving maps featuring the key sites of the massacre. There are also exhibits on the Buffalo Soldiers, an African American regiment of the United States Army.

To get there, head south on Route 66 (Military Ave.) turn left (east) on 7th Street. The museum is one block ahead on the right (south) side.

Bilke's Western Museum

Texas cattleman drove herds of longhorns across the Red River to ship east. Baxter Springs was a popular spot for ranchers since it was the closest town to Texas, making it the first "cow town" in Kansas. This was a critical trading center for Texas cattle, but when the longhorn trail moved further west, Baxter Springs lost its livelihood. A full-size mural of the longhorn cattle drive lives on the side of **Bilke's Western Museum** (1041 Military Ave., 620/856-5707, 9am-6pm Mon.-Sat., free). A museum with a collection of antique saddles, bits, and spurs is located upstairs.

Food

Angels on the Route (1143 Military Ave., 620/856-2266, www.angelsontheroute. homestead.com, 7am-6pm Mon.-Tues. and Thurs., 7am-5pm Fri., 9am-4pm Sat., 10am-3pm Sun., $6-$13) is located in one of the oldest structures in town. The 1865 brick building was a pharmacy in the early 1900s; today, delicious sandwiches, tasty lemonade, great root-beer floats, and cookie-dough custard pies are the cures on offer.

◈ Back on 66

Head south on Military Avenue. The Oklahoma border is less than 2 miles away.

Oklahoma

Oklahoma has some of the best Route 66 attractions: the earliest roadbeds, the most memorable roadside landmarks... and more drivable miles than any other state.

KANSAS

MO

Quapaw

Chelsea

Tulsa

AR

Clinton

Oklahoma City

Texola

OKLAHOMA

TEXAS

Woody Guthrie Center

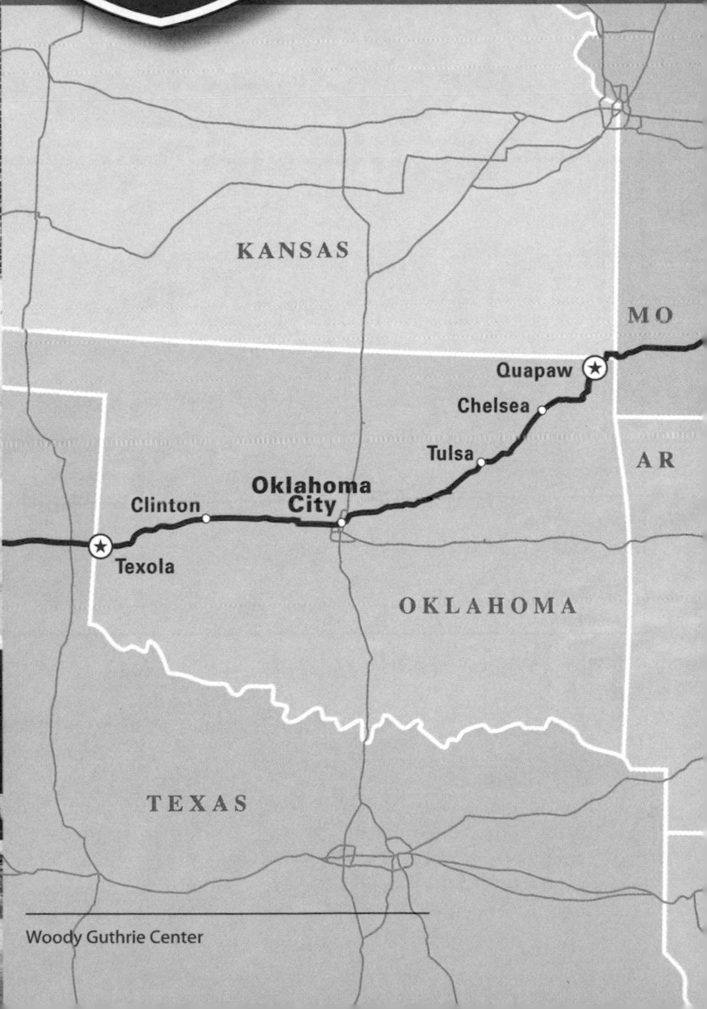

Oklahoma

© AVALON TRAVEL

The concept of the Mother Road was born right here in Oklahoma.

Tulsa native Cyrus Avery, often called the "Father of Route 66," was a board member of the Federal Highway System and founded the U.S. 66 Highway Association. Avery coined Route 66 as the "Main St. of America;" it can be argued that, without Avery's influence, Route 66 may not have become the celebrated icon it is today. In the late 1920s, less than one-quarter of the 400 miles of Route 66 through Oklahoma were paved. From 1926 to 1951, the Mother Road was rerouted, realigned, straightened, widened, and ultimately shorted to about 380 miles.

Three major migrations color the history of this state. From 1828 to 1887, the

Highlights

★ **Sidewalk Highway, Miami:** Tackle one of the earliest segments of the Mother Road (page 132).

★ **Will Rogers Memorial Museum, Claremore:** Nearly 20,000-square feet of exhibits memorialize this Route 66 icon (page 137).

★ **Greenwood Cultural Center, Tulsa:** This museum and memorial commemorates one of the worst race riots in U.S. history (page 139).

★ **Pops, Arcadia:** Browse more than 600 different kinds of soda pop in one the brightest, coolest, and newest landmarks on Route 66 (page 153).

★ **William H. Murray "Pony Bridge," Geary:** This 1930s engineering marvel is one of the longest bridges on Route 66 (page 162).

★ **Oklahoma Route 66 Museum, Clinton:** Learn about Route 66's myth, history, and lore in one of its best museums (page 165).

U.S. government began the process of forcing American Indians off their native land and onto the Trail of Tears to walk to the "Indian Territory," what eventually became the state of Oklahoma. The forced migration resulted in relocating 67 tribes to Oklahoma; today about 38 tribes remain. In 1887, the federal government realized the Indian Territory could be farmed and passed the Dawes Act, opening up nearly 2 million acres of land to white settlement. The historic Land Runs attracted more than 50,000 land-hungry prospectors.

During the Great Depression, overuse of the soil coupled with severe drought eroded the earth. Strong winds blew away the topsoil, forming dark clouds of dust that made working, living, and even breathing nearly impossible. The resulting Dust Bowl saw more than 200,000 survivors use Route 66 to escape poverty. Author John Steinbeck labeled Route 66 as a "migrant road" and the "path of people in flight" as families headed west. Folk musician Woody Guthrie wrote in his song *Dust Bowl Disaster*, "We loaded up our jalopies and piled our families in. We rattled down that highway to never come back again."

Planning Your Time

With selective planning, you can make it across Oklahoma in **two days.** From the state line, this road trip hits Miami, Afton, and Foyil before reaching Tulsa, where you'll spend the night. The next day travels 107 miles to Oklahoma City, where you'll spend the second night. Then it's just 115 miles to the Texas state line.

Driving Considerations
If pressed for time, I-44 from the eastern edge of the state to Oklahoma City will be the alternate option for speedy transport. West of Oklahoma City, I-40 becomes the freeway option.

Route 66 passes through several small towns with gas stations, so there's no need to worry about running out as long as you keep the tank at least half full. To save money, fill up in Tulsa and Oklahoma City, where gas is less expensive. Be forewarned that Oklahoma weather can be intense and unpredictable; in November, Oklahoma can be colder and windier than Chicago.

Getting There

Starting Points
Car
The original alignment of Route 66 entered the state from the west at the Kansas border and continued through Quapaw, Commerce, and Miami, a stretch of Route 66 primarily labeled Highway 69. Once you hit Afton, the road becomes Highway 60/69 into Vinita, then is mostly labeled

Best Accomodations

★ **Campbell Hotel, Tulsa:** Built in 1927, this hotel includes 26 theme rooms—including the ultimate Route 66 room (page 145).

★ **Mayo Hotel, Tulsa:** Even if you don't spend the night at this historic hotel, stop to take a peek at the opulent lobby (page 145).

★ **Aloft Hotel, Oklahoma City:** A stay here provides a bit of mid-century *Mad Men* atmosphere in Oklahoma City (page 158).

★ **Skirvin Hilton Hotel, Oklahoma City:** The "finest hotel in the Southwest" once hosted presidents and move stars (page 158).

Route 66 into Tulsa and Oklahoma City. West of the city capital, rolling tree-studded hills give way to wide-open plains as Route 66 heads straight into the Texas panhandle.

Interstate 44 (also called the Will Rogers Turnpike) enters Oklahoma near Afton and is the major east-west artery through the state; I-44 also runs alongside much of Route 66, so it's a good alternate road to use if you're short on time. I-40 enters the state on the east side south of Tulsa and runs directly to Oklahoma City. From Oklahoma City, I-35 is the major north-south route from Dallas, Texas, to Wichita, Kansas.

Car Rental

If you need a rental car, the Tulsa Airport is a good place to go. **Enterprise** (2228 E. 11th St., 918/583-4880, 7:30am-6pm Mon.-Fri., 9am-noon Sat., noon-3pm Sun.) has the best customer service. **National Car Rental** (7777 Apache St., 855/237-4219, 6am-midnight Mon.-Fri., 7am-11pm Sat., 7am-midnight Sun.) tends to be a little pricier, but they generally have a good fleet to choose from and they're open longer hours.

Air

The two major airports closest to Route 66 fly out of Tulsa and Oklahoma City.

Tulsa International Airport (7777 E. Apache St., www.tulsaairports.com, 918/838-5000) is small but serves most of the major airlines including United, American, Delta, and Southwest. It's located five miles northeast of downtown.

The **Will Rogers World Airport** (7100 Terminal Dr., 405/316-3200, www.flyokc.com) in Oklahoma City is larger than Tula International, with 21 nonstop flights to 18 cities. It's the only airport in the country to use the word "World" in its name and not reference the city in the title; there's also an art space, outdoor garden and bronze statue of its namesake. Alaska, Allegiant, United, American, Delta, US Airways, and Southwest Airlines fly out of here.

Train and Bus

The Heartland Flyer on **Amtrak** (100 South E.K. Gaylord Blvd., 800/872-7245, www.amtrak.com) makes daily trips to Oklahoma City from Fort Worth, Texas. The station is located in the historic Santa Fe Depot in the Bricktown District.

The **Greyhound Bus** (1948 E. Reno Ave., 405/606-4382, www.greyhound.com, daily 24 hours) serves Oklahoma City and Tulsa (317 S. Detroit Ave., 918/584-4428, www.greyhound.com, daily 24 hours).

Best Restaurants

★ **Waylan's Ku-Ku, Miami:** This is the last remnant of a 1960s chain restaurant that once had about 200 locations throughout the Midwest (page 131).

★ **Clanton's Cafe, Vinita:** Clanton's is the oldest continually owned family restaurant on Route 66 in Oklahoma (page 133).

★ **Molly's Landing, Catoosa:** Dine in a log house filled with rustic, whimsical decor (page 138).

★ **Burn Co. Barbeque, Tulsa:** Get in line early for the best BBQ in Tulsa (page 146).

★ **Rock Cafe, Stroud:** This cafe opened in 1939 and has been run by women for much of its existence (page 149).

Quapaw

As you enter Oklahoma on U.S. 69, you'll pass through the quiet mining town of Quapaw. For more than 140 years, Quapaw has hosted one of the oldest **Indian powwows** in the United States at Beaver Springs State Park (5681 S. 630 Rd.). If you happen to be visiting the first week of July, don't miss it. For more information, contact Mike Shawnee of the Quapaw Tribe (918/542-1853, www.quapawtribe.com).

In downtown Quapaw, **murals** depicting the town's lead and zinc mining history adorn several buildings along Route 66. Look for these as you drive toward the town of Commerce.

◈ Back on 66

Follow Main Street through Quapaw. As the road curves west, it turns into E. 50 Road (Hwy. 69) and dips south into Commerce. Before you get to Commerce, you might want to take a quick side trip to the ghost town of Picher.

◈ Side Trip: Picher

In the 1920s, Picher was a leading producer of zinc and lead. Then, in 1967, the local Tar Creek turned red from contaminated water that was loaded with toxic heavy metals and had leached into the ground water. The chat piles (mountains of crushed limestone, dolomite, and silica) had risen to more than 300 feet. Families picnicked, played, practiced sports, and rode four-wheelers on the poisonous mounds. Karen Harvey, who lived in Picher from 1960 to 2002, remembers swimming in the ponds: "Our hair would turn orange, and it didn't wash out." Even though 34 percent of the children had lead poisoning, authorities didn't declare Picher uninhabitable until 2006, when the Army of Engineers found the town was at risk of collapsing

Conoco Hole in the Wall, Commerce

due to instability of the underground mine shafts.

During its heyday, Picher had a population of nearly 20,000; by 2013, nearly all the residents had accepted federal buyouts and moved away. Picher was mostly demolished and officially dissolved on November 26, 2013. The government has spent more than 300 million dollars trying to clean up the mess, but the waters still run red from heavy metal runoff in Tar Creek.

In 2014, there were 10 fearless (and possibly foolish) citizens left. Gary Linderman, the owner of the Ole Miner Pharmacy became the "the last man standing." He said, "I'll stay here until I draw my last breath." And he did, at the age of 60 in June of 2015. Today Picher is an abandoned toxic wasteland, a brutal reminder that we have to do better.

✦ Back on 66
Picher is only three miles from Route 66. Once the road curves west from Quapaw and turns into E 50 Road, the next major road is Hwy 69. Turn right (north) and drive 3 miles to Picher. If you're not visiting Picher, then stay west on E. 50 Road from Quapaw. Follow Highway 69 as it heads south into the town of Commerce.

Commerce

Commerce marks the end of the Ozark Plateau and the beginning the Prairie Plains. This is also Oklahoma's Tornado Alley, with about nine tornado watches a year. Driving into town, an old silo welcomes Route 66 visitors.

✦ Route 66 through Commerce
Enter Commerce on Mickey Mantle Boulevard. Soon after the curve, turn west (right) on 4th Street and left (south) on N. Main Street.

Sights
Bonnie and Clyde Monument
Commerce is where outlaws Bonnie and Clyde Barrow, along with accomplice Henry Methvin, got stuck in the mud. A passerby called the local police, and once the police arrived, violence broke out. The outlaws murdered Constable William C. Campbell, who was their thirteenth and last victim. They kidnapped police chief Percy Boyd and released him in Fort Scott, Kansas. A **monument** (Main and 3rd Sts.) commemorates the event.

Dairy King
Dairy King (100 N. Main St., 918/675-4261, 10pm-6pm Mon.-Fri., 11am-3pm Sat., $5-8) was once a Marathon service station. Today they sell burgers, ice cream, and Route 66-shaped cookies. There's also a drive-through, if you just want an edible souvenir for the road.

Mickey Mantle Sights
Commerce was the **childhood home** of

legendary Hall of Fame baseball switch-hitter Mickey Mantle. Mantle lived at 319 S. Quincy Street in the 1930s and '40s. The dents in the side of the tin barn are from hours spent honing his skills to become one of the best baseball players in America. From Main Street, turn left (east) on C Street and then left (north) onto S. Quincy Street.

A nine-foot tall **statue** of Mantle is on the south side of town, located at the entrance of the Mickey Mantle field at Commerce High School (420 E. D St., dusk-dawn daily).

Conoco Hole in the Wall

The 1929 **Conoco Hole in the Wall** (101 S. Main St., 918/533-2079) is a cottage-style service station built right into a brick wall. In the late 1930s, it became a Phillips 66 station and later a beauty shop.

◆ Back on 66

Leave Commerce driving south on Main Street and join U.S. 69 for three miles into the town of Miami.

Miami

The town was named after the Miami (pronounced My-Am-Uh) Indian tribe. In 1891, Dr. W. I. McWilliams was the first white man to receive an official title to own land in the Indian Territory.

Mining played a major part in Miami's growth. Lead and zinc were discovered here in 1905; by 1909, the town had nine miles of cement sidewalks, three bakeries, three newspapers, 13 churches, two railroads, a public school system, and a three-story hotel. In 1929, mining millionaire George L. Coleman built the Coleman Theater with the intent of bringing culture to Miami.

Coleman Theater, Miami

◆ Route 66 through Miami

Route 66 enters Miami on Main Street (U.S. 69) and continues south for 3.5 miles.

Sights
Coleman Theater

The **Coleman Theater** (103 N. Main St., 918/550-2425, tours: 10am-4pm Tues.-Fri., 10am-2pm Sat., free) is a beautiful 1600-seat theater that was built right before the Great Depression hit; it was considered the most elaborate entertainment venue between Dallas and Kansas City. Will Rogers, The Three Stooges, and Vaudeville entertainers all performed here. The stucco facade, ornate arched windows, hand-carved terra-cotta detailing, wrought-iron railing, red-tile roofs, and bell towers make this one of the best surviving examples of a Spanish Revival building in Oklahoma. Step inside to see the original chandelier, gilded statues, and carved winding staircase. Today, the theater hosts tours, films, and performing arts.

Vintage Iron Motorcycle Museum

The **Vintage Iron Motorcycle Museum** (128 S. Main St., 918/542-6170, www.route66vintageiron.com, 10am-6pm Mon.-Sat., noon-5pm Sun. May-Oct., 10am-5pm Mon.-Sat. Nov.-Apr., free) is a 2,000-square-foot gallery with a collection of more than 40 vintage motorcycles. Highlights include Evel Knievel memorabilia, vintage helmets, a 1917 Harley, a 1949 Indian Scout, and World Record Jump Bikes. This is a must-see for any motorcycle enthusiast.

Marathon Oil Company Service

The 1929 **Marathon Oil Company Service Station** (331 S. Main St. at 4th St., free) is an example of the Neoclassical Revival style. Though the gas pumps have been removed, the property has been restored to look as it did in the 1930s, with Greek columns holding up a bright red and white canopy.

Food

★ **Waylan's Ku-Ku** (915 N. Main St., 918/542-1696, 10am-11pm Sun.-Thurs., 10am-midnight Fri-Sat., $6-10) opened up the first drive-through in town; today they are loved by locals and tourists alike and serve about 2,000 burgers a week. The tasty quarter-pounder burgers are cooked-to-order and take a little bit longer, but they're worth the wait because they're absolutely delicious. Also on the menu: deep-fried dill pickles, fried-green tomatoes, and fried squash. This greasy goodness is the perfect complement to a once-in-a-lifetime road trip. Look for the giant green and yellow neon sign with a cuckoo clock (it used to chime every hour).

◆ Back on 66

Follow U.S. 69 south from Miami through Narcissa. You'll pass under I-44; soon afterward, the road curves west to

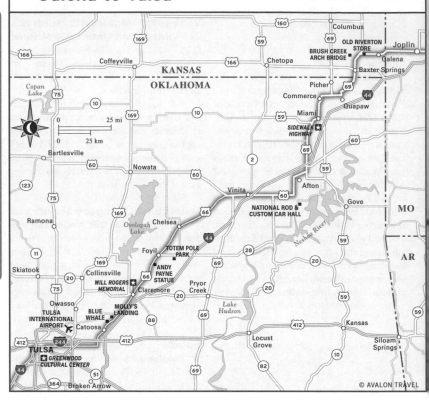

Galena to Tulsa

reach the mining town of Afton. Or, if you're brave, consider a side trip on the Sidewalk Highway.

★ Sidewalk Highway

The 1922 Sidewalk Highway stretches between Miami and Afton and is one of the oldest roadbeds that is still drivable on Route 66. This three-mile long, nine-foot wide roadbed was built from stone and Topeka asphalt and laid over a concrete base with five-foot gravel shoulders. Today, the rough and narrow road is covered with dirt and gravel, and the original curbing is still visible in some places.

As you leave Miami, continue south on Main Street (OK-125). (Don't follow U.S. 69, which turns at 3rd Street). The road curves right (southwest) to become E Street SW. Continue heading south. Once you reach E 120 Road (20th Avenue SW), keep going straight for another mile. Turn right (west) onto E 130 Road. Drive 1.5 miles, then turn left (south) onto S 540 Road and make a right (west) on E 140 Road. After one mile, turn left (south) on U.S. 69 (OK-66).

Do not drive the Sidewalk Highway when it's wet, and take it slow, especially if you have a low-clearance vehicle.

Afton

Afton is a small town with early 1900s buildings, rusted motel signs, fading auto courts, vintage gas stations, and two really awesome car museums.

Route 66 through Afton

Route 66 enters Afton on 1st Street (U.S. 60/69) and heads southwest for about 1 mile.

Sights
Afton Station Packard Museum
The red, white, and blue Approved Packard Service logo in front of the **Afton Station Packard Museum** (12 SW First St., 918/257-4044, www.postcards-fromtheroad.net, 9:30am-3pm daily, free) is a blast from the past. This restored 1930s D-X filling station opened in 1933 and was one of the first 24-hour filling stations on Route 66. Owners Laurel and David Kane have an impressive collection of almost 20 Packards. An honorable tribute to the Mother Road, the museum here includes an official program from the International-Transcontinental Foot Race and items from the now-demolished Buffalo Ranch Trading Post (the Buffalo Ranch sponsored Indian tribal dances and had live elk, deer, goats, sheep, and bison).

Darryl Starbird's National Rod & Custom Car Hall of Fame Museum
Darryl Starbird's National Rod & Custom Car Hall of Fame Museum (55251 E. Hwy. 85A near Hwy. 125, 918/257-4234, www.darrylstarbird.com, 10am-5pm Wed.-Mon. Mar.-Oct., $10) is a 40,000-square-foot facility with more than 40 custom-built cars, many of which look like something out of a science fiction film—Starbird's Galaxy x2000, for example, is a custom bubble-topped 1957 Caddy. These cars have more than clean lines and chrome-tipped fins—some of them look like they could fly.

From Route 66 (U.S. 69), drive south on U.S. 59 for 5 miles. Turn right (south) on Highway 125 and drive another 5 miles. Starbird's is on the left (south) side of the road.

Back on 66
Leaving Afton, Route 66 (U.S. 69/60) curves south. After about 4 miles, turn right (west) at E 270 Road to follow U.S. 69. The town of Vinita is less than 10 miles away.

Vinita

This former railroad town was home to the Will Rogers Memorial Rodeo. Many homes built here in the late 1800s are still standing today; however, the once very popular Harvey House is now gone.

Route 66 through Vinita
Route 66 enters Vinita on U.S. 60/69 and heads northwest for about 1 mile. Turn left (southwest) to follow U.S. 60/69.

Sights
The Eastern Trails Museum (215 W. Illinois Ave., 918/323-1338, www.easterntrailsmuseum.com, 11am-4pm Mon.-Fri., 11am-3pm Sat., free) has several exhibits about the town's early railroad, ranching, and military history. There are also vintage photographs and artifacts of Route 66. The museum is one block west of Highway 60.

Food
★ **Clanton's Cafe** (319 E. Illinois, 918/256-9053, www.clantonscafe.com, 6am-8pm Mon.-Fri., 7am-2pm Sat., 11am-2pm Sun., $5-14) is the oldest continually owned family restaurant on Route 66 in Oklahoma. Clanton's has been serving their famous chicken-fried steak to locals and Route 66 travelers since 1927 (one year after the birth of Route 66). The creamy mashed potatoes and hand-breaded "Calf Fries" served with horseradish sauce should not be missed. The restaurant interior is lined with old photos on the walls depicting its longstanding history.

⬥ Back on 66

Leave Vinita heading southwest on U.S. 60/69 (Wilson St.). Continue onto U.S. 69/60 as it curves to the right (west). After about 5 miles, Route 66 curves southwest through the town of White Oak, then heads south for about 10 miles to Chelsea.

Chelsea

You wouldn't know it by the looks of it, but Chelsea used to be one of the largest towns in Oklahoma. In 1889, it was incorporated under the law of the Cherokee Nation in Indian Territory. That same year, Edward Byrd secured mineral leases from the Cherokee Nation and drilled the first non-commercial oil well in Indian Territory. By the early 1900s, Chelsea became an important site for cattle ranching, shipping, and farming oats, corn, pecans, and wheat. Chelsea also reportedly had the first state bank in the Indian Territory in 1896.

⬥ Route 66 through Chelsea

Route 66 enters Chelsea on Walnut Street, then curves southwest for about 1 mile.

Sights
Pryor Creek Bridge

The original 1926 **Pryor Creek Bridge** is an iron truss bridge 123 feet long and 18 feet wide. This six-panel bridge has beams that run diagonally forming an "X" pattern; it's also a "through truss" bridge, which means that the beams cover the top of the bridge, making it look more like a tunnel. The bridge carried Route 66 traffic until 1932. Although it's rusted, the single-intersection lattice guardrail is intact and the structure retains its historic significance and integrity. It is no longer open to traffic, but you can walk across it. The bridge is located on the

top to bottom: Dairy King, Commerce; Sidewalk Highway, Miami; Clanton's Cafe, Vinita

Hogue House

The **Hogue House** (1001 Olive St.) is believed to be the first Sears "kit home" in Oklahoma, and was one of the first to be built west of the Mississippi River. Between 1908 and 1940, more than 70,000 kit homes were sold in the United States. The kit contained all the materials needed to construct the Sears pre-fab house: the 2,400 square-feet home cost $1,663 and had a 14-foot living room, a 12-foot dining room, a 10-foot kitchen, four bedrooms, and a 30-foot porch. Lumber was measured and cut to size, then shipped to consumers on railcars.

The "Sears Saratoga" Hogue House is one of the best examples of the Sears Modern Home series. The house remained in the same family since 1912 until it was sold for $137,000 in 2014. The house is located one block northwest of Route 66. Turn right (northwest) on E. 10th Street, then make another left (southwest) on Olive Street. This is a private residence, so please be respectful and do not disturb the owners.

south side of Route 66 at S 4260 Road, before you reach downtown Chelsea.

Pedestrian Tunnel

As Route 66 became more popular, it became more difficult and dangerous to cross it on foot. As a result, several underground **pedestrian passages** were built throughout the route. You can still see the one in Chelsea (Walnut St. near 6th St.). Other Oklahoma pedestrian tunnels were built in in Tulsa, El Reno, Sayre, and Oklahoma City.

Food

Breakfast is served all day at **Pat's Main St. Diner** (251 W. 6th St., 918-789-2001, 6:30am-9pm Mon.-Sat., 7am-3pm Sun., $5-10), where the hand-battered onion rings and pies are made from scratch. The waitresses will make you feel right at home with their friendly coffee "warm ups." (They also warm up your syrup—that doesn't even happen at home.) From Route 66, Pat's is two blocks northwest (turn right) on W. 6th Street.

The rooms at the **Chelsea Motor Inn** (325 E. Layton St., 918/789-3437, $50-60) are clean and well-maintained and an excellent value for the money. Rooms are furnished with microwaves, refrigerators, and flat-screen televisions. Even if the Route 66 room is booked, the whole experience has the charm of bedding down at a classic roadside motel.

Back on 66

Leaving Chelsea, drive southwest for 6 miles on Route 66 to the town of Bushyhead. Before reaching Foyil, turn east on Highway 28 and drive 3.5 miles to Totem Pole Park. If you don't have time to see Totem Pole Park, keep heading south on Route 66 to the town of Foyil.

Side Trip: Totem Pole Park

One of the largest folk-art monuments in the country, **Totem Pole Park** (21300 E. Hwy 28A, 918/342-9149, 11am-3pm Mon.-Sat., 12:30pm-4pm Sun., free) was built by the late Ed Galloway between 1937 and 1961 as a tribute to the American Indian. The park features four 9-foot Indians, each representing a different tribe. The largest totem pole is 90 feet tall, with 200 carved images and a turtle at its base. It is estimated to have taken 28 tons of cement, 6 tons of steel, and 100 tons of sand and rock to build. Galloway died in 1961 and the Rogers County Historical Society took over the property in 1989. Restoration efforts are underway.

◆ Back on 66

Drive west on Highway 28 for 3.5 miles to return to Route 66. Continue south to Foyil.

Foyil

As you approach Foyil, turn left (south) on Andy Payne Boulevard to take the **1926 alignment**. Andy Payne Boulevard is named after an incredible Cherokee man who won the Transcontinental Foot Race in 1928.

Sights

Andy Payne loved to run the 5 miles from his family farm to school. The year after he graduated, he decided to run clear across the country in the **Transcontinental Foot Race** from Los Angeles to New York City. The path he ran between Los Angeles and Chicago was on Route 66.

The Transcontinental Foot Race (dubbed the "Bunion Derby") was created by Lon Scott and promoted by Charles C. Pyle, known as the P.T. Barnum of professional sports. Pyle's marketing efforts, product endorsements, and media coverage helped make Route 66 into a household name.

This unique race captured the attention of the public: It was the first footrace across the United States, and it was also racially integrated during the height of the Jim Crow era. Five African Americans, a Jamaican-born Canadian, American Indians, Pacific Islanders, and many Latinos participated.

On March 3rd, 1928, Andy Payne (#43) lined up with 275 other runners and set off on a grueling adventure, running through the heat of the Mojave desert, across freezing mountain passes, and in torrential rain. One runner was hit by a car; another was struck by a motorcycle. By the third day, more than half of the participants had dropped out—but Payne kept running. The race ended 84 days later with 55 people crossing the finish. First across the finish line was Andy Payne, who had run 3,423.5 miles in 573 hours, 4 minutes, and 34 seconds at an average of about 6 miles an hour. When he won, he set a world record.

Payne won the grand prize of $25,000 (equal to about $350,000 dollars today) and used the money to pay off his family's farm. Then he ran for public office and was elected to serve as a clerk to the Supreme Court in Oklahoma City. A **monument** commemorating Payne and his victory is located on the south end of town.

There's no official address, but the monument can be found in a small park on the south end of Andy Payne Boulevard. It's located on the right side (north) of the street near the highway where Andy Payne Boulevard rejoins Route 66.

◆ Back on 66

Heading southwest through Foyil, Andy Payne Boulevard dead-ends into the newer alignment of Route 66. Turn left (south) and you'll pass through Sequoyah, a town named after the Cherokee chief who created the 86-symbol Cherokee alphabet. In less than 5 miles, Route 66 becomes Lynn Riggs Boulevard in the town of Claremore.

Claremore

Nestled into the hills of northeastern Oklahoma, Claremore is home to antiques shops and history museums.

◆ Route 66 through Claremore

The **pre-1958 alignment** runs parallel through Claremore one block north of Lynn Riggs Boulevard. Turn right (west) at J. M. Davis Boulevard (across from Stuart Roosa), and follow the road southwest for about 2 miles.

Sights
★ Will Rogers Memorial Museum

Learn about the life and work of Will Rogers at the **Will Rogers Memorial Museum** (1720 W. Will Rogers Blvd., 800/324-9455, www.willrogers.com, 10am-5pm daily, $7). Most people know Rogers as a movie star, but he was also a writer, speaker, philosopher, and comedian. His father was a Cherokee senator and judge who helped write the Oklahoma constitution, and his mother descended from a Cherokee chief. This museum delves into his early years and explores his legacy as a newspaper columnist and radio, film, and vaudeville star. Although Rogers is gone, his aphorisms live on. One still rings true for die-hard road trip fans: *"You would be surprised what there is to see in this great country within 200 miles of where any of us live. I don't care what state or what town."*

The museum is approximately one mile from Route 66. Turn right (northeast) onto Highway 88 (W. Will Rogers Blvd.).

Claremore Museum of History

Lynn Riggs was a Claremore-native playwright, poet, and author of *Green Grow the Lilacs*. The play produced from his book was adapted for the stage by Rodgers and Hammerstein and used as the basis for the musical *Oklahoma!* Several of the characters were based on Riggs' family and friends. The **Lynn Riggs Memorial** is located in the newly renovated **Claremore Museum of History** (Lynn Riggs Park, 121 N. Weenonah, 918/342-1127, www.rchs1.org/lynn-riggs-museum, 9am-noon and 1pm-4pm Mon.-Fri., free) and features photos and personal audio recordings of the famed playwright. From Route 66 head east on E. Will Rogers Boulevard. After four blocks, turn left (north) on N. Weenonah.

Food

The **Hammett House** (1616 W. Will Rogers Blvd., 918/341-7333, www. hammetthouse.com, 11am-9pm Tues.-Sat., 11am-8pm Sun., $7-15) has been serving comfort classics since 1969. They also serve a little taste of the South, with sweet tea, catfish Po' Boys, sweet potato fries, and fried okra.

The restaurant is less than a mile from Route 66 near the Will Rogers Museum. From Route 66, turn right (northeast) on Highway 88 (W. Will Rogers Blvd.).

Ron's Hamburgers and Chili (1220 S. Lynn Riggs Blvd., 918/283-0000, www.ronschili.com, 10:30am-8pm daily, $6-11) is a local chain that dishes out delectable hamburgers. The sausage burger featured sausage mixed with ground hamburger, adding even more flavor to the fried crispy edges. Don't skip the real draft root beer.

◈ Back on 66

Leaving Claremore, head southwest on J. M. Davis Boulevard until it rejoins Lynn Riggs Boulevard (Route 66). Turn right (south) onto Route 66 and continue for about 12 miles to Catoosa.

Catoosa

Catoosa was a wild, rough-and-tumble town where cowboys came to play after making money during the days of the cattle drives. Today, Catoosa is better known for its 80-foot long blue sculpture of a Sperm Whale sitting in a pond.

Sights
Blue Whale

The **Blue Whale** (2680 N. Hwy 66, 918/694-7390, www.bluewhaleroute66.com) is a quirky roadside attraction built in 1972 by zoologist Hugh S. Davis. Davis was 60 years old when he came up with the idea. He used more than 1,200 feet of pipe, 126 sacks of concrete, almost 20,000 pounds of rocks, and 15 tons of sand to build it over the two years it took to complete. Davis unveiled the whale as an anniversary gift for his wife Zelta, who collected whale figurines. The Blue Whale has since seen better days, but it's still worth a look.

Catoosa Historical Society Museum

Housed in an old depot, the **Catoosa Historical Society Museum** (207 S. Cherokee, 918/266-7156, www.bluewhaleroute66.com, 10am-3pm Tues, 10am-3pm Fri., free) displays information about Catoosa's train history, including a train depot log from 1897, a bank check dated in 1907, photographs of early residents, and an old mailbox from times when mail was delivered on horseback.

Food

For a dignified meal in an eclectic log house, try ★ **Molly's Landing** (3700 N. Hwy. 66, 918/266-7853, www.mollyslanding.com, 4pm-10pm Mon.-Sat., $18-40). Order the melt-in-your-mouth filet with peppercorn sauce, and enjoy the housemade bread or the roasted garlic bread. An extensive wine menu makes for a memorable meal. Lighted bridges lead into the rustic, whimsical decor and add to the fun.

From Route 66, cross the Verdigris River and turn right (northwest) onto Old Highway 66. Take the first right, which leads to Molly's Landing in about 700 feet.

✦ Back on 66

Leaving Catoosa, take Route 66 south for about 1 mile, then turn right (west) on Antry Drive. Take an immediate left (south) on S. Cherokee Street. After about 1 mile, turn left (south) on Highway 167. Continue under I-44 and then turn right (west) on 11th Street into Tulsa.

✦ Side Trip: Broken Arrow

Before you head into Tulsa, vintage car lovers should check out **Hot Rod Alley**

Gifts & Nostalgia (2300 N. 9th St., Broken Arrow, 918/355-6649, www.hotrodalleygifts.com, 9am-6pm Mon.-Fri., 9am-4pm Sat.), a museum and gift shop located in a replica of a 1930s filling station. On-site are a collection of gas pumps, porcelain signs, neon lights, clocks, jukeboxes, racing collectibles, and hot rods. It's also a fun place to shop for unique gifts.

From Route 66 (11th St.) south of I-44, turn left (south) onto 177th Avenue (S Lynn Lane Rd.) and drive about 6 miles south to E. Albany (E. 61st St.). Hot Rod Alley is on the right, about a 15-minute drive from Route 66.

Tulsa

Tulsa was created as part of the Indian Removal Act (the Trail of Tears). In the 1830s, Choctaw, Cherokee, Muscogee (Creek), Chickasaw, Cheyenne, Comanche, Apache, Seminole, and other tribes were relocated to this region after being forced to surrender their land east of the Mississippi River to the federal government. Their new land eventually became the state of Oklahoma.

At the turn of the 20th century, Tulsa changed from a small frontier settlement into a boomtown when oil was discovered. It soon became the "Oil Capital of the World," and oil barons built incredible skyscrapers and beautiful buildings. As a result, Tulsa has one of the largest concentrations of Art Deco architecture in the United States.

✦ Route 66 through Tulsa

West of U.S. 169, Route 66 follows 11th Street through downtown Tulsa past several neon Route 66 signs, murals, and old motor courts, including the Desert Hills (near Yale St.). An **older alignment** zigzags less than one mile north of 11th Street on Admiral Place, traveling west to Lewis Avenue, then south to 2nd Street—but the one-way streets make this route tricky to follow.

To take the more direct **post-1932 alignment,** follow 11th Street west all the way to the Arkansas River, where it turns south into Southwest Boulevard. Tulsa is fairly easy to navigate, and most sights are located less than a mile from Route 66.

Sights

Downtown Tulsa is encircled within a loop of freeways and highways—U.S. 244 (north), Highways 412 (north) and 75 (east), and State Route 51 (west and south). As Route 66 (11th St.) enters downtown, the road crosses Highway 75; turn north on S. Elgin Avenue to begin exploring the downtown area.

★ Greenwood Cultural Center

The **Greenwood District** in Tulsa is an area Booker T. Washington referred to as America's "Black Wall Street." The 35-block area was once a vibrant community with the wealthiest black neighborhoods in the south. Not only was it a hotbed of jazz and blues in the 1920s, it housed more than 300 black-owned businesses, including theaters, restaurants, hotels, and law offices.

In June 1921, one of the nation's worst acts of racial violence broke out in the Greenwood District. The **Tulsa Race Riot** was instigated by a rumor about a black man assaulting a white woman—and then spun out of control. No one knew what really happened, but most people believe that a 19-year old black man tripped while exiting an elevator and grabbed a white woman's arm to steady himself. She screamed, and he ran. As the story spread through the town, with each version getting more creative, jealousy over black economic success coupled with inflammatory false reporting led to a riot by an angry white mob. The mob set the Greenwood District on fire

top to bottom: Totem Pole Park; Philbrook Museum of Art, Tulsa; John Hope Franklin Reconciliation Park, Tulsa

Tulsa

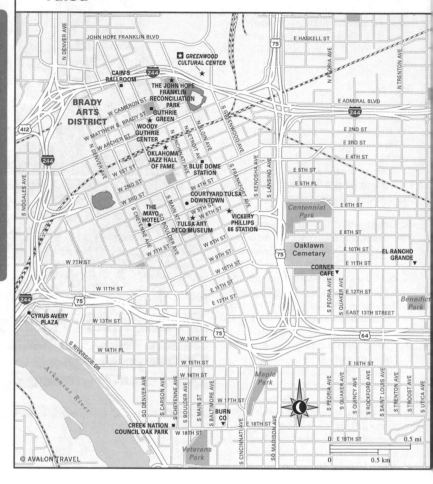

and prevented the firefighters from saving the buildings. After 16 hours of rioting, looting, and complete mayhem, hundreds died as Black Wall Street burned to the ground. An estimated 10,000 black people were left homeless, and the riot was responsible for wiping out nearly all of the prosperity and success the Greenwood district had achieved up to that time.

The **Greenwood Cultural Center** (322 N. Greenwood Ave., 918/596-1026, www. greenwoodculturalcenter.com, 9am-5pm Mon.-Fri., free) has a valuable collection of historical memorabilia and photos of the area before, during, and after the riot. Although most of Greenwood District was burned to the ground, the black community persevered and opened businesses such as **The Warren Hotel** (105 N. Greenwood St.), located down the street from the cultural center. The Warren Hotel was listed in the historic Negro Motorist Green Book.

Art Deco Architecture

Born in the 1920s, Art Deco was characterized by bold geometric shapes and motifs of sharply defined chevrons ("v" shapes), terra-cotta details, stylized floral patterns, low-relief designs, strong colors, and forms inspired by Native American artwork. **Downtown Tulsa** is a great place for a concentrated collection of some of the most stunning examples of Art Deco architecture in the United States. The Philtower and Philcade buildings, the Tulsa Club, the Atlas Life building, the Public Service Company of Oklahoma, and the Boston Avenue Methodist Church are a great start.

For a list of almost 40 Art Deco buildings throughout Tulsa, visit the **Tulsa Preservation Commission** (175 East 2nd St., Ste. 570, 918/576-5687, www.tulsapreservationcommission.org). The **Tulsa Historical Society** (2445 S. Peoria Ave., 918/712-9484, www.tulsahistory.org, 10am-4pm Tues.-Sat., $5) provides Art Deco walking tours.

John Hope Franklin Reconciliation Park

Built as a space of healing and hope in response to the 1921 Tulsa Race Riot, the **John Hope Franklin Reconciliation Park** (321 N. Detroit, 918/295-5009, www.jhfcenter.org/reconciliation-park, 8am-8pm daily, free) opened in 2010 and presents the role of African-Americans in Oklahoma. A 25-foot memorial tower depicts the history of the African-American struggle—from Africa to North America—and stands near three 16-foot granite sculptures based on actual pictures from the 1921 riot.

Cain's Ballroom

Since 1924, **Cain's Ballroom** (423 N. Main St., 918/584-2306, www.cainsballroom.com, box office 10am-noon and 1pm-5pm daily, $16-45) has been the Carnegie Hall of country music. It has hosted a range of stars, including Bob Wills, Dolly Parton, Hank Williams, Bob Dylan, U2, Bonnie Raitt, and Willie Nelson. In 1978, the Sex Pistols even played here (Sid Vicious punched a hole in the wall). Today, expect a diverse group of talented performers like Christopher Stapleton, Morrissey, and the Smashing Pumpkins. Most tickets are less than $30, and while the theater is big enough to attract world-famous acts, it's small enough to offer an intimate experience. There are two bars, a BBQ restaurant, balcony seating, great lighting, and kicking acoustics.

Guthrie Green

Guthrie Green (111 E. Brady St., 918/574-2421, 6am-11pm daily) is an urban garden filled with activities such as outdoor Zumba, yoga, and bocce ball classes as well as storytelling sessions, film screenings, and concerts. If you happen to visit on a Wednesday, **food trucks** line up around 11:30am. Guthrie Green is located in the Brady District, between Brady and Cameron and Boston and Cincinnati Avenues.

Woody Guthrie Center

Woody Guthrie's progressive political views rustled the feathers of Cold War conservatives, but it can't be denied that he composed some of the most iconic, patriotic songs of our nation; his anthems about the Dust Bowl gave a voice to so many who had lost so much. The **Woody Guthrie Center** (102 E. Brady St., 918/574-2710, www.woodyguthriecenter.org, 10am-6pm Tues.-Sun., 10am-9pm First Fridays, $8) offers a comprehensive archive of more than 10,000 photos, journals, notes, illustrations, and sketches, as well as the lyrics to "This Land is Your Land" written in Guthrie's own hand. The 12,000-square foot facility, on a corner of the Brady District, includes exhibits, a research facility,

The Green Book

Being black and traveling Route 66 during the Jim Crow era was a potentially life-threatening undertaking that involved a considerable amount of planning and hope. The *Negro Motorist Green Book* was a trusted travel guide. This critical roadside companion (dubbed the "Green Book") was considered the "Bible of black travel." Published from 1936 to 1966 by Victor H. Green, a black postal worker in Harlem, the Green Book was distributed by Esso gas stations. Green featured restaurants, hotels, barbershops, beauty parlors, taverns, garages, and gas stations that were willing to serve black people during Jim Crow. Green wanted to "give the Negro traveler information that will keep him from running into difficulties and embarrassments."

educational programs, field trips, and songwriting sessions.

Oklahoma Jazz Hall of Fame

The **Oklahoma Jazz Hall of Fame** (5 South Boston, 918/928-5299, www.okjazz.org, $15-20), once housed in the Greenwood Cultural Center, now lives in the historic Art Deco Union Depot. They host an ongoing concert series, cultural events, and blues, gospel, and jazz performances. An on-site museum exhibits memorabilia, photographs, and historical information about greats like Chet Baker and Jimmy Rushing.

Tulsa Art Deco Museum

Tulsa Art Deco Museum (511 S. Boston Ave., 918/804-2669, www.tulsaartdecomuseum.com, 8am-6pm Mon.-Fri., 11am-6pm Sat.) is a small but informative museum about the design and era of Art Deco culture. A collection of artifacts such as jewelry, advertising artwork, silverware, and clothing show how pervasive the style was and how it became a part of everyday life. The museum is located in the lobby of the gorgeous Philcade Building; a gift shop and docent-led tours are available upon request.

Underground Pedestrian Tunnel

Located on the pre-1930s alignment northeast of downtown is an **underground pedestrian tunnel** (Admiral Place and Harvard Ave.). This tunnel was built sometime from the late 1920s to the early 1930s for pedestrian safety after the Sequoyah Elementary school opened a couple of blocks north in 1927. Look for it on the corner near the Crosstown Church of Christ; it resembles a subway train entrance with a metal cage. The rusted concrete base has exposed rebar, old lighting fixtures, and Art Deco accents. The tunnel is usually locked on weekends, but it's worth a gander as a reminder of the old days of Route 66.

Creek Nation Council Oak Park

Located south of the Highway 64/51/75 interchange and near the Arkansas River is **Creek Council Oak Park** (1750 S. Cheyenne Ave.), where a large burr oak tree marks the traditional ceremonial ground chosen by the Lochapoka clan of the Creek Indians. After being forced off their land in 1836, and losing 161 members on the horrific Trail of Tears, 469 tribe members arrived on this hill overlooking the Arkansas River. They named this place Tulasi (Tulsa is derived from the Lochapoka word tulasi, which means "old town"). The Tulsa-Lochapoka gathered here for ceremonies until 1896. The park is often referred to as Tulsa's first City Hall, and commemorative tribal ceremonies are held each year.

Philbrook Museum of Art

The **Philbrook Museum of Art** (2727 S. Rockford Rd., 918/749-7941, www.

Car Culture

The 1932 **Vickery Phillips Station** (602 S. Elgin Ave., 918/582-2534), leased to Virgil Vickery in 1946, is a pristine example of signature Cotswold Cottage design by the Phillips Petroleum Company. These cottage-style brick properties featured pitched roofs and a central tapered chimney; many were painted dark green with orange and blue trim. They were popular, and by 1930 there were 6,750 of them in 12 states. The Vickery property has been restored with a cost-share grant from the Route 66 Corridor Preservation Program. Today the building is used as an Avis Rental Car company.

philbrook.org, 10am-5pm Tues.-Sun., 10am-8pm Thurs., $9) was a 72-room mansion built during Tulsa's gilded age, when oil barons had more money than they knew what to do with. Built in 1926, the mansion was designed to look like an Italian villa. Today, the property is surrounded by 23 acres of beautifully manicured gardens and houses collections of art from all over the world. To get there from E. 11th Street (Route 66), turn left (south) on S. Peoria Avenue and drive 1.5 miles. Turn left (east) on E. 27th Place; the Philbrook will be one block straight ahead.

Golden Driller

At the entrance of the Tulsa Expo Center is a 76-foot tall, 22-ton statue of an oil worker standing over a (real) oil derrick. The **Golden Driller** (4145 E. 21st St., 918/596-2100, www.exposquare.com, free) was built in 1966 as a monument for petroleum industry workers at a time when Oklahoma was considered the oil capital of the world. The Golden Driller was built to withstand 200-mph tornadoes; although he has been vandalized and assaulted by shotgun blasts, the city patches him up and slaps on a new paint job. It's a Tulsa icon that is built to last.

To get there from E. 11th Street (Route 66), turn left (south) on S. Sandusky Avenue. In one mile, turn right (west) on E. 21st Street. Take an immediate right into the Tulsa Expo Center parking lot. The Golden Driller is in the front of the Expo Center.

Gilcrease Museum

The **Gilcrease Museum** (1400 N. Gilcrease Museum Rd., 888/655-2278, www.gilcrease.utulsa.edu, 10am-5pm Tues.-Sun., 10am-8pm Thurs., $9) sits on 460 acres with 23 themed gardens and features more than 10,000 paintings, prints, drawing, and sculptures by 400 artists from colonial times to the present. They also have an unparalleled collection of Native American artifacts, historical manuscripts, and art.

To get there from E. 11th Street (Route 66), turn right (north) on S. Denver Avenue and drive one mile. Turn left (west) on W. Edison Street. Drive one mile to N. Gilcrease Museum Road and turn right (north). The museum will be on the left.

Cyrus Avery Plaza

As Southwest Boulevard crosses the Arkansas River leaving downtown, larger-than-life bronze sculptures, flags from the eight Route 66 states, and a huge Route 66 sign hang over the Mother Road at **Cyrus Avery Plaza** (Southwest Blvd. and Riverside Dr., dawn-dusk daily, free), which pays homage to the man considered by many to be the "Father of Route 66." A sculpture by Robert Summers depicts Avery climbing out of his Model T to help a farmer in a horse-drawn carriage coming west from Tulsa's oil fields; Avery's wife, daughter, and cat are also in the car. The sculpture is about 60 feet long and 15 feet high and weighs nearly 20,000 pounds. Free

Cyrus Avery, The "Father of Route 66"

Cyrus Avery Plaza, Tulsa

Cyrus Avery (1871-1962) was born in Stevensville, Pennsylvania; his family moved to the Indian Territory of Cherokee Nation in Oklahoma when he was a teenager. In 1924, Avery became the chairman of the State Highway Commission, and in 1925 he was selected by the Department of Agriculture as one of four board members to assist in numbering the nation's highways. Avery was determined to bring business and tourism to Oklahoma. He and his wife owned the Old English Inn, a tourist court and restaurant located on what is now the traffic circle at Mingo and Admiral Place.

A more direct diagonal route for Route 66 would have passed through the middle of Kansas, but it was Avery's passion and vision that led state and federal highway officials to build Route 66 right through his home state of Oklahoma. Avery's convincing argument was that the road followed an important trade route between Chicago and Tulsa. It was originally going to be called Route 60, but the states of Kentucky and Virginia had their hearts set on the number 60, and won the battle; Avery and his board members settled on 66 because it had not yet been assigned.

parking is available near the pedestrian bridge that crosses 11th Street.

Route 66 Village
Train enthusiasts will appreciate **Route 66 Village** (3770 Southwest Blvd., 918/609-0405, www.route66village.org, dawn-dusk daily, free), home to a restored Frisco 4500 steam engine that carried passengers from St. Louis through Tulsa to Oklahoma City from 1940 to 1947. A business lounge car was built in 1929 with six rooms, a kitchen, and a lounge area. Also on-site is an oil tank car built in 1917 and a 154-foot tall oil derrick, currently the largest in North America.

Blue Dome Station
The **Blue Dome Station** (313 E. Second St.) is a 1924 Gulf Oil gas station that was converted into office space. The rounded brick building with the sky-blue dome on top has become the iconic landmark of the Blue Dome entertainment district east of downtown Tulsa. Efforts are underway to restore the building back to its original glory.

Brady Arts District
The Brady Arts District is the oldest section in Tulsa, with red-brick buildings and an urban garden. This walkable neighborhood is a vibrant hotspot for artists, craftspeople, and merchants, with restaurants, nightclubs, galleries, and a popular food truck court. The **Art Crawl** (www.thebradyartsdistrcit.com) occurs the first Friday of every month with live music, chocolate-making, and glass-blowing demonstrations.

Admiral Twin Drive-In
The **Admiral Twin Drive-in** (7355 E. Easton St., 918/392-9959, www.selectcinemas.com, opens at dusk, $7) is located on the pre-1930s alignment of Route 66. This classic drive-in from the early 1950s shows blockbuster films on two nine-story screens. Two tickets, popcorn, and a drink will run you less than $20—a better deal than most indoor movie theaters. Your car must have FM radio to hear the movie. Get there early, as this place is popular.

Circle Cinema
For documentaries, foreign films, or an indie flick, **Circle Cinema** (10 S. Lewis Ave., 918/592-3456, office 918/585-3405, www.circlecinema.com, $6.50-9.50) is the place. This is the oldest historic movie theater in Tulsa: The theater opened in 1928, when the price of a ticket was only a dime, and a nickel would buy an orange juice and a funnel-shaped cup of peanuts.

Accomodations
For modern-day comfort in a classic setting, try the beautifully restored ★ **Campbell Hotel** (2636 E. 11th St., 855/744-5500, www.thecampbellhotel.com, $139-209), located right on Route 66. Built in 1927, this hotel spans an entire block with 26 theme rooms, including one inspired by the Rat Pack and a Route 66 suite complete with vintage roads signs and memorabilia. There are spa services available on-site and

Maxxwells (918/748-5550, www.maxxwellsrestaurant.com, 6am-10pm daily), attached to the hotel, serves delicious fare. What could be better after a long day on the road?

Marriott Courtyard Tulsa (415 S. Boston Ave., 918/508-7400, www.marriott.com, $84-150) is housed in the historic Atlas Life Building with a beautiful Art Deco lobby. Book a room on the 7th floor to see the original features from 1922. Rooms are fairly spacious for a historic property, giving you get the best of both worlds—modern amenities surrounded by history. The hotel is located next to the Philtower Building, one block away from the Tulsa Art Deco Museum.

Built in 1925, the ★ **Mayo Hotel** (115 W. 5th St., 918/582-6296, www.themayohotel.com, $118-289) has hosted celebrities such as John F. Kennedy, Charles Lindbergh, Babe Ruth, and Charlie Chaplin. Though the hotel closed in 1981, it was resurrected in 2009 after a $42 million restoration. It is now the pinnacle of modern elegance, with custom linens, 47-inch flat-screen TVs, Keurig coffee makers, and spa showers will full-body sprays. The property is an architectural gem with a fascinating history: It was home to oilman J. Paul Getty, and many famous deals among oil barons happened here.

Food
Hanks Hamburgers (8933 E. Admiral Place, 918/832-1509, www.hankshamburgers.com, 10am-2pm Mon., 10am-7pm Tues.-Sat., $4-8) has been frying their legendary hash house burgers since 1949. The half-pound "Hank's Special" takes about 15 minutes to cook and is definitely worth the wait, while the "Big Okie" is a full one-pound burger layered with one-quarter pound onion burgers. If that seems like too much food, you're probably right—but this burger's texture of thin-layered patties marbled with cheese and caramelized onions is unlike any other. You don't have to eat the whole

thing by yourself; split it with someone and then finish it off with a chocolate-peanut butter bon bon.

Maxxwell's (2636 E. 11th St., 918/748-5550, www.maxxwellsrestaurant.com, 6am-10pm daily, $8-16) serves veggie omelets, sweet potato tater tots, meatloaf, pork chops, and creamy garlic mashed potatoes. Even better, if you stay the Campbell Hotel next door, your breakfast is free.

Get your Tex Mex on at **Rancho Grande** (1629 E. 11th St., 918/584-0816, www.elranchograndemexicanfood.com, $9-14). Since 1953, Route 66 road trippers have been loving the cheese enchiladas, refried beans, tamales, and queso-topped tacos served here. The vintage neon sign with a saguaro cactus and a *vaquero* in a sombrero completes the experience.

The best thing about the **Corner Cafe** (1103 S. Peoria Ave., 918/587-0081, 6am-9pm daily, $6-14) is that it's not pretending to be anything other than what it is:

an old-school diner serving up a home-style breakfast. This is regular people enjoying regular food.

★ **Burn Co. Barbeque** (1738 S. Boston Ave., 918/574-2777, www.burnbbq.com, 10:30am-2:30pm Tues.-Sat., $8-18) owner Adam Myers always wanted to "make stuff," but he went to business school and never had a traditional culinary education. Apparently, he didn't need one to learn how to make some of the best BBQ in Tulsa. Each week the restaurant runs through 650 pounds of charcoal, 125 pounds of BBQ rub, and more than 40 gallons of BBQ sauce: The locally sourced meat is smoked daily and the brisket, pulled pork, smoked jalapeno sausage, and potato salad are all off the charts. Burn Co. closes early in the day, so plan to arrive before noon, when the line can stretch out the door.

◆ Back on 66

Leaving Tulsa, Route 66 heads south on Southwest Boulevard. After crossing

Mayo Hotel, Tulsa

I-244, continue driving south through Oakhurst, where Route 66 turns into Frankoma Road. After about 4 miles, Route 66 joins OK 66 (Mission St.) heading south into the town of Sapulpa.

Sapulpa

Sapulpa's first permanent settler was Creek Indian Chief Sapulpa in 1850. Later, the town turned into an important site for cattle shipping. Ninety percent of the buildings in the historic district were built between 1904 and 1952 and designed in the Classical and Tudor Revival styles. There used to be a Fred Harvey Restaurant and railroad station, but that was torn down in the early 1960s.

◆ Route 66 through Sapulpa
In Sapulpa, head south on Mission Street and turn right (west) onto Highway 33 (Dewey Ave.) to the west side of town.

Sights
Waite Phillips Filling Station Museum
The Sapulpa Historical Society restored this beautiful 1923 **Waite Phillips Filling Station Museum** (26 E. Lee Ave., 918/224-7765, 10am-3pm Tues.-Sat., donations appreciated). Not to be confused with the Phillips 66 in Tulsa, this station was run by Frank Phillips' brother Waite. The station is located on the southwest corner about one block south on Route 66. Also on-site is a collection of interesting artifacts and cars from the 1920s.

Sapulpa Historical Society Museum
Across the street from the Wait Phillips Filling Station is the **Sapulpa Historical Society Museum** (100 E. Lee Ave., 918/224-4871, www.sapulpahistorical-society.com, 10am-3pm Tues.-Sat., donations accepted) with three floors of exhibits depicting Sapulpa's history. A re-created village showcases an early blacksmith shop, general merchandise store, the Rock Creek Indian Methodist Church, a boarding school, and railroad shops that were popular in the early 1900s.

Rock Creek Bridge #18
In the 1920s, when Route 66 travelers crossed **Rock Creek Bridge #18,** it was a memorable experience. It may not look like much today, but truss bridges were quite impressive for their time. This one had brick decking, which was unusual and made it even more special. The bridge is located on W. Ozark Trail, 1.2 miles west of Main Street (Hwy. 97). Turn right (north) on W. Ozark Trail and the bridge will be after the turn.

Food
Happy Burger (215 N. Mission St., 918/224-7750, 11am-8pm Mon.-Sat., $3-7) serves great burgers and incredible peanut butter shakes under a fun retro sign that rivals all knock-offs. The restaurant was originally built as a Tastee

Tulsa to Oklahoma City

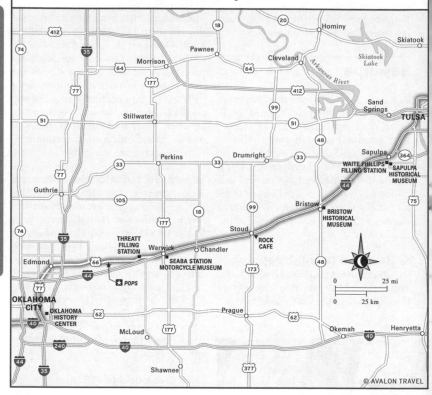

© AVALON TRAVEL

Freeze in 1957, but the owner changed the name to Happy Burger.

❖ Back on 66

Depart Sapulpa via West Dewey Avenue (Route 66) to head west and follow Route 66 south toward Kellyville. After five miles, the road veers west as it crosses under I-44 into the town of Bristow, where Route 66 becomes Main Street.

Detour: Ozark Trail

Definitely worth a slight detour, take West Dewey Avenue west to follow a narrow, bumpy 3.3-mile section of the 1926 alignment via the Ozark Trail. You'll see a 120-foot concrete steel truss bridge (now closed) that served Route 66 travelers

from the birth of the road until the construction of a new alignment in 1952.

Leaving Sapulpa, head west on West Dewey Avenue (Route 66). Turn right (north) on W. Ozark Trail and follow it for 3 miles until it rejoins the newer alignment. Turn right (southwest) to rejoin Route 66.

Bristow

Bristow was once a small trading post in the Creek Indian area at the turn of the 20th century. It quickly became a railroad town when the Oklahoma City Railroad (which later became the San Francisco Railway) extended its line from Sapulpa to Oklahoma City. There were several cotton gins in the area, and oil was discovered around 1915. By the late 1920s, Route 66 brought even more business to town. Many of the garages, auto dealers, and service stations, such as the streamlined modern **Beard Motor Company** (210 E. 9th St.), were built to accommodate Route 66 travelers. After the turnpike was built in the 1950s, the route bypassed Bristow and, like many Route 66 towns, Bristow lost its shine and took on a more weathered patina.

⊕ Route 66 through Bristow

Route 66 enters Bristow on Main Street (Hwy. 48), traveling south for about 0.5 mile to head west (right) on 4th Avenue for 0.5 mile.

Sights

Railroad enthusiasts will enjoy checking out this 1923 restored depot. The **Bristow Historical Museum, Depot, and Town Square** (199 E. 6th Ave., 918/367-5151, 10am-2pm Mon.-Fri., donations accepted) has railroad-related exhibits, displays, and information about Bristow's history from the time of the Indian Territory to the present in a one-story brick building.

⊕ Back on 66

Leaving Bristow, head south on Main Street and then turn right (west) on 4th Avenue. After about four blocks, Route 66 curves south on Roland Street. From this point to the town of Stroud, you're driving over a massive underground natural gas storage facility that was built in 1950. Follow Route 66 west for about 7 miles to Depew.

Depew

You would never know it today, but in the mid-1920s Depew was a busy town with several grain mills, three lumber-yards, three grocery stores, three service

stations, four hotels, a bakery, a Chevrolet dealership, a drugstore, and a dentist. All the roads were dirt until Route 66 came through in 1926. However, Depew suffered like so many other towns during the Great Depression. By the late 1930s, there were only two grocery stores, one bank, a couple of gas stations, a hardware store, and a few other businesses. Today, the town is lined with historic yet empty buildings and businesses.

Route 66 made a loop though downtown Depew for only two years, from 1926 to 1928. To follow through the route through town, turn left (south) on Flynn Avenue and then make a right (west) on Main Street. Turn left (north) on Ladd Avenue, which leads back to Route 66.

⊕ Back on 66

Complete the Depow Loop, then from Ladd Avenue turn left onto Route 66 and drive west for 10 miles to Stroud.

Stroud

In the 1890s, Stroud was a hell-raising party town for cattlemen and cowboys; it was forced "dry" by Oklahoma law in 1907. Today, there are a number of old buildings along Main Street. Route 66 enters Stroud on Main Street and travels west for about 1.5 miles. Don't miss the great neon sign at the **Skyliner Motel** (717 W. Main St.).

Food

When Route 66 came through Stroud in the 1920s, several businesses popped up, but the only one that remains today is the ★ **Rock Cafe** (114 W. Main St., 918/968-3990, www.rockcafert66.com, 7am-8pm daily, $8-11). Owner Dawn Welch is a powerhouse and long-time promoter of Route 66. (The character Sally Carrera in the Pixar film *Cars* is reportedly patterned after her.) They keep things simple at the Rock Cafe, but this place is far from predictable. You can order alligator burgers, beignets, Indian fried rice, chicken and waffles, and German favorite "Jagerschnitzel," a breaded and fried pork cutlet covered with creamy mushroom sauce, bacon, and onions.

Like many places on Route 66, it's the history of this place that makes it special. The Rock Cafe opened in 1939 and has been run by women for much of its existence. In the 1940s, during World War II, the restaurant doubled as a busy Greyhound bus stop. From 1959 to 1983, it was a 24-hour restaurant run by Mamie Mayfield until she retired at age 70. When a tornado almost took it out in 1999, the National Park Service Route 66 Corridor Preservation Program stepped in and helped with a cost-share grant. When a disastrous fire happened in 2008, funding from the National Park Service and the National Trust Southwest Office helped restore this place to its former glory. Hopefully this is just one of those places that will never die.

◈ Back on 66

Heading west out of Stroud, Route 66 dips south and curves through Davenport. From Davenport, continue another 6 miles west to Chandler.

Chandler

Chandler was settled during the 1891 Land Rush (the land had previously been occupied by Sac, Fox, and Iowa tribes, but was then opened up for homesteading). A tornado wiped out much of Chandler in 1897. After that, sturdier brick and stone structures were built. Many of these historic brick and sandstone buildings can still be seen throughout the town. One of the most impressive is the Chandler Armory, which houses the Route 66 Interpretive Center.

As you head into town, keep an eye out for the **Lincoln Motel** (740 E. 1st St.), which has a great neon sign. It's on the right (north) side of the highway.

◈ Route 66 through Chandler

Route 66 enters Chandler on 1st Street and heads south. After passing under the railroad, it then merges with Manvel Avenue heading south to 15th Street.

Sights
Route 66 Interpretive Center

The **Chandler Armory** was built between 1935 and 1937 for the Oklahoma National Guard as part of the Works Progress Administration (WPA). The Chandler Armory was one of 54 Oklahoma armories built by the WPA. More than 250 laborers chiseled its sandstone outer walls by hand; 20 inches thick, they were built to withstand tornado winds. As a job site, it offered desperately needed employment during the Great Depression. Once the armory opened, it housed more than 60 men of the 45th Infantry Division. This was also the site where Reverend Burton Z. "Lee Lee" Lewis, the first black person ever to serve in the Oklahoma National Guard, was sworn in.

Decades later the building fell into disrepair and suffered water damage. The armory's windows and parts of the roof were missing, and the plumbing and electric systems did not work. Although it was a mess, the property was listed in the National Register of Historic Places in 1992; it took another 10 years before the armory received a much-needed restoration. In 2007, the **Route 66 Interpretive Center** (400 E. 1st St. 405/258-1300, www.route66interpretivecenter.org, 10am-5pm Tues.-Sat., 1pm-5pm Sun., closed Sun. Oct.-Apr., $5) opened featuring exhibits, vintage billboards, and videos of the Mother Road.

McJerry's Route 66 Gallery

Artist and painter Jerry McClanahan has been touring, researching, documenting, mapping, and writing about Route 66 for more than 30 years. The **McJerry's Route 66 Gallery** (306 Manvel Ave., 903/467-6384, www.mcjerry66.com, no set hours, free) showcases his paintings, postcards,

Car Culture

Phillips Petroleum Co. was founded in 1917, but the trademark Phillips 66 was created one year after the birth of the Mother Road. Legend has it that Phillips executives happened to be driving 66 miles per hour with their new gasoline, which had a high gravity mark of 66, so they thought this was the perfect name brand for their stations.

This early 1930s **Phillips 66 Station** (701 Manvel Ave., 405/258-5305, www. patinaproperties.com, free) is a Tudor Revival, cottage-style gas station with a steep roof, tall windows, and a chimney. Behind the station is a 1958 **Valentine Diner,** also under restoration. Valentines were tiny, portable, pre-fab diners that seated 8-12 people. They were popular during the Depression because their modest size made it possible to operate a business with very limited funds. Valentine Diners were also unique because most diner manufacturers were located on the East Coast; Valentines were made in Wichita, Kansas, and transported throughout the West.

and prints, which capture special moments from the Mother Road. You can even commission him to record your own personal Route 66 road trip experience in paint. There are no formal hours for the gallery; McClanahan suggests folks call head or just drop by. He loves to chat about Route 66 history and the lore of the highway.

The gallery is located one block north of Route 66 after its merge with Manvel Avenue.

Lincoln County Museum of Pioneer History

Housed in three buildings more than 100 years old, the **Lincoln County Museum of Pioneer History** (717 Manvel Ave., 405/258-2425, www.skypoint.com, 10am-4pm Tues.-Sat., donations accepted) features children's marionettes and historical paintings of the arrival of the American Indians. Cattle trails, the Land Run, and the life of early settlers are depicted in Route 66 exhibits, along with replicas of an old-fashioned dental office, milliner and seamstress shops, and a general store with items typically sold during the early 1900s.

✦ Back on 66

Manvel Avenue (Route 66) curves right (west) onto West 15th Street for 7 miles to Warwick.

Warwick

Even if you're not a motorcycle fan, the **Seaba Station Motorcycle Museum** (336992 Oklahoma 66, 405/258-9141, www.seabastation.com, 10am-5pm daily, donations accepted) is a fun place to stop. It's housed inside a restored 1921 brick gas station and a great example of an early rural service station along Route 66. The station was owned by John Seaba. He employed about 18 people in the late 1930s, worked on Model T Fords, and ran an engine repair shop. Today the museum has an eclectic collection of 65 vintage motorcycles from 1908 to the present. Antique signs line the old brick walls, and there's also a gift shop inside.

✦ Back on 66

Route 66 heads west from Warwick and in approximately 10 miles you'll reach Luther.

Luther

Luther is a small agricultural township with a deep and layered history. The town shipped the largest amount of cotton of any Oklahoma town. The Booker T. Washington School for blacks was built here in 1916 and then destroyed by a fire in December 1930. The school was rebuilt in 1931 and its graduates (including Elizabeth Threatt, whose family owned the Threatt filling station) went on to colleges throughout the United States. The high school closed in 1957 when the school system integrated.

During the Jim Crow era, black travelers were often not welcome at restaurants, hotels, and service stations along Route 66. The **Threatt Filling Station** (N. Countryline Rd.), at the intersection of Route 66 and Pottawatomi Road, was an exception. A small, unassuming, one-story sandstone bungalow with a slightly pitched gabled roof, wide eaves, and a wooden door, it served blacks from 1915 to the 1950s. Owner Alan Threatt Sr., a black man, had a homestead in the Luther area from which his family quarried native sandstone to build the filling station, which bordered their property. Though it is not open to the public, it is still visible from the road.

Food

The Boundary (16001 Oklahoma 66, 405/277-3532, www.theboundaryon66. com, 11:30am-7:30pm Thurs., 11:30am-8pm Fri., noon-8pm Sat., noon-7pm Sun., $5-15) got its name because it sits on the border of the eastern boundary of the 1889 Land Run. The restaurant serves excellent BBQ pulled pork, brisket, and black-eyed peas in a rustic, vintage gas station.

◆ Back on 66

Leaving Luther, Route 66 turns into to E. Danforth Road. Arcadia is about 8 miles west.

Arcadia

Soon after the Land Rush, Arcadia was established and attracted both white and black cotton farmers. At the turn of the 20th century, the Deep Fork Township Census reported that the area was 50

Pops, Arcadia

percent black, and it remained that way for decades. When Route 66 came through, it generated business and more income for locals, but many left Arcadia to move to larger towns during the Great Depression. The one mainstay that keeps people coming to visit Arcadia is the Round Barn, built in 1898.

Sights
Biker Shak
The **Biker Shak** (208 Oklahoma 66, 405/396-2100, 10am-5:30pm Wed. and Fri.-Sat., 10am-7pm Thurs.) has all kinds of stylish biker accessories that make the road safer and more comfortable. Choose from jackets, headwear, helmets, leg warmers, and chaps, or have custom patches made for your own MC.

Round Barn
William H. Odor's neighbors him told it couldn't be done, but he proved them wrong, and in the process created what many consider an architectural marvel.

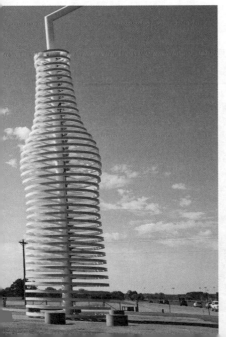

In 1898, Odor soaked and bent lumber to construct the 60-by-45-foot tall **Round Barn** (107 Oklahoma 66, 405/396-0824, www.arcadiaroundbarn.org, 10am-5pm daily, free). It was so special that it couldn't be used to just store hay. Instead, the barn hosted all kinds of community gatherings, even dances. Once Route 66 came through in 1926, the Round Barn became one of the most-photographed landmarks on the Mother Road. As traffic slowed on Route 66, the barn went through a rough period of neglect, but retired building contractor Luke Robinson has saved the barn from total ruin. Today, the walls are lined with images of other unusual shaped barns, and there's a gift shop inside.

Southwest Collectibles
For authentic American Indian wall hangings, flutes, peace pipes, drums, knives, furs, and hides, stop at **Southwest Collectibles** (135 W. First St., 405/396-2202, 11am-4:30pm Mon.-Sat.). Southwest Collectibles is located one block west of the Round Barn. From Route 66, turn right (north) on Division Street, and it's one block up at 1st Street.

★ Pops
Even though this soda pop utopia opened in 2007, it's quickly become one of the most "pop"ular sights on Route 66. **Pops** (660 Oklahoma 66, 405/233-2020, www.pops66.com, 6am-10pm daily; restaurant 10:30am-9pm daily, breakfast 7am-10:30am Sat.-Sun., $8-13) has to be one of the coolest modern gas stations in America. The colossal 66-foot tall, steel, LED-lit sculpture of a bottle emerges over the horizon on the roadside. Architect Rand Elliott designed this slick neo-futuristic service station, which looks like something out of the *Jetsons*. The four-ton soda bottle towers over the glass-and-steel building; the massive cantilevered canopy will make you feel like you should have landed here instead of driven on

four wheels. Inside, the walls shoot overhead at a sharp angle, and jewel-toned bottles of soda line the window in perfect succession, like a neo-pop version of stained glass.

The diner serves breakfast all day, as well as burgers, shakes, and dessert—and it's usually pretty crowded. (Plan to wait about an hour for a table, especially on the weekends.) But you don't have to eat here to experience this place. Come in and just cruise the huge selection of sodas. There are more than 600 different flavors—from butterscotch to peanut butter—from brands like Al Capone Soda and Round Barn Root Beer.

Route 66 has a long tradition of roadside tourist traps that use every stunt in the book to grab your attention and make you pull off the road and spend your money. In many ways, Pops is no different. It's flashy and a little gimmicky, but it's definitely worth the stop. This place proves you don't have be old to be an instant classic.

◆ Back on 66

Traveling west, Route 66 ends at I-35. Keep heading west and follow U.S. 77 into Edmond. After 3 miles, turn left (south) on Broadway (U.S. 77) and drive 3 more miles to the Memorial Road/Kelley Avenue exit. Turn left on Kelley Avenue and drive 5 miles to join I-44 West. Take the next exit for Lincoln Boulevard (Exit 128A). Turn left and head south on North Lincoln Boulevard into Oklahoma City.

Oklahoma City

In Bobby Troup's Route 66 anthem, "Oklahoma City looks mighty pretty," but this city has more than just good looks. Oklahoma City is layered with a complicated history that has defined America, for better and for worse. Thousands of American Indians were forced off their land in the eastern United States and relocated here in exchange for their original homeland. The government believed this

the Gold Dome Building, Oklahoma City

land had no value; however, it wasn't long before modern agricultural and ranching techniques ensured the land could be profitable. Then, everything changed.

The Dawes Act of 1887 opened up nearly 2 million acres of land to white settlement. Under a cloudless, cerulean sky, at high noon on April 22, 1889, more than 50,000 land-thirsty Americans lined up along the state border. At the crack of a whip, they rushed into Indian Territory on horseback, wagons, and on foot. As one observer described, "it wasn't human at all, but like thousands of wild animals." By that evening, thousands of plots had been claimed. Some considered this to be a display of pioneer spirit and an opportunity to claim free land—however, the tribes had lost their land again, and their way of life. The reservations were dissolved, and the tribes forced to assimilate.

Over the following decade, legal battles filled the courts with people fighting over property ownership. A lottery system was put in place to designate claims, and by 1905, as a result of the Land Rush, Oklahoma City had become one of the biggest boomtowns in the state. Two years later, this area was no longer called Indian Territory: "Oklahoma" became the 46th state of the Union.

◈ Route 66 through Oklahoma City

The pre-1930's alignment passed through the northern part of the city. Head south on Lincoln and turn west (right) on 23rd Street. In less than 2 miles, turn right (north) on North Classen Boulevard. After about one mile, follow signs marked "OK 66 NW 39th Expy." If you have the time, venture off Route 66 and explore the city. There's a lot to do and see.

Sights

At 622.5 square miles, Oklahoma City is the third-largest U.S. city in terms of acreage. But the city isn't just big in terms of space; they also have big ideas about how to create a vibrant city. For 20 years, the city imposed a limited-term penny sales tax to raise funds for services, the arts, and sports arenas. The city has since spent $176 million of the funds renovating the streets in order to make them more pedestrian-friendly and adding landscaping, public art, bike lanes, a canal, and a waterfront area.

Oklahoma History Center

Smithsonian-quality exhibits tell the history of Oklahoma in this 215,000 square-foot, 18-acre site. The **Oklahoma History Center** (800 Nazih Zuhdi Dr., 405/522-0765, www.okhistorycenter.org, 10am-5pm Mon.-Sat., $7) explores everything from aviation, transportation, and commerce to heritage and geology. There are five state-of-the-art permanent galleries, an outdoor oilfield exhibit with drilling derricks, and more than 200 interactive exhibits to educate and entertain.

Once Route 66 came through, traffic congestion in Oklahoma City became a problem for tourists and locals. In 1913, there were an estimated 3,000 cars; by the 1930s, there were more than 500,000. To handle parking issues, the city placed time limits on parking, but it was difficult to enforce them. That is, until Carl C. Magee designed the Park-o-Meter, the world's first parking meter, which cost a nickel an hour. It inspired a huge debate: opponents called it "un-American" to have to pay for parking. Regardless, the invention caught on quickly: Within five years, there were 140,000 parking meters in the United States. Today, the **Park-O-Meter No. 1** is on display at the Oklahoma History Center. There are other exhibits on travel, along with a fairly extensive oral history of the Mother Road.

Milk Bottle Building

The **Milk Bottle Building** (2426 N. Classen Blvd., 24 hours, free) harkens back to a time when diary was king, cows were hormone-free, and Lactaid didn't exist. A former grocery store, this intimate, triangular-shaped, red-brick building is home to a huge sculpture of a milk bottle. This is what a real milk bottle used to look like, with a long tapered neck and a rounded bottle cap.

Gold Dome Building

The 1958 **Gold Dome Building** (1112 NW 23rd St.) is a geodesic dome based on famous futurist Buckminster's Fuller's design. The Route 66 landmark with a 625 gold-paneled roof looks like a glowing spacecraft that landed smack in the middle of suburban America. Originally a Citizens State Bank, over the years it has housed a cultural center, office space, restaurant, and art gallery. Though it's not currently open to the public, it's still worth a stop. More recently, it has been in danger of being demolished.

Oklahoma City National Memorial and Museum

In 1995, Oklahoma City became infamous for the terrorist bombing by U.S.

Centennial Land Run Monument, Oklahoma City

veteran Timothy McVeigh. About 800 people were maimed, and 149 men and women and 19 children were killed. It was the deadliest domestic terrorist attack in U.S. history. The **Oklahoma City National Memorial and Museum** (620 N. Harvey Ave., 405/235-3313, https://oklahomacitynationalmemorial.org, 9am-6pm Mon.-Sat., $15) honors those who lost their lives. The memorial park contains two massive monoliths, a shallow 318-foot long reflecting pool, and a "survivor tree" that stands at the highest point of the memorial. A field is filled with 168 chairs engraved with the name of each person who died. The 24,000 square-foot museum offers powerful oral histories, videos, and bomb-damaged artifacts.

Centennial Land Run Monument

The **Centennial Land Run Monument** has 36 life-size sculptures re-enacting the Land Rush. The energy of the event is captured in the artwork, whose level of detail is impressive, but the scene it's commemorating is a disturbing reminder of how this pivotal moment in history forever changed the life and ways of tribal members. More sculptures are being added each year. When completed, it will be one of the largest freestanding bronze sculptures in the world.

The monument is located in the South End of Bricktown Canal. The entrance is at 200 Centennial Avenue, just off Reno Avenue and between the Bass Pro Shops and the Residence Inn Hotel.

Riversport

Do an 80-foot free fall off a 700-foot zipline across the Oklahoma River at **Riversport** (725 S. Lincoln, 405/552-4040, www.boathousedistrict.org, 1pm-8pm Sun.-Thurs., 10am-10pm Fri.-Sat. May 25-Aug 9, 1pm-8pm Sat.-Sun. Aug. 10-Dec. 31, from $35). This adventure park is located right on the water in the Boathouse District, so you can also row, boat, kayak, long board, and paddle board or take kayaking lessons. Not only is this world's tallest adventure course, it is also a designated U.S. Olympic and Paralympic Training Site.

Bricktown

The Bricktown entertainment district is just east of downtown between the Bricktown Ballpark and the Oklahoma River. This former warehouse district is now filled with restaurants, hotels, shops, and a ballpark. **Automobile Alley,** just north of downtown, used to be the city center for car dealerships. Now the area has been revamped into some of Oklahoma's best dining and shopping. A street festival is held every third Thursday of the month. The **Paseo District** has almost 20 galleries and more than 60 artists with restaurants, coffee houses, boutiques, and gift shops. A **Gallery Walk** happens the first Friday and Saturday of every month.

Shopping

Authenticity, quality, and a strong sense of origin are the values **Plenty Mercantile** (807 N. Broadway Ave., 405/888-77470, www.plentymercantile.com, 10am-7pm Tues.-Sat., noon-4pm Sun.) carries in both their products and their businesses. The store features goods and toys that are handmade in the United States; they also make an effort to work with companies that give back to their community. The store's cool digs are located inside the former Scott-Chevrolet Dealership in Automobile Alley.

Want to decorate your house like Don Draper's swinging pad in *Mad Men?* **Perch'd** (14 NW 9th St., 405/494-0419, www.perchdmodern.com, noon-7pm Tues.-Sat., noon-4pm Sun.) sells fashionable and fresh mid-century modern home decor and goods crafted by artisans, architects, and designers. The fun store is housed in a teal-colored shipping container whose floor is covered with Astroturf.

Inter-Tribal Designs (1520 N. Portland Ave., 405/943-7935, www.okitd.com, 10am-6pm Mon.-Sat.) is American Indian-owned and -operated. The shop sells authentic clothing, pottery, blankets, *kachinas*, sterling silver and turquoise jewelry, beading, and craft supplies. Built to resemble an old trading post, the store has large murals by a Choctaw artist.

Foodies will appreciate **Super Cao Nguyen** (2668 N. Military Ave., 405/525-7650, www.caonguyen.com, 9am-8:30pm daily), which has hard-to-find Asian foods, bamboo, art, cookware, dishware, furnishings, and clothing such as cheongsam, a traditional dress from China.

Accommodations

The ★ **Aloft Hotel** (209 N. Walnut Ave., 405/605-2100, www.aloftoklahomacity-bricktown.com, $140-240) offers accommodations that sport bold, loft-inspired designs with comfortable beds, nine-foot ceilings, 42-inch flat-screen televisions, rainfall showerheads, and plug-and-play connectivity stations for your electronics. The two-story, 1,900-square-foot celebrity suite looks like it was designed by the producers of *Mad Men,* with a curved staircase, starburst chandeliers, sleek modern furniture, and floor-to-ceiling windows. Amenities include an outdoor pool and a rooftop lounge with city views, along with beds, toys, and treats for canine traveling companions. Oh and yes, you're still in Oklahoma.

The historic 1911 ★ **Skirvin Hilton Hotel** (1 Park Ave., 405/272-3040, www.skirvinhilton.com, $169-355) has hosted presidents, actors, politicians, and athletes, including Dwight Eisenhower, Harry Truman, Elvis, Frank Sinatra, and Jimmy Hoffa. Rooms feature solid wood doors, elegantly stuffed chairs with ottomans, beds with tall, statement headboards, and 32-inch flat-screen televisions. It's within walking distance to Bricktown District shops and restaurants.

For something a little more traditional with an upscale Art Deco vibe, try the **Ambassador Hotel** (1200 N. Walker Ave., 405/600-6200, www.ambassadorhotel-collection.com, $200-240) in Midtown. This boutique hotel is in a historic building yet offers modern amenities such as iPod docks, high-thread-count linens, and Keurig coffeemakers. The spacious rooms sport city views and a decidedly understated, simply sublime decor.

Food

The **Iguana Mexican Grill** (9 NW 9th St., 405/606-7172, www.iguanamexicangrill.com, 11am-10pm Mon.-Fri., 10am-10pm Sat.-Sun., $8-16), in Automobile Alley, has one of the most extensive selections in the state with more than 200 kinds of tequila. Temper your blood-orange margarita with some good, stick-to-your-ribs black beans that are seasoned just right. The grilled veggies, sizzling steak fajitas, and enchiladas with smoked pork and green sauce are all delicious.

Brown's Bakery (1100 N. Walker Ave.,

405/232-0363, 5:30am-3pm Mon.-Fri., 5:30am-noon Sat., $2-8) is one of those family-owned places that have been around forever. Since 1946, Brown's has enticed locals with cake donuts, maple long johns, cinnamon rolls, pies, cheesecake, pecan bars, and thumbprint cookies.

In the 1970s, Vietnamese immigrants flocked to Oklahoma City, and today it has some of the most authentic Asian food you'll find. Most of the restaurants are located around 23rd Street and Classen Boulevard (near the Milk Bottle Building). **Lido Restaurant** (2518 N. Military Ave. #101, 405/521-1902, www.lidorestaurantokc.com, 10:30am-9pm Mon.-Thurs., 10:30am-9:30pm Fri., 11am-9:30pm Sat., $7-14) blends Vietnamese and colonial French dishes. Vermicelli bowls are loaded with fresh mint, bean sprouts, carrots, and peanuts. The Pho, pork in a clay pot, and spring rolls with peanut sauce are delicious.

If you're mad about Pho, you must try **Pho Lien Hoa** (901 NW 23rd St., 405/521-8087, 9am-9pm daily, $5-10). This no-frills, cash-only restaurant has set the benchmark for the best Pho in the state with generous portions, fresh veggies, perfectly cooked noodles. The broth is pure bliss, with tons of flavor but not too much salt.

Classen Grill (5124 N. Classen Blvd., 405/824-0428, 8am-2pm Mon.-Fri., 7am-3pm Sat.-Sun., $5-10) is a hole-in-the wall joint with funky decor and some of the best pancakes around. The "Elvis" has cinnamon pancakes with peanut butter and bananas, while the "Biscuit Debris" has gravy, melted cheddar, and sausage. Finish it off with freshly squeezed orange juice.

Cattlemen's Steakhouse (1309 S. Agnew Ave., 405/236-0416, www.cattlemensrestaurant.com, 11am-8:30pm Tues.-Sat., $10-35) is the oldest continuously operating restaurant in Oklahoma City. The restaurant opened in 1910 in Stockyards City and served thousands of people who worked in the stockyards; during Prohibition, they brewed their own liquid libations. Gene Autry, John Wayne, and Reba McEntire have stopped in for meals. Of course, the featured menu item is steak, but it doesn't really matter what you order—the history of this place makes it worth it.

Pinkitzel Cupcakes & Candy (1309 S. Agnew Ave., 405/236-0416, www.pinkitzel.com, 11am-8:30pm Tues.-Sat., $10-35) is a combination boutique gift store, bakery, and candy-store extravaganza. This sugar-filled wonderland sells taffy, pralines, truffles, lollipops, and freshly baked cupcakes. Wash them down with pink lemonade, espresso, or hot cocoa flavored with peppermint, salted caramel, or bacon. The store name means tickled pink; it's a play on the words pink and *kitzel* (Yiddish for tickle.)

Ann's Chicken Fry Steakhouse (4106 Northwest 39th St., 405/943-8915, 11am-8:30pm Tues.-Sat., $6-12) has perfected the art of the sizzle, deep-frying everything from steak, okra, and green tomatoes to olives and even peaches. Nothing here escapes a golden bath of oil.

◈ Detour: Lake Overholser Bridge

The 1925 Lake Overholser Bridge was a critical link for Route 66 travelers until the 1950s. Once the volume of traffic increased and tail-finned cars got heavier, a newer, wider four-lane highway was built just north of the bridge. Today the bridge carries local traffic, but it's also a cool reminder of old Route 66.

As you leave Oklahoma City on NW 39th Expressway (and before you cross the North Canadian River, about 0.5-mile west of North Council Road), keep an eye out for this old bridge south of the highway.

◈ Back on 66

From Oklahoma City, head west on Route 66 (NW 39th Street) for about 10 miles,

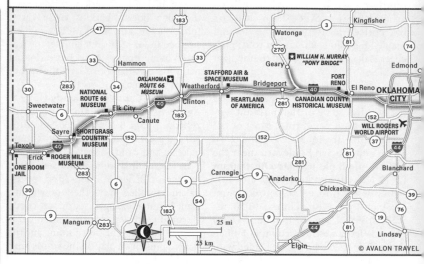

Oklahoma City to Texola

© AVALON TRAVEL

passing Yukon. After 13 miles, Route 66 curves north and turns into South Rock Island Avenue.

El Reno

Route 66 brought a lot of life to El Reno. By the mid-1930s, there were 10 hotels, 8 tourist camps, 24 grocery stores, 27 barber shops, 20 gas stations, and 31 restaurants. When the railroad came through in the 1890s, the town became a major crossroads for the north-south and east-west transcontinental lines railway lines. By the 1950s, the railroad industry employed about 1,300 people in El Reno until the railroad went bankrupt in 1980. The railway yards now sit vacant on the north side of town.

◈ Route 66 through El Reno

Drive north on South Rock Island Avenue and turn left (west) at East Wade Street. After a few blocks, turn right (north) on Highway 81 (Choctaw Avenue), then take the next left (west) on Sunset Drive.

Sights

The **Canadian County Historical Museum** (300 S. Grand Ave. 405/262-5121, 10am-5pm Wed.-Sat., 1pm-5pm Sun., free) is located on the 98th Meridian, the border site where the eastern lands were open for settlement. (The western side of the border was settled by Arapaho and Cheyenne tribes.) The museum has a jail, barn, church, one-room schoolhouse and fully restored depot with memorabilia, including a Red Cross canteen from 1918. The on-site cabin was General Sheridan's headquarters and is the oldest structure in county.

Food

For a truly authentic Oklahoma experience, don't drive through El Reno without trying an onion burger. In the 1920s, onion burgers were born out of economic necessity brought on by the Depression. To stretch the meat farther, razor-thin ribbons of onions were grilled and then added to the ground beef with a flat 90-degree spatula resembling a brick trowel tool. As the onions caramelized, they formed a tasty crust on the patty. People were pleasantly surprised to find the cost-saving measure actually improved the flavor and texture of the burger.

The onion burger captures the spirit of Route 66: taking an everyday item and turning it into something great. Three restaurants in El Reno specialize in onion burgers, but it might be hard to choose just one—they all serve excellent burgers. Fortunately, they're all within a block of each other.

Johnnie's Grill (301 S. Rock Island Ave., 405/262-4721, 6am-8pm Mon.-Sat., 11am-8pm Sun., $3-7) is the largest of the three. It's more utilitarian, with booths and tables, and resembles a fast food joint.

Robert's Grill (300 S. Bickford Ave., 405/262-1262, 6am-9pm Mon.-Sat., 11am-7pm Sun., $3-6) is a classic hole in the wall that dates back to the birth of the Mother Road. This tiny place has no tables and only 14 stools; they also serve a great breakfast.

Sid's Diner (300 S. Choctaw Ave., 405/262-7757, 7am-8pm Mon.-Sat., $5-10) is roomier than Robert's, with historic pictures lining the walls and decoupage on the counter and the tables.

◆ Back on 66

The 18-mile segment between El Reno and Hydro is where the road opens up and the vast expanse of the American West begins to emerge. In the 1930s, the standard road width was 20 feet; in 1935, this segment was straightened and shortened to create a more direct route. The new road bypassed Bridgetown, which became a ghost town as a result.

To take the 1926 alignment, leave El Reno driving west on Route 66 (Sunset Drive). As the road begins to curve south, take a right on East 1020 Road, which is the two-lane alignment of Route 66. Fort Reno is a few hundred feet past the turn.

◆ Detour: Fort Reno

The eastern part of El Reno opened up for settlement in the Land Run of 1889; the western section was designated as Cheyenne and Arapaho land. To monitor the situation, **Fort Reno** (7101 W. Cheyenne St., 405/262-3987, www.fortreno.org, 10am-4pm daily, $2) was established as an Army post in 1847. The Buffalo Soldiers, an all-Black regiment of the Army, were also stationed here. Later, during World War II, Fort Reno became an internment camp for 1,300 German prisoners of war. Seventy German and Italian soldiers are buried in the western part of the cemetery.

Fort Reno is located four miles west of El Reno, near I-40 (Exit 119). From the pre-1930s alignment of Route 66, it is just after the turn off Sunset Drive. Note: Entering Fort Reno into GPS may take you to the wrong place; be sure to consult a map.

◆ Back on 66

From Fort Reno, continue west on East 1020 Road. In about four miles, turn right (north) on U.S. 270 (North Calumet Rd.). Drive 4.5 miles, turn left and continue following I-270 for 6 miles to the town of Geary.

Geary

Geary was Arapaho and Cheyenne country until 1892, when 3.5 million acres were opened to settlement by the U.S. government. Almost 80 percent of the land wasn't claimed, however, when a terrible drought lasted until 1896. Today, this rural farming community is home to a few historic buildings.

◆ Route 66 through Geary

Route 66 enters Geary via 150th Street NW and continues 0.5 mile before heading south (left) on Broadway.

Sights

Upon entering Geary, turn right (north) on Broadway (SR-270) to see the historic **Gillespie Building** (100 E. Main St.). Built in 1903, it later became the American State Bank, which failed during the Great Depression.

Turn right on Main Street and, at the intersection of Canadian and NE Boulevard, is an old **water trough** that was used by horses and visitors who came through here in the early 1900s.

✛ Back on 66

Drive south on Broadway Avenue, which turns into U.S. 281. In 4 miles, turn left (southwest) to follow Highway 8/U.S. 281. Drive 2.5 miles, and as you approach the Canadian River, you'll see one of the most significant bridges on Route 66.

★ William H. Murray "Pony Bridge"

The 1933 **William H. Murray Bridge** (what locals call the "Pony Bridge") is the longest truss bridge on Route 66, with a span of nearly 4,000 feet. The bridge got the nickname for its 38 pony trusses, each 100 feet long. The camelback design has a curved arch that makes the bridge strong and light. At the time, it was an engineering marvel. At the west end of the bridge is where a scene in the 1940 film *The Grapes of Wrath* was shot.

✛ Back on 66

Head south on U.S. 281. When the road begins to curve right (west), stay straight to continue on Route 66 (don't follow Highway 8). The next town is Hydro, about 10 miles west.

top to bottom: Milk Bottle Building, Oklahoma City; Pinkitzel Cupcakes & Candy, Oklahoma City; National Route 66 Museum, Elk City

Hydro

Sights
Nutopia
Nutopia Nuts 'N More (206 W. Main St., 405-663-2330, www.nutopianuts.com, 10:30am-4:30pm Mon.-Fri.) has been supplying critical road-trip munchies to Route 66 travelers since 1942. They sell every kind of peanut you can imagine—salted, raw, ballpark, shelled, naked, Spanish, and spicy—as well as peanut butter, peanut brittle, pecans, and candy.

Nutopia is located less than a mile north of Route 66 on Highway 58 (Arapaho Ave.) and Main Street.

Lucille's Service Station
Two-story **Lucille's Service Station** was built in 1929. In 1941, Lucille Hamons bought the station with her husband and made it a celebrated stop on Route 66. Then, in 1971, Route 66 moved to I-40. Despite the hardships she faced, Lucille stuck it out, working here seven days a week for 59 years until her passing in 2000. She was stubborn, resilient, and a survivor, and people called her the "Mother of the Mother Road."

Lucille's is only one of two stations like it on Route 66 in Oklahoma. Though the station is no longer operating, you can still admire the two large, distinctive, tapered piers that support the property, with its out-thrust porch, exposed rafter tails, and overhanging eaves in the Craftsman style. Vintage gas pumps sit outside, and the owner's living quarters were upstairs. Lucille's is located 0.5 mile west of Highway 58 to the right (north) of Route 66.

❖ Back on 66
Drive west on Route 66 (the I-40 frontage road) for 5 miles to Weatherford.

Weatherford

Soon after Route 66 came through Main Street in Weatherford, the Works Progress Administration funded the construction of the National Guard Armory. By the 1960s, the company 3M employed many of the folks who lived here. Today, Weatherford has one of the largest wind farms in Oklahoma.

❖ Route 66 through Weatherford
Route 66 enters Weatherford on Main Street and heads south. Turn left (south) on North Washington Avenue, and then take an immediate right (west) onto Main Street/Business 40 through downtown.

Sights
Stafford Air & Space Museum
The **Stafford Air & Space Museum** (3000 Logan Rd., 580/772-5871, www.staffordmuseum.com, 9am-5pm Mon.-Sat., 1pm-5pm Sun., $7) is named after astronaut Thomas P. Stafford, who is from Weatherford. Stafford piloted Gemini VI, commanded Apollo, and received a Congressional Space Medal of Honor. The museum that bears his name has 3,500-square feet of actual rocket displays, as well as numerous articles on loan from the Smithsonian such as space food, survival items, and a Gemini flight suit.

From Route 66 (Main St.), turn right (north on Jim Cobb Dr.). The museum is a few blocks away.

Heartland of America Museum
The **Heartland of America Museum** (1600 S. Frontage Rd., 580/774-2212, www.oklahomaheartlandmuseum.com, 9am-5pm Tues.-Fri., $6) is a local history museum that gives visitors a glimpse into small-town America from the late 1800s through the 1950s. Several artifacts are on display—a collection of vintage cars, wedding dresses, and

aprons—and there are more than 30 exhibits, including a well-stocked general store, diner, pharmacy, a school house, and s blacksmith shop.

Doc's Longhorn Trading Post
Stop at **Doc's Longhorn Trading Post** (1511 E. Main St., 580/772-2277, 9am-5pm Tues.-Sat.) for unique vintage furniture, home decor, glassware, Navajo weavings, flatware, turquoise jewelry, and cowboy collectibles like old spurs, tack, and saddles. Also on-site is the artwork of Indian artist Robert Redbird and more than 50 alabaster sculptures by local Arapaho, Kiowa, and Cheyenne artists.

Weatherford Wind Energy Center
In the midst of oil and gas country, it's refreshing to see a field of wind-loving turbines. These enormous wind turbines generate energy for more than 44,000 homes. Each turbine stands 262-feet tall with blades that are 122-feet long. To see a turbine blade up close, visit the **Weatherford Wind Energy Center** (522 W. Rainey Ave., http://cityofweatherford. com) across from City Hall. The outdoor display panel includes information about the wind energy industry and how these turbines work.

Food
Tired of burgers, shakes, and fries? Then the tasty Mexican food at **Casa Soto** (115 SW Main St., 580/772-0232, http://casa-soto-dgo.com, 11am-9pm Mon.-Thurs., 11am-10pm Fri.-Sat., $6-13) will hit the spot. This immaculate setting serves good home-cooked and freshly prepared food from "Mama's" family recipes at reasonable prices. The locals love it.

✥ Back on 66
Drive west on Main Street leaving Weatherford. Turn left (south) on 4th Street (Highway 54); the road curves right and heads west for about 6 miles. Turn right (north) at N2330 Road and take the next left (west) at East 1030 Road. In 2 miles, turn left (south) on N2310 Road. The Cherokee Trading Post is on the left (east) side of the road before you reach I-40.

Cherokee Trading Post

After gold was discovered in Georgia in 1829, an estimated 16,000 Cherokees were forced at gunpoint to leave their homes and *walk* to Oklahoma. More than 4,000 died. The Cherokee Nation rebuilt itself in Oklahoma, and you can learn how at the **Cherokee Trading Post** (23107 N. Frontage Rd., 888/572-0001, www.cherokeegifts.com, 7am-10pm daily). The family-owned business offers a wealth of knowledge about Cherokee history, including a list of the Cherokee alphabet with a pronunciation guide, and sells clothing, knives, jewelry, and other accessories. This is a great place for a one-of-a-kind memento of the Mother Road.

✥ Back on 66
Drive west on the north I-40 Frontage Road for 3 miles, then join Business 40 into the town of Clinton.

✥ Side Trip: Indiahoma

Wichita Mountains Wildlife Refuge (32 Refuge Headquarters, Indiahoma, 580/429-3222, www.fws.gov/refuge/ Wichita_Mountains, free) is the perfect place to rejuvenate the road-weary soul. Established in 1901 with almost 60,000 acres of wilderness, the refuge is home to more than 250 species, including bald eagles, whooping cranes, black-tail prairie dogs, and lizards. In 1907, 15 bison were brought here from the New York Bronx Zoo; today, there are 650. There are also about 700 elk and 300 longhorns. This wild and rugged landscape invites hiking, rock climbing, biking, fishing, and camping.

Exhibits at the **visitor center** (Hwy. 115 and Hwy. 49, 9am-5pm daily) include dioramas, art, sculptures, taxidermy, and an auditorium. Hiking maps, books, and park pamphlets are available in the gift shop. The **Doris Campground** (gates open 8am-10pm Sun.-Thurs., 8am-11pm Fri.-Sat. Apr.-Oct.; 8am-8pm Sun.-Thurs., 8am-10pm Fri.-Sat. Nov.-Mar., $10-20), located west of the visitor center, has drinking water, fire grills, picnic tables, tent sites, a shower/restroom facility, and electoral hookups for RVs. Campsites are first-come, first-served, and backcountry camping is by reservation/permit only.

The Wichita Mountain Refuge is a two-hour drive south of Weatherford. From Route 66 west of Weatherford, take Highway 54 south for 15 miles. Turn right (west) on Highway 152 and continue 7 miles. Turn left (south) on Highway 54 and drive 38 miles. Turn left (east) on Highway 49 to enter the refuge. Arrive with plenty of gas and observe posted speed limits in order to protect wildlife (and yourself).

Clinton

Cotton was the leading crop in Clinton's early years. About 10 years after Route 66 came through Clinton, the Swift meat packing company (later Bar-S) became the largest employer here, with 500 workers. Clinton's claim to fame today is that it's home to one of the most popular Route 66 museums on the Mother Road and has one of the oldest trading posts in the state.

◈ Route 66 through Clinton

Enter Clinton via Business 40 and turn left (south) on 4th Street (U.S. 183). Turn right (west) on Opal Avenue, then turn left (south) on 10th Avenue, which turns into Neptune Drive. After about 1 mile, turn right (west) onto Commerce Road.

Sights
Mohawk Lodge Indian Store

The **Mohawk Lodge Indian Store** (22702 Route 66 N, 580/323-2360, www.clintonokla.org, 9am-5:30pm Mon.-Fri., 9am-5pm Sat.) originally opened in a different location in 1892; it moved to its current location in Clinton in 1940. The store was a place where Cheyenne women made and sold their handmade wares. Today, it doubles as a museum and store. Historical artifacts and antique photos display its incredible history, and tribal treasures are sold across the same counter used in 1892. Items include everything from tanned hides to handwoven blankets and handmade pottery, and everything is authentic.

McLain Rogers Park

McLain Rogers Park (10th St. and Bass Rogers Dr., 580/323-4572, dawn-dusk daily, free) sits on 12 acres and was home to several Works Progress Administration projects. During the 1930s and '40s, Route 66 road-trippers picnicked here, swam in the Olympic-size swimming pool, and played in the children's park. Today, there's also a large amphitheater, an 18-hole miniature golf course, and a distinctive Art Deco entrance with zigzag brickwork and a neon sign.

★ Oklahoma Route 66 Museum

Oklahoma Route 66 Museum (2229 W. Gary Blvd., 580/323-7866, www.route66.org, 9am-7pm Mon.-Sat., 1pm-6pm Sun. Memorial Day-Labor Day; 9am-5pm Mon.-Sat., 1pm-5pm Sun. Labor Day-Memorial Day, $4) is one of the best museums dedicated to the Mother Road. Operated by the Oklahoma Historical Society, it is filled with exhibits, vintage cars, and an indoor "drive-in theatre." Best-selling author and storyteller Michael Wallis narrates the tumultuous history of the fabled road, tracing the major cultural and social changes that have taken place over the past 80 years.

The museum is a great place to learn more about Cyrus Avery's role in creating Route 66 and the impact of the numerous racial and class migrations that happened along the Mother Road. There's also a fully restored pre-fab **Valentine Diner** that dates back to the late 1940s, with a grill, counter, and stools. Don't miss the well-stocked gift shop with books, videos, scale model cars, dishware, and memorabilia.

The Route 66 Museum is one mile west of Route 66. From Route 66 (SR-183), turn right (west) onto Modelle Avenue and turn left (south) on Business 40 (West Gary Blvd). The museum is on the right.

Food

For a sophisticated and memorable meal, eat at the **White Dog Hill Restaurant** (22901 Old 66 Frontage Rd., 580/323-0059, 5:30pm-9:30pm Wed.-Sat., $9-30). The steaks are popular, but it's not just the food that makes this place special—the view, vibe, and rustic ambiance add another dimension to the experience. The restaurant is housed in a native red-stone clubhouse that used to be the Clinton Country Club, with a large deck that has a perfect view of soul-stirring sunsets. The restaurant fills early in the evening, so call ahead and make reservations.

To get to the White Dog, head west on the I-40 Frontage Road about 3 miles east of Clinton. Turn right (north) on N2290 Road; at the fork immediately after the turn, go right. The restaurant is about 900 feet up the road. (Look for an old olive-green and buttercream-yellow Ford truck out front.) Note: Do not use GPS to find the White Dog Hill Restaurant.

In the 1970s, Jiggs Botchlett opened **Jiggs Smokehouse** (22203 N. Frontage Rd., 580/323-5641, www.jiggssmokehouse.com, 11am-7pm Tues.-Fri., 11am-5pm Sat., $6-10) as a retail outlet for his popular smoked turkeys, ham, and cheeses. Today, the family-run restaurant specializes in sandwiches stacked high with hickory-smoked meats and slathered in barbecue sauce. The Wooly Burger weighs in at 31 ounces of smoked ham, summer sausage, relish, and cheddar cheese. This place is truly for carnivores—the only veggies on offer are lettuce, tomatoes, onions, and pickles—and sells about 4,000 pounds of jerky a year.

◆ Back on 66

Leaving Clinton, drive west on Commerce Road, which becomes South Frontage Road. In less than 5 miles, turn right (north) on N2170 Road (Exit 57 near I-40) and cross the freeway. Turn left (west) at North Frontage Road and drive past the town of **Foss** to Exit 50. Turn left to go back across the freeway, then head west (right) on South Frontage Road. Drive 3 miles west to Canute.

Canute

◆ Route 66 through Canute

South Frontage Road becomes Old U.S. Hwy. 66 through Canute. Continue west to the intersection of Main Street.

Sights

As you drive about 10 blocks through the small community of Canute, there are a few roadside sights on the east side of town. Located next to the cemetery as you enter Canute from the east is **Oklahoma's first state park,** built on Route 66 by the Works Progress Administration.

Near Main Street, the mid-century neon signs of the derelict **Cotton Boll** and **Washita Motels** still stand as fading remnants of the roadside, though the motels are no longer open.

On the northwest corner of Main Street and Route 66 is the 1930s **Canute Service Station,** built in a Pueblo Deco style with a gabled roof and canopy sporting triangular pediments and decorated with red diamonds.

Located in an alley north of Scheidel Avenue (at Main Street) is an old **jailhouse** that dates to 1918.

On Route 66, about three blocks west of the Canute Station, is the abandoned **Kupka's Service Station** with a canopy whose signature, curve-hugging corners exemplify the traditional 1930s Streamline Moderne style.

⚐ Back on 66

From Canute, head west on Route 66 for 6 miles to Elk City.

Elk City

Before Elk City was established in 1901, cattle drives from Texas to Kansas came through here, making it a popular place to stop. By 1918, Elk City had an ice plant, two flour mills, and two broom factories. By the 1930s, nine cotton gins were in operation and the first cooperative community hospital opened; local farmers could pay $50 for one share of stock, then pay $25 a year for free medical care for their immediate family.

When the U.S. Highway 66 Association held its annual convention here in 1931, more than 20,000 people came. After Route 66 was rerouted, Elk City didn't suffer like other towns bypassed by the Mother Road; it remained busy thanks to its rich history in the oil and gas industry. (Elk City's biggest claim to fame is that it was considered the natural gas capitol of the world.) Today, the biggest Route 66 attraction is the Old Town Museum complex, which houses the National Route 66 Museum.

⚐ Route 66 through Elk City

Route 66 enters Elk City via North Van Buren Avenue, then dips south before curving west on 3rd Street (Business 40), the main drag through town.

Sights
National Route 66 Museum

The **National Route 66 Museum** (2717 W. 3rd St., 580/225-6266, www.visitelkcity.com/museums, 9am-5pm Mon.-Sat., 2pm-5pm Sun., closed Sun. Jan-Apr., $5), in the Old Town Museum complex, offers travel exhibits and memories of the Mother Road along with mock-ups of a chapel, bank, general store, doctor's office, grist mill, and an opera house. The 6,500-square foot museum takes visitors though the eight states on the Mother Road and features a glimpse into the lives of early settlers and pioneers who lived and worked on Route 66. Learn through historical documents, narratives, and artifacts how their livelihood was impacted by the many changes that happened over the decades.

Casa Grande Hotel

The 1928 **Casa Grande Hotel** (103 E. 3rd St.) was the site of one the first meetings of the U.S. Highway 66 Association. Back in its heyday, the Casa Grande was advertised as the largest and only fireproof hotel between Amarillo and Oklahoma City. Today the building is closed, however there are talks of renovating the structure into apartments.

Parker Drilling Rig

Located behind the Casa Grande Hotel is the **Parker Drilling Rig # 114**. At 179 feet (the approximate height of a 22-story building), this is the world's tallest, non-operating oil rig. The Parker Drilling Rig was built in the mid-1960s to drill shafts in order to test-detonate atomic bombs underground; it was later used for oil and gas drilling.

Hedlund Motor Company

The **Hedlund Motor Company** (206 S. Main St.) was established in 1913 and is the second oldest Ford dealership in Oklahoma. The 1918 building, a striking stucco Mission Revival with red clay tiles, is located on Main Street, about two blocks south of Route 66.

Food

A charming ladies-who-lunch tea room, the **Country Dove Tea Room** (610 W. 3rd St., 580/225-7028, 9am-5:30pm Mon.-Sat., $8-14) is located in a renovated 1920s house on Route 66. In addition to tea, the savory chicken and avocado croissant, creamy vegetable soup, and French silk pie are fabulous. They're also known for their lemon Jello dessert, a thin layer of Jello blended with cream cheese and pears on a bed of lettuce.

Family owned **Lupe's Mexican Restaurant** (905 N. Main St., 580/225-7109, 11am-9pm Mon.-Sat., 11am-2pm Sun., $6-17) serves up tasty and top-quality Tex-Mex dishes; the crispy chile rellenos and chimichangas are something to write home about. It's located just a few blocks north of Route 66 on Main Street.

◈ Back on 66

Leave Elk City heading west on Business 40. Soon after passing Highway 34 (about 4 miles from Elk City), take the next right and then a quick left to North Frontage Road. Follow it for about 10 miles to I-40 (near Exit 25) and turn right (west) on Business 40, which leads into the town of Sayre.

◈ Side Trip: Flying W Guest Ranch

The **Flying W Guest Ranch** (10874 N. 1920 Rd., 580/660-1033, www.flyingwguestranch.com) is a 500-acre dude ranch, Old West town, and the largest bison kill site ever found in the southern plains. Between 300 BC and AD 300, spear-wielding hunters herded an estimated 800 bison over this 30-foot sandstone cliff. Today, archeologists from the University of Oklahoma are excavating their remains. An accurate re-creation

Beckham County Courthouse, Sayre

of an 1880s general store is also on-site; historical guides will walk you through the store and discuss the primitive medications and healing herbs used during the period.

To reach the ranch, leave Elk City heading southwest on Route 66. Turn right (west) on Highway 6 and drive almost 5 miles to North 1920 Road. Turn right (north), and the ranch will be about 2 miles up the road.

Sayre

Sayre once served as a major shipping point for wheat, cotton, corn, and livestock; the town promoted itself as the place where the "Spirit of the West is still alive." By the 1930s, there were five oil companies and a gasoline plant keeping people employed. Today, a giant, rusted, grain elevator by the railroad tracks near downtown is a reminder of Sayre's rich agricultural history.

✦ Route 66 though Sayre

The Mother Road enters via Business 40 and turns left (south) on 4th Street (U.S. 283). Route 66 continues through the historic downtown district.

Sights

As you head into town, look for the **Western Motel** (315 NE Hwy. 66), which has an extraordinary vintage yellow-and-blue neon sign with a distinctive typeface and a neon cactus. There's also a **WPA Pedestrian Tunnel** (4th and Elm Sts.), built to help pedestrians safely cross under the steady stream of traffic on Route 66.

Beckham County Courthouse

The three-story brick **Beckham County Courthouse** (302 E. Main St., 580/928-3330, 8am-4pm Mon.-Fri., free) was built in 1911 and is one of the few domed courthouses in Oklahoma. The traditional neoclassical style was designed to impress railroad travelers. (It might look familiar: The building was featured in the 1940 film *The Grapes of Wrath*.)

WPA Land Run Mural

Located inside the post office is a 1940 **WPA Mural** (201 N. 4th St., 8:30am-4:30pm Mon.-Fri., 10am-noon Sat., free) by Vance Kirkland. The mural depicts the 1887 Land Run, with whips cracking, horses rearing, and people being trampled when the Cheyenne and Arapaho land was opened up to settlement.

Shortgrass Country Museum

Located in the former Rock Island railroad depot, the **Shortgrass Country Museum** (106 E. Poplar Ave., 580/928-5757, 2pm-4:30pm Tues.-Fri., donations welcome) documents the history of the Cheyenne tribes and the arrival of settlers.

Sayre City Park

Sayre City Park (Hwy. 283 S., 580/928-2260, www.sayreok.net, dawn-dusk daily, free) is home to two WPA projects: a 1940 red-stone, pueblo-style pool house and a red-stone rock wall, both frequented by early Route 66 travelers. It also offers plenty of amenities, including a golf course, miniature golf, tennis, basketball, and volleyball courts, and an RV campground with hookups and a dump station. The park is located 1 mile south of Sayre off Business 40.

◆ Back on 66

From Sayre, head south on Highway 283. In one mile turn right (west) on BK Q, then left (south) on BK 21. Drive south and turn right (west) on North Frontage Road before reaching I-40. Drive west through the town of **Hext**. Route 66 crosses under I-40 and continues south. In less than 2 miles, the road curves west into the town of Erick.

Erick

Erick sits right on the edge of the high plains of the Texas Panhandle. Route 66 passed through the north end of Erick, which was lined with cafes, service stations, and motels. Today, it's just a quiet western Oklahoma town lined with old brick buildings, and mostly known for being the home of Roger Miller, the singer and songwriter of the finger-snapping tune, "King of the Road."

Sights

As you enter Erick on the east side of town, keep an eye out for a graveyard of rusting cars and windmills. (They're located on private property, but are visible from the road.)

Roger Miller Museum

The **Roger Miller Museum** (101 S. Sheb Wooley Ave., 580/526-3833, www. rogermillermuseum.com, 10am-5pm Wed.-Sat., 1pm-5pm Sun., $3) is a charming tribute to the man who wrote

one of most popular road songs of all time. "King of the Road" was written in 1964 and was an instant crossover hit on the Billboard charts. The tune has been covered by everyone from Dean Martin to The Chipmunks. The museum gives visitors a glimpse into Miller's life growing up in western Oklahoma and his life as a celebrity. His Honda motorcycle, lots of photos, and some of his musical instruments are on display.

Sandhills Curiosity Shop

Sandhills Curiosity Shop (201 S. Sheb Wooley Ave.) was one of the places Pixar producers went while researching the film *Cars*; it's a good, old-fashioned junk shop with early 20th-century oak furniture, artwork, and vintage musical instruments. Owner Annabelle Russell and her husband Harley had a wacky music act called the "Mediocre Music Makers." They wrote more than 300 songs and performed them for anyone who stopped by. Annabelle passed away in 2014 after a three-year battle with cancer; as of this writing, the shop has closed, but it is still worth seeing. The building's exterior is covered with old road signs and vintage advertisements. Stop by and pay your respects to an amazing woman who entertained thousands of Route 66 travelers from all over the world.

The Sandhills Shop is one block south of Route 66 near 3rd Street and Sheb Wooley Avenue.

◆ Back on 66

Leave Erick traveling west on Roger Miller Boulevard and follow Route 66 (Business 40) for about 7 miles to the lonely border town of Texola.

Texola

This is one of those unreal places where a shell of what once-was haunts the roadside. In 1910, the census recorded 361 people living in Texola; the 2013 census estimated a population of 38. Driving through, you may not see a single soul.

As Route 66 runs west through town, look for a 1910 **one-room cinderblock jail,** a block north on Main Street. It's a solid, tomb-like building; it's said the walls continue several feet underground so that prisoners couldn't dig their way out. Other abandoned buildings nearby may have been a school, a gas station, and a garage.

Despite being a near-ghost town, some life still percolates in this place. **Tumbleweeds Grill and Country Store** (Route 66 and Oklahoma Ave., 580/526-3914, www.tumbleweedstexola.com, 7am-7pm daily, $4-9) sits tucked inside the Water Whole #2 building. You'll find friendly service and simple food in a clean environment.

As you head west out of town, look on the south side of the highway. Printed on the side of an abandoned metal corrugated building is one of the best signs you'll see on the road:

THERE'S NO OTHER PLACE
LIKE THIS PLACE
ANYWHERE NEAR THIS PLACE
SO THIS MUST BE THE PLACE

Mediate on that as you drive straight into Texas.

Texas

Following Route 66 through the Texas panhandle, you'll drive past skillet-flat plains, huge rusted grain silos, and rickety oil rigs that dot the horizon.

COLORADO

KANSAS

OKLAHOMA

NM

Adrian

Vega

Groom

Glenrio

Amarillo

McLean

Shamrock

TEXAS

Cadillac Ranch

Texas

© AVALON TRAVEL

Texas isn't just big—it's gi-normous. Anyone who's driven I-10 across the Lone Star State knows that you can roll on for what feels like forever.

Fortunately, this is not the case for Route 66 travelers. Texas actually has the second-shortest Route 66 alignment. (Kansas claims first place with only 13 miles of the Mother Road.) And although Texas is only the runner-up, driving through the "Panhandle"—the rectangular outcrop that sits atop the state—is not necessarily a quick jaunt either.

Despite Texas's reputation as a rough-and-tumble state, bursting with ego and pride, the Panhandle is an out-of-the-way region with its own pace and attitude. Most Route 66 towns are lined up along a quiet, lonely, two-lane highway and hold fewer than 500 residents. Large Texas cities like Dallas or Houston are nowhere near Route 66; Amarillo, the largest city in the Panhandle, is about one-third of the size of Austin. This is a quiet, dare-I-say humble area of Texas.

Route 66 originally stretched 178 miles through Texas; today, about 150 miles are actually drivable. Most of Route 66 lies under the I-40 Frontage Road. The road trip through Texas will follow I-40 between Jericho and Alanreed as well as the last 18 miles as you exit the state from Adrian to Glenrio. But don't fret—even this frontage road still offers a rural, middle-of-nowhere feel.

Planning Your Time

Driving through the Texas Panhandle is a straight shot and can be done in a **one day.** Route 66 sights start to appear in Shamrock and McLean, but you can push onward to spend the night in Amarillo. The next day, it's a little more than 100 miles for the final stretch to New Mexico.

Driving Considerations

Route 66 runs alongside I-40, so if time is a factor, it's easy to jump on the freeway as needed. Though you'll be passing through several small towns, most of the gas stations are defunct and nonoperational. Plan to **fill up the tank in Shamrock;** the next major gas stop will be **Amarillo**, approximately 90 miles west.

Highlights

★ **Tower Station and U-Drop Inn Café, Shamrock:** This former Conoco station is landmark Americana—and one of the most beautifully restored art deco buildings on Route 66 (page 176).

★ **Devil's Rope Museum and Old Route 66**

Museum, McLean: This quirky museum and captivating tribute to barbed wire has more than 450 different examples on display (page 178).

★ **Palo Duro Canyon State Park, Canyon:** This second-largest canyon in the United States is considered

the "Grand Canyon of Texas" (page 181).

★ **Cadillac Ranch, Amarillo:** This surreal and powerful public art installation consists of vintage Cadillacs buried nose deep in a wheat field (page 184).

Getting There

Starting Points
Car
I-40 enters Texas near the town of Shamrock and is the only major east-west highway through the Panhandle. Leaving Texola, Oklahoma, head northwest on SR-30 and drive until the road turns into the southern frontage road. From this point, it's a straight shot into Shamrock.

Highway 27 runs south from Amarillo to Lubbock; beyond that, there is no major north-south U.S. interstate nearby.

Car Rental
Budget (10800 Airport Blvd., 806/335-2812, www.budget.com, 8am-midnight daily) operates out of the Rick Husband Amarillo International Airport. **Enterprise** (3001 W. 26th Ave., 806/353-9227, 7:30am-6pm Mon.-Fri., 9am-2pm Sat.) is centrally located in Amarillo, less than 2 miles south of Route 66.

Air
The only major airport in the Texas Panhandle is the **Rick Husband Amarillo International Airport** (10801 Airport Blvd., Amarillo, 806/335-1671, http://airport.amarillo.gov), named after a NASA astronaut who died on the *Columbia* space shuttle mission. The airport is about 10 miles east of downtown Amarillo and served by Southwest, United, and American Airlines with nonstop service to Dallas-Fort Worth, Denver, Houston, and Las Vegas.

Train and Bus
The Texas Panhandle has no Amtrak service. Amarillo has a **Greyhound** (700 S. Tyler St., 806/374-5371, www.greyhound.com, daily 24 hours) bus station, with service throughout the United States.

Shamrock

Shamrock, Texas was named after an Irish Immigrant for both luck and courage. Comanche and Kiowa herded bison here until the Anglos arrived in the late 1800s. Eventually the bison were replaced with sheep and cattle. By the time Route 66 came through in the late 1920s, agriculture and oil were the two biggest industries. About a decade later, Route 66 was paved and the iconic U-Drop Inn was built.

Sights
★ Tower Station and U-Drop Inn Café
Tower Station and U-Drop Inn Café (101 E. 12th St., www.shamrockedc.org/u-drop-inn, free) was the first commercial business to open when Route 66 came through Shamrock; it was the only café within 100 miles. This art deco marvel was built in 1936 with glazed brick, zigzag motifs, neon light, and a four-sided obelisk. The stucco towers are decked

---

Best Restaurants

★ **Golden Light Café and Cantina, Amarillo:** Established in 1946, this is the oldest restaurant in Amarillo (page 183).

★ **The Stockyard Cafe, Amarillo:** Chow down with the cowboys in the Amarillo stockyards (page 183).

★ **Rooster's, Vega:** Look for the large sheet-metal rooster outside to find this hole-in-the-wall restaurant serving great enchiladas (page 185).

★ **MidPoint Café, Adrian:** Stop for a photo op and a slice of "ugly pie" at the geographic midpoint of Route 66 (page 186).

out with gold-glazed terra-cotta tiles and the largest pillar in the front rises nearly 100 feet above with geometric detailing crowned with a signature metal "tulip" on top. The entire site is a treasure. It's arguably one of the most architecturally significant buildings of its kind and one of the few art deco buildings like this from the 1930s. Most Depression-era cafés were not this decorative.

Today, the U-Drop is the city's **Chamber of Commerce** and a **Route 66 Visitor Center** (806/256-2501, 8am-5pm daily) with a gift shop inside. If you show up at night, you're in for another treat—the lit green neon is fabulous. Tower Station was featured in the animated film *Cars* as the inspiration for Ramone's body shop. A replica is also at Carsland in Disneyland. It's truly unlike any roadside café and, what's more incredible, is that it's in the middle of Nowhere, Texas.

Magnolia Gas Station

A 1930s-era **Magnolia Gas Station** (204 N. Madden St. at 2nd St.) has been restored, with three tall gravity-feed gas pumps and a cool sign with two signature flying red Pegasus' on the front.

Pioneer West Museum

Next to the Magnolia Station, the **Pioneer West Museum** (204 N. Madden St., 806/256-3941, www.shamrocktexas. net/museum, 9am-noon and 1pm-5pm Mon.-Fri., free) is housed on two floors of the former 1925 Reynolds Hotel. Approximately 25 rooms showcase the culture and history of the Great Plains, including vintage weapons, cowboy exhibits, old farm and ranching equipment, and a pioneer kitchen.

The 1910 **Bernice Zeigler** house is part of the Pioneer West Museum. Zeigler was one of the only doctors to serve the community during both world wars, and he had an operating room in his office. His medical tools, desk, and operating table are all preserved and on display. To reach the house, head west on Route 66 and turn left (south) on U.S. 83. Continue driving for less than 1 mile and turn left on 2nd Street. The house is one block down and on the left.

Food

For a really juicy steak, stop in at **Big Vern's Steakhouse** (200 E. 12th St., 806/256-2088, www.bigvernssteakhouse. weebly.com, 11am-10pm daily, $8-30), where the grilled zucchini, corn muffins, and beer bread are also good. This is no-frills dining, just good food in a dusty Texas town.

⏺ Back on 66

Leaving Shamrock, continue west on the south I-40 Frontage Road. In about 6 miles, you'll pass through the town of Lela. Continue driving about 15 miles to Exit 146. Turn right to cross the freeway and then turn left to drive the North Frontage Road. At the "Y", take First Street into the town of McLean.

McLean

The town of McLean was donated in 1901 by Alfred Rowe, an English rancher who traveled to and from Europe until his fateful trip on *Titanic*. When Route 66 arrived in McLean in 1927, the 22 auto-related businesses and gas stations were the primary industry that drove the local economy. McLean was also known as the "Uplift City" after the local bra factory, where women earned $1 for an eight-hour shift. Danny Douglas, who grew up in McLean, says "Many of us had small, fancy bras hanging from our car mirrors—given to us by local girlfriends who worked in the factory. I still have mine."

In its heyday, McLean had tourist cabins, car dealerships, motels, movie theaters, and restaurants—today most are gone. As Amarillo became popular, McLean struggled to stay relevant. Once Route 66 bypassed the town in 1982-1984, the nail was in the coffin.

Devil's Rope

In the late 1800s, before settlers arrived, the West was all "open range." Millions of bison, cattle, and horses freely roamed the grasslands eating everything in their path; there were so many of them that they blackened the plains. The animals trampled and destroyed crops; regular fencing couldn't corral them. So, in the 1870s fencing was a hot topic. The Land Office at the U.S. Department of Agriculture feared it would be impossible to settle the West because there was no practical solution to controlling the cattle and bison. That was … until the invention of barbed wire. Michael Kelly came up with the basic design, and then Joseph Glidden improved on it by locking the signature sharp metal barbs in place. The invention, referred to as the **"Devil's Rope,"** proved so popular that by 1876, nearly three million pounds of barbed wire were being sold annually.

The new barbed wire helped farmers maintain control over their property, but the ranchers were furious. As a result, a series of battles broke out resulting in "fence-cutting wars." It was an all-out brawl, but bison paid the ultimate price. Their numbers were already being decimated by hunters, but barbed wire played a critical role by blocking access to water and food.

Ironically, it is this isolation and lack of activity that has preserved the town as one of the more popular stops on Route 66. McLean stands today like a perfectly aged film set and something out of a time capsule.

Sights

To cruise the **Historic District,** drive Route 66 (1st St.) through Main, 2nd, and Gray Streets. While in town, be sure to check out the **1929 Phillips Petroleum** (219 Gray St.), a quaint cottage-style Tudor Revival building with a red roof, rounded orange gas pumps, and an exterior brick chimney. This was the first Phillips Petroleum filling station that opened in Texas, and it was in business for more than 50 years.

★ Devil's Rope Museum and Old Route 66 Museum

The **Devil's Rope Museum** (100 Kingsley St., 806/779-2225, www.barbwiremuseum.com, 9am-5pm Mon.-Fri., 10am-4pm Sat. Apr.-Oct., free) has the largest collection of barbed wire with 450 different types and more than 2,000 samples and a gallery of artworks made from the "Devil's Rope."

Right next door, the **Old Route 66 Museum** (100 Kingsley St., 806/779-2225, 10am-4pm Tues.-Sat. Mar.-Dec., free) housed in a former bra factory, has a modest collection of artifacts donated from Texas Route 66 businesses including road signs, advertising souvenirs, and a huge snake from the famed but now-closed Reptile Ranch. The gift shop also sells little fragments of pavement from the Mother Road.

McLean Alanreed Museum

During World War II, there was a prisoner-of-war camp right outside McLean. The **McLean Alanreed Museum** (116 N. Main St., 806/779-2731, 9am-5pm Mon.-Fri., free), located downtown, has a POW display, pioneer costumes, farming equipment, vet supplies, a fire truck, and a vintage barber shop. To visit the area of the POW camp, take I-40 east of town to Exit 146. There is a historical marker about one mile north on McCarty Street (County Line Rd.).

Accommodations and Food

The **Cactus Inn** (101 Pine St., 806/779-2346, $45-55) is a good value with basic accommodations and a friendly staff in a convenient location. Built in 1956, the inn has a great big emerald green and yellow cactus sign. The Red River Steak House is right next door.

The hand-cut rib eye at **Red River Steak House** (101 W. Hwy. 66, 806/779-8940, www.redriversteakhouse.com, 11am-9pm Tues.-Sat., $8-22) is big—just like everything else in Texas—juicy and tender. Pescatarians can opt for the hand-breaded catfish, which is full of flavor. (The restaurant is located in the building where the old Reptile Ranch used to be.)

⊕ Back on 66
Head west from McLean following 1st Street and cross Highway 273. After about 1 mile, turn left (south) on County Road 26 and follow the road as it curves east (left). Take the next right (south) to cross under I-40 and then curve right (west) to take the South Frontage Road. In 6 miles, you'll reach the town of Alanreed.

Soon after Alanreed, the **pre-1930s alignment** turns into a dirt road that leads to Jericho Gap, an area notorious for stranding motorists in the mud. Back when this dirt road was the only option, people were often forced to stay in private homes waiting to be towed out.

From Alanreed, you'll follow to the **post-1930s alignment** instead. Turn right (north) on Main Street and take I-40 West to Exit 124. Turn left (south) and drive under the freeway, then take the first right (west) to follow the South Frontage Road for 3.5 miles. At the next I-40 exit (Exit 121), take a quick left to continue following the South Frontage Road for 6 miles into Groom.

Groom

Groom was named after Colonel B. B. Groom, a cattle breeder from Kentucky who imported Angus from Scotland and bought thousands of feet of barbed wire to manage the livestock.

Sights
As you drive deeper into Texas, the land gets drier, the vegetation sparser, and every structure that sits on the smooth flat prairie looms large over the horizon. Rambling through this old Texas town with nothing but abandoned service stations and the huge mint-green **Wheeler-Evans Grain Elevator** is one of those wonderful iconic moments on the Mother Road.

On the north side of I-40 (near Exit 114) is the **Leaning Water Tower,** which looks like it's going to fall over. However, it was actually built that way. Ralph Britten, a Groom native and Army Air Corps engineer, bought the water tower and moved it here around 1980 as a joke. The water tower really only leans about 10 degrees, but our eyes trick us into overestimating the angle. If you look a little closer, you'll notice that it has three legs anchored like a tripod, so it's not going anywhere. But it still made you look twice.

On your way out of town, you won't be able to miss the 19-story **Giant Cross** (2880 County Rd., www.crossministries. net) on the north side of Route 66, just west of County Road 295. Erected in 1995, the cross towers over the highway and is one of the largest in the United States; it weighs about two million pounds and lights up at night.

Food
The Grill (407 Front St., 806/248-0202, www.thegrill-groomtx.com, 6:30am-2pm Tues.-Wed. and Sun., 6:30am-8pm Thurs.-Sat., $6-15) is a simple, rural eatery with wood-paneled walls, good comfort food, and friendly service. The California club with chicken, bacon, and guacamole on warm Texas toast hits the spot, while the fried biscuit with blackberries and cream cheese will leave you smiling.

⊕ Back on 66
Leave Groom driving west on Route 66/Bus-40 (Front St.) and follow the South

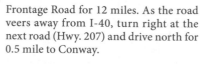

Frontage Road for 12 miles. As the road veers away from I-40, turn right at the next road (Hwy. 207) and drive north for 0.5 mile to Conway.

Conway

When Route 66 came through Conway, the population grew from 25 people to 125. Today, the population is back down to about 20, but the simplicity and grace of a landscape dotted with dirt county roads and windmills makes it look the same as it did nearly a century ago.

As a quirky tribute to the Cadillac Ranch (outside Amarillo), the **VW Slug Bug Ranch** buried five graffiti-coated Volkswagen Beetles nose first in the earth. The windows and wheels are missing, so the shells of the cars are pretty much all that remains. Stop here for a photo op, with a deserted gas station the perfect backdrop. The VW Slug Bug Ranch is 0.5 mile north of Route 66 on Highway 207 and the I-40 Frontage Road. It's on the left.

❖ Back on 66

The 7.2-mile segment between Highway 207 and I-40 is among the best-preserved and untouched sections on Route 66 in Texas. The drive offers miles of wide-open prairie alongside an abandoned railroad track. In 1900, this was a dirt road; after it was paved in the 1940s, it became a major throughway for Route 66 travelers. Today, Texas Farm Road 2161 is listed on the National Register of Historic Places.

From the Bug Ranch, head south on Highway 207 (Bus-40). After 0.5 mile, turn right (west) on County Road 2161. After County Road L, the road splits; stay right to follow County Road 2161, which

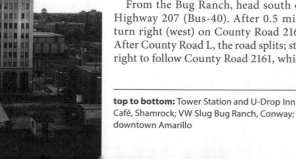

top to bottom: Tower Station and U-Drop Inn Café, Shamrock; VW Slug Bug Ranch, Conway; downtown Amarillo

heads north to I-40. In less than 2 miles, cross I-40 and turn left (west) to drive on North Frontage Road for about 4 miles. At Exit 85 (Amarillo Blvd.), the road curves left to follow Highway 2575 for 4 miles into Amarillo (do not take Bus-40 into Amarillo).

◈ Side Trip: Canyon

★ Palo Duro Canyon State Park

At 120 miles long and 600 to 800 feet deep, **Palo Duro Canyon State Park** (11450 Park Rd., Canyon, 806/488-2227, www.tpwd.texas.gov, $5) is the second-largest canyon system in the United States (the Grand Canyon is the first). The 27,173 stunning acres of crimson-hued spires and jaw-dropping beauty formed over the past 250 million years. Start your exploration at the **Visitor Center** (8am-8pm Sun.-Thurs., 8am-10pm Fri.-Sat. Apr.-May and Sept.-Oct.; 8am-10pm daily June-Aug.; 8am-6pm Sun.-Thurs., 8am-8pm Fri.-Sat. Nov.-Mar.), where you can buy books, pottery, jewelry, and souvenirs as you consider hitting a few trails.

The **Lighthouse Trail** (about 2.5 miles one-way) is a moderately difficult trail that leads to the Lighthouse rock formation. The **Rojo Grande trail** (1.17 miles) is a little easier as it travels through rust-red geological formations at the bottom of the canyon. Also easy, but longer, the **Rylander Fortress Cliff trail** (3.73 miles) leads to several scenic overlooks with incredible views of the canyon bottom.

Getting There

Palo Duro is about 30 miles south of Route 66 in Amarillo. From I-40 as it enters Amarillo, take I-87 south toward the town of Canyon. After 14 miles, take Exit 110 to follow I-27 south for 3.5 miles. Turn left (east) on Highway 217 and drive 13 miles to the park.

Amarillo

At the turn of the 20th century, the roads in Amarillo were mostly dirt; driving the 110 miles from Amarillo to Tucumcari, New Mexico, took an entire day. The 1920s oil boom called for easier and faster transport, and Amarillo businesspeople went to Congress to secure government funding to build better roads. Two hundred laborers were put to work, widening and paving the road—including the infamous Jericho Gap (the mud trap near the town of Groom). After the roads were paved, the trip to Tucumcari only took a few hours.

Amarillo was the only city along Route 66 in Texas, and it became a major cattle feeding and shipping center. The oil industry helped Amarillo become the commercial and corporate center of the Panhandle. Today, you can check out a former Harvey House, cruise the historic district, eat at one of the many steak houses, and stay downtown.

◈ Route 66 through Amarillo

Route 66 (CO 2575) turns into NE 8th Avenue and then curves north on B Avenue. In about 1.5 miles, turn left (southwest) on Amarillo Boulevard. Follow Amarillo Boulevard for 4 miles; when the road curves south, it turns into Bus-40 and crosses Highway 335. Turn right to follow Indian Hill Road.

Sights

6th Street Historic District

Amarillo's 13-block historic district was added to the National Register of Historic Places in 1994 and offers a great peek into the town's Route 66 and art deco heritage.

Before hotel chains dominated every commercial corner, there were few overnight options for travelers; it wasn't unusual for people to sleep in their cars or camp beside the road. As Amarillo grew in popularity, it built "Tourist Camps"

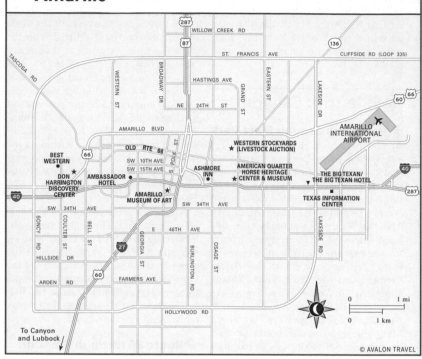

Amarillo

and motels on 6th Avenue along Route 66. The adobe **Ranchotel** (2501 W. 6th St.), which eventually became an apartment building, is a good example of the U-shaped roadside lodging that lined Amarillo streets from 1928 to 1953.

The 1922 Natatorium, called the **"Nat" Ballroom** (2705 SW 6th Ave., 806/367-8908, www.thenatroute66.com, 10am-6pm Mon.-Sat.), was built in the Gothic Revival style. The two-story stucco exterior includes turrets and deep-set windows and doors, with a nautical theme carried through the north side of the building and along the roofline. The Natatorium originally housed an indoor swimming pool, but was converted into a ballroom and hosted "big band" greats Duke Ellington and Tommy Dorsey.

Today the "Nat" features 100 antiques dealers in 20,000 square feet of space.

Automotive relics include the Streamline Moderne **Adkinson-Baker Tire Co.** (3200 W. 6th Ave.), which still has its original canopy, while **Taylor's Texaco Station** (3512 W. 6th St.) has white porcelain enameled panels on the walls and a canopy supported by pipe columns. **Martin's Phillips 66 Station** (3821 W. 6th Ave.) features glass-plated walls and an exaggerated, soaring, triangular canopy.

Accommodations

The **Courtyard Amarillo Downtown** (724 S. Polk St., 806/553-4500, www.marriott. com, $159-190) offers the best of both worlds. It's located in the beautiful historic Fisk building, yet has all the contemporary creature comforts, such as free

Harvey House

The **Santa Fe Depot and Hotel** (401 S. Grant St.) was built in 1910 as a Harvey House. The depot covered six acres and served passengers until the trains stopped running in 1971. The on-site Harvey House restaurant—considered the most refined place to eat in town—remained open until 1940.

The city of Amarillo purchased the depot in 2013. It's unclear exactly what will happen with the building, but plans intend to honor and preserve the historic complex, possibly turning it into a convention center.

To get there from Route 66: Travel south on SR-87, then turn left (east) on SE 3rd Avenue and turn right (south) on Grant Street after a few blocks. The station will be on the left.

Wi-Fi, crisp linens, and pillow-top mattresses. The spacious rooms are decorated in warm tones of yellow and paprika. Be sure to ask for a room with a view of the Santa Fe Building, with neon that lights up at night. It will make you wonder if you're still in the Texas Panhandle.

Food

Everything at the **Big Texan Steak Ranch** (7701 E. I-40, 806/372-6000, www.big-texan.com, 7am-10:30pm daily, $15-30) is—you guessed—big. There's a massive sculpture of a steer out front, tall Texas flags are lined up outside the building, and the interior includes a huge two-story dining room with a gift shop, a bar, a shooting range, and slot machines. The food is fine, but that's not the main draw. This place is legendary for its free 72-ounce steak dinner. But it's only free if you eat the entire 4.5-pound steak—with a baked potato, salad, and shrimp cocktail—in less than one hour. Since 1965, thousands have tried and failed the food challenge. One who *has* succeeded is Molly Schuyler, world-record holder for the fastest completion of the challenge. This 120-pound mom-of-four from Sacramento, California scarfed the entire meal down in 4 minutes 16 seconds ... then ate *two* more, totaling three steak dinners in 20 minutes. Only in Texas.

From Route 66, travel south on State Route 87 and turn left (east) on SE 3rd Avenue. Make a right (south) on Big Texan Road and the restaurant will be on the left before I-40.

The ★ **Golden Light Café and Cantina** (2906 SW 6th Ave., 806/374-9237, www.goldenlightcafe.com, 11am-10pm Mon.-Wed., 11am-11pm Thurs.-Sat., $3-9) was established in 1946; it's the oldest restaurant in Amarillo. The hickory-smoked Gooney's shroom burger and the all-natural buffalo burger are delish. Vegetarians can go for the grilled cheese with onions and mushrooms. The service is good but things do move a little slower here, so just relax. You're on vacation. What's the hurry? Also, if you happen to be staying overnight in Amarillo, they host weekly music acts here too.

If you want to eat with real cowboys, ★ **The Stockyard Cafe** (100 S. Manhattan St., 806/373-7999, www.amarillostock-yardscafe.com, 6am-2:30pm Mon.-Sat., 5pm-9:30pm Fri., $5-12) is the place to go. The biscuits and gravy, huevos rancheros, and flapjacks are standard favorites; if the chicken-fried steak isn't on the menu, ask (it's usually available). The restaurant is right in the middle of a huge barn where thousands of heads of beef are auctioned off every week in the Amarillo stockyards.

From Route 66, travel south on State Route 87, turn left (east) on NE 3rd Avenue. Turn right (south) on Bull Road and the auction house will be on the left.

◈ Back on 66

Driving west on Amarillo Boulevard, Route 66 curves south and turns into Bus-40 as it crosses Highway 335. About 1.5 miles after passing Highway 335, turn right and then make a quick left onto Indian Hill Road and drive west for 4.5 miles. Turn left (south) on South Blessen Drive and take the next right (west) on the I-40 North Frontage Road. Drive 20 miles through **Bushland** and **Wildorado**, past massive concrete silos, old military bases, and windmills—and hold your nose for a foul, can't-believe-how-bad-it-smells cattle yard on the way to Vega.

★ Detour: Cadillac Ranch

Some of the best art is unexpected. **Cadillac Ranch** (I-40 Frontage Rd. near Exit 60, dawn-dusk daily, free) is an awe-inspiring public art installation by the Ant Farm art collective. In a Texas wheat field 10 miles west of Amarillo stand 10 tail-finned and graffiti-soaked Cadillacs, manufactured between 1948 and 1964, planted nose deep in perfect succession facing west.

However, this wasn't the original site of the installation. As the suburbs of Amarillo encroached on the area near Cadillac Ranch, the land suddenly became valuable and in 1997 Cadillac Ranch was moved 2 miles west. The new location remains sparse and uncluttered, a Zen backdrop with a horizon line so straight the cars look like they are sprouting from a blank canvas framed by the sky.

Walking forward, the angled and abstract shapes slowly take form as you approach. These aren't Fords, Chevys, or Buicks—these are Cadillacs for a reason. The Cadillac was the ultimate symbol and celebration of the American Dream. The artwork could be a metaphor for burying commerce and materialism; or it could be viewed as a monument to commercialism and American excess. You decide.

Over the past several decades, the cars have become defaced with layers of Day-Glo spray paint and have been battered to the point that they barely resemble Cadillacs anymore. Hudson Marquez, one of the Ant Farm artists who designed and built Cadillac Ranch, said he wishes the site was more protected and that people wouldn't litter and spray paint the cars. Though other Route 66 guides may encourage folks to continue this tradition, it's best to leave the spray paint at home.

Getting There

Cadillac Ranch is west of Amarillo near I-40 (Exit 60) on the South Frontage Road. As Amarillo Boulevard (Route 66) curves south, it turns into Bus-40. Turn left (south) on Hope Road, cross I-40, then turn right (west) on the South Frontage Road. Drive east 1 mile and Cadillac Ranch will be on the right (south) side. Park along the shoulder and enter the pasture through the unlocked gate. Pets are welcome.

◈ Back on 66

Leaving Cadillac Ranch, turn left (west) onto the South Frontage Road. Take your next right (north) on Arnot Road. Cross I-40 and turn left (west) on Indian Hill Road.

Vega

Route 66 gracefully flaunts its scars amidst fragments of broken cement and hollowed out rubble in the small, wind-whipped town of Vega. At one time, Vega was a sizable town for the Panhandle, with more than 500 people and several gas stations, cafés, and a few auto courts. But it needed Route 66 to survive, so when the Mother Road was decommissioned, Vega lost its shine. Today most of the businesses under the weathered woodened awnings are closed.

Car Culture

The Route 66 Corridor Preservation Program restored the **1920s Magnolia Service Station** (southeast corner of N. Main St./U.S. 385 and Coke St., 806/267-2828, 9am-5pm Mon.-Fri. June-mid-Oct., free); it's one of the few two-story stations that look more like a house and less like a cottage. The station sat for many years in a dilapidated state so the restoration was fairly involved; the canopy had to be completely reconstructed and the doors, windows, roof, and stucco were replaced. Today, the building has historic artifacts and photographs of the early days in Vega.

To get there from Bus-40, turn right (north) on U.S. 385 (Main St.) and the station is about four blocks on the right.

✦ Route 66 through Vega

The oldest alignment of Route 66 went through U.S. 385 (Main St.) and turned on West Main Street. But today this segments dead-ends into a dirt road west of town, so follow the post-1930s alignment instead. As you enter Vega from the North Frontage Road, Bus-40 splits off to the north and turns into Vega Boulevard. Follow Vega Boulevard west through town.

Sights

Roark's Hardware

Roark's Hardware (214 S. Main St., 806/267-2102, 8am-noon and 1pm-5pm Mon.-Fri., 8am-noon Sat.) may be the oldest hardware store still in operation in the Texas Panhandle. The store mostly sells farming and household supplies, but there may be a gift or two hidden away—you never know what you'll find. The most fun part is talking with the locals and listening to their stories.

From Bus-40, turn right (north) on U.S. 385 (Main St.). The store is one block up on the right.

Dot's Mini-Museum & Boot Tree

Dot's Mini-Museum & Boot Tree (105 N. 12th St., 806/267-2367, dawn-dusk daily, free) includes three small buildings filled with random oddities the late Dot Levitt collected over the years. Dot came to Vega in 1940s with her husband; now her daughter Betty Carpenter runs the place.

Items range from Avon perfume bottles to old hats, pistols, and a tree with cowboy boots hanging from the branches. Stop by and say hello.

From Bus-40, turn right (north) on U.S. 385 (Main St.). Turn left (west) on West Main Street, then make a right (north) on North 12th Street.

Vega Motel

The 1947, U-shaped **Vega Motel** (1005 Vega Blvd.) was built during the prosperous years of Route 66, with two wings, 12 units, and a small house in the central courtyard. As Route 66 got busier, the exterior was covered with permastone and eight more units with garages and kitchenettes were added. By the late 1940s, there were about 30,000 motor courts along the American roadside. The Vega Motel remains a rare example of these classic old-school motor courts.

Food

You might pass by ★ **Rooster's** (1300 Vega Blvd., 806/267-0113, 8am-8pm Mon.-Sat., 10am-2pm Sun., $6-12) if you didn't know how good it was. This small, rustic, hole-in-the-wall of a restaurant is located in an old gas station with a large sheet-metal rooster outside. The service is great, the enchiladas are yummy, and the margaritas are on point. Try the stuffed avocado—amazing.

Feel like you're eating on the film set of a Western at the **Boot Hill Saloon and Grill** (909 Vega Blvd., 806/267-2904,

11:30am-2am daily, $11-30). The green chili wontons, rib eyes, brisket sliders, and sweet potato fries are on point. Finish the meal with warm bread pudding smothered in caramel and dollop of vanilla ice cream.

⬧ Back on 66

Leave Vega heading west on Bus-40 until it rejoins the North Frontage Road in 1 mile. Keep an eye out north of the railroad for the old concrete remnants of the unpaved 1926 alignment. From Vega, it's about 11 miles west to Adrian.

Adrian

Adrian was founded in 1909; in 1915, the town had a population of 50 people. When Route 66 came through in 1926, tourism became a steady source of income for the community. Today, the most exciting thing about Adrian is its location. Adrian sits 1,139 miles west of Chicago and 1,139 miles east of Los Angeles, making it the geographic midpoint on Route 66. You'll know you've made it when you see the MidPoint Café. You're halfway there!

Food

The ★ **MidPoint Café** (305 W. Rte. 66, 805/536-6379, 8:30am-4pm daily Apr.-mid-Nov., $8-14) was serving hungry travelers 10 years before Route 66 was even paved. This was a one-room, greasy spoon with a dirt floor called Zella's; after that it was Jesse's Café. Today, the MidPoint serves fresh (never frozen) Angus-beef burgers and homemade "ugly pies," made with a bumpy crust that are utterly delicious—try the Texas Pecan and Elvis Pie. Leave some time to browse the gift shop and don't forget to take a photo of the sign outside.

abandoned service station, Glenrio

◈ Back on 66

Leave Adrian in the rearview mirror, heading west on the North Frontage Road for 4.6 miles to Exit 18 (Gruhlkey Rd.) and jump on I-40 West.

Glenrio

Glenrio sits right on the **Texas-New Mexico border.** For many years the early Route 66 alignment was just a dirt road; it wasn't paved until the late 1930s. Today, Glenrio is a desolate border town that's fading into the flat Panhandle plains. The tourist courts, cafés, and gas stations are gone and most of the buildings have fallen down. As we head west in New Mexico, prepare to be swooned by the Land of Enchantment.

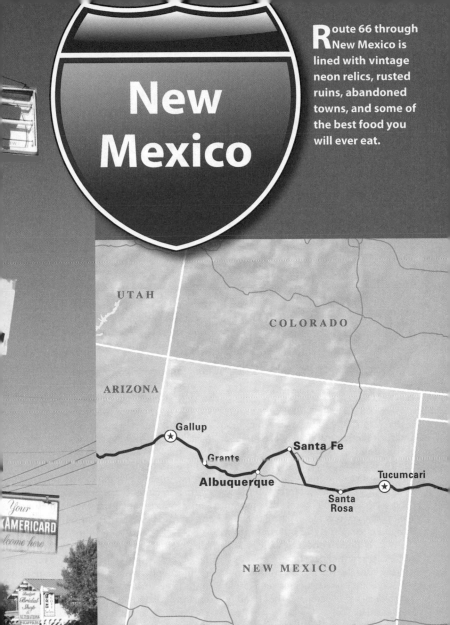

New Mexico

Route 66 through New Mexico is lined with vintage neon relics, rusted ruins, abandoned towns, and some of the best food you will ever eat.

UTAH

COLORADO

ARIZONA

Gallup

Grants

Santa Fe

Albuquerque

Tucumcari

Santa Rosa

NEW MEXICO

TEXAS

MEXICO

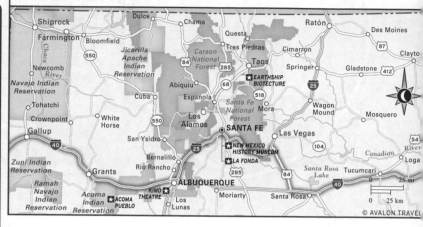

New Mexico

N ew Mexico's culture, food, and landscape set it apart from any other place on Route 66.

Here you'll see the oldest community in the country, one of the oldest churches, and the oldest continuously used public building in the United States. As Route 66 crosses New Mexico, it passes over three distinct topographies, with elevations ranging from 3,800 to 7,500 feet; these include the Pecos and Canadian Valleys of the Great Plains, the Basin and Range Plateau, and the Intermountain Plateau. Hidden amid the valleys and curves are quaint Spanish villages, soul-stirring sunsets, rustic adobe-brick chapels, and sun-kissed pueblos set against a cerulean sky. Welcome to the "Land of Enchantment."

New Mexico was the wildest part of the West—nothing compared to the all-out revolts that took place here. The state's deep, multicultural history encompasses the Spaniards, Mexicans, and Indians who fought to claim the territory and retain their independence. Once the violence subsided, the state was filled with native communities that were walled off like fortresses. Today, New Mexico is home to 19 pueblos, each of which has its own distinct culture and traditions, as well as two Apache tribes and about 107,000 members of the Navajo Nation.

In 1912, there were only 28 miles of paved roads in New Mexico. Between 1933 and 1941, government spending to build roads increased, but the state's diverse topography gave early highway engineers quite a challenge. Originally, Route 66 zigzagged northwest along the Santa Fe Trail, from Santa Rosa to Santa Fe, and then dipped south to Albuquerque and Los Lunas before heading west to Gallup. Then in 1937, a major realignment changed Route 66's north-south trajectory into an east-west corridor (and made Albuquerque one of the few Route 66 towns with two alignments that intersect). The new, more direct road shortened the route through the state from 506 to 399 miles. After all was said and done, Route 66 became New Mexico's first completely paved highway.

Highlights

★ **New Mexico History Museum, Santa Fe:** This fascinating museum delves into the diverse cultural layers of New Mexican history (page 203).

★ **La Fonda, Santa Fe:** One of the few remaining Harvey Houses is still going strong right in the heart of Santa Fe (page 204).

★ **Earthship Biotecture, Taos:** At this revolutionary and self-sustaining community in the high desert, off-the-grid homes resemble stunning out-of-this-world art sculptures (page 212).

★ **KiMo Theatre, Albuquerque:** This opulent Pueblo Deco theater plays classic Hollywood films and

hosts live performances, operas, and more (page 219).

★ **Acoma Pueblo:** Tour this 12th-century Pueblo Indian village, one of the oldest communities in North America (page 227).

Planning Your Time

This trip speeds across New Mexico in **2-3 days,** but there's a lot to do. Route 66 enters the state near Glenrio. Spend the night in Tucumcari, just 40 miles west. The next day follows the pre-1937 alignment along the scenic "Santa Fe Loop" (rather than following I-40 between Santa Rosa and Albuquerque), ending in Santa Fe for a second overnight. From Santa Fe, a side trip to Taos will add a day, but is completely worth it to visit the Earthship Biotecture. Another overnight—either Taos or Albuquerque—is recommended so that there's time to visit the Acoma Pueblo before zipping through Gallup to cross the border into Arizona.

Driving Considerations

There's so much to see and do in New Mexico that you could easily spend two weeks here. Plan ahead in order to experience much as you can in one of the most magnificent states on the Mother Road. If time is running out, I-40 and I-25 will quickly get you to the next destination. **Gas** is available in Tucumcari, Santa Rosa, Santa Fe, Albuquerque, Taos, and Gallup.

If you happen to be driving through New Mexico from mid-June through September, this is **monsoon season.** Practically every afternoon, the sky opens up like clockwork to rain for about an hour. Sometimes the showers are quite dramatic with lightning and thunder. But as soon as the storm passes, the sun usually comes out and the skies are even more gorgeous.

Getting There

Starting Points
Car

In New Mexico, I-25 joins Route 66 north-south, while I-40 follows it east-to-west. The recommended **pre-1937 alignment** travels north from I-40 toward Santa Fe via U.S. 84 and I-25. From Santa Fe, I-25 then dips down into Albuquerque before meeting I-40 to head west toward Gallup. If time is an issue, take the **post-1937 alignment,** which follows I-40 east/west from Santa Rosa to Albuquerque.

Car Rental

The Albuquerque Sunport is the best place to rent a car. **Enterprise** (3400 University Blvd., 505/765-9100, www.enterprise.com, 6am-midnight daily) is another good choice. **Avis** (4770 Montgomery Blvd. NE, 505/842-4080, 5am-1am daily) is another in-town option with longer hours.

Best Accommodations

★ **Blue Swallow Motel, Tucumcari:** Stay at a pristine example of a pre-WWII tourist court on Route 66 (page 196).

★ **Earthship Biotecture, Taos:** Spend the night in one of these fantastic self-sufficient homes made of recycled materials (page 213).

★ **Hyatt Regency Tamaya Resort and Spa, Bernalillo:** The Hyatt's love of nature shows in this resort's green practices (page 215).

★ **Los Poblanos Inn, Albuquerque:** This is a place to remember for years to come (page 222).

★ **Enchanted Trails RV Park, Albuquerque:** Stay in a vintage Airstream trailer at the former trading post (page 223).

★ **El Rancho Hotel, Gallup:** The choice of 1930s A-listers, this three-story plantation-style hotel still retains a gorgeous yet historic feel (page 230).

Air

Nearly five million people fly in and out of **Albuquerque International Sunport** (ABQ, 2200 Sunport Blvd., 505/244-7700, www.abqsunport.com) every year. This is the largest commercial airport in the state with nonstop service to 23 cities via Alaska, American, Delta, JetBlue, Southwest, US Airways, and United Airlines. The airport is about 3 miles southeast of downtown Albuquerque.

Train and Bus

Amtrak's *Southwest Super Chief* (www. amtrak.com, 800/872-7245) passes through some fabulous southwestern scenery on its way through stations in Albuquerque (320 1st St. SW) and Gallup (Gallup Cultural Center, 201 E. Rte. 66).

Greyhound (www.greyhound.com) bus service is available at stations in Tucumcari (McDonald's, 2608 S. 1st St., 575/461-1350, 5am-8pm daily), Albuquerque (320 1st St. SW, 505/247-0246, 1am-noon, 2pm-6pm, and 9pm-midnight daily), and Gallup (Route 66 Mini Mart, 3060 W. Hwy. 66, 505/863-9078, 24 hours daily).

◆ Route 66 to Tucumcari

As you enter New Mexico on I-40 take Exit 369, turn right (north) and then take the first left at Quay Road to follow the North Frontage Road southwest for about 10 miles. As the road curves west, turn left (south) on Highway 469, cross I-40 heading south, and then turn right (west) in San Jon to join Route 66 on South Frontage Road. Many small communities that once thrived on the Mother Road became ghost towns after I-40 came along. **San Jon** once had a reputation as a rough-and-tumble town in the early 1900s, but this town is now all but a memory with fragments of failed auto shops and ghost signs.

Follow Route 66 west for the next 20 miles through the irrigated farmlands and the former Ozark Trail to Tucumcari.

While there is a dirt road option that travels south of I-40 from Glenrio to San Jon, the formerly paved road is not recommended; the road is not maintained and can be dangerous when muddy.

Tucumcari

Tucumcari was notorious for being a rowdy western town with wild saloons and outlaws that earned it the nickname "Six Shooter Siding." Tucumcari was memorialized in the television show *Rawhide,* and it was the setting for one of the first scenes in the Sergio Leone

Best Restaurants

★ **Comet II Drive-In, Santa Rosa:** This former carhop serves up some serious green chile (page 200).

★ **Santa Fe Bite, Santa Fe:** Bite into the best green-chile cheeseburger in New Mexico (page 207).

★ **Tia Sophia's, Santa Fe:** This locals' hangout serves New Mexican cuisine and some of the best green chile in Santa Fe (page 209).

★ **Sugar Nymphs Bistro, Peñasco:** It's worth the drive just to dine on locally sourced cuisine served by the former executive chef of the famed Greens Restaurant in San Francisco (page 211).

★ **Jerry's, Gallup:** Don't leave New Mexico without trying the chiles rellenos at this classic (page 231).

Tucumcari to Santa Fe

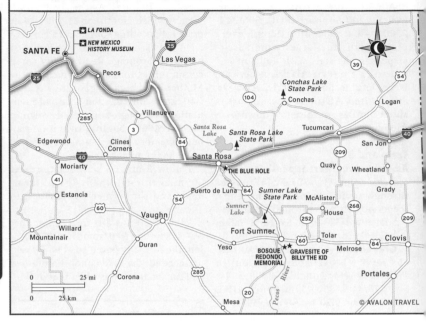

"Spaghetti Western" classic *For a Few Dollars More*. During Route 66's heyday, Tucumcari posted billboards inviting travelers to TUCUMCARI TONITE!, with claims of 2,000 motel rooms (this was later changed to 1,200). Today, only a fraction of these places remain open; however, the streets are lined with the classic neon signs of the Blue Swallow, Cactus Motor Lodge, and Route 66 murals and landmarks such as Teepee Curios and La Cita Restaurant with its huge rooftop sombrero.

◈ Route 66 through Tucumcari

From the I-40 South Frontage Road, turn right (north) on Bus-40; the road will cross I-40, curve, and head west for 3.5 miles along Tucumcari Boulevard. On the west side of town, turn left onto State Route 54 and then join I-40 West at Exit 329.

Sights
Mural Tour

Artists Sharon and Doug Quarles painted most of the **40 murals** throughout Tucumcari over a 10-year period. The Blue Swallow's James Dean mural portrays the Porsche Spyder that cost him his life, while "The Legendary Road" mural outlines the conflicting story of America's western migration—one of the largest Route 66 murals on the Mother Road, with two beautiful bovine skulls with an image of the wide-open road. Pick up a mural map at the **Chamber of Commerce** (404 Rte. 66, 575/461-1694, www.tucumcarinm.com, 8:30am-5pm Mon.-Fri., free).

Route 66 Photo Museum

The **Route 66 Photo Museum** (1500 W. Rte. 66, 575/461-1641, www.nmrt-66museum.org, 9am-1pm Mon.-Thurs., 9am-4pm Fri.-Sun., free) captures key

Odeon Theatre

Built in 1937, the classic art deco **Odeon Theatre** (123 S. 2nd St., 575/461-0100, call for movie times, $6) may be the oldest continuously used theater in New Mexico. The original owner liked that the word Odeon—a Greek term meaning a building with musical performances—only had five letters, which made the sign more affordable. Locals just called it the "New Theater."

New owners Christy Dominguez and Robert Lopez put in a lot of money and sweat equity to restore the theater, which reopened in 2014. They sanded every seat; some of the seats that were too old were replaced with longer and wider converted bus seats sprayed with a coat of Emron automobile paint and then upholstered in denim. The original art deco features have also been restored, and updated modern equipment now screens feature flicks.

To get there from Route 66, turn right (north) on Highway 104, then turn left (west) on West Center Street. The theater is one block down on the right.

moments along the Mother Road. Photographer Michael Campanelli's 166 framed photographs are on exhibit along with vintage cars, old gas pumps, historical Tucumcari Route 66 artifacts, and more. The museum is in the back of the Tucumcari Convention Visitors Center parking lot. In front is artist Tom Coffin's 1997 **sculpture** dedicated to the Mother Road; it looks like a massive hood ornament with the number 66 in chrome with Cadillac tail fins sitting on a stylized sandstone pyramid-shaped base.

Mesalands Community College Dinosaur Museum

The **Mesalands Community College Dinosaur Museum** (222 E. Laughlin St., 575/461-3466, www.mesalands. edu, 10am-6pm Tues.-Sat. Mar. 1-Sept.; noon-5pm Tues.-Sat. Sept.-Feb., $6.50) claims to house the world's largest collection of life-sized *bronze* skeletons. The size, scope, and power of these fossil replicas comes through in 10,000 square feet of exhibition space. An on-site museum shop sells rocks and minerals, fossils, games, clothing, teaching aids, and scientific and educational books.

The museum is located two blocks north of Route 66. Heading west on Route 66, turn right (north) on 1st Street (Hwy.

209). Drive two blocks, then turn right (east) on Laughlin Avenue.

Tucumcari Historical Museum

Learn about the rise and fall of Tucumcari and the early railroad years at the **Tucumcari Historical Museum** (416 S. Adams St., 575/461-4201, www.cityof-tucumcari.com, 9am-3pm Tues.-Sat., $5). A wide range of artifacts are spread across three floors of a 1903 schoolhouse with five indoor and outdoor exhibits, including newspapers, family scrapbooks, and bootleg liquor stills. There's also an original chuck wagon and old Firehouse with a 1926 Chevrolet fire truck that still works.

The Historical Museum is three blocks north of Route 66. Heading west on Route 66, turn right (north) on Adams Street. The museum will be on the right.

Shopping

The **Tucumcari Trading Post** (1900 Tucumcari Blvd., 575/461-3889, www.tucumcaritradingpost.com, 8am-5pm Mon.-Sat.) sells more than 4,000 square feet of all kinds of collectibles—western relics, gas station antiques, clothing, art, books, knives, old license plates, and porcelain signage. Stop by and pick up a souvenir.

The **Trade Station** (1201 Tucumcari Blvd., 575/708-0551, www.

rt66tradestation.com, call to schedule a visit) pays homage to a Texaco gas station with Fire Chief and Sky Chief fuel pumps and great murals by Doug Quarles. Inside, you can browse unique antiques, postcards, pottery, and collectibles. They are always looking to buy and trade gold, silver, diamonds, vintage guns, watches, toys, motorcycles, cars, and scooters.

In the 1940s, when Route 66 was a wide two-lane road through Tucumcari, **Tee Pee Curios** (924 Tucumcari Blvd., 575/461-3773, 8am-5pm Mon.-Sat., 1pm-5pm Sun.) was a gas and grocery store. When the road widened, the shop lost its gas pumps, but today they still sell coonskin caps, rubber tomahawks, jewelry, pottery, and Route 66 souvenirs under a big concrete tepee.

Accommodations

The ★ **Blue Swallow Motel** (815 Tucumcari Blvd., 575/461-9849, www. blueswallowmotel.com, $70-130) opened around 1940 and is a pristine example of a pre-WWII tourist court on Route 66. Lillian Redman, the former owner of the Blue Swallow, came to New Mexico in 1915 in a covered wagon to homestead near Santa Rosa. Redman was a waitress and a cook for Fred Harvey. When she married Floyd Redman, her engagement present was the Blue Swallow. Together they served many passengers on the Mother Road; for those who couldn't pay, they often waived the room fee. Each room portrays a copy of a letter written by Lillian Redman that states the Blue Swallow is a:

"... human institution to serve people and not solely a money-making organization . . . We are all travelers. From 'birth till death.' We travel between the eternities. May these days be pleasant for you, profitable for society, helpful for those you meet and a joy to those you know."

Still in operation today, the motel features an L-shaped layout with 14

Blue Swallow Motel, Tucumcari

nicely restored rooms and attached garages. Rooms are decorated with 1950s furniture from the Franciscan Manufacturing Company and include chenille bedspreads, art deco accents, and rotary phones. A classic car is parked in front of the motel underneath one of the best neon signs on Route 66. The Blue Swallow's bird-in-flight symbol harkens back to the classic sailor tattoo: When sailors saw this bird, they knew land was near.

The **Historic Route 66 Motel** (1620 E. Tucumcari Blvd., 575/461-1212, www. rte66motel.com, $44-65) has a minimalist Palm Springs cool factor built in the International Style. Rooms are dated (in a good way), spacious and clean with floor-to-ceiling windows. The Circa Espresso Bar is right next door, and they get bonus points for being pet-friendly.

The **Motel Safari** (722 E. Tucumcari Blvd., 575/461-1048, www.themotelsafari. com, $55-95) was established in 1959 and is the perfect mix of modern amenities (pillowtop mattresses, 32-inch flat-panel TVs) with the vintage charm of a mid-century motor court. The Rockabilly Suite features wood floors and stone tile, a living room with a leather sofa, and a 50-inch plasma television. All rooms are non-smoking, pets re not allowed, and there are no check-ins after 10pm. Look for the sign with a camel, which pays homage to Edward Fitzgerald Beale's 1857 Camel expedition when the U.S. Army uses 70 camels as pack animals to survey the southwest.

Food

The **Del's Restaurant** (1202 E. Tucumcari Blvd, 575/461-1740, www.delsrestaurant.com, 11am-9pm Mon.-Sat., $8-18) steak house has been serving Route 66 travelers since 1956. But if you've had enough red meat after driving through Texas, the vegetables are fresh, the soup is homemade, and the Mexican dishes are also good.

Kix on 66 (1102 E. Tucumcari Blvd, 575/461-1966, www.kixon66.com, 6pm-2pm daily, $6-12) is a cheerful and charming eatery in a mid-century era coffee shop with an open floor layout and a counter lined with cantilevered stools. The omelets and hash browns are great, but the menu also includes biscuits and gravy, chicken cubes, and ice cream. A pet-friendly patio offers a special "Canine Cuisine" menu (all items less than $3) for your pooch; it's a great way to spend some time with your four-legged family member.

Many folks go to **La Cita** (820 S. 1st St. and Rte. 66, 575/461-7866, 11am-8pm Mon.-Sat., 11am-2pm Sun., $7-12) just so they can walk into a restaurant sitting under a giant sombrero sculpture—a rare example of quirky mid-century western vernacular architecture. Once inside, order the chicken enchiladas.

For really good chiles rellenos and burritos smothered with green chile sauce, go to **Pow Wow** (801 W.

Tucumcari Blvd, 575/461-2587, www. powwowlizard.com, 7am-10pm daily, $8-30). Inside there is Route 66-themed artwork and a lounge in case you want to take a load off with a Blue Swallow Margarita. If you've enjoyed a few too many, and you're staying at a local motel, take advantage of their lifesaving hotel shuttle service.

Watson's BBQ (502 S. Lake St., 575/461-9620, www.tucranchsupply.com/watsons-bbq.html, 9am-5pm Mon.-Fri., 9am-4pm Sat., $6-$14) is decked out in railroad decor, with wood picnic tables under a large canopy. The smoked brisket, meaty ribs, green-chili stew, and juicy fruit cobblers are all outstanding. Watson's is located three blocks north of Route 66 on S. Lake Street.

◆ Back on 66

The road west of Tucumcari makes its way along a shallow valley with sandstone mesas in the distance near Montoya and Newkirk. Leaving Tucumcari, join I-40 West at Exit 329 and drive 17 miles. Take Exit 311 and turn left to cross I-40, then follow the South Frontage Road for 6 miles. Cross I-40 again (no exit) to follow the North Frontage Road for 14 miles through **Newkirk,** a small ranching community that today is little more than a ghost town.

The next town, **Cuervo,** lies 8.5 miles from Newkirk. The road between Newkirk and Cuervo can be kind of rough, so take it slow. There are many places where the road dips; if there is deep or running water, do *not* cross it. Turn around and take I-40 instead.

Cuervo was a railroad town and ranching district. Trains stopped here in the early 1900s, and once Route 66 came through, a few gas stations and grocery stores opened. Today there are remnants of an abandoned stone church, but avoid going inside as the interior is unsafe. In Cuervo, join I-40 West at Exit 291 and drive to Exit 277 at Santa Rosa.

◆ Side Trip: Fort Sumner Historic Site

In the 1860s, more than 8,500 Navajo and 500 Mescalero Apache were interned on the one-million-acre Bosque Redondo reservation along the banks of the Pecos River overseen by the troops of **Fort Sumner.** After the U.S. Army forced the Mescalero Apache people to leave their homeland, they brought them to Bosque Redondo in 1863. The Navajo were forced to walk hundreds of miles here, starving along the way. Upon arrival, they were then forced to build the fort, a dam, dig ditches, and plant cottonwood trees. The plan was to "teach" the Navajo and Mescalero Apache how to be self-sufficient—but they had already been self-sufficient for centuries before the Europeans arrived. No shelter was provided; instead the Navajo lived in pits and used tree branches for protection. As the U.S. government severely underestimated the amount of food needed to feed the population at the fort, approximately 20 percent of the American Indians starved to death.

Bosque Redondo Memorial

The site today is the **Bosque Redondo Memorial** (3647 Billy the Kid Rd., 575/355-2573, www.nmmonuments. org/bosque-redondo, 8:30am-4:30pm Wed.-Sun., $3). Navajo architect David Sloan designed the Mescalero Apache and Navajo memorial in the shape of an Apache teepee. Take the 0.75-mile outdoor interpretive trail to see the Indian Commissary where crops were stored, the area where the 1868 Navajo treaty was signed, and the entrance to the Fort Sumner Military Center and barracks with 30-inch adobe walls that housed 637 soldiers. There's also a plaque at the site where Bill the Kid was killed by Sherriff Pat Garrett in 1881. The museum is being redesigned, but there are informative panels and a video recapping the

Car Culture

New Mexico has the perfect weather for preserving classic cars: The dry, temperate climate keeps the rust at bay and the paint job intact. The **Route 66 Auto Museum** (2866 Will Rogers Ave., 575/472- 1966, 7:30am-5:30pm daily, $5) has a small but impressive collection of more than 30 lovingly restored and rebuilt vintage cars—from flame-kissed roadsters to hot rods and trucks.

history of the site. The on-site gift shop sells hand-woven rugs, pottery, books, mugs, clothing, and tribal jewelry.

From I-40 in Santa Rosa, take Exit 277 to get on U.S. 84 South. Drive 40 miles to the village of Fort Sumner. Turn left (east) on Highway 60 and continue on U.S. 84. Turn right (south) on Billy the Kid Road. The site is 3.5 miles on the right (west).

Billy the Kid's Gravesite

Also in Fort Sumner is **Billy the Kid's gravesite;** the famous outlaw was killed here in 1881. There are several signs claiming to have the "real grave of Billy the Kid"; it's still unclear where he actually is, but his headstone is in the graveyard behind the Old Fort Sumner Museum. It was stolen more than once so now it's caged up. The **Billy the Kid Museum** (1435 E. Sumner Ave., 575/355-2380, www.billythekidmuseumfortsumner.com, 8:30am-5pm daily, $5) has more stories about the infamous teenage outlaw's life. Also on-site are his chaps, spurs, rifle, and other memorabilia.

The gravestone is in the Old Fort Sumner Cemetery in the Fort Sumner Park near Billy the Kid Drive and Old Fort Park Road. The museum is on U.S. 60/84 in the east side of the town of Fort Sumner.

Santa Rosa

Santa Rosa was an agrarian community until the railroad came to town in 1901. When Route 66 arrived in 1930, it became an official transportation hub. The original Route 66 alignment took a sharp turn north here toward Dilia and Romeroville then headed toward Santa Fe. Santa Rosa remained a part of the east-west alignment after 1937.

In an otherwise arid land, Santa Rosa stands out for its sapphire lakes. Called the "City of Natural Lakes," this area is also home to the Santa Rosa Sink, sinkholes connected by an underground network of water-filled tunnels. The phenomenon formed from water erosion over millions of years creating a large basin of wetlands. As the geologic strata weakened, collapsed, and dissolved, an artesian well formed. Today it is a part of a large system of seven lakes that are connected underground. This refreshing watering hole was a great find for nomadic tribes and cattle ranchers in the middle of such a dry area.

Today Santa Rosa is primarily ranch country, with picturesque stone buildings and a quaint historic downtown. Santa Rosa was featured the film *The Grapes of Wrath* as the site where Henry Fonda watches a freight train cross the Pecos River. The bridge portrayed in the film is on the right after 1st Street on the west side of town.

◆ Route 66 through Santa Rosa

From I-40 West, turn right off of Exit 277 and follow Bus-40 (Will Rogers Dr.) through downtown. Soon after you cross the Pecos River at the fork, stay right and follow Bus-40 northwest to rejoin I-40 West.

Blue Hole

Take a reprieve from the hot car with a swim in the **Blue Hole** (1085 Blue Hole Rd., 575/472-3763, www.santarosabluehole.com, 10am-7pm daily with lifeguards on duty, $5), a round, bell-shaped lake. On a hot summer day, it's fun to cliff dive into the crystal-blue water with its craggy limestone walls; but that water is a crisp 62°F, so prepare for a chilly dip. The 81-foot deep artesian spring-fed lake and sinkhole experiences an outflow of 3,000 gallons per minute. The Blue Hole is known as one of the best natural swimming holes in the state, and it's the scuba diving capital of the Southwest. It attracts visitors from around the world, so it can get really busy on weekends.

Heading west on Route 66 turn left (south) on Lake Drive and make another left (east) on Blue Hole Road.

Food

★ **Comet II Drive-In** (1257 E. Rte. 66, 575/472-3663, 11am-9pm Tues.-Sun., $8) is a quaint, no-frills restaurant serving good Mexican food in a former carhop. The original Comet Restaurant opened in 1929 and has been family-run for three generations. Owner John Martinez began as the cook more than six decades ago. Martinez is serious about his green chile: it's a unique strain grown in Puerto de Luna (commonly called PDL) that has been cultivated in New Mexico for more than a century. (But he says it's no match for the popular Hatch green chile from southern New Mexico.) Maybe that's what brings in the locals and celebrities like Dan Aykroyd and the late, great Johnny Cash. Martinez says, "My customers are the most important thing in my life. I'll die here with a spatula in my hand."

All the food is made here from scratch; the refried beans are delicious (I always rate a Mexican restaurant by how good the refried beans are; if the beans are good, the rest of the menu items are usually great.). The carnitas burrito swimming in red-chile sauce is a winner.

⬥ Back on 66

Leaving Santa Rosa, you have a decision to make: Take the longer, more scenic pre-1937 alignment toward **Santa Fe,** or the post-1937 alignment heading west toward **Clines Corners** (much of this route is only accessible via I-40). The **pre-1937 alignment** that travels north to Santa Fe is my recommendation. It is more of a commitment, but it's well worth the time, effort, and expense.

If time is a factor, take I-40 West to **Albuquerque** where the two alignments cross and pick the route up in Albuquerque instead.

The Santa Fe Loop

⬥ Pre-1937 Alignment to Santa Fe

Leaving Santa Rosa, join I-40 West, and take Exit 256 to follow U.S. 84 north for 41 miles. You'll cross the Pecos River right before **Dilia.** There really isn't anything to "do" on this trek to Santa Fe except enjoy the beautiful alfalfa pastures, roaming cattle, and multihued mesas in the distance. In Dilia, there's an old, buttercream-yellow Catholic church and a bar on the side of the road. Once you reach I-25, continue on to Santa Fe traveling north on U.S. 84 and cross I-25. Turn left (southwest) on the Frontage Road and in less than 5 miles, you'll reach **Tecolote** (the Aztec word for "owl"). As you pass over Tecolote Creek on the south end of town, look back to see several concrete bridge supports where the original Route 66 crossed the creek.

Keep heading south on the Frontage Road for another 5 miles to the blink-and-you-could-miss-it town of **Bernal.** There's not much more than a church and small store on the west side of the highway. The next town, **San Jose,** is about 7 miles west and sits on the south side of the frontage road; dirt roads lead off to old sun-soaked adobe homes and a church. On the east side of San Jose, keep an eye out for a rusty truss bridge with dusty wooden planks and no railings—its weathered state is a scenic moment on the Mother Road.

Leaving San Jose, the Frontage Road crosses to the south side of U.S. 84 and climbs to the top of the **Glorieta Mesa** with extensive views of the valley below. After 13 miles, you'll reach **Rowe;** right after Railroad Way, turn right (northwest) to cross under U.S. 84. Turn left (north) on Highway 63 and in less than 3 miles you'll come to Pecos National Historic Park.

Pecos National Historical Park
Tucked away in the Sangre de Cristo Mountains, **Pecos National Historical Park** (Hwy. 63 and Ranger Ln., Pecos, 505/757-7241, 8am-6pm daily Memorial Day-Labor Day, 8:30am-4pm daily Labor Day-May 30, $7) features majestic ruins of an ancient pueblo that dates to AD 800. This area was a trading crossroads, and the remains of pueblos stand as majestic reminders. Trail ruts, a stage stop from the Santa Fe Trail, and a Civil War battlefield tell the story of the West and its role in shaping and redefining the United States. In 1862, Confederate soldiers tried to take Santa Fe; after a three-day battle at Glorieta Pass, it was clear New Mexico would remain a Union state. Look for the 2.3-mile Civil War Battlefield Trail map at the visitors center, which also offers other trail maps, information about ranger-led pueblo tours, exhibits, and a 10-minute introductory film.

✪ Back on 66
Head north for 3 miles on Highway 63 and drive through the town of **Pecos**. Turn left (west) on Highway 50 and climb 7,500 feet to Glorieta Pass, the highest point on the pre-1937 alignment of Route 66. In 5.5 miles, join

I-25 West/U.S. 85 and drive 5 miles to Exit 294/Cañoncito. Turn left (southwest) on Old Las Vegas Highway (Hwy. 300), which parallels I-25. Stay on Old Las Vegas Highway for about 10 miles, then turn right (north) on Highway 466/Old Pecos Trail (near Exit 284 on I-25). Drive north 1.2 miles, and then bear right to continue following Old Pecos Trail north. In about 1.5 miles, the road merges with Old Santa Fe Trail, which leads into the heart of Santa Fe.

Santa Fe

Santa Fe is *the* oldest capital city in the United States. Nomadic Paleo-Indians arrived in northern New Mexico around 10,000 BC, and their descendants created the iconic Pueblo-style adobe structures that define Santa Fe today.

From 1926 to 1937, Route 66 came through Santa Fe. Today the route goes right through downtown, two blocks south of the historic Plaza along tight winding streets lined with ancient adobe buildings. A distinctive culture and aesthetic—formed by a mix of 17th-century buildings, world-renowned cuisine, southwestern art, and relaxing spas—draw outcasts, eccentrics, New Agers, and artists to Santa Fe. This is a place that keeps you grounded and ethereal at the same time—it's simply magical.

✪ Route 66 through Santa Fe
Entering Santa Fe, head north on Old Santa Fe Trail and turn left (west) on East Alameda Street. Drive two blocks west and then turn left (south) on Galisteo Street. Continue 1 mile to turn right (west) on Alta Vista Street. At Cerrillos Road (Hwy. 14), turn left (southwest) and drive about 7 miles; pass under I-25 and continue straight for another 2 miles. Turn right (west), then make a quick left (south) to follow the South Frontage Road.

Santa Fe

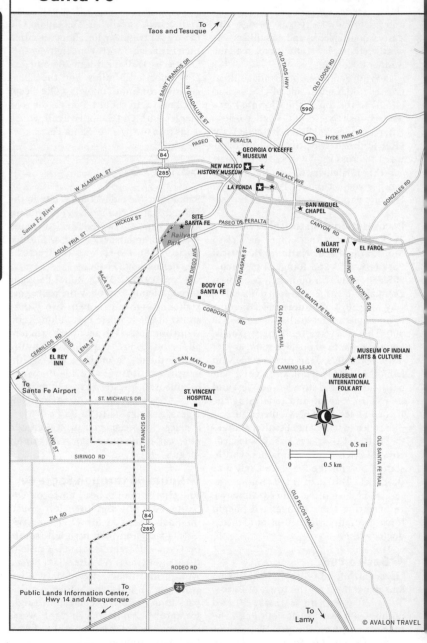

To Taos and Tesuque

OLD TAOS HWY
OLD LODGE RD
590
HYDE PARK RD
475
N SAINT FRANCIS DR
N GUADALUPE ST
PASEO DE PERALTA
84
285
W ALAMEDA ST
GONZALES RD
GEORGIA O'KEEFFE MUSEUM
NEW MEXICO HISTORY MUSEUM
PALACE AVE
LA FONDA
SAN MIGUEL CHAPEL
Santa Fe River
HICKOX ST
CANYON RD
AGUA FRIA ST
SITE SANTA FE
PASEO DE PERALTA
Railyard Park
DON DIEGO AVE
NÜART GALLERY
EL FAROL
CAMINO DEL MONTE SOL
BACA ST
DON GASPAR ST
BODY OF SANTA FE
OLD SANTA FE TRAIL
CORDOVA RD
OLD PECOS TRAIL
CERRILLOS RD
2ND ST
LENA ST
E SAN MATEO RD
CAMINO LEJO
MUSEUM OF INDIAN ARTS & CULTURE
EL REY INN
To Santa Fe Airport
MUSEUM OF INTERNATIONAL FOLK ART
ST. MICHAEL'S DR
ST. FRANCIS DR
ST. VINCENT HOSPITAL
LLANO ST
SIRINGO RD
0   0.5 mi
0   0.5 km
OLD SANTA FE TRAIL
ZIA RD
84
285
OLD PECOS TRAIL
RODEO RD
To Public Lands Information Center, Hwy 14 and Albuquerque
25
To Lamy

© AVALON TRAVEL

One Day in Santa Fe

Have breakfast at **Tia Sophia's** and then head to the **Palace of the Governors.** Explore the **New Mexico Museum** before walking a few blocks to visit **La Fonda.** For lunch, have a green-chile burger at **Santa Fe Bite.** From there, walk about 1 mile to **The Railyard District,** a newly revitalized area with contemporary art galleries, bookstores, cafes, boutiques, outdoor music venues, and an excellent farmers market. Walk up Guadalupe Street and at night, have dinner at **Tomasita's.** If you're still up for some fun, see if there's any live entertainment at **El Farol.**

Sights

Santa Fe has at least 11 museums and more than 200 galleries, making it the third-largest art market in the United States. There are some great places to see both traditional southwestern and contemporary art.

The Plaza

The Plaza (San Francisco St. at Old Santa Fe Trail, free) was the terminus of the Santa Fe Trail and has been a gathering place to shop, eat, and socialize since 1610. This cultural epicenter has some of the oldest landmarks and best hotels in Santa Fe. You can spend an entire afternoon shopping among the authentic American Indian art and jewelry stores, or grab an ice-cream cone and a patch of grass to relax in the most serene of city centers.

The Palace of the Governors

If only these four-foot-thick adobe walls could talk. **The Palace of the Governors** (105 W. Palace Ave., 505/476-5100, www.palaceofthegovernors.org) is the oldest continuously occupied public building in the United States, predating the White House by 200 years. Built in 1610, the Palace of the Governors served as the original seat of government for Spain's northernmost American colony and was the capitol of New Mexico during the Spanish Colonial era (1610-1680). In the late 1600s, Spain tried to force the Pueblo Indians to convert to Christianity, and they revolted in 1680. Spaniards fled from the surrounding area and took refuge in the Palace of the Governors. After the Pueblo Indians cut off their water supply, they were able to take back Santa Fe. During this time, about 1,000 Pueblo Indians lived here and added a multistory pueblo-style construction on top of the building that stands today.

When the Spanish returned to New Mexico in 1693, they destroyed the addition. Spanish rule continued until Mexico claimed independence in 1821 and took control of the region. In 1848, the Americans claimed it as a U.S. territory. Today the building shows remnants of both Spanish and Native constructions with Territorial elements and Spanish Colonial-Pueblo Revival style. Outside the building, dozens of American Indian artists and tribal members sell authentic handmade crafts and jewelry as part of a regulated marketplace. The New Mexico History Museum is inside.

★ New Mexico History Museum

The **New Mexico History Museum** (113 Lincoln Ave., 505/476-5200, www.nmhistorymuseum.org, 10am-5pm daily May-Oct.; 10am-5pm Tues.-Sun. Nov.-Apr., $9) is housed on the Plaza adjacent to the Palace of Governors with an entrance around the corner on Lincoln. Three and a half floors of exhibits explore New Mexican heritage and the history of the Southwest, offering insight into the region's indigenous people, stories along the Santa Fe Trail, and the role Spanish

colonization played in shaping Santa Fe's culture and identity.

Also on-site is New Mexico's first printing press (dating from 1834), a noncirculating library with approximately 40,000 books, 6,000 maps, and more than 750,000 photo archives from as early as 1850, and a beautiful Works Progress Administration wall mural by Olive Rush.

New Mexico Museum of Art

Located across the street from the Palace of the Governors, the **New Mexico Museum of Art** (107 W. Palace Ave., 505/476-5072, www.nmartmuseum.org, 10am-5pm daily May-Oct.; 10am-5pm Tues.-Sun. Nov.-Apr., $9) was one of the first spaces to encourage local artists to showcase their work. Today the museum displays work from New Mexican and Taos Society artists, as well as and Santa Fe Art colony members and Hopi pottery makers.

★ La Fonda

La Fonda (100 E. San Francisco St., 800/523-5002, www.lafondasantafe. com, $240-475) is a sophisticated luxury hotel in the heart of downtown Santa Fe. Located on the same site as the city's first inn, La Fonda opened in 1922. In 1925, the building changed hands and Fred Harvey leased the property. Famed architect Mary Colter renovated the interior—adding the San Francisco street entrance and enclosing the front patio—and the site operated as a Harvey House until 1968.

Today, La Fonda is the perfect blend of old southwestern character and modern amenities. Guest rooms feature original Puebloan artwork, hand-painted furniture, luxurious bathrobes, and a nightly turndown service. The rooftop bar is a wonderful place to have a drink and

top to bottom: La Fonda, Santa Fe; Georgia O'Keeffe Museum, Abiquiu; San Miguel Chapel, Santa Fe

Harvey House

Don't miss the *Setting the Standard: The Fred Harvey Company and its Legacy* exhibit at the New Mexico History Museum (113 Lincoln Ave., 505/476-5200, www.nmhistorymuseum.org, 10am-5pm daily May-Oct., 10am-5pm Tues.-Sun. Nov.-Apr., $9). The show uses artifacts from the museum's collection as well as loans from other museums to tell the story of the Fred Harvey Company and the cultural imprint it left on the American Southwest.

On exhibit are original track signs, Harvey Girl uniforms, furniture designed by Harvey House architect Mary Colter, Fred Harvey's original datebook, and artworks inspired by Harvey Houses. An interpretive station shows with interviews of Harvey Girls conducted by Katrina Parks, who produced the best documentary on the subject, *The Harvey Girls: Opportunity Bound*.

watch the sunset, and the 1920s patio still has the original skylights, terra-cotta tiles, and hand-stamped chandeliers. The Fred Harvey Package includes breakfast, two passes to the History Museum, and an autographed copy of *Appetite for America*, by Stephen Fried.

Even if you don't stay overnight, stop for a bite at **La Plazuela Restaurant** (505/995-2334, 7am-2pm and 5pm-10pm Mon.-Fri., 7am-3pm and 5pm-10pm Sat.-Sun., $8-35) and eat in the historic dining room under beautiful skylights, 460 hand-painted windows, and a romantic wrought-iron chandelier. The tempura-fried squash blossoms stuffed with goat cheese are delicious, and the guacamole is made tableside. Reservations are recommended.

San Miguel Chapel
The original **San Miguel Chapel** (401 Old Santa Fe Trail, 505/983-3974, 10am-2pm Mon.-Fri., 11am-3pm Sat., 2pm-5pm Sun., $1) was built between 1610 and 1626, making it the oldest church in Santa Fe. Erected by Tlaxcalans under the direction of Franciscan friars, the chapel was partially destroyed in 1640; then again in 1680 during the Pueblo Revolt. The present structure dates to 1710.

Inside the chapel are images of Christ on the Cross and St. John the Baptist painted in the 1630s by the Franciscans; these were used as teaching aids to try to convert the indigenous peoples to Christianity. Regardless of your faith, stepping inside this piece of history is astounding.

Museum of International Folk Art
The **Museum of International Folk Art** (706 Camino Lejo, 505/476-1200, www.internationalfolkart.org, 10am-5pm daily May-Oct.; 10am-5pm Tues.-Sun. Nov.-Apr., $9) has the world's largest collection of cultural art, with 150,000 artifacts from more than 100 nations. The museum has documented and preserved creative works from folk artists around the world since 1953, championing folk art and its impact on cultural identity before "outsider art" became hip.

Museum of Indian Arts & Culture
The **Museum of Indian Arts & Culture** (710 Camino Lejo, 505/476-1250, www.indianartsandculture.org, 10am-5pm daily May-Oct.; 10am-5pm Tues.-Sun. Nov.-Apr., $9) offers a good introduction to the American Indian communities in northern New Mexico, focusing on the history and contemporary life of the Pueblos, Navajo, and Apache. There's a huge repository of more than 10 million artifacts, with 80,000 archaeological, ethnographic, and fine arts objects.

Georgia O'Keeffe Museum
Georgia O'Keeffe was born in Wisconsin,

studied art in Chicago, and lived in New York, but it was New Mexico that changed the course of her life. O'Keeffe visited Ghost Ranch near Abiquiu in the 1930s and 1940s, and it was here that she painted some of her most famous works. The **Georgia O'Keeffe Museum** (217 Johnson St., 505/946-1000, www.okeeffemuseum.org, 9am-5pm Sat.-Thurs., 9am-7pm Fri., $12) is home to the largest collection of her art, with 1,149 paintings, drawings, and sculptures. Serious O'Keeffe fans can sign up for the **Abiquiu home & studio tour** (505/946-1098, by reservation only Mar.-Nov., $35), about one hour north of Santa Fe.

SITE Santa Fe

For a break from the traditional southwestern style, **SITE Santa Fe** (1606 Paseo de Peralta, 505/989-1199, www.sitesantafe.org, 10am-5pm Thurs. and Sat., 10am-7pm Fri., noon-5pm Sun., $10) offers a contemporary art space with experimental and innovative exhibits. You never know what you'll see here, and their forward-thinking curatorial design keeps visitors engaged, curious, and captivated.

Galleries

Sante Fe galleries are clustered within three hubs: Canyon Road, the Railyard, and downtown. The **Canyon Road Arts district** (Paseo de Peralta and Canyon Rd., southeast of the Plaza) is home to more than 40 galleries alone. Strolling Canyon Road is a popular pastime for art lovers. For contemporary art fans, the **Nüart Gallery** (670 Canyon Rd., 505/988-3888, www.nuartgallery.com, 10am-5pm daily) represents an exclusive group of talented artists whose work ranges from abstract to figurative to magical realism.

Accommodations

Inn and Spa at Loretto (211 Old Santa Fe Trail, 866/582-1646, www.destination-hotels.com/inn-at-loretto, $154-280) sits one block from bustling Santa Fe Plaza

Inn and Spa at Loretto, Santa Fe

and is walking distance to galleries, museums, and boutiques. The large and impressive hotel offers 136 guest rooms in an adobe building inspired by the Taos Pueblo. Rooms blend old-world charm and southwestern sophistication, with four-poster beds, plush robes, fireplaces, and balconies. On-site are three art galleries, a tranquil garden, a heated outdoor pool, and a full-service spa with a private elevator so you can slip downstairs for a facial, full body scrub, and massage without changing out of your robe and slippers. It's been a long trip—you deserve a little pampering.

One block from the historic Plaza is the **Hotel Chimayó** (125 Washington Ave., 505-988-4900, www.hotelchimayo. com, $108-252), a beautiful boutique hotel that honors the sacred New Mexico village of Chimayó. The hotel donates a portion of every room fee to artistic and cultural programs, events, community organizations, nonprofits, and scholarships that preserve and advance New Mexican cultural heritage. Rooms feature original artwork by more than 70 local artists; many have wood-burning fireplaces with private balconies that overlook a hacienda-style courtyard. Pets are welcome.

The town of Chimayó was once the center of lowrider culture, as exemplified by the **Low 'n Slow Lowrider Bar** (2pm-midnight Mon., 11am-midnight Tues.-Sat., 11am-11pm Sun.) in the Hotel Chimayó. The bar is decorated with tricked-out hubcaps that hang from the ceiling, tables made with chain-link steering wheels, and framed photos of lowriders hang over the diamond-tuck vinyl booths.

A classic property right on Route 66, the **El Rey Inn** (1862 Cerrillos Rd., 505/982-1931, www.elreyinnsantafe.com, $93-165) is situated on five acres with patios, fountains, gardens, and a Spanish Colonial courtyard. The 86 rooms offer a variety of choices and amenities, such as kiva fireplaces, kitchenettes, original paintings and prints, ornate tinwork, and signature southwestern wood-beamed ceilings. The Pantry restaurant is just a block away.

Food

You can make a night of it at **El Farol** (808 Canyon Rd., 505/983-9912, www. elfarolsf.com, 11am-midnight Mon.-Sat., 11am-11pm Sun., $7-36), Santa Fe's oldest cantina. The restaurant serves Spanish tapas and hosts live entertainment with world-class flamenco dancers. Make reservations in advance when going during a live performance, as it gets busy. Once there, try the grilled rib-eye skewers and the flash-fried avocado. Delish.

The ★ **Santa Fe Bite** (311 Old Santa Fe Trail, 505/982-0544, www.santafebite. com, 11am-9pm Tues.-Fri., 8am-9pm Sat., 8am-8pm Sun., $8-17) is owned by John and Bonnie Eckre, the former owners of the beloved Bobcat Bite, famous for having the best green-chile cheeseburger in New Mexico. Fortunately the

Local Eats

New Mexico grows more chile peppers than any other state in the United States. In fact, it takes its chile so seriously that it's even spelled differently (Chil is an Aztec word that means pepper; the Spanish added the "e" at the end). Chile is both the state vegetable and its largest agricultural crop. **New Mexican chiles** have a distinct and delicious flavor—perhaps it's the convergence of 400 years of Spanish and American Indian history. Farmers have been perfecting the art of growing, drying, and roasting chiles in the southwestern sunshine for centuries.

The climate of warm days and cool nights with a steady wind produce the best-tasting chile. If you visit in the fall during roasting season, the air is perfumed with their sweet, earthy aroma.

Route 66 road-trippers will have a big decision to make with each meal: whether to order red or green chile. Green has a tangy flavor, similar to a green tomato, while red is imbued with a rich, deep, earthy flavor. If you can't decide, just order "Christmas-style" for a bit of both.

food is still just as delicious. The burger is a mix of chuck and sirloin from Clovis, New Mexico, that is ground fresh daily. A cast-iron grill (built by John) cooks the meat slowly, bringing out the savoriness and elevating the flavor. The green chiles are from Hatch, New Mexico, and are roasted until they have a firm al dente texture; when you bite into them, the subtle, smoky flavor is sublime. Santa Fe Bite keeps winning awards every year—whatever they're doing, it's working.

The Shed (113½ E. Palace Ave., 505/982-9030, http://the-shed-restaurant. myshopify.com, 11am-2:30pm and 5pm-9pm daily, $8-24) is a family-owned business that's been going strong since 1953. The Shed is famous for their spicy red-chile enchiladas and blue-corn dishes. The restaurant is housed in an adobe hacienda that dates back 1692, with nine rooms and a sunny brick courtyard shaded with trumpet vines. Though quite popular (almost annoyingly so), the charming, relaxing atmosphere makes dining here a memorable Santa Fe experience worth the hassle. But save yourself the grief—call ahead and make a reservation.

With a tin ceiling, old-fashioned, black-and-white checked floors, and the comforting scent of warm *sopaipillas* (pillows of fried dough), the **Plaza Café** (54 Lincoln Ave., 505/982-1664, www.santafeplazacafe.com, 7am-8pm Mon.-Thurs., 7am-9pm Fri.-Sun., $8-17) makes you want to grab a seat and soak up some history. Locals from the nearby courthouse stop by every day to enjoy blue-corn pancakes for breakfast, tortilla soup for lunch, and green-chile meat loaf for dinner. This place has been owned by the same family since 1947, and the staff has been working here for decades.

Santa Fe is best experienced on foot. If you don't want set aside an hour to sit down to eat, grab a Frito pie (chili and cheese in a bag of Fritos) at the **Five & Dime** (58 E. San Francisco St., 505/992-1800, www.fiveanddimegs.com, 8am-10pm Mon.-Fri., $8) and keep walking as you munch away.

Café Pasqual's (121 Don Gaspar, 800/722-7672, www.pasquals.com, 8am-3pm daily, dinner 5:30pm-close, $10-33) sits tucked away in a historic pueblo-style adobe. The festive dining room, decorated with hand-painted Mexican tiles and murals, serves delicious food. Ingredients are meticulously selected; the beef, pork, eggs, dairy, and produce are organic and the bread, ice cream, and chile sauces are made on-site. The corned-beef and trout hash is moist and full of flavor, and the quinoa burger is fantastic. This is one of the most popular restaurants in Santa Fe, so call ahead to reserve a table.

For authentic New Mexican cuisine, and some of the best green chile in Santa Fe, ★ **Tia Sophia's** (210 W. San Francisco St., 505/983-9880, 7am-2pm Mon.-Sat., 8am-1pm Sun., $6-12) is a true locals hangout with great prices, friendly service, and delicious food. They possibly serve the best breakfast burrito in town, and any dish smothered with their homemade sauces will be a hit. Don't worry if there's a line out front, as it usually moves quickly and it's definitely worth the wait. Don't forget to order some flaky *sopaipillas.*

Tomasita's (500 S. Guadalupe St., 505/983-5721, www.tomasitas.com, 11am-9pm Mon.-Thurs., 11am-10pm Fri.-Sat., $10-20) specializes in northern New Mexican food and has won awards for the best green and red chile. The blue-corn enchiladas and the sangria swirl margarita are amazing. The restaurant has been owned and operated by the same family for more than 40 years; they plan to step into the future with the installation of a solar-powered carport.

The Pantry (1820 Cerrillos Rd., 505/986-0022, www.pantrysantafe.com, 6:30am-8:30pm Mon.-Sat., 7am-8:30pm Sun., $6-18) has been a Santa Fe staple since 1948. Go for breakfast and choose between the *"buenos dias"* with potatoes, green chile, two eggs, and cheese, or the breakfast burrito (but red or green?). Either way, you'll eat your way to nirvana.

◈ Back on 66

Exit Santa Fe driving south on Cerrillos Road (Hwy. 14) until you cross US 84/285. At this point, determine whether to take the side trip and head north to **Taos,** follow the post-1937 alignment to **Albuquerque,** or take the detour to **Turquoise Trail.**

The side trip to **Taos** is recommended. From the south end of Santa Fe, there are two options. Staying on Highway 599, which bypasses Santa Fe and rejoins U.S. 84 on the north side of town, is the faster route. Or take Cerrillos Road (Highway 14) north through town until it merges with U.S. 84 on the north side of the downtown area.

For those following the post-1937 alignment, the most direct route to **Albuquerque** is to keep heading south on Cerrillos Road (Hwy. 14) and join I-25 south for 1.7 miles. Turn right (west) onto Highway 599 and take the next left to follow the South Frontage Road for I-25. Drive approximately 9 miles south to Exit 267 where you will join I-25 to follow the post-1930s alignment to Albuquerque.

At the junction of Highways 599 and 14 and I-25, you can follow the **Turquoise Trail** detour south along Highway 14.

◈ Side Trip: Taos

The High Road to Taos

The northern New Mexico landscape is layered with colorful skies over a stunning view of mountains and multihued mesas; you'll pass by peach and apple orchards and chile farms on the way to Taos.

Follow I-84 north for 20 miles to its junction with Highway 68 near Española. Turn north (right) onto Highway 68, then in 0.5 mile turn east (another right) onto Highway 76. In 7 miles, you'll reach the village of Chimayó.

Chimayó

The village of Chimayó, nestled in the Sangre de Cristo foothills, was settled around 1740. This region has a long history of beautiful fiber arts and talented weavers that spans generations. En route, you'll pass by the picturesque **Santuario del Señor de Esquipulas** (15 Santuario Dr., 505/351-9961, 9am-5pm daily Oct.-Apr.; 9am-6pm daily May-Sept., free), built around 1814.

Stop for lunch at the **Rancho de Chimayó Restaurante** (300 Santa Fe County Rd. 98, 505/351-4444, www.

ranchodechimayo.com, 11:30am-9pm daily May-Oct.; 11:30am-9pm Tues.-Sun. Nov.-Apr., $9-22), a New Mexican restaurant and inn housed in a historic renovated home. To get here from Highway 76, turn right (south) on County Road 98. The restaurant is 0.5 mile south on the left (east) side of the highway.

Cordova

Highway 76 climbs west for 5 miles to Cordova, a town popular for its wood carving. The **Castillo Gallery** (181 County Rd. 80, 505/351-4067, www.mulert.com) doesn't have regular hours, but if it's open, stop in to see the intricately patterned metal sculptures, contemporary wood carvings, and soft-muted abstract paintings.

Truchas

Highway 76 keeps climbing for 4 miles to Truchas, a Spanish Colonial outpost perched on an 8,000-foot mesa with spectacular views. There are many arts and crafts locales along the road here; to get a sense of the caliber of artists in this area, visit the High Road Artisans (1642 NM 76, http://highroadnewmexico.com/map) for a list of workshops, art classes, and information about the art and history of this area.

The **High Road Marketplace** (1642 Hwy. 76, 505/689-2689, www.highroadmarketplace.com, 10am-5pm daily) co-op sells jewelry, art, pottery, quilts, leather, metals, homemade soaps, and other great gift items created by 70 local artisans. **Cordova's Handweaving Workshop** (32 County Rd. 75, 505/689-2437) has been producing gorgeous blankets, place mats, and rugs in striking designs for four generations. **Hand Artes Gallery** (137 County Rd. 75, 505/689-2443, www.handartesgallery.com) features an eclectic range of artwork from abstract painters and glass

top to bottom: Rio Grande Gorge Bridge; the San José de Gracia chapel, Las Trampas; Truchas, NM

artists, as well as sublime furniture and steel sculptures.

Las Trampas

Keep driving northeast on Highway 76 for 7 miles to the town of Las Trampas. At one time, a defensive wall surrounded the town and its central plaza in an attempt to protect inhabitants from Ute, Comanche, and Apache attacks. For centuries, Las Trampas was an isolated and remote village; the community was completely cut off from popular culture. As a result, the Spanish heritage here goes back several generations and is pure and particular to this region. Today there are no remains of the defensive wall, but you'll know you are in Las Trampas when you see one of the most elegant, ancient Spanish Colonial churches in New Mexico. The **San José de Gracia** (505/351-4360) chapel, on the east (right) side of Highway 76, was built in 1780. Today you can see the original wide-plank wooden floors, an original transverse clerestory window, and a wood-beam ceiling painted with designs from the 18th and 19th century.

Peñasco

Highway 76 keeps climbing 6 miles north through Chamisal to dead-end into Highway 75. Turn right (south) onto Highway 75 and drive 1.5 miles east toward Peñasco. Here you can stop at ★ **Sugar Nymphs Bistro** (15046 Hwy. 75, 505/587-0311, www.sugarnymphs. com, 11:30am-3pm Mon.-Wed., 11:30am-3pm and 5pm-8pm Thurs-Sat., 11am-2:30pm Sun. in summer, call for winter hours, $8-18) for tasty sandwiches made with fresh, home-made bread as well as red-quinoa salads and pasta with green-chile cream sauce. Owner Kai Harper is the former executive chef of the famed Greens Restaurant in San Francisco. She uses locally sourced and seasonal ingredients, and the food is excellent. Wash it all down with a cranberry lemonade then try the carrot cake for dessert.

From Peñasco, follow Highway 75 east for a few more miles, then take Highway 518 north. Drive 12 miles through Talpa to Highway 68, where you will turn right (northeast). Taos is only a few miles away.

Taos

Taos is a small high-desert art colony with a rich cultural history tucked away in the hills of northern New Mexico. The town was constructed in the Spanish tradition as a fortified plaza surrounded by a defensive wall. Shortly after Spanish occupation, the Pueblo Indians who were already here led a revolt against the missionaries in 1680. The Spanish fled, only to return in 1692. These cross-cultural clashes are apparent in the downtown Historic District where Territorial Mission Revival, Spanish Colonial style, and Pueblo Revival buildings stand side by side.

Artists started to come to Taos in the late 19th century, and it has since become a spiritual mecca for creatives. A quaint town with winding streets and adobe buildings, it's easy to spend a whole weekend here.

Sights
Millicent Rogers Museum

The **Millicent Rogers Museum** (1504 Millicent Rogers Rd., 575/758-2462, www.millicentrogers.org, 10am-5pm Tues.-Sun. Apr.-Oct., $10) is a must for those interested in the history of pueblo pottery making. The private collection of oil heiress and model Millicent Rogers, the museum holds 20 galleries and exhibition spaces that feature Mexican folk art, modernist and historic jewelry, Navajo weavings, and black-on-black pottery from the San Ildefonso Pueblo.

Heading north on Highway 64, and turn left (west) on Millicent Rogers Road. The museum is 0.5 mile south on the right.

Taos Pueblo

The San Geronimo de Taos, commonly known as **Taos Pueblo** (505/758-1028, www.taospueblo.com, 8am-4:30pm daily, $16), has been occupied for more than 1,000 years. This multistory pueblo is the only existing American Indian community designated as both a UNESCO World Heritage Site and a National Historical Landmark. Built between AD 1000 and 1450, today the pueblo is home to about 150 people; it is considered one of the oldest continuously inhabited communities in the United States. To visit, contact tribal members who lead walks through the village of adobe dwellings.

To reach the pueblo, follow Paseo Del Pueblo Street until the road curves left (northwest) and turn right (east) on Paseo Del Pueblo Norte (the highway to the town of Taos). The Taos Pueblo is 2 miles up the road.

Rio Grande Gorge Bridge

The **Rio Grande Gorge Bridge** (El Prado, 575/758-8851, www.blm.gov) is a steel deck arch bridge that overlooks the magnificent Rio Grande. Construction began in 1963, and the bridge opened in 1965 (it was originally called the "bridge to nowhere" because there wasn't enough funding to finish it). Today, it is one of the highest bridges in the United States—a 650-foot drop into a 1,300-foot wide gorge. Be careful as the chest-high guardrail will not prevent you from falling over. To find the bridge, take Highway 64 north (west) about 10 miles from Taos.

★ Earthship Biotecture

Earthship Biotecture (2 Earthship Way, 575/751-0462, www.earthship.com, 10am-4pm daily, $7-15) is a community of off-the-grid homes located in the world's largest self-sufficient residential development. The Earthships are fantastic sculptural homes with curved walls and whimsical roofs topped by playful

Earthship Biotecture

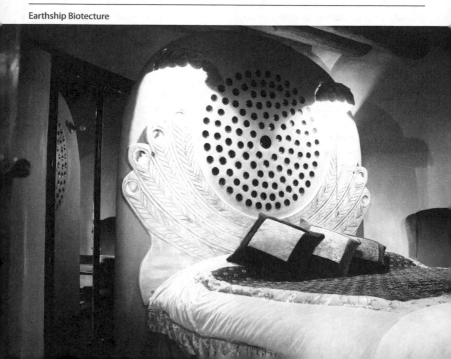

appendages that spin like weather vanes. They are also incredibly efficient. Walls are made from compacted earth, tires, and cans in order to create "thermal mass," an efficient insulation. Despite the range of temperatures here (from 100°F to -20°F), Earthship homes average a pleasant interior temperature of 70°F without benefit of heating or cooling. Power is generated by solar panels and wind-powered devices and then stored in batteries. Water is collected on the roof and used up to four times (sink and shower water becomes gray water which then feeds the plants; that water is pumped back to the toilets where it is flushed into a septic tank.) With only eight inches of water collected per year, this resourceful system ensures there is enough water to run the entire home.

The **Visitor Center tour** ($7) includes a 15-minute video, a 20-minute slide-show, and a wall of literature and photos. A longer, more involved **tour of the community** ($15) includes visits to several

homes and must be scheduled at least two weeks in advance. You can also stay overnight in an Earthship, which is highly recommended.

The Earthship Biotecture is outside Taos on the way back to Santa Fe by the loop route through Tres Piedras. Heading north (west) on Highway 64, the Visitor Center is about 2 miles after crossing the Rio Grand Gorge Bridge; turn right (east) on Lava Lane. The Visitor Center will be the first building on your left.

Accommodations

El Pueblo Lodge (412 Paseo del Pueblo Norte, 866/582-1646 www.elpueblolodge. com, $113-190) is a charming and reasonably priced hotel with the laid-back vibe you would expect in Taos. Some rooms include fireplaces and *viga* wood beams on the ceiling. It's within walking distance to the Plaza, shops, and restaurants.

El Monte Sagrado (317 Kit Carson Rd., 575/758-3502, www.elmontesagrado. com, $179-439) offers rustic elegance and resort-style living. Choose from 48 Taos Mountain Rooms, 18 Native American Suites, 6 Casitas, and 12 Premier Suites. All rooms feature plush bedding, original artwork, soaking tubs, and fireplaces.

For a once-in-a-lifetime experience, spend the night at ★ **Earthship Biotecture** (2 Earthship Way, 575/751-0462, www.earthship.com, $175-410). These strange and beautiful self-sustaining homes are made from recycled materials and are fronted by a two-story, glass-walled greenhouse. Some homes feature fully stocked kitchens, living rooms, ornate handmade bed frames, and the bathrooms with bottle walls that resemble jewels of light.

Food

Love Apple (803 Paseo del Pueblo Norte, 575/751-0050, www.theloveapple.net, 5pm-9pm Tues.-Sun., $14-25) uses locally sourced organic produce and free-range meat to create some exciting and interesting dishes. Don't miss the blue-corn muffins or the stone-fruit salad with goat cheese. Reservations are recommended, and the restaurant is cash only.

Love Apple is housed in a quaint 19th-century chapel with thick adobe walls and a steeple. Look for it 1 mile north of Taos Plaza, on the right between Laughing Horse and Lotaburger North. Do not use GPS for directions.

La Cueva (135 Paseo del Pueblo Sur, 575/758-7001, www.lacuevacafe.com, 10am-9pm daily, $7-14) may be tiny in size, but it's big in flavor. The enchiladas and the trout and garlic shrimp tacos are great, and the menu includes a good selection of gluten-free and vegetarian options. Even New Mexicans can't get enough of this place.

For a break from New Mexican food, **Sushi a la Hattori** (1405 Paseo Del Pueblo Norte, 575/737-5123, $10-30) is a good alternative. The salmon sashimi is rich and buttery, the Seafood Sunomono Salad is fresh and delicious, the octopus is sweet and chewy, the noodle dishes are full of umami flavor, and the solid sake selection rivals most urban, ocean-adjacent sushi restaurants. This is an authentic, classic Japanese place, but the fantastic views of Taos Mountain will remind you that you're still in New Mexico.

This restaurant is north of the town of El Prado as you leave Taos on Highway 64. It's located behind the Overland Sheepskin Company; look for a wooden porch swing and a rusted tractor out front.

✦ Back to Santa Fe

To return to Santa Fe, head north on State Route 64 out of Taos. (Note: this loop route also passes by the Earthship Biotecture.) Drive 28 miles to Tres Piedras and take State Route 285 south (left). Follow State Route 285 south for 47 miles to State Route 84. Turn south (left) onto State Route 84 and drive 8 miles through Española. Just north of Santa Fe is the junction with Highway

Hyatt Regency Tamaya Resort and Spa, Bernalillo

599. Take Highway 599 (Veterans Memorial Hwy.) south for 13 miles to join I-25 South. From I-25, you'll follow the post-1937 alignment south to Albuquerque.

Post-1937 Alignment to Albuquerque

On I-25 as you approach Exit 264, look west to see **La Bajada Hill** where Route 66 zigzagged through a steep elevation change from 1926 to 1932. This was quite treacherous terrain for early horse- and wagon-era travel. Inmates from the nearby penitentiary took sand from the Rio Santa Fe and used a cut-and-fill method to carve 23 hairpin curves. Today, this road is too rough for passenger vehicles, so we'll stay on I-25. In 20 miles, take Exit 248; turn right (northwest) and then left (southwest) onto Highway 313 and in about 6 miles you'll reach the town of Bernalillo.

Bernalillo

Before the Spanish arrived, Bernalillo had at least two Tiwa-speaking pueblos built alongside the river, where there was plenty of water for crop irrigation. Today, the Santa Ana Pueblo owns the Hyatt Regency.

Silva's Saloon

Back in the early 1930s, Felix Silva was a bootlegger and moonshiner, and when he went legit after Prohibition, he opened **Silva's Saloon** (955 S. Camino Del Pueblo, 505/867-9976, 11am-8pm Mon.-Sat., noon-6pm Sun.) right on Route 66. When his son took it over, there were still some illicit activities like card games and liquor sales on Sunday, which was illegal in New Mexico at the time. In 1949, some customers started a fight with Felix, and he ended it by hitting one of them with a pipe. The blood splatter on the ceiling is still there. Today the saloon is a local favorite. The hats hanging from the ceiling are from loyal patrons who have passed away, and the bottles lining the wall that have been dipped in wax have been there since the 1930s.

Accommodations and Food

Set on 500 acres alongside the Sandia Mountains and the Rio Grande River, the ★ **Hyatt Regency Tamaya Resort and Spa** (1300 Tuyuna Trail, 505/867-1234, www.tamaya.hyatt.com, $190-304) in Bernalillo is unique. The 350 pueblo-style guest rooms are decorated with handmade, natural materials created by tribal artisans. On-site amenities include three heated outdoor pools, two tennis courts, horseback riding, and the Tamaya Mist Spa & Salon. More unusual are the colony of 80,000 bees used to pollinate the surrounding gardens. Eighty pounds of wild honey and natural beeswax have been produced and are used in the resort's spa products and even in dishes at their **Corn Maiden Restaurant** (5:30pm-9pm Wed.-Thurs., 5:30pm-10pm Fri.-Sat., 5:30pm-9pm Sun., $35-50), such as honey-vanilla ice cream topped with candied green-chile bits. The Hyatt's love of nature keeps going with other green-friendly efforts, such as composting, recycling, and water-conservation practices.

To get there from Highway 313 South, turn right (west) onto State Route 550. After about 2 miles, turn right (north) on Tamaya Boulevard and follow the signs to the Hyatt.

The **Range Café** (925 Camino Del Pueblo, 505/867-1700, www.rangecafe. com, 7am-9:30pm Sun.-Thurs., 7am-10pm Fri.-Sat., $8-16) has only been around since 1992, but with food this good they'll be around for more decades to come. The regional comfort food (such as green-chile hollandaise sauce) is made from scratch and desserts—from green-chile apple pie to coconut cream pie to Almond Joy cheesecake—are innovative and delicious. A bar and live music make it fun and memorable … even President Obama stopped here in 2008.

⬥ Back on 66

Leaving Bernalillo, drive south on Highway 313 for 7 miles. After passing Highway 556, the road curves west and dips south onto 4th Street. Continue about 7 miles into Albuquerque.

⬥ Detour: The Turquoise Trail

The Turquoise Trail (Hwy. 14) connects the high country of Santa Fe with Albuquerque. If you'd rather not take I-25 south from Santa Fe to Albuquerque, this 60-mile detour offers a nice alternative. Highway 14 travels south for 42 miles through several mining towns to the quirky Tinkertown tourist attraction and the lovely arts community of Madrid before reaching I-40 just east of Albuquerque. (It's called the Turquoise Trail because the nearby mines were filled with the signature stone.) To

access Highway 14 from I-25 South, take Highway 599 east (left) and turn south (right) onto Highway 14 South.

Madrid

Madrid (pronounced MA-drid) is a budding artist colony reminiscent of Santa Fe before it became commercialized. The former mining town has a rich history that dates back to the 1800s. It's unique in that there are only two other mines in the world where both hard and soft coal could be mined from the same shaft. Once coal was no longer primary commodity, Madrid became a ghost town. But in the early 1970s, artists began moving here and converted many of the old buildings into shops, studios, and galleries. Today, it's a great place to shop for blown-glass, clothing, and turquoise jewelry.

Shopping

Seppanen & Daughters Fine Textiles (2879 Hwy. 14, 505/424-7470, www.fine-textiles.com) features absolutely gorgeous Tibetan carpets, Navajo and African textiles, and Oaxacan rugs in a variety of sizes, colors, and patterns.

Weasel & Fitz (2878 Hwy. 14, 505/474-4893, 10am-5pm most days, closed Tues.-Wed. in winter) represents more than 30 artists. Artworks are created from recycled and found objects and the work ranges from ethnographic and contemporary painted forms to unique nightlights and funky lamps and shades.

Cowgirl Red (2865 Hwy. 14, 505/474-0344, 11am-5pm most weekdays and Sat.-Sun., www.cowgirlred.com) sells antiques, fine art, jewelry, collectibles, and more than 400 pair of vintage and new cowboy boots.

Food

Jezebel Soda Fountain (2860 Hwy. 14, 505/471-3915, 10am-5pm daily) is housed in a 1920s-era soda fountain. The shop, which sells jewelry, clothing, furniture, lighting, and paintings, is also a small

The DeAnza Motor Lodge

When black travelers came through Albuquerque on Route 66, only 6 percent of the nearly 100 motels along Central Avenue would open their doors. The **DeAnza Motor Lodge** (4301 Central Ave. NE) was one of them. Built in 1939 and run by C. G. Wallace, a prominent Zuni trader, the DeAnza was a gathering spot for artisans, traders, and those who loved southwestern Indian crafts. Comprised of seven separate buildings in the Spanish Colonial-Pueblo Revival style, it was the largest motel on Central Avenue. The original 30 rooms eventually expanded to 67 and offered modern amenities such as private telephones and air-conditioning. The on-site Turquoise Room diner featured thousands of pieces of turquoise embedded in the linoleum floor. Seven murals painted by Zuni artist Tony Edaakie for the basement conference room depicted a sacred Zuni Shalako ceremony.

Wallace sold the building in 1983 and after several changes in ownership, the property sat empty for more than a decade. The city of Albuquerque purchased the hotel in 2003, saving it from demolition; in 2004, the DeAnza was named a city landmark. Today, it is recognized as one of the best remaining mid-century motels along Central Avenue and has been listed on the State Historic Register. It even made an appearance in an episode of the television series *Breaking Bad*. An $8-million-dollar plan to convert the property into a condo-hotel hybrid with shops and restaurants has been approved and is scheduled to open in 2016.

restaurant. So you can get uniquely flavored milk shakes, sodas, and gelato (like caramel green chile) along with your Santa Fe souvenir.

Known locally as "Madrid's living room," the **Mine Shaft Tavern** (2846 Hwy. 14, 505/473-0743, www.themineshafttavern.com, 11:30am-8pm Sun.-Thurs., 11:30am-9pm Fri.-Sat.) serves roadhouse food (including burgers made from local Waygu beef) along with 12 beers on tap and live music on weekends.

◆ Back on the Turquoise Trail

Keep heading south on Highway 14 for 20 miles, winding past Placer Mountain and through the towns of Golden and San Antonio. Turn right on Highway 536 (west) for 1 mile to visit Tinkertown.

Tinkertown

Tucked away in Sandia Park is an Americana wonderland of curiosities. For more than 40 years, folk artist Ross Ward collected, carved, and constructed an eclectic assortment of miniature figurines in a 22-room museum. **Tinkertown** (121 Sandia Crest Rd., 505/281-5233, www.tinkertown.com, 9am-6pm daily, $3.50) portrays a myriad of miniature scenes that include a 1940s big-top circus, a blacksmith shop, a western town with old-fashioned storefronts, a fortune teller, and walls made with more than 50,000 glass bottles.

◆ Back on 66

Head south on Highway 14 for 5 miles to join I-40 West. Follow I-40 west for 7 miles to Exit 167. Turn right (west) onto Central Avenue (Rte. 66) in Albuquerque.

Albuquerque

New Mexico's biggest city has a long, deep Route 66 history. During the Dust Bowl years, migrants had their vehicles checked out at the Jones Motor Company. Black travelers who had been driving through sundown towns in the Ozarks and Texas did their best to time their overnight stay in Albuquerque because the town had hotel options. A drive down Central Avenue was exciting—there were about 100 motels, many of them

Outside Albuquerque

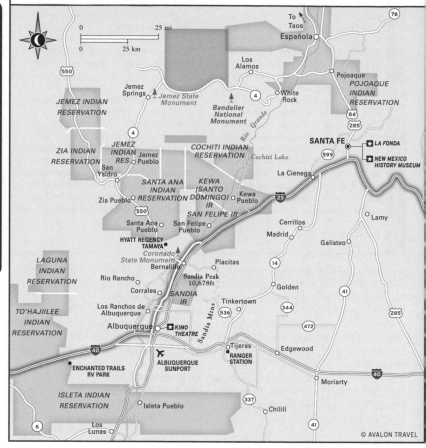

To Taos
Española
76
Los Alamos
Pojoaque
POJOAQUE INDIAN RESERVATION
550
Jemez Springs
Jemez State Monument
4
White Rock
JEMEZ INDIAN RESERVATION
Bandelier National Monument
84
285
Rio Grande
SANTA FE
LA FONDA
NEW MEXICO HISTORY MUSEUM
ZIA INDIAN RESERVATION
JEMEZ INDIAN RES.
Jemez Pueblo
COCHITI INDIAN RESERVATION
Cochiti Lake
599
4
San Ysidro
La Cienega
SANTA ANA INDIAN RESERVATION
KEWA (SANTO DOMINGO) IR
Kewa Pueblo
Zia Pueblo
25
Lamy
550
SAN FELIPE IR
Cerrillos
Santa Ana Pueblo
San Felipe Pueblo
Madrid
Galisteo
HYATT REGENCY TAMAYA
Coronado State Monument
Bernalillo
Placitas
14
Golden
41
LAGUNA INDIAN RESERVATION
Rio Rancho
Sandia Peak 10,678ft
Corrales
SANDIA IR
Tinkertown
344
285
TO'HAJIILEE INDIAN RESERVATION
Los Ranchos de Albuquerque
536
472
Albuquerque
KIMO THEATRE
Sandia Mtns
Tijeras
RANGER STATION
Edgewood
40
ENCHANTED TRAILS RV PARK
ALBUQUERQUE SUNPORT
337
Moriarty
40
ISLETA INDIAN RESERVATION
Isleta Pueblo
Chilili
6
Los Lunas
41

0   25 mi
0   25 km

© AVALON TRAVEL

lit up with huge neon signs. However, since only about 6 percent of those hotels served blacks, the Green Book was a critical traveling companion.

Today, fewer than 40 of the motels along Central Avenue remain. As Albuquerque spread outward in the 1960s, parts of downtown were abandoned and many historic buildings were razed for high-rises and parking lots. While some are being restored, others sit crumbling on the roadside (although some were actually used in the television series *Breaking Bad*.)

◆ Route 66 through Albuquerque

The original 1926 alignment of Route 66 traveled from north to south on 4th Street. In 1937, Route 66 was realigned along Central Avenue. For the post-1937 alignment (and the quickest route traveling west on I-40), take Exit 167 to cross under the freeway, then turn right (west) on Central Avenue. Follow Central Avenue through Albuquerque until it rejoins I-40.

If you opted to take the pre-1937 alignment through Santa Fe, you'll be traveling south on 4th Street as you enter Albuquerque. Turn right (west) on Central Avenue.

Sights

Albuquerque is popular for hosting **Balloon Fiesta** (www.balloonfiesta.com), the world's largest hot-air balloon event. If you want to see the balloons, plan to arrive the first week in October; otherwise, it's best to avoid visiting in early October, as the whole state gets flooded with tourists.

Tewa Motor Lodge

Entering Albuquerque via I-40 and Central Avenue (via the post-1937 alignment), keep an eye out for the 1946 **Tewa Motor Lodge** (5715 Central Ave. NE), built in the Pueblo Revival style with projecting *vigas* (wooden roof beams) and rounded parapets. Though the neon sign looks original, unfortunately it isn't (but it's still great for a photo op).

Madonna of the Trail

If following the pre-1937 alignment, you'll drive into town along 4th Street. At the corner of Marble Avenue, look for the 18-foot tall **Madonna of the Trail** statue. This monument of the Mother Road was dedicated to pioneer women who traveled the National Old Trails. There were 12 installed; this one is identical to the one in Upland, California.

Telephone Museum of New Mexico

Look at your tiny cell phone, then marvel at how far we've come in the world of communications at the **Telephone Museum of New Mexico** (110 4th St. NW, 505/842-2937, www.telcomhistory.org 10am-2pm Mon., Wed., and Fri., $2). Three floors of unique exhibits showcase the variety of communication devices made in the past century—everything from switchboards to teletype machines and hundreds of telephones are on display. This place will undoubtedly make you appreciate your cell phone, even when you can't get a signal during rush hour traffic.

★ KiMo Theatre

The **KiMo Theatre** (421 Central Ave. NW, 505/768-3544, www.kimotickets.com, 11am-8pm Wed.-Sat., 11am-3pm Sun.) came to life a year after the birth of Route 66. Opulent film palaces were popular in the 1920s, and the KiMo was one of the most unique. It was built to feature both stage productions and motion pictures and the first theater to fuse art deco with American Indian style. The interior is flanked with seven murals; iconic American Indian motifs include air vents designed to resemble Navajo rugs, chandeliers shaped like drums, and kiva, bird, clouds, and Navajo symbols throughout.

In 1961, a fire destroyed parts of the theater. It fell into disrepair and eventually closed in 1968. Slated for destruction, it was thankfully saved, restored, and revitalized in the 1990s. Today, the KiMo screens classic movies like *High Noon* and *Dirty Harry*, as well as more modern films like *The Dark Knight*. Even if you don't have time to see a show here, stop in to view the stunning entryway and gaze at this historic treasure.

Old Town

Albuquerque began as a farming community that was the sheepherding center of the West. When Spain established a military presence here in 1706, they built a town in the Spanish tradition with a central plaza surrounded by government buildings. Today, this area is Albuquerque's historic Old Town, with more than 150 shops, galleries, and restaurants housed in adobe buildings along winding brick paths. It's a great place to stretch your legs and step way back into the past. One of the most impressive structures is the 1793 **San Felipe de Neri Church** (2005 N. Plaza St. NW, 505/243-4628, www.sanfelipedeneri.org, free), the oldest chapel in Albuquerque. The adobe walls are five feet thick and still home to

Albuquerque

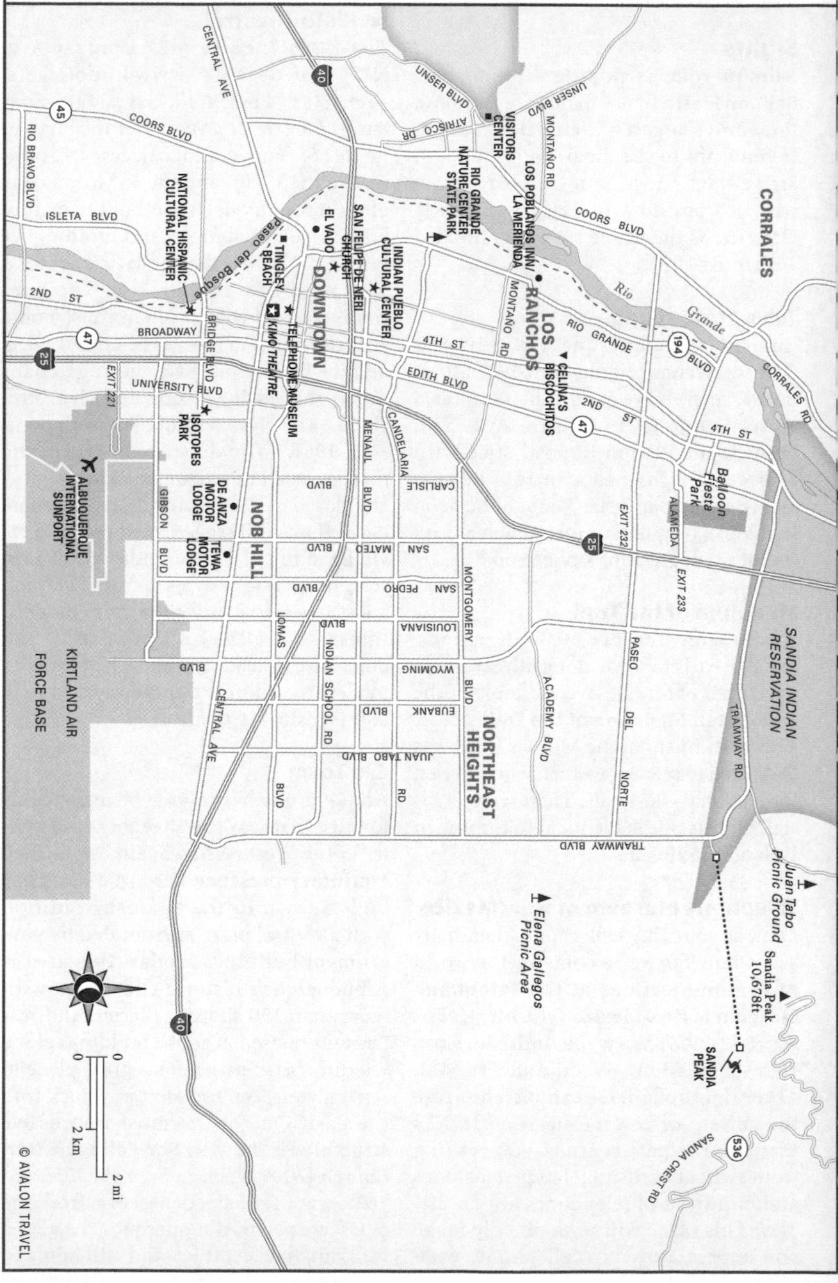

CORRALES

RIO BRAVO BLVD

COORS BLVD

CENTRAL AVE

UNSER BLVD

VISITORS CENTER

ATRISCO DR

MONTAÑO RD

LOS POBLANOS INN/ LA MERIENDA

RIO GRANDE NATURE CENTER STATE PARK

ISLETA BLVD

NATIONAL HISPANIC CULTURAL CENTER

Paseo del Bosque

EL VADO

SAN FELIPE DE NERI CHURCH

TINGLEY BEACH

DOWNTOWN

INDIAN PUEBLO CULTURAL CENTER

2ND ST

BROADWAY

TELEPHONE MUSEUM

KIMO THEATRE

BRIDGE BLVD

UNIVERSITY BLVD

ISOTOPES PARK

DE ANZA MOTOR LODGE

TEWA MOTOR LODGE

GIBSON BLVD

NOB HILL

ALBUQUERQUE INTERNATIONAL SUNPORT

KIRTLAND AIR FORCE BASE

MENAUL BLVD

CANDELARIA

CARLISLE

SAN MATEO BLVD

SAN PEDRO BLVD

MONTGOMERY BLVD

LOUISIANA BLVD

LOMAS BLVD

INDIAN SCHOOL RD

WYOMING BLVD

EUBANK BLVD

NORTHEAST HEIGHTS

JUAN TABO BLVD

CENTRAL AVE

LOS RANCHOS

CELINA'S BISOCHITOS

4TH ST

EDITH BLVD

2ND ST

4TH ST

ALAMEDA

Balloon Fiesta Park

Rio Grande

CORRALES RD

MONTAÑO RD

RIO GRANDE BLVD

PASEO DEL NORTE

ACADEMY BLVD

SANDIA INDIAN RESERVATION

TRAMWAY RD

TRAMWAY BLVD

SANDIA PEAK

Juan Tabo Picnic Ground

Sandia Peak 10,678ft

Elena Gallegos Picnic Area

SANDIA CREST RD

EXIT 221

EXIT 232

EXIT 233

0 2 km

0 2 mi

© AVALON TRAVEL

Nob Hill District

The **Nob Hill District** (Central Ave. between Washington St. to Girard Blvd.) spans about 15 blocks lined with boutique shops. This area was New Mexico's first drive-in shopping center, built in 1947 with streamline modern architecture, white stucco walls, and decorative brick course with bands of terra-cotta tiles, curved corners, neon, and large plate-glass windows. The heart of the shopping center sits at the corner of Central Avenue and Carlisle Boulevard.

One the west side of the district is a police station housed in a restored **Valentine Diner** (2970 Monte Vista Blvd. NE), which formerly operated as the Little House Diner (1942-1992). The station is one block from Route 66 off Dartmouth Drive NE.

pastoral, community worship, with educational and church services.

Albuquerque Museum of Art and History

The **Albuquerque Museum of Art and History** (2000 Mountain Rd. NW, 505/842-0111, www.albuquerquemuseum.org, 9am-5pm Tues.-Sun., $4), located in the heart of Old Town, has exhibits that celebrate the diverse history and culture of the Southwest. Interactive exhibits present local stories, geography, culture, and history. There is also an area where visitors can electronically send a Route 66 postcard to friends and family.

American International Rattlesnake Museum

Normally, a rattlesnake is something you try to avoid on a road trip, but the **American International Rattlesnake Museum** (202 San Felipe St. NW, 505/242-6569, www.rattlesnakes.com, 10am-6pm Mon.-Sat., 1pm-5pm Sun. June-Aug., 11:30am-5:30pm Mon.-Fri., 10am-6pm Sat., 1pm-5pm Sun. Sept.-May, $5) in Old Town offers the best way to have a safe and painless encounter. At this educational center, you can learn everything you'd ever want to know about snakebites, strike positions, head shapes, fangs, and those signature rattles.

Red's Old School Hydraulics

At the lowrider garage, **Red's Old School Hydraulics** (2220 Central Ave. SW, www.redshydros.com), owner Eppie Martinez has some incredible, classic lowriders in various stages of beautification. When I was there, the car out front had just been used in George Lopez's latest film. It's not really open to the public as a showcase, but just walking by and chatting with Eppie was exciting enough for me.

Nearby is the recently restored neon sign of a cowboy lassoing the words **"El Don"** (2222 Central Ave. SW) and leaping over a turquoise sign.

El Vado Auto Court Motel

An Irishman built the 1937 **El Vado Auto Court Motel** (2500 Central Ave. SW) in the Pueblo Revival style with exposed wooden roof beams, irregular-shaped windows, varying buttresses, covered carports, and a colorful neon sign of an American Indian. It's a pristine example of an unaltered pre-1940s era motor court and one of the few left along Route 66 in New Mexico. Listed on the National Register of Historic Places in 1993, it has been closed for many years. A company recently stepped up to redevelop the property into a boutique motel with a food court, pool, shops, and an amphitheater. Let's hope they preserve the integrity of this architectural gem.

Indian Pueblo Cultural Center

To understand the distinctions between the state's 19 pueblos, visit the **Indian Pueblo Cultural Center** (2401 12th St. NW, 505/843-7270, www.indianpueblo.

org, 9am-5pm daily, $6) where you can learn about the Pueblo Revolt of 1680 and discover the storytelling traditions and evolving histories of the Pueblo people from pre-Columbian to modern times. The Shumakolowa (the retail store of the Cultural Center) sells traditional and contemporary arts and crafts by internationally renowned tribal artists.

From Central Avenue (Route 66), turn right (north) on 12th Street NW and drive 1.5 miles. The Indian Pueblo Cultural Center will be on the left.

National Hispanic Cultural Center

Those interested in Latin American and Hispanic culture could spend all day at the **National Hispanic Cultural Center** (1701 4th St. SW, 505/246-2261, www. nationalhispaniccenter.org, 10am-5pm Tues.-Sun., $3), which houses an eclectic and dynamic collection of multicultural exhibitions and performances. The permanent collection includes work by contemporary and cutting-edge artists from New Mexico, Latin American, and other regions from the Spanish diaspora. An on-site comprehensive research library includes a genealogy center with more than 12,500 books, magazines, and journals on the history and culture of the American Southwest, Central and South America, Spain and Portugal. The fun doesn't stop at night, with music, dance, film, and theater productions.

The **Torréon Fresco** *Mundos de mestizaje* (noon-5pm Sat.-Sun., 10am-5pm Wed. upon request, free) at the National Hispanic Cultural Center is a cultural treasure. This 4,000-square-foot and 45-foot-tall tower houses a bright, bold, mural that depicts 3,000 years of Hispanic history. Muralist Frederico Vigil ground the natural pigments himself then applied the plaster by hand, painting every inch. The result is largest concave fresco in North America and a piece that took 10 years to complete.

From Central Avenue (Route 66), turn left (south) on 8th Street SW and drive one mile. Cross Bridge Boulevard and the National Hispanic Cultural Center will be straight ahead.

Shopping

For unusual gifts and one-of-a-kind pieces handmade by local artists, stop at the **Mariposa Gallery** (3500 Central Ave. SE, 505/268-6828, www.mariposa-gallery.com, 11am-6pm Mon.-Sat., noon-5pm Sun.) in Nob Hill. The gallery has been exhibiting contemporary art, ceramic, jewelry, blown-glass, and found-objects sculptures since 1974.

After Route 66 was rerouted through Albuquerque in 1937, **Maisel's Indian Trading Post** (510 Central Ave. SE, 505/242-6526, www.kellysbrewpub. com, 9am-5:30pm Mon.-Sat., 8am-midnight Fri.-Sat.) was built to capitalize on the tourist trade. This was the only Pueblo Deco building that commissioned pieces by Navajo and Pueblo artists and the large display windows framing murals of Indians in ceremonial clothing and glazed terra-cotta floor tiles with Indian designs, added to the authenticity. By the 1940s, there were more than 300 American Indian artisans on-site, making it the largest trading post on Route 66. Today, the shop sells Acoma, Jemez, Kewa, Isleta, Santa Clara, Ohkay Owingeh, Zuni, Hopi and Navajo pottery, rugs, and jewelry.

Accommodations

★ **Los Poblanos Inn** (4803 Rio Grande Blvd., 800/326-6317, www.lospoblanos. com, $161-570) is special for so many reasons. The romantic entrance features a long driveway flanked by enormous cottonwood trees. Lush gardens, 25 acres of organic lavender fields, and the fabulous peacocks that roam the property all served to enchant. Guest rooms are refreshingly understated, with kiva fireplaces, carved ceiling beams, and hardwood floors. A full gourmet breakfast includes eggs, honey, and fruit and vegetables that are straight off the farm. An on-site shop features lavender spa products, artisan foods, garden tools, gifts, books, and more.

Sleep in a vintage 1969 Airstream trailer, a 1956 Teardrop, or a sprawling 1974 Silver Streak at the ★ **Enchanted Trails RV Park** (14305 Central Ave. NW, 800/326-6317, www.enchantedtrails.com, $56-86). The well-maintained trailers are decked out with retro furnishings, double beds, baths, and kitchens. With reasonably priced classic campers and a 1940s Trading Post on-site, a stay here offers a unique and memorable experience on the Mother Road.

Hotel Parq Central (806 Central Ave. SE, 505/242-0040 or 888/796-7277, www.hotelparqcentral.com, $135-272) is located in a renovated 1926 hospital that once served railroad employees and tuberculosis patients. The exterior still looks like an old health institution, but thanks to a $21-million-dollar renovation, the interior is a posh, modern hotel. Rooms feature high ceilings with furnishings decorated in soothing, understated tones. The on-site Apothecary Lounge serves classic Prohibition-era drinks with a wide selection of bitters. Buildings on the property are linked via pathways through landscaped gardens that once calmed ailing souls many decades ago.

The **Route 66 Casino Hotel** (14500 Avenue SW, 505/352-7866, www.rt66casino.com, $99-129) is a fun stop for Route 66 roadsters who love to gamble. This is a fully functioning casino with 1,600 slot machines, card tables, a bingo hall, five restaurants, three lounges, and a faux-retro diner Johnny Rockets. Rooms are modern with comfortable king- or queen-size beds, a flat-screen TV, and free Wi-Fi, and an indoor pool and workout room are also on-site.

top to bottom: El Don Motel; KiMo Theatre; Red's Old School Hydraulics

Food

Loyola's Family Restaurant (4500 Central Ave. SE, 505/268-6478, www.loyolasfamilyrestaurant.com, 6am-2pm Tues.-Fri., 6am-1pm Sat., 7am-1pm Sun., $6-10) serves great breakfast burritos with a green-chile sauce that will make you sweat. If the dining room looks familiar, it might be because scenes from the TV series *Breaking Bad* were filmed here.

In the 1930s, **Kelly's Brew Pub** (3222 Central Ave. SE, 505/262-2739, www.kellysbrewpub.com, 8am-10:30pm Sun.-Thurs., 8am-midnight Fri.-Sat., $7-14) was the Jones Motor Company, one of the most modern service stations in the West. This was the first station Dust Bowl migrants saw upon arrival in Albuquerque. The original owners built a canopy off the side of the building so that the weighted-down jalopies could unload in the shade before being serviced.

Today this restored landmark is a full-service restaurant and bar with more than 20 in-house brews, wine specials on Wednesday, and half-priced margaritas on. Look for the vintage Fire Chief gas pumps outside.

If you're up for a retro 1950s setting with blue-plate specials and handmade milk shakes, the **66 Diner** (1405 Central Ave. NE, 505/247-1421, www.66diner.com, 11am-10pm Mon.-Thurs., 11am-11pm Fri., 8am-11pm Sat., 8am-10pm Sun., $8-14) is the place. The signature dish is the Pile Up, with pan-fried potatoes, bacon, green-chile, eggs, cheddar, and red or green chile sauce. Whatever you do, leave room for the banana-cream pie with a strawberry-rhubarb or chocolate malt shake.

Housed in a renovated 1938 Texaco station, the **Standard Diner** (320 Central Ave. SE, 505/243-1440, www.standardiner.com, 7am-9:30pm Sun.-Thurs., 7am-10pm Sat., $8-16) offers a retro, yet upscale restaurant diner experience. The menu features innovative takes on classic comfort food with made-from-scratch fare like southern-fried pickles, short-rib sliders, and bacon-wrapped meat loaf.

For a sweet treat, try the state cookie. A *biscochito* (also spelled *bizcochito*) is a light and flaky anise-flavored cookie dusted in cinnamon sugar and with a hint of brandy. Locals say **Celina's Biscochitos** (400 Osuna Rd. NW, 505/269-4997, www.celinasbiscochitos.com, 9am-3pm Mon.-Thurs., noon-3pm Fri.) are the best. Their recipe is based on how the owner's grandma, Maggie, used to make them. She says Maggie would bake with "her whole heart and soul." To find Celina's from Central Avenue (Rte. 66), turn right (north) on Highway 47 (Broadway Blvd.) and cross I-40. Turn west (left) on Menaul Boulevard then, and after a few blocks, turn north (right) to continue on Highway 47. Drive 3 miles then turn west (left) on Osuna Road.

The diner in the back of the **Duran Central Pharmacy** (1815 Central Ave. NW, 505/247-4141, http://durancentralpharmacy.com/restaurant, 9am-6pm Mon.-Fri., 9am-2pm Sat.-Sun., $7-10) dishes out good red chile that is full of flavor, yet not too spicy. The Frito pies are also yummy, and the huevos rancheros and tortillas are made to order. Don't forget to check out the unique gifts and locally made items in the pharmacy out front.

◆ Back on 66

Leave Albuquerque driving west on Central Avenue and cross the Rio Grande. After about 6 miles, the road runs alongside I-40. Near Exit 149, turn north (right) to cross I-40, then take the North Frontage Road to Exit 140. **Nine Mile Hill** offers stunning views of the Sandia Mountains and beyond. To the west, the valley is framed by mountains that rise more than 10,000 feet—this is the view early Route 66 travelers wrote about many decades ago.

As you continue on the North Frontage Road, look for a Parker-through

Albuquerque to Gallup

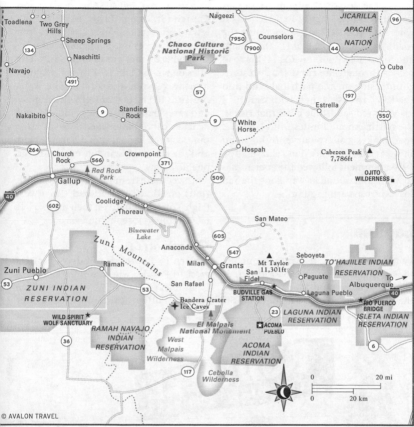

© AVALON TRAVEL

truss-bridge at Exit 140 perched over the eroded banks of the Rio Puerco.

Rio Puerco Bridge

The Rio Puerco is a river notorious for flooding. All the other bridges that had been built here had washed away, so when travelers encountered this area after a storm or during the monsoon season, there was no choice but to wait for the water to subside to cross. In 1933, the current **Rio Puerco Bridge** was built. The 250-foot-long steel-truss bridge was the longest of its kind in New Mexico. The 10 panels set at varying angles made a "camelback" arch, a popular design during the late 1920s and early 1930s. This additional support made the bridge strong enough to handle the Rio Puerco's massive flooding. The truss was remodeled in 1957, and some of the struts were replaced with lighter ones to allow for a higher clearance. Today the bridge is closed to car traffic, but it's open as a pedestrian bridge and offers a great excuse to get out of the car and stretch your legs.

◆ Back on 66

Continue driving west on I-40 West, following the **post-1937 alignment** and ignore the Route 66 sign at Exit 126 (this is where the pre-1937 alignment joins the road). At Mesita, take Exit 117, turn right, and follow Old Route 66 Road. This road passes through the rural southwestern countryside of Acoma tribal land and the Rio San Jose Valley, with beautiful views of red sandstone cliffs that rise in the north. About 2 miles from I-40, the road makes a sharp curve to the right; this was called "Dead Man's Curve." The 1926 alignment followed the ancient native trail and wound its way along the San Jose River toward Laguna.

Laguna

Laguna is a late 17th-century pueblo, the full name of which is San Jose de la Laguna, set on a sandstone bluff north of the San Jose River and south of Route 66.

Laguna Pueblo was one of the few pueblos visible from the highway. Today these are private homes, but the **San Jose Mission Church** (St. Joseph Blvd., 505/552-9330, www.lagunapueblo-nsn.gov, 9am-3pm Mon.-Fri., free) is a public place of worship where tours are offered daily. The mission was built in 1701 from fieldstone, mortar, plaster, and adobe. The walls measure 105 feet by 22 feet with original and rare Spanish paintings, murals, and ornately carved woodened doors. A large multicolored animal skin covers the altar and the choir loft window overlooks the pueblo below.

To get there from Route 66, turn south (left) on Rio San Jose Road. Turn west (right) on Capital Road, then make a left (south) on St. Joseph Boulevard.

◆ Back on 66

Return to Route 66 and drive 5 miles west to **Paraje**, where Route 66 curves back toward I-40 in 2 miles. Continue west to follow Route 66 or consider

Budville Gas Station

making a detour south here to visit Acoma Pueblo.

★ Acoma Pueblo

Acoma Pueblo (Pueblo of Acoma, 800/747-0181, www.acomaskycity.org, 9am-5pm daily, $23) is considered the oldest continuously inhabited settlement in North America. Its iconic village of 250 structures is situated on a 367-foot sandstone bluff. The Acoma people have lived here since AD 1150, growing corn, tanning deerskin and buffalo hides, domesticating turkeys, and weaving cotton. Despite Spanish rule and colonial oppression, including the destruction of their village in 1599, the Acoma fought to preserve their culture, spiritual practices, and rituals, eventually rebuilding the village into an impressive architectural masterpiece.

The 40,000-square-foot **Sky City Cultural Center** (open year-round, guided tour required) sits below the mesa and echoes the ancestral architectural design

of mud-plastered adobe and natural stacked stone used by the Acoma. Inside, the **Haak'u Museum** (tours available daily, call for hours) showcases exhibits about the life, art, and language of the Acoma. Native pottery, arts, and crafts are sold at the **Gaits'i** gift shop, while the **Y'aak'a Café** (9am-4pm daily) offers the opportunity to dine on Acoma traditional cuisine as prepared by tribal members.

The **San Esteban Del Ray Mission** was founded in 1629 by Friar Juan Ramirez to force assimilation of the Acoma people. Located on the mesa (and part of the tour), the church stands 150-feet long and 40-feet wide with an adobe roof and *vigas* beams that were transported 30 miles from the San Mateo Mountains.

The Acoma Tribal Council requests that visitors do not wear revealing clothing (short skirts, halter or tank tops) and avoid photographing tribal members or their artwork. Rock climbing, camping, and off-roading are strictly prohibited.

Getting There

From Route 66 in Paraje, turn south (left) on Casa Blanca Road (Hwy. 22/23/ Kaatsiima Dr.) and drive 13 miles south. The Cultural Center and Museum is on the right (north) at Indian Service Route 38. Turn left on Indian Service Route 38t to reach the San Estevan del Rey Mission Church (about 0.5-mile away).

Budville

Back on Route 66, (near I-40 Exit 104) west of Paraje, keep an eye out for some native stone ruins and the 1920s gas station in Budville, on the left (southwest) side of the road.

Budville was named after H. N. "Bud" Rice. In 1928, Rice and his wife Flossie operated the **Budville Gas Station**, a car service and trading post. Most of the cars that ended up stranded between Albuquerque to Grants were towed here. The store was held up in 1967, and Bud was murdered. His wife ran the business into the late 1970s. Today the station is closed, but the large gravity-feed gas pump on-site makes it worth a photo op.

✦ Back on 66
The pre-1937 alignment climbs 1.5 miles north toward **Cubero,** then curves west to **San Fidel** where towering 11,306-foot Mount Taylor frames the north side of the landscape. Route 66 approaches I-40 again in 3 miles. Cross over I-40 at Exit 96 and follow Highway 124 west, which runs alongside the South Frontage Road through McCartys.

McCartys

About 1 mile after crossing I-40, look for the stone 1933 Spanish Colonial **Santa Maria de Acoma Church** sitting on a hillside south of Route 66.

In 5 miles, Route 66 makes a sharp right turn under I-40 to parallel the North Frontage Road. This stretch passes through several miles of lava flow, locally called *malpais.* Much of Route 66 was rerouted around this rugged terrain of ancient magma. To get a closer look, consider adding a visit to **El Malpais National Monument** (123 E. Roosevelt Ave. NW, visitors center 8am-5pm daily, free), accessed via Highway 117.

✦ Back on 66
Route 66 continues to parallel I-40 for 3.5 miles. Near Exit 89, the road curves right and climbs 6.5 miles north. Route 66 then becomes Santa Fe Avenue as it runs through Grants.

Grants

Grants is a true-blue Route 66 town with vintage motels and roadside diners with cool neon signs. This former railroad town grew into a farming community. Then in 1950, a Navajo sheepherder

discovered uranium on Haystack Mountain—it turned out to be one of the largest uranium reserves in the world. A recession in 1983 eventually forced the uranium mines and mills to close.

Sights
Learn about the rich legacy of uranium mining and visit a re-created mine shaft at the **New Mexico Mining Museum** (100 N. Iron Ave., 505/287-4802, www.grants. org, 9am-4pm Mon.-Sat., $3). The self-guided tour offers a rare and educational experience about specialized drilling tools and blasting equipment.

Heading west on Route 66 (Santa Fe Ave.), turn right (north) on Iron Avenue. The museum will be on the right.

Accommodations
Compared to the shabby roadside motels that line Route 66, the **South West Motel** (1000 E. Santa Fe Ave., 505/287-2935, $40-53) offers welcome relief, with clean and comfortable rooms at rock-bottom prices. A bright yellow and orange neon sign of a sun rising over the building adds to the fun.

The **Sands Motel** (112 E. McArthur St., 505/287-2997, $45-55) has a classic 1950 motor court sign and offers basic accommodations with a personable staff. Elvis supposedly stayed in Room 123.

Food
Honey bottles sit at every table in **El Cafecito** (820 E. Santa Fe Ave., 505/285-6229, 7am-9pm Mon.-Fri., 7am-8pm Sat., $6-10) awaiting fresh *sopaipillas.* Savory *sopaipillas* are stuffed with beef, beans, and guacamole and then smothered with red chile. (The green chile is tasty too). So good.

Breakfast at **First Street Café** (1600 W. Santa Fe Ave., 505/287-7111, 7am-2pm Tues.-Sat., 8am-2pm Sun., $6-10) is fresh and delicious. The biscuits are made on-site, the pancakes are huge, and the homemade pies and cinnamon rolls are amazing. It may look a little worn on the outside, but don't let that deter you—it's all good once you step inside.

⏺ Back on 66

Traveling west on Route 66, **Milan** is only a couple of miles away. There's a big Love's Travel Stop if you need to gas up and replenish the snack collection. This pre-1930s alignment was originally the National Old Trails Highway heading to the Continental Divide.

Route 66 (Hwy. 122) heads north for about 14 miles to **Prewitt**, then curves west for about 10 miles to Thoreau (pronounced "thu-ROO").

Thoreau

Just west of I-40 (Exit 53) sits one of the oldest remaining gas stations on Route 66 in New Mexico. This Standard Oil franchise was originally located 30 miles east in Grants. After Route 66 was realigned in 1937, it was moved to Thoreau, becoming the first business on the realigned section of Route 66. Roy Herman bought the station in 1950; by 1963, Herman and his son stopped selling gas and moved the station to the west side of town where it became a car repair and service station. After all these decades, **Roy's Garage** has retained its historic character. The one-story building features a section of white enamel coverings and three white-rounded 1940s gas pumps.

⏺ Back on 66

Keep driving west on Highway 122 for 5 miles to the Continental Divide, the second-highest point on Route 66 with an elevation of 7,263 feet. Piñon and juniper dot the landscape amid Navajo homesteads and crimson cliffs that extend to the Arizona border. Route 66 joins I-40 West at Exit 47. Traveling west on I-40, in 11 miles take Exit 36 and drive straight to follow Route 66 (Hwy. 118/North Frontage Rd.) into Gallup.

Gallup

In the 1880s, Gallup was a railroad town. Today the historic highway is well-preserved with vibrant vintage neon signs, including that of the Blue Spruce Lodge—a rare and wonderful treat.

Sights

Gallup is one of the most significant trading centers in the Southwest and is known as the "Indian Capital of the World." Navajo Nation land wraps around the northwestern edge of Gallup; the Zuni Reservation sits just to the south. Although Gallup isn't as charming as Santa Fe, the prices, quality, and authenticity of the Pueblo pottery, handcrafted jewelry, and hand-loomed Navajo textiles can't be beat.

Gallup Cultural Center

The Southwest Indian Foundation and the city of Gallup formed the **Gallup Cultural Center** (201 E. Rte. 66, 505/863-4131, www.southwestindian.com, 9am-5pm Mon.-Fri. late May-early Sept.; 9am-4pm Mon.-Fri. early Sept.-late May, free) to teach visitors about Gallup's rich cultural heritage. The center is located in a former Harvey House Santa Fe Depot designed by Mary Colter. Exhibits cover train travel, westward expansion, sandpainting, weaving, silversmithing, and Route 66. The Storyteller gift shop sells tribal clothing, jewelry, pottery, and handbags.

El Morro Theatre

Catch a cowboy flick in the 1928 Spanish Colonial-style **El Morro Theatre** (207 W. Coal Ave., 505/863-1250, www.elmorrotickets.com, $5). The space has loads of charm and history and also hosts musical performances and cultural events.

The theatre is one block south (left) from Route 66. At South 3rd Street, turn left (east) and drive one block to West Coal Street.

Rex Museum

Housed in a former brothel and grocery store, the **Rex Museum** (300 W. Historic US 66, 505/863-1363, www.ggsc.wnmu. edu/mcf/museums/rex.html, 8am-3:30pm Mon.-Fri., free) explores Gallup's colorful mining and railroad history and its earliest residents. Exhibits include old hotel registers, books, and newspapers dating 1886-1919.

Shopping

The commercialization of American Indian jewelry started in the late 1800s when Fred Harvey bought rings, bracelets and earrings from the Navajo to sell to tourists from his Harvey Houses. Until then, tribal members made silver for their own use and would occasionally sell it to soldiers stationed on reservations. During the heyday of Route 66, these trading posts became all the rage— there was no shortage of Hopi *kachina* dolls and Navajo Yei deities made into kitschy ashtrays, flowerpots, bookends, spittoons, and jewelry.

Times have changed and it is now possible to purchase authentic American Indian arts and crafts from traders with a connection to the tribal communities. Today, Gallup's shops are filled with sacred objects, symbols, and depictions of rituals that mean something to the people who made them.

Pick up quality western wear at **Zimmerman's** (213 W. Hwy. 66, 505/863-3142, 9am-6pm Mon.-Sat.). **Silver Dust Trading Company** (121 W. Hwy. 66, 505/722-4848, www.silverdusttrading. com, 9am-6pm Mon.-Fri., 9am-5pm Sat.) has a nice collection of Zuni Pueblo turquoise, as well as other jewelry and specialty beads. **Richardson's Trading Co.** (222 W. Hwy. 66, 505/722-4762, www. richardsontrading.com, 9am-6pm Mon.-Sat.) sells rare and unique heirlooms including concha belts, Zuni needlepoint, chief blankets, Apache and Navajo baskets, Tohono O'odham trays, and bold paintings that depict ceremonial dancers.

Accommodations

Film director D. W. Griffith's brother, Joe Massaglia, opened the ★ **El Rancho Hotel** (1000 E. Rte. 66, 505/863-9311, www.el-ranchohotel.com, $98-166) in the late 1930s. It became a premier hotel and a temporary home for Hollywood's A-list movie stars, such as Katharine Hepburn, Humphrey Bogart, John Wayne, Kirk Douglas, Jane Wyman, and Mae West. The three-story plantation-style building with a pitched-wood shake roof, stone chimneys, and a second-floor balcony conjures the Old West mixed with the Deep South. The rustic yet elegant hotel offered superior service by a Fred Harvey-trained staff.

By the mid-1960s, the fascination with the American West began to fade and the once-glamorous El Rancho appeared more dated. After Route 66 was rerouted through I-40, the property fell into decline. Thankfully Armond Ortega, a well-known Indian trader, purchased the El Rancho and has kept it going. The lobby is swathed with Navajo rugs with dark wood furniture and an enormous brick and stone fireplace. A wooden staircase curves up to several rooftop patios that showcase photographs of western film scenes in the 1950s. Rooms are tastefully decorated with western accents and burgundy drapes. The window-lined Ronald Reagan Suite has a beautiful rock-wall bathroom with a gorgeous vanity and cobalt-blue tiles.

An on-site store sells handmade jewelry, rugs, and *kachina* dolls created by Hopi, Navajo, and Zuni artists. Ortega is a fourth generation trader and knows how to select pieces with excellent craftsmanship and quality.

Food

The Navajo tacos with Indian fry bread, beans, meat, green chile, cheese, and tomatoes are big enough to share at **Earl's Restaurant** (1400 E. Hwy. 66, 505/863-4201, www.66diner.com, 6am-8:30pm

Mon.-Sat., 7:30am-6:30pm Sun., $8-14). Or opt instead for the green-chile enchiladas with a slice of smooth and extra creamy coconut-cream pie for dessert. Earl's has been the place for Gallup since 1947. It's also a tourist spot that supports Navajo artisans who sell their handcrafted works tableside.

Tucked away in the old Harvey House train depot, **Angela's Café** (201. E. Hwy. 66, 505/722-7526, 8am-9pm Mon.-Sat., $8-11) serves fresh green salads, gyros, sandwiches on homemade bread, and house-made hummus. It's a great place to have coffee and dessert, and there's live jazz music at night.

Before you leave the state, you should eat at ★ **Jerry's** (406 W. Coal Ave., 505/722-6775, 9am-3pm Mon., 9am-4pm Tues.-Sun., $8-12), a tried-and-true locals place with dark vinyl booths,

wood-paneled walls, a classic neon sign, and some of the best New Mexican food in the area. The chiles rellenos with green-chile sauce are amazing and try not to fill up on the addictive *sopaipillas*.

From Route 66, turn left (south) on 4th Street; drive one block and turn left on Coal.

❖ Back on 66

Leave Gallup heading west on Highway 118 for about 15 miles to **Manuelito**. The last 8 miles on the pre-1930s alignment is lined with gorgeous yellow and red sandstone cliffs. The road climbs above the railroad as it makes its way around the Devil's Cliff mesa. Approaching Arizona, Route 66 passes through a narrow part of the valley alongside deep canyons and brick-red earth. Overhead, the sunrays seem to go on forever.

Arizona

Arizona features some of the best surviving stretches of the Mother Road. Drive through red-rock canyons, lush green forests, ancient volcanoes, historic mining towns, and wide-open spaces that embody the rugged spirit of the American Southwest.

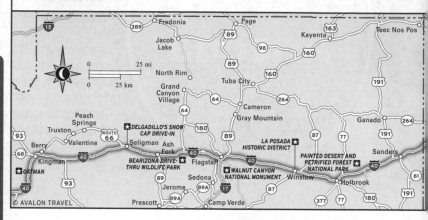

Arizona

A merican Indians, Spanish explorers, cattle wranglers, and outlaws all discovered this multicultural, sunkissed lunar landscape.

Route 66 through Arizona is laid over age-old paths that were developed to facilitate trade and access to critical resources between the Great Plains and California. In the late 1850s, Lieutenant Edward Fitzgerald Beale was ordered by the U.S. war department to build the Beale Wagon Road across Arizona. It was the shortest route to the West and became a well-traversed immigrant trail that guided thousands of folks in the 1860s and 1870s. The Beale Wagon Road was later followed by the Santa Fe Railway, and then became Route 66. When Route 66 opened in 1926, most of the Arizona portion was unpaved. In 1933, President Roosevelt's National Recovery Administration gave Arizona $5 million to pave the route. The Federal Highway Act of 1956 brought I-40 to the state, which bypassed several sections of Route 66.

Planning Your Time

Plan at least **two days** for the drive across Arizona. After crossing the state line, spend the first night at La Posada in Winslow. The next day, stop in Flagstaff, 160 miles from the eastern border; the mountain town has the best variety of restaurants, shops, and services along Route 66 in Arizona. It's also a hub for detours to the Grand Canyon and Sedona. Continue east to Williams and Seligman before driving the pristine, two-lane stretch of Route 66 through Peach Springs to spend the night in Kingman. From Kingman, you'll leave Arizona via the Oatman Highway, which requires every driver's patience and concentration.

Driving Considerations

To really experience the major attractions Route 66 has to offer, you may want to add two extra days for a side trip to the Grand Canyon or Sedona, or allocate an extra day to leisurely stroll the historic districts of Williams and Oatman.

Gas is scarce in the western part of the state along Route 66, so make sure to gas up in Kingman before heading to Oatman.

Highlights

★ **Driving tour through Painted Desert and Petrified Forest National Park:** See colorful badlands, mesas, ancient petroglyphs, petrified wood, and fossils that date back 225 million years (page 238).

★ **La Posada Historic District, Winslow:** Step back in time at this Harvey Hotel, trading post, and restaurant built in 1929 (page 242).

★ **Walnut Canyon National Monument, near Flagstaff:** Curved canyon walls, incredible geological formations, and ancient pueblos are just a few of the jewels in this stunning monument (page 245).

★ **Bearizona Drive-Thru Wildlife Park, Williams:** A roadside view of black bears, bison, bighorn sheep and wolves roaming the landscape in their natural habitat (page 267).

★ **Delgadillo's Snow Cap Drive-In, Seligman:** This quirky, classic roadside restaurant built by local resident Juan Delgadillo in 1953 is one of the most celebrated stops on Route 66 (page 274).

★ **Oatman:** A gold rush mining town has been brought back to life along the original alignment on Route 66 (page 281).

Getting There

Starting Points
Car
Route 66 enters Arizona at Lupton then climbs through the Kaibab Plateau near Flagstaff before dropping in elevation through Ash Fork. On the eastern side of the state, much of the original alignment from Lupton to Flagstaff is not continuous or intact; unfortunately, you will have to take I-40. Once you reach Seligman, 159 miles of unspoiled Route 66 await on a pristine two-lane highway. Past Kingman, be sure to take the original alignment via the Oatman Highway, a scenic winding road through the Black Mountains. Drive this stretch with caution: the Oatman Highway is fraught with hairpin turns, steep mountain grades, and 15-mph switchbacks, earning it the notorious nickname "Bloody Route 66."

Car Rentals
Car rentals are available at both the Flagstaff and Phoenix airports. **Enterprise** (2136 E. Rte. 66, Flagstaff, 928/526-1377, www.enterprise.com, 8am-6pm Mon.-Fri. 8am-3pm Sat., 9am-1pm Sun.) has a location right on Route 66.

Air
The two major airports in the region are in Phoenix and Flagstaff. The **Flagstaff Airport** (FLG, 6200 S. Pulliam Dr., 928/556-1234, www.flagstaff.az.gov) is served by US Airways and American Airlines with daily flights to and from Phoenix. **Phoenix Sky Harbor International Airport** (PHX, 3400 E. Sky Harbor Blvd., 602/273-3300, www.sky-harbor.com) is one of the 10 busiest airports in the country and serves about 20 airlines with roughly 1,200 daily flights to more than 100 domestic and international destinations. Phoenix is a 2.5-hour drive from Route 66 in Flagstaff.

Train or Bus
Greyhound (800/231-2222, www.greyhound.com) stops in the towns of Holbrook, Flagstaff, and Kingman.

Since Route 66 was laid out alongside the train tracks, **Amtrak** (www.amtrack.com) offers easy access. The **Southwest Chief** line stops in Winslow at the **La Posada Hotel** (303 E. 2nd St. on Rte. 66), in Flagstaff at the **Station Building** (1 E. Rte. 66), in **Williams** (corner of Railroad Ave. at Rte. 66 and Grand Canyon Blvd.), and in **Kingman** (402 Andy Devine Ave.).

Lupton and Houck

As you enter Arizona, colorful American Indian trading posts flank both sides of I-40 near the Navajo Reservation, Allentown, Querino, Houck, and Sanders. Little remains of Route 66

Best Accommodations

★ **Wigwam Motel, Holbrook:** This 1930s tepee-shaped motel is one of only two left standing on Route 66 (page 241).

★ **La Posada Hotel & Gardens, Winslow:** Spend the night in a historic Harvey House designed by Mary Colter in 1929 (page 243).

★ **Little America Hotel, Flagstaff:** Rooms in this classic lodge, set amid a 500-acre ponderosa pine forest, feature a 1970s French-themed decor (page 251).

★ **Red Garter B & B Inn, Williams:** Stay in an 1897 Victorian saloon and bordello with balconies overlooking the Grand Canyon Railway depot (page 270).

today, but the deteriorating billboards along the frontage road show this was once a bustling area. Much of Route 66 through the eastern section of Arizona sticks to I-40; detours to explore segments of the old alignment at Allentown, Sanders, and Chambers tend to follow gravel roads that are difficult to navigate and not worth the effort.

Part of the 1926-1931 alignment remains along the **Querino Bridge,** which spans a rugged canyon. This early example of truss design (with a concrete-decked trestle and three Pratt deck trusses) is located along a bumpy, but drivable county road. From I-40, take Exit 346 and turn right (north), then take a left (west) at Querino Dirt Road (County Rd. 7250). Proceed with caution and avoid when wet.

◆ Back on 66

In about 4 miles Querino Dirt Road (County Rd. 7250) rejoins I-40 via the Frontage Road. Follow I-40 west for 2 miles to Exit 339. Turn right (north) and then take an immediate left (west) to take the Frontage Road to Sanders.

Sanders

Established in 1881, Sanders was named after C. W. Sanders, an office engineer at the Atchison Topeka and Santa Fe Railway. This unincorporated town was an education center for displaced Navajo; the Navajo-Hopi land dispute started in the 1860s and was in the courts for 25 years. Today, little remains of Sanders. The once-popular 66 Diner, an old Valentine diner, has since closed.

◆ Back on 66

Drive 6 miles west on the I-40 Frontage Road and turn left (south) on U.S. 191. Join I-40 west and drive 21 miles to Exit 311 (Painted Desert/Petrified Forest).

Painted Desert and Petrified Forest National Park

The **Painted Desert and Petrified Forest National Park** (Exit 311 off I-40 in Navajo, 928/524-6228, www.nps.gov/pefo, 8am-5pm daily, hours vary seasonally, $10) has the world's largest and most colorful collection of petrified wood. It is also the only national park in the United States that protects a portion of Route 66. The northern section of the park encompasses the Painted Desert—approximately 146 square miles of colorful badlands and multihued mesas of stratified layers of mudstone, shale, and siltstone pigmented by iron and magnesium deposits. The southern section of

Best Restaurants

★ **Joe & Aggie's Café, Holbrook:** Established in 1943, Joe & Aggie's is the oldest restaurant in Holbrook (page 241).

★ **Turquoise Room Restaurant, Winslow:** Dine on award-winning southwestern cuisine in the former Harvey House lunchroom at La Posada (page 243).

★ **E&O Kitchen, Winslow:** Enjoy some of the most authentic and delicious Mexican food in Arizona (page 244).

★ **Satchmos, Flagstaff:** This Flagstaff favorite serves heavenly BBQ, Cajun, and Creole cuisine (page 252).

★ **The Oatman Hotel & Restaurant, Oatman:** More than 100,000 dollar bills line the ancient walls of this Wild West saloon and restaurant (page 281).

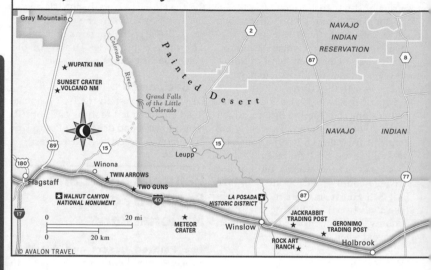

Lupton to Flagstaff

the park contains the Petrified Forest with historic structures, archaeological sites, and fossils that date back more than 200 million years.

It takes at least 45 minutes to drive the 28-mile road through the park, but to truly experience it try to allow at least a couple of hours to drive Blue Mesa Road, take a hike, and stop at the spectacular viewpoints along the way. Tiponi, Tawa, and Kachina Points feature overlooks with panoramic views, all located less than 2 miles north of the Painted Desert Visitor Center. There are no camping facilities or overnight parking allowed in the park.

★ Driving Tour
Painted Desert Visitor Center

Less than 0.5 mile from the I-40 exit is the **Painted Desert Visitor Center** (8am-5pm daily Sept. 20-Apr. 4, 7am-7pm daily Apr. 5-Sept. 19), which houses books, petrified wood exhibits, and park information. A film about the park is shown continuously throughout the day. The visitors center is adjacent to a restaurant,

gift shop, and gas station; restrooms are available.

Painted Desert Rim Trail

The **Painted Desert Rim Trail** has remarkable views of the Painted Desert. Approximately one mile after the northern park entrance is the pull-off for **Tawa Point,** where the Painted Desert Rim Trail begins. The trail travels along the canyon rim and includes several information panels about the wildlife, geology, and ancient people of the region. In 0.5 mile, you'll reach the **Painted Desert Inn** and then **Kachina Point** with its panoramic views of the red, orange, pink, and purple rocks. From Kachina Point, the trail enters a 5- to 8-million-year-old volcanic area. Once you reach Kachina Point, turn around and head back to the Tawa Point parking lot.

Painted Desert Inn

The restored 1924 **Painted Desert Inn** (928/524-6228, 9am-5pm daily) is 2 miles north on the park road. The inn was built with wood and stone in the Pueblo

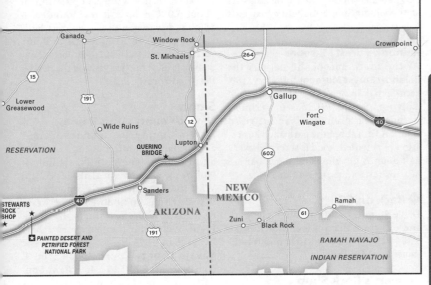

Revival style with flagstone terraces and earth-textured walls that are two feet thick. In 1940, the Fred Harvey Company managed the place to serve passengers traveling the Santa Fe Railway, then it closed in 1942.

In 1947, architect Mary Jane Colter renovated the inn with a new color scheme and glass windows to display the surrounding landscape—a pioneering style of architecture that brought inside the essence of the outdoors. The interior lunchroom, where the Harvey Girls served hungry train passengers, features murals painted by Hopi artist Fred Kabotie. The inn closed again in 1963 and was scheduled for demolition in 1976. The National Park Service stepped in to list it on the National Register of Historic Places and saved it. In 1987, the secretary of the interior designated the inn a National Historic Landmark.

The Painted Desert Inn reopened in 2006. Though it no longer operates as a hotel and restaurant, the **museum** and **bookstore** feature extraordinary architectural details, such as hammered-tin chandeliers, local pottery, and a vivid mountain lion petroglyph, one of the finest in the region.

Route 66 Studebaker

The park road circles back toward I-40 heading south; however, you cannot access the interstate at this point. Right before you approach I-40, look west on the right side of the road for a rusted **1932 Studebaker** (Stop Number 4) that marks an old Route 66 alignment.

Newspaper Rock

Heading south on the park road, you will reach **Newspaper Rock** (Stop Number 6) on the west (right) side of the road. Newspaper Rock contains more than 650 petroglyphs etched into its boulders and offers a glimpse of the people who lived here in the Puerco River Valley close to 2,000 years ago.

Blue Mesa Trail

The **Blue Mesa Trail** (Stop Number 7) is a moderately strenuous 1-mile hike among bluish-bentonite clay badlands and petrified wood. The trailhead starts at the Blue Mesa sun shelter just past Newspaper Rock.

Rainbow Forest Museum

At the south end of the park is the **Rainbow Forest Museum** (off Hwy. 180, 8am-5pm daily Sept. 20-Apr. 4, 7am-7pm daily Apr. 5-Sept. 19). Museum exhibits include prehistoric animals and petrified wood. A film about the park and the creation of petrified wood is screened every half hour. A gift shop and snack bar are nearby; restrooms are available.

◈ Back on 66

Drive 28 miles south through the park and exit from the south entrance. Take U.S. 180 for 19 miles north to rejoin I-40/Route 66 at Holbrook.

Stewart's Rock Shop

Since it's a big no-no to take any petrified wood from the park, you can get some at **Stewart's Rock Shop** (Hwy I-40 Exit 303, Washboard Rd., Holbrook, www.petrifiedwood.com, 800/414-8533, 9am-5pm daily), 13 miles east of Holbrook. It's part trading post, part garage sale sitting in a strange folk art sculpture garden. They sell meteorites, dinosaur bones, tree stumps, bookends, and jewelry made from petrified wood. The property also has ostriches (with eggs for sale), sunblasted vintage cars, quirky dinosaur sculptures like a T. rex with a mannequin hanging out of its mouth. This place is so awesomely odd with a tinge of creepiness it makes it worth a stop.

◈ Back on 66

From I-40, take Exit 289 and follow the Route 66 signs. Turn right (west) on Hopi Drive.

Holbrook

Holbrook is sited along the banks of the Little Colorado River as the seat of Navajo County with a population of about 5,000 people. It was founded in 1882 and was one of the wildest hell-raising towns in Arizona. Once Route 66 came through in 1926, Holbrook became a tourist hub for visiting the nearby Petrified Forest.

Sights
Navajo County Court House

Navajo County was founded in 1881 as a farming, railroading, lumber, and ranching community. Its hub of Holbrook was a typical lawless Wild West town and the locals brought in a new sheriff, Commodore Perry Owens, to deal with the criminals. By 1896, Frank Wattron had taken over as sheriff, and in 1898 the county built the **Navajo County Court House** (100 E Arizona St., 800/524-2459, 8am-5pm daily, later hours in summer, free). This is where the notorious prisoners were caged in small gloomy jail cells. The first man to be hanged in the county was George Smiley on January 8, 1900, and it was a major event. An invitation was printed on gilt-bordered paper and wired to the Associated Press. It made news around the world reaching as far as London and Berlin. Today it is believed that his ghost is pacing the halls, walking up and down the stairs, closing doors and moving objects. Another ghost of a former prisoner named Mary who died in one of the jail cells has been seen peering out the window.

There is a museum inside detailing the history, and courtrooms and offices upstairs. Aside from sweeping the property, the docents have left the jail as it was over a century ago. Prisoners' artwork is also displayed. Today the historic building houses the **Navajo County Historical Museum,** the Holbrook Chamber of Commerce, and a visitor's center.

The courthouse is a couple of blocks north of West Hopi Drive. From I-40 take

Exit 286, and go left (south) on SR 77 to Arizona Street.

Rainbow Rock Shop

For a fun photo op, check out the huge dinosaur statues made from chicken wire and concrete at the **Rainbow Rock Shop** (101 Navajo Blvd., Holbrook, 928/524-2384, 10am-5pm Mon.-Sat.). They also sell specialty rocks, souvenirs, petrified wood, and if you want a snapshot with the dinosaurs, there is a charge of $0.75.

It's located a couple of blocks south of West Hopi Drive. Heading north on Highway 180 from the Petrified Forest, it's right on the highway on the left (west) side of the road.

Accommodations and Food

The concrete and steel tepee-shaped ★ **Wigwam Motel** (811 W. Hopi Dr., 928/524-3048, $70) was part of a chain built in the 1930s. (Frank Redford put up the first one in 1937; he disliked the word "tepee" so he called them wigwams.) There were seven Wigwam Villages in Alabama, Florida, Kentucky, Louisiana, Arizona, and California. Only three Wigwam Villages survive today and two of them are on Route 66 (the other one is in San Bernardino, California). Wigwam Village #6 in Holbrook offers 15 free-standing wigwams, each 21 feet wide at the base and 28 feet high with a private bathroom, shower, TV, and air-conditioner. A vintage Studebaker sits out front along with a museum of American Indian artifacts, Route 66 collectibles, petrified wood, and Civil War memorabilia.

If you'd rather not sleep in a tepee, a pleasant place to bed down in Holbrook is the **Globetrotter Lodge** (902 W. Hopi Dr., 928/297-0158, $75) one block west of the Wigwam Village on the north side of 180. They have Route 66 themed-rooms decorated in a 1970s Americana meets Native American style. Every room is different with an original handmade sink and flat-screen TVs.

On the main drag through Holbrook is ★ **Joe & Aggie's Café** (120 W. Hopi Dr., 928/524-6540, www.joeandaggies-cafe.com, 6am-8pm Mon.-Sat., $5-15), a classic Route 66 institution that is famous for delicious green- and red-chile dishes. Established in 1943, this is the oldest restaurant in town. The owners (Joe and Aggie) operated the restaurant during the heyday of Route 66. Their daughter Alice Gallegos (who passed away in 2012) said of the restaurant:

"When we first moved here, traffic out front was terrible. When those truckers put on their brakes to make the turn at the corner, they made so much black smoke that we would have to come in early to wipe the soot off our tables."

If you're craving pizza and chicken saltimbocca, try the **Mesa Italiana Restaurant** (2318 Navajo Blvd., 928/524-6696, 11am-2pm Mon.-Fri. and 4pm-9pm daily, $11-30). Their linguine with clam sauce is reportedly some of the best in northern Arizona. It's on the east end of Holbrook; from I-40 take Exit 289 Navajo Boulevard. If you are coming from the Petrified Forest loop, continue north on Navajo Boulevard and cross under I-40.

◈ Back on 66

Join I-40 westbound at Exit 289 and take Exit 280 to the Geronimo Trading Post.

Joseph City

Sights
Geronimo Trading Post

West of Holbrook in Joseph City, off the 280 exit, the **Geronimo Trading Post** (5372 Geronimo Rd., 928/288-3241, 8am-5pm daily) is well stocked with Route 66 memorabilia for sale. They also allege to have the world's largest petrified tree (apparently the largest petrified tree trunk is in Thailand), which weighs about 80 tons. In any case, it's big and it's free. To get there from I-40 past Joseph City, take Exit 269.

Jackrabbit Trading Post

The **Jackrabbit Trading Post** (3386 Rte. 66, 928/288-3230, www.jackrabbit-tradingpost.com, 9am-6pm daily in summer, 9am-5pm Mon.-Sat., noon-5pm Sun. in winter) is famous for its "HERE IT IS" sign, featured in the film *Cars* along with a graphic of the soft-curved silhouette of a jackrabbit. A man named James Taylor built the Jackrabbit Trading Post and painted 30 twelve-inch jackrabbits along the roof. The Geronino Trading Post, about 10 miles away, had large decorated tepees that attracted visitors, so Taylor decided to amp up his marketing strategy. He plastered billboards of hopping rabbits for more than 1,000 miles from here to Springfield, Missouri, making this jackrabbit a running mascot of Route 66. On-site, there's a gift shop with roadside souvenirs and a giant fiberglass sculpture of a jackrabbit.

Rock Art Ranch

Rock Art Ranch (tours by reservation, 928/288-3260, May-Oct., $35) is a private cattle ranch situated on land that was inhabited by Puebloan, Mogollon, and Sinaguan cultures with some of the best preserved collections of ancient petroglyphs in the world dating back to 6000 BC. The rock art covering the cliffs of Chevelon Canyon has captured attention from researchers at the Smithsonian Institution. The 5,000-acre ranch is run by Brantley Baird—a real Arizona cowboy—and a small heard of bison roam the property.

The ranch is in a remote area between Winslow and Holbrook about 13 miles from La Posada. Before the Rock Art Ranch turnoff, a recently restored 1913 bridge crossing Chevelon Creek is one of Arizona's oldest and listed on the National Register of Historic Places. To get there, take Exit 257 (E. 3rd St.) off I-40 and head south (left) on Highway 87 (N. Williamson Ave.). After about 1.5 miles, turn east (left) onto Highway 99. Stay on Highway 99 for about 6 miles, then head east (left) on Territorial/McLaws Road. It's 2.2 miles southwest to the ranch entrance.

◆ Back on 66

From I-40 in Joseph City, drive 20 miles west to Exit 257 for Winslow. Turn left (south) and then right (west) on East 3rd Street (Hwy. 87). Turn left again (south) on North Williamson Avenue (Hwy. 99), then make another quick left (east) onto 2nd Street. Look for the La Posada entrance on your right.

Winslow

Winslow was founded in 1882 and operated primarily as a railroad hub. After World War II, the automobile took precedence over rail travel and that spurred Winslow's economic decline. With the I-40 bypass and decommission of Route 66 in 1985, Winslow appears to be a depressed, deserted, run-down place; however, just beneath the surface there is an underground art scene simmering to a boil. Winslow has hosted the hip Station-to-Station Art on Rails project featuring Cat Power, Jackson Browne, and artist Ed Ruscha.

Sights

The La Posada Harvey House is Winslow's diamond in the rough. It also has a gallery with Tina Mion's cutting-edge contemporary art, so when you arrive in Winslow this should be your first stop.

★ La Posada Historic District

For an unforgettable experience, go to **La Posada Hotel & Gardens** (303 E. 2nd St., 928/289-4366, www.laposada.org, $119-169). The hotel is a stunning Harvey House designed by Mary Colter in 1929. This 11-acre Spanish Colonial property was the favorite project of this head architect for Fred Harvey and one of the most important female architects in the early

20th century. Most Americans at the time valued European culture and design; however, Colter felt that the southwestern style rooted in Native American, Spanish, and Mexican influences was undervalued and ignored. Colter loved the look of the great Spanish and Mexican haciendas in the Southwest, which inspired the design of La Posada.

La Posada opened during the Depression, which is mainly why it never prospered. The hotel and restaurant closed in 1957, and the Santa Fe Railway used it for office space until 1994. Soon after it was slotted for demolition, but thankfully, Allan Affeldt purchased the property and took on a $12-million-dollar renovation transforming it into a magical place and one of the crown jewels of Route 66.

If you can't stay the night, purchase the souvenir guide and walking tour map ($3) at the gift shop. Stroll the art gallery, flowering gardens, see the world's largest Navajo rug, and browse the gift shop for Fred Harvey jewelry, *kachinas,* textiles, iron, tinwork, and pottery.

Old Trails Museum
A few blocks east of La Posada is the **Old Trails Museum** (212 Kinsley Ave., 928/289.5861, www.oldtrailsmuseum. org, 10am-4pm Tues.-Sat. Apr.-Oct., 11am-3pm Tues.-Sat. Nov.-Mar.), which features the railroad history of Winslow along with an extensive collection of photographs, textiles, and documents that have been donated by locals.

Standing on the Corner Park
Ron Adamson's bronze statue *Standing on the Corner in Winslow, Arizona* (Kinsley and 2nd Ave., http://standinonthecorner.com) pays homage to the Eagles song *Take it Easy.* Backed by a two-story trompe-l'oeil mural by John Pugh (of store windows reflecting a girl driving by in a flatbed Ford), the bronze statue displays a life-size man standing with his guitar in his hand. Songwriter

Jackson Browne was actually traveling Route 66 and standing on a corner in Flagstaff, Arizona, but the word "Winslow" was easier on the ears. It's amazing, and a little unsettling, how easily history rewrites itself, but it's fun see the sculpture and hum that classic 1970s anthem.

Snowdrift Art Space
A block west of Standing on the Corner Park is the **Snowdrift Art Space** (120 W. 2nd St., 928/289-8201, www.snowdrift-art.com, call 24 hours in advance for an appointment). The 22,000-square-foot multipurpose community art space is run by sculptor and La Posada partner Daniel Lutzick and his wife Ann Mary. A 7,000-square-foot gallery features Lutzick's large-scale sculptures using corrugated tin, plywood, roofing tar, and rebar.

Accommodations and Food
If you choose to stay overnight (which is highly recommended), every room at ★ **La Posada Hotel & Gardens** (303 E. 2nd St., 928/289-4366, www.laposada. org, $119-169) is special and unique. Many feature handmade ponderosa pine beds, Mexican tin and tile mirrors, six-foot cast-iron tubs, hand-painted tile murals, whirlpool tubs, hand-woven Zapotec rugs, and antique, hand-painted furniture. With most of the rooms under $150, it's a four-star experience for the price of a Holiday Inn.

On-site at La Posada is the award-winning ★ **Turquoise Room Restaurant** (303 E. 2nd St., 928/289-2888, www. theturquoiseroom.net, 7am-2pm and 5pm-8:30pm daily, $10-42) serving contemporary southwestern cuisine. The churro lamb meatballs with green chile tomatillo mint dipping salsa are heavenly. The restored dining room is in the former Harvey House lunchroom, with has tall ceilings, turquoise-colored beams, and backlit transparent paintings by resident artist Tina Mion. The entire property is

an absolute treasure and one of the most exquisite places to see on Route 66—don't miss it.

Tucked away behind the Winslow Airport, the ★ **E&O Kitchen** (703 Airport Rd., 928/289-5352, 11am-6pm Mon.-Thurs., 11am-6:30pm Fri., 11am-5pm Sat. in winter; 11am-6:30pm Mon.-Fri., 11am-5pm Sat. in summer, $4-11) serves some of the most authentic and delicious Mexican food in Arizona. They have delectable blue-corn enchiladas, a fresh salsa bar to die for, and comforting refried beans full of flavor.

It takes a little effort to find, but it's worth it. From downtown Winslow, take State Route 99 (N. Williamson Ave.) south and then turn right (west) onto Airport Road. Follow Airport Road all the way to the end and turn left behind the airplane hangar. If you can't find the restaurant, call.

◈ Back on 66
From I-40, drive 16 miles west to Exit 233 and drive 6 miles south on Meteor Crater Road.

Meteor Crater

About 50,000 years ago, a meteor weighing several hundred thousand tons that had been traveling through space for 500 million years crashed into the Earth at 26,000 miles per hour. You can see the 550-foot-deep hole it left at **Meteor Crater** (I-40 Exit 233, Meteor Crater Rd., 800/289-5898, www.meteorcrater.com, 8am-5pm daily Labor Day-Memorial Day, 7am-7pm daily Memorial Day-Labor Day, $18). It's the best-preserved meteorite impact site on Earth. There are also more than 25 exhibits in the onsite museum.

top to bottom: El Rancho Restaurant, Holbrook; La Posada hotel; La Posada restaurant, Winslow

⬥ Back on 66

Back on I-40, go 14 miles and take Exit 219 to Twin Arrows. Traveling westbound, take the overpass to the South Frontage Road then head west. A concrete barrier blocks direct access to the town ruins, but you can park a little farther east.

Two Guns and Twin Arrows

On a sleepy stretch of Route 66, all that remains of the Wild West theme park and tourist town of **Two Guns** are a few crumbling ruins. The roadside zoo with a large sign featuring "Mountain Lions," is on the southern frontage road of I-40 but is difficult to access. The KOA and Shell station are now closed, and their ruins are on private property.

The **Twin Arrows Trading Post** built in 1937, was originally called Padre Canyon Trading Post. In 1955, the Troxell family transformed it into a Route 66 icon by planting two feather-tipped telephone poles made to look like twin arrows crashing into the earth. The curio shop, **Valentine Diner,** and gas station have been shut down and heavily vandalized. Route 66 enthusiasts and Hopi tribe members restored the arrows with a fresh paint job.

⬥ Back on 66

From Twin Arrows, return to I-40 heading west for 10 miles to get to Winona.

Winona

Although the Route 66 theme song sings "...don't forget Winona," today there is really not much to see. Back in the day it was believed to be the first campsite for tourists in the 1920s.

⬥ Route 66 through Winona
Pre-1947 Alignment

If you have time, you can drive a pre-1947 alignment of Route 66. From I-40, take Exit 211. Turn right (north) and follow Townsend Winona Road (394) for about 10 miles. Townsend Winona Road leads to the **Walnut Canyon Bridge,** which is listed on the National Park Service Register of Historic Places. The bridge featured a Parker truss with an upper polygonal chord, concrete abutments, wing walls, and steel lattice guardrails—a type of bridge construction that was common for the time, but is now rarely found on Route 66. The bridge is on a short stretch of abandoned roadbed and is closed to traffic.

Keep heading west for 10 miles on Townsend Winona Road and turn left (south) onto U.S. 89 West heading into Flagstaff.

1947-1968 Alignment

From I-40, take Exit 204 to follow a 1947-1968 alignment via Santa Fe Avenue (U.S. 180 and U.S. 66). This road can be a little bumpy, but it passes the eastern edge of the largest **ponderosa pine forest** in the world. The road dead-ends in 4.5 miles at U.S. 89. Turn left (southwest) onto U.S. 89 to reach Flagstaff in 4 miles or turn right (north) to visit to Sunset Crater in 15 miles.

Taking Exit 240 also provides an opportunity to visit Walnut Canyon Monument before exploring the 1947-1969 alignment. From Exit 204, head south (left) for 3 miles on Walnut Canyon Road.

★ Walnut Canyon National Monument

Geological cliff formations, limestone ledges, curved buff sandstone walls, and ancient ruins are the impressive features at **Walnut Canyon National Monument** (3 Walnut Canyon Rd., 928/526-3367, 9am-5pm daily Nov.-May, 8am-5pm daily May-Oct., $8). Archaeologists labeled indigenous people who lived in the area as "Sinagua," a term from the old Spanish name for the area Sierra de Sin Agua ("mountains without water"). In the 1880s, the canyon was looted by "pot hunters," which led to establishing a national monument as protection in 1915.

The **Island Trail** (1 mile round-trip) leads directly to the dwellings with access to 25 rooms; however, the climb back is 240 steps at 6,690 feet in elevation, so it's a good workout. It also gets windy, so bring a jacket. Note that pets are not allowed on any park trails or in buildings.

❦ Side Trip: North on U.S. 89

From I-40, take Exit 201 and turn right (northwest) on Highway 180 toward U.S. 89 North. Turn right and follow signs for the Loop Road (Rte. 395). The **Loop Road** takes about an hour to drive—from the juniper grasslands, ponderosa pine forests, and open meadows to Sunset Crater and the red rocks of Wupatki National Monument.

Note: Avoid using GPS, as it may direct you to the monument's administrative offices or on a dirt road through the forest.

Sunset Crater Volcano National Monument

About 900 years ago a volcano erupted north of Flagstaff and reshaped the entire surrounding landscape. The 34-mile scenic loop through **Sunset Crater Volcano National Monument** (6082 Sunset Crater Rd., 9am-5pm daily Nov.-May, 8am-5pm daily May-Oct., $5, under 16 free) passes the scene of the eruption and offers views of an enormous volcanic cinder cone.

The **Sunset Crater Volcano National Monument Visitor Center** (6082 Fire Rd. 5454, 928/526-0502, 9am-5pm daily Nov.-May, 8am-5pm daily May-Oct.) has natural history and seismograph exhibits that outline the powerful forces behind earthquakes and volcanoes.

Allow at least an hour to hike the **Lava Flow Trail** (1 mile round-trip). The lava is sharp and brittle so be cautious. The trailhead is 1.5 miles west of the visitors center. For a more challenging hike, take the **Lenox Crater Trail**, found one mile east of the visitors center. The steep one-mile loop provides close-ups of the lava flow and basalt formations.

Wupatki National Monument

Located on the loop road through the Sunset Crater Monument, **Wupatki National Monument** (6400 N. Hwy. 89, 928/679-2365, visitors center 9am-5pm daily, dwellings dawn-to-dusk, $5) is one of the driest and hottest spots on the Colorado Plateau. The monument's 35,422 acres include dramatic vistas, geologic volcanic formations, desert wildlife, 900-year-old artifacts, and pueblos from ancient southwestern cultures. The Wupatki ruins lay scattered throughout the park and offer a glimpse into the lives of the Cohonina, Sinagua, and Kayenta cultures from the 1100s. The freestanding three-story **Wupatki Pueblo** was one of the lushest and most significant pueblos in the area, home to 85-100 people. In the early 13th century, all the settlements were abandoned.

❦ Back on 66

The Loop Road (Rte. 395) returns to U.S. 89, exiting Wupatki National Monument. Drive south on U.S. 89 for 25 miles into Flagstaff.

Flagstaff

Flagstaff is a convenient hub with access to seven national parks and monuments, including the Grand Canyon 80 miles northwest. Rather than a desert or red-rock landscape, Flagstaff sits smack in the middle of the world's largest ponderosa pine forest. While the rest of Arizona may experience sunny 60-degree days October through April, Flagstaff's almost

Flagstaff

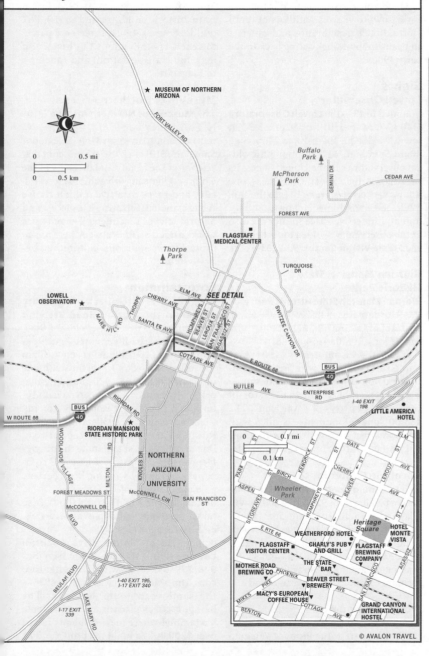

MUSEUM OF NORTHERN ARIZONA

FORT VALLEY RD

Buffalo Park

McPherson Park

GEMINI DR

CEDAR AVE

FOREST AVE

0   0.5 mi
0   0.5 km

FLAGSTAFF MEDICAL CENTER

TURQUOISE DR

Thorpe Park

LOWELL OBSERVATORY

MARS HILL RD

THORPE

CHERRY AVE

ELM AVE   SEE DETAIL

HUMPHREYS

BEAVER ST

LEROUX ST

SAN FRANCISCO ST

AGASSIZ ST

SANTA FE AVE

SWITZER CANYON DR

COTTAGE AVE

E ROUTE 66

BUS 40

BUTLER   AVE

ENTERPRISE RD

I-40 EXIT 198

BUS 40

RIORDAN RD

W ROUTE 66

WOODLANDS VILLAGE

LITTLE AMERICA HOTEL

RIORDAN MANSION STATE HISTORIC PARK

KNOLES DR

MILTON RD

NORTHERN
ARIZONA
UNIVERSITY

FOREST MEADOWS ST

McCONNELL CIR

SAN FRANCISCO ST

McCONNELL DR

BEULAH BLVD

LAKE MARY RD

I-40 EXIT 195,
I-17 EXIT 340

I-17 EXIT 339

Detail

0   0.1 mi
0   0.1 km

ELM

DATE ST

KENDRICK ST

PARK ST

CHERRY ST

LEROUX AVE

AVE

BIRCH

AVE

BEAVER

ASPEN

Wheeler Park

HUMPHREYS

AVE

SITGREAVES AVE

Heritage Square

SAN FRANCISCO ST

AGASSIZ

HOTEL MONTE VISTA

E RTE 66

WEATHERFORD HOTEL

FLAGSTAFF VISITOR CENTER

CHARLY'S PUB AND GRILL

FLAGSTAFF BREWING COMPANY

MOTHER ROAD BREWING CO

THE STATE BAR

PHOENIX AVE

BEAVER STREET BREWERY

MIKES PIKE

MACY'S EUROPEAN COFFEE HOUSE

COTTAGE AVE

GRAND CANYON INTERNATIONAL HOSTEL

BENTON

© AVALON TRAVEL

7,000-foot elevation means an average snowfall of about 108 inches annually.

Once you arrive, don't miss the historic downtown area with lots of retail stores, hotels, restaurants, and galleries in beautiful buildings dating back to the early 1900s.

Sights
Lowell Observatory
Founded in 1894 the **Lowell Observatory** (1400 W. Mars Hill Rd., 928/233-3211, www.lowell.edu, 10am-10pm Mon.-Sat., 10am-5pm Sun., $12) is among the oldest observatories in the United States. Its original 24-inch Alvan Clark telescope allows viewers to stare right into the sun. Wide-screen multimedia shows, exhibits, and an immersive space theater are also at the observatory. Guided tours begin at the **Steele Visitor Center** (928/233-3212).

Riordan Mansion State Historic Park
Riordan Mansion State Historic Park (409 W. Riordan Rd., 928/779-4395, www.azstateparks.com, 9:30am-5pm daily May-Oct., 10:30am-5pm daily Nov.-Apr. $10) is an impressive 1904 Arts and Crafts mansion with log-slab siding and volcanic stone arches designed by Charles Whittlesey, the creator of the Grand Canyon's El Tovar Hotel. The 13,000-square-foot manse is filled with 40 rooms that are furnished with original artifacts. Guided tours are available.

Coconino Center for the Arts
The **Coconino Center for the Arts** (2300 N. Fort Valley Rd., 928/779-2300, www.fllagartscouncil.org, 11am-5pm Tues.-Sat., fees vary) is the largest exhibit space in northern Arizona with a wide range of exhibits from regional artists and a 200-seat indoor amphitheater with films, performances, and concerts year-round.

Pioneer Museum
Imagine what it was like to live a settler's life in Flagstaff at the **Pioneer Museum** (2340 N. Fort Valley Rd., 928/774-6272, www.arizonahistoricalsociety.org, 9am-5pm Mon.-Sat., $6). A 1929 Baldwin train, historic buildings, and a 1950s D-7 bulldozer are set on a three-acre parcel to teach visitors about the history of logging, transportation, and ranching in Flagstaff.

Museum of Northern Arizona
The **Museum of Northern Arizona** (3101 N. Fort Valley Rd., 928/774-5213, www.musnaz.org, 10am-5pm Mon.-Sat., noon-5pm Sun., $10) is a 200-acre museum that celebrates the beauty and diversity of the Colorado Plateau with exhibits, research labs, and more than five million Native American artifacts, fine art pieces, and natural science specimens. The museum works directly with Native Americans to protect their traditions, culture, and belief systems.

Entertainment
Named after Steinbeck's signature surname, the **Mother Road Brewing Company** (7 S. Mikes Pike, 928/774-9139, www.motherroadbeer.com, 2pm-9pm Mon.-Thurs., 2pm-10pm Fri., noon-10pm Sat., noon-10pm Sun.) is on the south side of Flagstaff inside a 1920s building that originally housed a commercial laundry on a lost portion of Route 66. During the Depression, a 1930s alignment of Route 66 traveled under the railroad line one block west to handle the heavier Depression-era traffic. Today, the company brews award-winning IPAs, porters, pale ales, and a Kolsch-style beer with a dry, malty, and slightly fruity finish. Also on the menu are seasonal, anniversary, and barrel-aged ales.

The **Hotel Monte Vista Cocktail Lounge** (100 N. San Francisco St., 928/779-6971, www.hotelmontevista.com, 1pm-2am daily) was built in 1926—the same year Route 66 began. The lounge is attached to the historical Monte Vista hotel where local residents raised over $200,000 to build the property. The

Lounge was a speakeasy in the 1920s and hosted Humphrey Bogart, Carole Lombard, Gary Cooper, John Wayne, and Clark Gable. (Allegedly Wayne was so drunk he tried to put his horse in the elevator.) It's also rumored to be haunted with moving bar stools and ghosts dancing without a care in the world. Good times.

The **Museum Club** (3404 E. Rte. 66, 928/526-9434, www.themuseumclub. com, 11am-2am daily) is housed in a log cabin that was built in 1931 as a taxidermy curio cabinet. In 1939, it morphed into a country roadhouse, and today, it's a classic honky-tonk filled with history and tradition. Tanya Tucker played her first gig here at age 14, and country legends Willie Nelson and Waylon Jennings have graced the stage. It remains an all-American cowboy bar where folks square dance and do the two-step to national and regional acts.

Heritage Square (928/853-4292, www.heritagesquaretrust.org, free) is an 11,000-square-foot plaza and Flagstaff's only open-air amphitheater showcasing local artists, performers, events, movie screenings, and concerts. Located on Aspen Avenue (between Leroux and San Francisco Sts.) in the heart of historic downtown, it's a great place to grab a gelato, shop, sit, and watch people walk by.

The **Orpheum Theater** (15 W. Aspen Ave., 928/556-1580, www.orpheum-flagstaff.com) is a local landmark and Flagstaff's premier entertainment venue offering unique film screenings and some of the best regional and national music acts in the area. They have an expansive balcony, plush seating, a full bar and lounge.

Shopping

Historic Downtown Flagstaff (1 E. Rte. 66, 928/774-9541, www.flagstaffarizona. org) is a quaint, pedestrian-friendly area filled with clothing boutiques, bookstores, art galleries, restaurants, cafés, outdoor outfitters, and nightlife nestled in a picturesque historic downtown with buildings from the early 1900s. An **art walk** takes place the first Friday of every month, and there are other annual events, including **Flagstaff Route 66 Days** (928/451-1204, www. route66carclub.com), a three-day event with more than 400 restored classic cars that is held in September. Venture south of the railroad tracks near downtown to the **Historic Southside District,** a popular spot with a collection of restaurants, tattoo shops, coffee shops, and breweries.

Bookman's (1520 S. Riordan Ranch Rd., 928/774-0005, 9am-10pm daily) is an extensive used bookstore with music, DVDs, audio books, magazines, comic books, collectibles, and board and video games with Amazon prices. Pets are welcome to shop with you as long as they're on a leash.

For practically everything you might need for an outdoor adventure check out **Peace Surplus** (14 W. Rte. 66, 928/779-4521, 8am-9pm Mon.-Sat., 8am-6pm Sun.). It's conveniently located right on Route 66 and stocked with huge selection of camping, hiking, skiing, fishing, and exercise gear.

Flagstaff Soap Company (21 N. San Francisco St., 928/774-9178, 11am-6pm Mon.-Thurs., 11am-7pm Fri., 10am-7pm Sat., 10am-5pm Sun.) features hand-crafted, 100 percent cruelty-free products for the whole family. The salves, lip balm, and dog-bone-shaped soaps are the best.

Aspen Place at the Sawmill (Butler Ave. and Lone Tree Rd., www.aspenplace.com) has almost 70,000 square feet of shops and restaurants—from Chico's to Wildflower Bread Company to REI.

Earthbound Trading Company (22 N. San Francisco St., 10am-9pm Mon.-Thurs., 10am-10pm Fri.-Sat., 10am-9pm Sun.) has an eclectic global, gift line from Eastern Indian to Native American beaded jewelry, bath products, dream catchers, mosaics, backpacks, purses, and more.

Knitting is the ultimate relaxation activity for the road and **Purl in the Pines** (2544 N. 4th St., 928/774-9334, 10am-5:30pm Mon., Wed., and Fri.-Sat., 10am-7:30pm Tues. and Thurs.) has a wonderful, well-organized selection of quality knitting products including hand-dyed luxury yarns, needles, and books.

Recreation

Flagstaff is an outdoor-enthusiasts paradise with world-class biking, skiing, and hiking in the surrounding Coconino National Forest. There are several favorite excursions in the area.

Lava River Cave

Discover the ancient underground **Lava River Cave** (Coconino National Forest, FR-171B, 928/526-0866, www.fs.usda. gov, 10am-5pm daily May, 9am-5pm daily late May-Sept., closed in winter, $5), which was formed about 700,000 years ago. Wavelike ripples are frozen in the floor from molten rock and stone icicles hang from the ceiling where volcanic heat partially melted the ceiling that dripped and dried. It's pitch-black so bring two sources of light in case one fails. Dress warm (it's about 42 degrees inside) and tread carefully, the rocks are sharp and slippery.

To access the cave, drive 9 miles north of Flagstaff on U.S. 180 and turn west (left) on FR 245 (at milepost 230). Continue 3 miles to FR-171 and turn south for 1 mile to where FR-171B turns left and then it's a short distance to Lava River Cave. The cave is open year-round but FR-171 and FR-245 may be closed in the winter.

Hiking

Stretch your legs on the **Kachina Trail,** a moderate 5-mile hike in the Kachina Peaks Wilderness area about 17 miles north of Flagstaff. The trail crosses several canyons before descending into a lava cliff with eroded volcanic rocks. It's an especially popular hike in fall due to the brilliant foliage in the aspen groves.

From Flagstaff, drive 7 miles northwest on U.S. 180. Turn right (north) onto Forest Road 516 (Snowbowl Rd.). Follow this road for about 7 miles to the Snowbowl Ski Area and park in the first parking lot on the right (south) The trailhead is at the south end of the parking lot.

Biking

The mountain bike trails in the Coconino National Forest range from easy to technical rocky single-track downhill routes. **Absolute Bikes** (202 E. Rte. 66, 928/779-5969, www.absolutebikes.net, 9am-7pm Mon.-Fri., 9am-6pm Sat., 10am-4pm Sun. Apr.-Dec.; 10am-6pm Mon.-Sat., 10am-4pm Sun. Jan.-Mar.) is a full-service bike shop with an assortment of mountain, road, town cruiser, and tandem bike rentals. They work with a local bike advocacy group and the Coconino Forest to build new routes, and they are the best resource for local info about bike trail rides in the Flagstaff area. Bike rentals ($20-65) include a helmet, pump, repair kit, spare tube, choice of pedals, and personalized fit service. Reservations are not necessary, but are recommended.

Flagstaff Nordic Center

For cross-country skiing, snowshoeing, camping, hiking, biking, and wildlife-viewing, the **Flagstaff Nordic Center** (Hwy. 180 at mile marker 232, 928/220-0550, www.flagstaffnordiccenter.com, 9am-4pm daily) hosts some of the best outdoor recreation activities in the area. There are more than 35 miles of ski and snowshoe trails ranging from beginner to expert; many of these trails are also used for hiking and biking in summer, and bike rentals are available on-site ($20-30). Accommodations include cabins and yurts with woodstoves (up to 8 people, www.offgridgetaways.com, $40-90).

Horseback Riding

Breathe in the fresh mountain air while

on horseback or in a horse-drawn wagon at the **Hitchin' Post Stables** (4848 Lake Mary Rd., 928/774-1719, www.hitchin-poststables.com, $55-220), just south of Walnut Canyon. One-, two-, three-, and four-hour trails gallop through the home of cliff- and cave-dwelling American Indians through 10,000 acres. Rides with lunch and dinner included are also available.

Winter Sports
With an average of 260 inches of snow, it would be a shame to miss the **Arizona Snowbowl** (Snowbowl Rd., off Hwy. 180, 928/779-1951 or 928/779-4577 for snow report, www.arizonasnowbowl.com). Ski more than 32 trails with five lifts with a 2,300-foot vertical drop. When it's not snowing, ride the Scenic Skyride with fabulous views at 11,000 feet and play disc golf.

Accommodations
★ **Little America Hotel** (2515 E. Butler Ave., 800/865-1401, www.flagstaff.littlecamerica.com, $105 190 is a classic hotel and lodge set in a 500-acre ponderosa pine forest. The rooms are immaculate and decorated in a 1970s French-themed decor which may sound dated but it's classic and traditional in all the right ways—that perfect warm, elegant, yet cozy experience you want on vacation.

The **DuBeau** (19 W. Phoenix Ave., 800/398-7112, www.modubeau.com, $58-84) is an affordable and charming historic motel and hostel located on a pre-1934 alignment of Route 66 in downtown Flagstaff. (The route traveled west of the railroad tracks on Beaver Street, then north on Phoenix). The DuBeau was also listed in historic guides published for African American travelers during Jim Crow. Economy rooms feature a double bed, a desk, and a mini-fridge, but no television. Deluxe rooms are larger with one double bed, a flat-screen cable TV, and a lounge chair. Premium rooms include two double beds and a kitchenette with a microwave.

For road-trippers on a budget, the **Grand Canyon International Hostel** (19 1/2 S. San Francisco St., 888/442-2696, www.grandcanyonhostel.com, $25) is a good choice. Set right in historic downtown Flagstaff, it's meticulously clean with five shared bathrooms, guest laundry, and two kitchens on the property.

Sonesta ES Suites (1400 N. Country Club Rd., 928/526-5555, www.sonesta.com/flagstaff, $58-84) is a spacious, all-suite hotel. Each suite sleeps 4-6 people and has a fully equipped kitchen; some studio suites come with a fireplace. Pets are allowed for an additional fee.

For modern amenities with panoramic views of the San Francisco Mountain Range, book a room at the **Twin Arrows Navajo Casino Resort** (22181 Resort Blvd., 877/630-9530, www.twinarrows.com, $90-180), a full-service gaming hotel with dining and entertainment. Rooms are stylishly decorated in sophisticated neutrals with maize, paprika, and turquoise accents, and include state-of-the-art entertainment centers.

Food
The smothered chicken-fried steak is legendary at the **Grand Canyon Café** (110 E. Rte. 66, 928/774-2252, $6-12), a true-blue diner that hasn't changed for decades. It's owned and operated by the Wongs, a wife and husband team who are praised for making the best homemade egg rolls in Flagstaff.

For vegans and those with dietary restrictions, **Macy's European Coffeehouse** (14 S. Beaver St., 928/774-2243, 6am-8pm daily, $4-8) serves up delicious dairy-, nut-, egg-, gluten-, and wheat-free options. Breakfast features couscous with fruit, raisins, almonds, cinnamon, and brown sugar. The coffee is roasted daily and served Americano-style from an espresso machine.

Tucked away behind a gas station in an older shopping center is the family-owned

★ **Satchmos** (2320 N. 4th St., 928/774-7292, 11am-8pm Mon.-Thurs., 11am-9pm Fri.-Sat., $6-12), serving up heavenly barbecue and Cajun and Creole faves like red beans and rice, po'boys, and jambalaya. The brisket sandwich served with Cajun-seasoned tater tots is unforgettable. Who knew a fried potato could taste so good?

For upscale, yet unpretentious American comfort food, the **Tinderbox Kitchen** (34 S. San Francisco, 928/226-8400, 5pm-9pm Sun.-Thurs., 5pm-10pm Fri.-Sat., $18-28) will not disappoint. Located in Flagstaff's historic Southside district, they welcome you to come dressed up or down. Just come as you are.

Eat with the locals right on Route 66 at **Miz Zips** (2924 E. Rte. 66, 928/526-0104, 6am-9pm Mon.-Sat., 7am-2pm Sun, $6-10 cash only), a tried-and-true old-school eatery that has been serving cowhands and construction workers since 1952. Enjoy great cheeseburgers and French dip sandwiches—the cherry pie is even better.

Along with an extensive variety of oatmeal stouts, IPAs, and lagers, the **Beaver St. Brewery** (11 S. Beaver St., 928/779-0079, 11am-11pm Sun.-Thurs., 11am-midnight Fri.-Sat., $9-28) serves yummy pesto and cream cheese dip, chicken potpie in a buttery crust, and mouthwatering pork chops.

The blackberry duck tacos with black bean salad at **Café Daily Fare** (408 E. Rte. 66, 928/774-2855, 11am-4pm Mon.-Sat., $8-12) are unlike anything you've ever tasted. This quaint, adorable hidden gem is located at the top of a gravel driveway off Route 66 before you get to North Elden Street (traveling west on Route 66), past the TitleMax Loan Company.

If you're in the mood for Indian, the best bet in the area is **Delhi Palace** (2700 S. Woodlands Village Blvd., Ste. 640, 11am-2:30pm and 5pm-930pm daily,

top to bottom: Museum Club, Flagstaff; Hotel Monte Vista Cocktail Lounge, Flagstaff; Meteor Crater

One Day in the Grand Canyon

First, ditch the car. Park near the **Grand Canyon Visitor Center** and walk the **Rim Trail** west, stopping at **Mather Point,** the **Yavapai Geology Museum,** and the **Hopi House** before lunching at **Bright Angel Lodge.** Afterward, explore the **Grand Canyon Village Historic District,** checking out the Harvey House history exhibit in Bright Angel Lodge, peeking through the lens at the **Kolb Studio,** and soaking in canyon vistas from **Lookout Point.**

From Grand Canyon Village, hop aboard the **shuttle bus** on the Hermits Rest Route to the West Rim. Stop off at **Hermits Rest** to view Mary Colter's masterpiece building and epic fireplace. The shuttle picks up again at several points along the West Rim. At night, make reservations for dinner in **El Tovar's** fabulous, historic dining room with views over the canyon.

Drivers who enter the park via the east entrance (Hwy. 64) can stop at the stunning **Desert View Watchtower** (another Mary Colter masterpiece) and the **Tusayan Ruin and Museum** before parking in the Grand Canyon Visitor Center lots.

$9-17). The creamy lamb korma, bold and spicy chicken *vindaloo*, and flaky garlic naan are out of this world.

Information and Services

The **Flagstaff Convention and Visitors Bureau** (1 E. Rte. 66, 800/842-7293, www.flagstaffarizona.org, 928/774-9541 or 800-842-7293, 8am-5pm Mon.-Sat., 9am-4pm Sun.) can be found in the historic train station downtown. Come for free maps and brochures, then explore the gift shop with Route 66 and train-themed souvenirs, books, clothing, and memorabilia.

At almost 7,000 feet in elevation, Flagstaff weather in may be a factor for drivers. To ensure you're prepared, contact the following for up-to-date status and conditions.

- National Weather Service (928/556-9161, http://weather.gov/flagstaff)

- Recorded Weather Information (928/774-3301)

- Road Conditions (888/411-7623, www.az511.com)

- Arizona Snowbowl Snow Report

(928/779-4577, www.arizonasnowbowl.com)

◈ Back on 66

Before leaving Flagstaff, consider a side trip to the Grand Canyon (1.5 hours away) or Sedona (about 45 minutes away). To continue on Route 66, drive west on Bus-40 (Route 66) for 4.5 miles to join I-40 West. Continue 14 miles past Bellemont and take Exit 178 to Parks. Turn right and take the next left on Old Route 66.

◈ Side Trip: Grand Canyon National Park

The **Grand Canyon National Park** (928/638-7888, www.nps.gov/grca, $30) is 277 miles long, nearly 18 miles wide, and 1 mile deep. The Grand Canyon is more than a geological nirvana with breathtaking vistas and colorful buttes—it also has a rich, deep cultural history that rivals almost any national park.

In 1540 when Spanish explorer Garcia Lopez de Cardenas gazed at almost 2 billion years of geology from the South Rim of the Grand Canyon he was not

ARIZONA

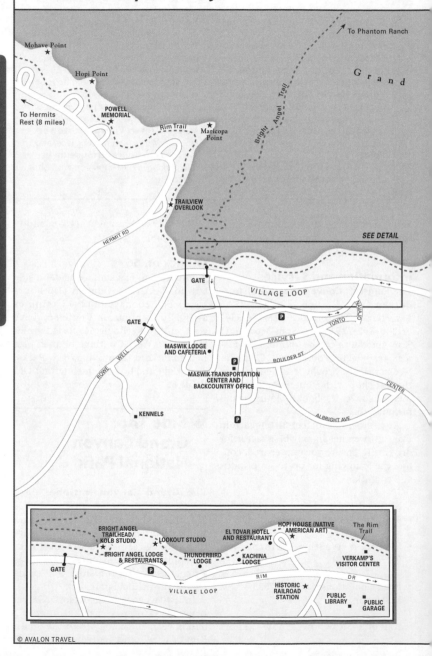

Grand Canyon Village

To Phantom Ranch

Grand

Mohave Point ★

Hopi Point ★

POWELL MEMORIAL ●

To Hermits Rest (8 miles)

Rim Trail

Bright Angel Trail

Maricopa Point ★

TRAILVIEW OVERLOOK ★

HERMIT RD

SEE DETAIL

GATE

VILLAGE LOOP

NAVAJO

TONTO

GATE

P

ROWE WELL RD

APACHE ST

MASWIK LODGE AND CAFETERIA ●

P

BOULDER ST

MASWIK TRANSPORTATION CENTER AND BACKCOUNTRY OFFICE

CENTER

ALBRIGHT AVE

KENNELS ■

P

BRIGHT ANGEL TRAILHEAD/ KOLB STUDIO

LOOKOUT STUDIO ★

EL TOVAR HOTEL AND RESTAURANT

HOPI HOUSE (NATIVE AMERICAN ART) ★

The Rim Trail

BRIGHT ANGEL LODGE & RESTAURANTS ●

THUNDERBIRD LODGE ●

KACHINA LODGE ●

VERKAMP'S VISITOR CENTER ●

GATE

P

RIM

DR

VILLAGE LOOP

HISTORIC RAILROAD STATION ★

PUBLIC LIBRARY ■

PUBLIC GARAGE ■

© AVALON TRAVEL

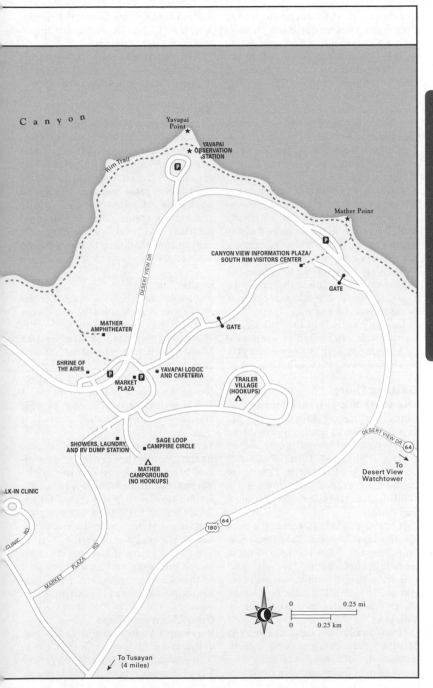

Canyon

Yavapai Point ★

★ YAVAPAI OBSERVATION STATION

Rim Trail

Mather Point ★

DESERT VIEW DR

CANYON VIEW INFORMATION PLAZA/ SOUTH RIM VISITORS CENTER

GATE

MATHER AMPHITHEATER

GATE

SHRINE OF THE AGES

MARKET PLAZA

YAVAPAI LODGE AND CAFETERIA

TRAILER VILLAGE (HOOKUPS)

DESERT VIEW DR 64

To Desert View Watchtower

SHOWERS, LAUNDRY, AND RV DUMP STATION

SAGE LOOP CAMPFIRE CIRCLE

MATHER CAMPGROUND (NO HOOKUPS)

LK-IN CLINIC

CLINIC RD

MARKET PLAZA RD

180 64

0   0.25 mi

0   0.25 km

To Tusayan (4 miles)

impressed with the view; he considered the area as a desert wasteland and was more concerned about finding a way to cross it. Cardenas and his 12 companions spent three days looking for a passage to the Colorado River below with no success. Hopi guides convinced the party to turn around, but some historians believe that the Hopis knew exactly how to access the river and they were protecting this sacred area. It would be another 300 years before Westerners attempted to explore the canyon again.

Hotelier and restaurant operator Fred Harvey knew the Grand Canyon would be a world-class tourist destination. In 1901, he convinced the Santa Fe Railway to run a rail line from Williams, Arizona. Although he died the same year, El Tovar Hotel, a Fred Harvey House, opened in 1905 at the South Rim at the end of the Santa Fe Railway line and was operated by his sons and grandsons.

It wasn't until 1919 that the Grand Canyon was established as a national park. Today more than five million visitors huddle along the South Rim.

Getting There

The **South Rim Entrance** (open year-round) is the most convenient access for Route 66 road-trippers. From Flagstaff, take U.S. 180 north for 50 miles to Highway 64. Turn right (north) onto Highway 64 and drive 22 miles to the South Entrance. Or, from I-40 in Williams, take Highway 64 north straight for 60 miles.

It is also possible to access the park via the less-crowded **East Entrance.** From Flagstaff, follow Highway 89 north for 46 miles to Cameron. Turn left (west) and drive 48 miles to the east entrance station. It is another mile west along Desert View Drive to Grand Canyon Village.

If you'd rather not drive, the **Arizona Shuttle** (1 E. Rte. 66, http://arizonashut-tle.com, 877-226-8060, $25 each way) provides round-trip shuttle service (twice daily in winter, three times daily in summer) from Flagstaff to the Grand Canyon from the Amtrak station.

After arriving in the park, leave your car at the visitors center and use one of the park shuttle buses to see the sights.

Sights
Grand Canyon Visitor Center

The **Grand Canyon Visitor Center** (8am-5pm daily year-round) has outdoor and indoor exhibits, including interactive trip planners, a large 3D relief map, videos, and films. A **café** (open year-round) and **bookstore** (8am-7pm daily) are on-site and bicycle rentals from **Bright Angel Bicycles** (928/638-3055, www.bikegrand-canyon.com, Mar.-Oct., $12/hr, $40/day) are available.

Mather Point

Just a short walk past the visitors center on the Rim Trail, **Mather Point** offers the first epic glimpse into the gaping canyon. The promontory, named after Stephan Mather (the first director of the National Park Service), juts out beyond the rim and gives first-time visitors a perspective of the canyon's depth. Picnic tables and a small stone amphitheater provide ringside seats to the views.

Yavapai Museum of Geology

Learn about the geology, origin, and history of Grand Canyon at the **Yavapai Museum** of **Geology** (928/638-7888, 8am-6pm daily), perched on the south rim of the Grand Canyon with panoramic views. Located a short walk east of Mather Point along the "Trail of Time," the museum features 3D models, photographs, and a scaled diorama of the canyon, fossils, and rock fragments, plus videos of the canyon floor.

Grand Canyon Village

Verkamp's Visitor Center (8am-6pm daily), east of El Tovar in Grand Canyon Village, details the pioneer history of the Grand Canyon. A bookstore and exhibits are on-site, and park rangers can answer any questions.

El Tovar

A former Harvey House, **El Tovar** sits front and center on the Rim Trail in Grand Canyon Village. The hotel opened in 1905 and continues to serve guests with quaint rooms, a stunning lobby, a stellar on-site restaurant, and a seasonal deck overlooking the rim. Designed by Charles Whittlesey and constructed with local limestone, the building has been designated a National Historic Landmark.

Hopi House

The **Hopi House** (928/638-2631, 8am-8pm daily) was built by Mary Colter for Fred Harvey. The Puebloan-style sandstone and adobe structure is a living museum for Hopi artisans to share their artistic process of making pottery, jewelry, and blankets and houses one of the best gift shops in the park.

Kolb Studio

At the trailhead for the Bright Angel Trail, the **Kolb Studio** (8am-6pm daily) details the history of the Kolb Brothers, two pioneering photographers who explored and promoted the canyon through films and photos. The Victorian building—the Kolb Brothers' former home and studio—includes an on-site museum with exhibits and was under renovation at time of publication. A gift shop (8am-7pm daily) is also on-site.

Lookout Studio

Mary Colter's **Lookout Studio** sits perched on the Grand Canyon's rim, its local stone and wood construction almost disappearing into the canyon walls. Built in 1914, its terraces offer a perfect opportunity to view the canyon's depths via telescope or spot the skies for California condors in flight. A gift shop (9am-5pm daily) is, of course, on-site.

West Rim

The best way to explore the canyon's **West Rim** is via **shuttle bus** (80 min. round-trip, hours vary daily Mar.-Nov., free), which picks up at the Village Route Transfer (on Village Loop Dr., below Bright Angel Lodge) and stops at nine viewpoints along the West Rim. **Hopi Point** juts farthest out into the canyon's rim and a stop at Hermits Rest should not be missed.

Hermits Rest

Built in 1914 by park favorite Mary Colter, **Hermits Rest** sits practically nestled into the canyon at the at the of the Rim Trail, its chunky stone blocks harmonizing with the surrounding environment. More impressive is the massive stone fireplace inside. A snack bar (9am-5pm daily), gift shop (9am-5pm daily), water refill station, and restrooms are also on-site. The start of the Hermit Trail leads steeply into the canyon below.

East Rim

Desert View Drive extends 25 miles east from Grand Canyon Village to the East Entrance on U.S. 64. Along the way are six canyon viewpoints, including Grandview Point and Lipan Point, four picnic areas, and a Mary Colter masterpiece.

Tusayan Ruin and Museum

The **Tusayan Ruin and Museum** (9am-5pm daily) contains the remains of a once thriving small 800-year old Puebloan village. The museum showcases handmade crafts from modern local tribes and includes figurines that are up to 4,000 years old. Tusayan is 3 miles west of Desert View Watchtower and 22 miles east of the Grand Canyon Village.

Desert View Watchtower

The **Desert View Watchtower** (8am-sunset daily) was designed by Mary Colter to be a replica of a four-story Indian tower; Colter spent six months researching archaeological construction techniques. Inside is a Kiva Room, interior murals painted by artist Fred Kabotie, and a rooftop observation area with 360-degree views of the Colorado River, the Painted Desert, and the San Francisco Peaks. The Watchtower is the tallest structure in the park and located 24 miles east of Grand Canyon Village. Nearby is a grocery store and snack bar, a gas station, and a seasonal campground.

Hiking

It's easy to be seduced by the magnificent views of the Grand Canyon. Although there are several trails from the South Rim, don't think you can hike to the river and back in less than one day; more than 250 hikers are rescued each year. There are no easy trails into or out of the Grand Canyon. Use common sense, be aware of your limitations, and always stay on the trail. Even the most experienced hikers say trekking through the Grand Canyon was more difficult than they expected due to the high altitude, elevation, and dry, desert climate.

Rim Trail

The **Rim Trail** follows the rim of the Grand Canyon for 13 miles (one-way) from the South Kaibab trailhead west to Hermits Rest. It's mostly flat, often paved, and offers excellent views of the inner canyon; many sections are suitable for wheelchairs. Popular sections include the 0.7 mile between Mather Point and Yavapai Geology Museum; the 1.3 miles between Yavapai and Verkamp's; and the 0.6 mile from Verkamp's to Kolb Studio in Grand Canyon Village.

Bright Angel Trail

The **Bright Angel Trail** descends from Grand Canyon Village to drop 12 steep miles to the Colorado River. While it is not possible to hike to the river and back in a day, some shorter sections are doable as a day hike. From the trailhead to the Upper Tunnel is 0.4 mile (round-trip); the

Lower Tunnel waits at 1.7 miles round-trip (1-2 hours). In 3 miles (round-trip, 2-4 hours) you'll reach 1 1/2 Mile Resthouse, which has restrooms and water (seasonally). Don't push your luck much farther than 3-Mile Resthouse, which is a brutal 6 miles round-trip (4-6 hours), with restrooms and water (seasonal). The trailhead is next to Kolb Studio along the Rim Trail and near Bright Angel Lodge.

South Kaibab Trail

The **South Kaibab Trail** offers the best views for a relatively short yet steep hike. Those in relatively good shape should make it to Ooh Ahh Point (1.8 miles round-trip, 1-2 hours), with a 600-foot change elevation. The views change around every bend, making it worth the effort. Extending down into the canyon to Cedar Ridge (3 miles round-trip, 2-4 hours) increases the elevation change to 1,120 feet. The hike back up to the rim is always harder; give uphill hikers the right of way. Dress in layers, wear good hiking boots, and bring water and food, as there is no water along this trail.

To reach the trailhead, park at the visitors center and take the free Kaibab/Rim Route shuttle bus to Yaki Point.

Accommodations

Accommodations tend to be full throughout the year so it's best to book rooms at least eight months in advance. Most **reservations** (928/638-2631 or 888/297-2757, www.grandcanyonlodges.com) can be made online at the six main lodges up to 13 months in advance.

The **Yavapai Lodge** (Market Plaza, 1 Main St., 877/404-4611, www.visitgrand-canyon.com, $142-178) offers rooms with clean basic necessities; choose from a king bed, two queen beds, and bunk beds that sleep 4-6 people. Internet access is available on-site (but not in the rooms). The prime location is what you're paying for—it's walking distance to the general store, visitors center, and the Rim Trail.

El Tovar Hotel (Grand Canyon Village, Apache St. and Center Rd., 888/297-2757, www.grandcanyonlodges.com, $197-489) is an elegant National Historic Landmark that was built in 1905 by Charles Whittlesey, the chief architect for the Atchison, Topeka, and Santa Fe Railway. The Fred Harvey Company owned El Tovar, and it's one of the few Harvey House facilities still in operation. The 78 rooms include many suites to choose from—no two rooms are alike. Amenities include TVs, Keurig coffeemakers, room service, and air-conditioning. An upscale restaurant is on-site.

Maswik Lodge (Grand Canyon Village, 888/297-2757, www.grandcanyonlodges.com, $107-205) is about 0.25 mile south of Grand Canyon Village in a ponderosa pine forest. The complex has 250 motel-style rooms, a gift shop, a food court, and a pizza pub. Rooms are located in two-story buildings (no elevators), and access is via exterior stairwells and walkways. Amenities include in-room coffeemakers, fridges, cable TV, and air-conditioning.

Thunderbird and **Kachina Lodges** (Grand Canyon Village, 888/297-2757, www.grandcanyonlodges.com, $215-232) offer contemporary lodging options close to the rim. Rooms include either one king or two queen beds with full baths; "canyonside" rooms have partial views. Amenities include coffeemakers, fridges, and flat-screen TVs. Each lodge is within walking distance of restaurants, gift shops, Kolb Studio, and the Bright Angel trailhead.

Bright Angel Lodge (Grand Canyon Village, 888/297-2757, www.grandcanyonlodges.com, $105-207) is a rustic landmark built by Mary Colter as a less expensive alternative to the elite El Tovar. Centrally located mere steps from the rim, the lodge offers 90 lodging options, from units with shared baths to standard lodge rooms and cabins. It was listed in the historic Negro Motorist Green Book and the on-site Bright Angel History Room features historic postcards, a 100-year old El Tovar menu, and exhibits about the Harvey Girls. Amenities include two restaurants, a bar and coffee nook, and a soda fountain (open seasonally). The trailhead for the Bright Angel Trail is nearby.

Camping

There are two campgrounds within the park. Reservations for each can be made up to six months in advance and are highly recommended.

Mather Campground (Market Plaza, 877/444-6777, www.recreation.gov, $18, year-round) is the largest campground in the park with 319 sites for tents and RVs. Centrally located south of Market Plaza, amenities here include fire rings at each campsite, drinking water, bathrooms with coin-operated showers, and laundry services; leashed pets are permitted. RV sites do not have hookups, but there is a dump station. The campground is serviced by the Village Route shuttle bus. From November-March, sites are available on a first-come, first-served basis; however, water may be turned off.

Desert View Campground (Desert View Dr., first-come, first-served, mid-Apr-mid-Oct., $12) is near Desert View Watchtower, 25 miles east of Grand Canyon Village. The 50 sites can accommodate tents and small RVs (less than 30 feet). Amenities include fire grills and picnic tables; drinking water and restrooms are available in the campground. Even though reservations are not accepted, sites fill by early afternoon in summer. A grocery store and snack bar are nearby. If entering the park via the East Entrance, this will be the first campground you come to.

If you are traveling with an RV, try **Trailer Village RV Park** (877/404-4611, www.visitgrandcanyon.com, $36, year-round), which is adjacent to Mather Campground near Market Plaza. Reservations are recommended for the 84 pull-through sites (up to 50 feet) with hookups. Amenities include

Wi-Fi, drinking water, and the bathroom and laundry facilities at Mather Campground.

Food

The Grand Canyon Visitor Center is home to the **Bright Angel Bicycle Rental and Café** (928/638-3055, http://bikegrandcanyon.com, 6am-8pm daily Apr.-Nov., 7am-7pm daily Dec.-Mar.), a coffee bar with prepackaged meals to go.

In the El Tovar Hotel, the **El Tovar Dining Room** (Grand Canyon Village, 928/638-2631, ext. 6432, www.grandcanyonlodges.com, 6:30am-10:45am, 11:15am-2pm, and 5pm-10pm daily, $20-35) offers a grand dining experience in a rustic yet classic ambience with native-stone and Oregon pine construction and Hopi, Apache, Mojave, and Navajo murals. Dishes merge traditional and southwestern influences, such as roasted duck with prickly pear orange glaze. It's the most popular dining spot in the Grand Canyon, so reservations are highly recommended. Although there is no formal dress code, shorts and flip-flops are discouraged.

For a less formal experience in the same property, opt for the **El Tovar Lounge** (928/638-2631, 11am-11pm daily), which offers a limited menu and creative concoctions like prickly pear margaritas. The outdoor deck is a prime people-watching spot and the perfect place to soak in the spectacular scenery of the park.

There are several dining options at Bright Angel Lodge. **Bright Angel Restaurant** (6:30am-10:45am, 11:15am-4pm, and 4:30am-10pm daily, no reservations, $10) is a casual family-style restaurant serving breakfast, lunch, and dinner. Entrée options include biscuits and gravy, burgers, and steak. More upscale is the grand **Arizona Room** (9 Village Loop Dr., 928/638-2631, 11:30am-3pm and 4:30pm-10pm daily, no reservations, $20), which puts a southwestern spin on hand-cut steaks, enchiladas,

and salads. Local artisan brewers and vintners are also featured. In the morning, the Bright Angel Lounge becomes the **Canyon Coffee House** (6am-10am daily, $3) serving coffee and continental breakfast items. In summer, **Bright Angel Fountain** (11am-5pm seasonally) is the place to take the kids for ice creams, sodas, and snacks.

Grab a snack or sit down for a meal at the **Maswik Food Court** (Maswik Lodge, 888/297-2757, 6am-10pm daily, $3-10) at the west end of Grand Canyon Village. Affordable menu options range from home-style dinner entrées to packaged lunches prepared "to go." With four televisions, the onsite **Maswik Pizza Pub** (11am-11pm daily, $20) is more like a sports bar, serving fresh-baked pizzas, salads, and cold beer.

The Market Plaza has the **Canyon Village Market** (928/638-2262, 6:30am-9pm daily May-Sept., shorter winter hours), which sells clothing and gifts, as well as groceries, and a **deli** (6:30am-8pm May-Sept., shorter winter hours), which builds made-to-order sandwiches or prepackaged meals. At **Yavapai Lodge**, the **Lodge Restaurant** (6am-10pm daily May-Sept., shorter winter hours, $15), **Coffee Shop** (5am-10pm daily May-Sept., shorter winter hours), and **Lodge Tavern** (11am-10pm daily July-Feb.) fulfills traveler needs.

Hermits Rest Snack Bar (8am-6pm daily in summer, 9am-5pm daily in winter) offers a unique spot for a quick snack. Enjoy sandwiches, ice cream, chips, cookies, and hot chocolate next to the enormous 1914 stone fireplace designed by Mary Colter.

Food options near the east entrance include **Desert View General Store** (928/638-2393, 8am-8pm daily in summer, shorter winter hours), which sells groceries and souvenirs. Nearby, the **Desert View Deli** (928/638-2360, 8am-7pm daily May-Sept., shorter winter hours) has a snack bar that serves chili, Indian tacos, salads, pizza, and chips.

Tours

Air Tours originate at the Grand Canyon Airport in Tusayan, Arizona, near the South Rim of the park. **Westwind Air Service** (888/869-0866, www.westwindairservice.com) offers 45-minute tours into the deepest part of the canyon with views of the Colorado River, the Painted Desert, and the Desert View Watchtower. **Grand Canyon Airlines** (866/235-9422, air tours start at $159) has been in business since 1927 and is one of the world's oldest air tour company. Another flight option is **Papillon Grand Canyon Helicopters** (888/635-7272, www.papillon.com).

Daily **bus tours** (888/297-2757, www.grandcanyonlodges.com) with guides outlining the history and geology of the canyon are also available.

⬥ Side Trip: U.S. 89 to Sedona

Nourish and heal your soul in the geological wonderland of Sedona. About 30 miles south of Flagstaff via U.S. 89, soaring monoliths straddle a town filled with dozens of spas, plentiful art galleries, boutiques, resorts, and wineries. The red-rock monoliths that flank Sedona are regarded as sacred and energy-harnessing vortexes that inspire spiritualists to travel from all over the world to access the mystical power of this area. But you don't have to be a crystal-loving hippie to get Sedona; it's also a hot spot for outdoor enthusiasts with lots of trails for hiking, biking, and off-roading. It's the perfect place to get in tune with nature, play hard, soak in the desert sun, and relax in the bosom of ultimate luxury.

Getting There

From Flagstaff and Bus-40, head south on S. Milton Road and turn right (west). Take your first left onto U.S. 89A. Follow U.S. 89A south for 25 miles into Sedona.

Scenic Drives
Oak Creek Canyon

Oak Creek Canyon Scenic Drive (Rte. 89A) is a 24-mile drive between Flagstaff and Sedona. From Flagstaff, take I-17 South to Highway 89A. The breathtaking road descends 4,500 feet from the top of the Mogollon Rim, winding through sandstone canyons and rock formations around every curve.

Along the way, visit one of the state's most beautiful swimming holes. **Slide Rock State Park** (1300 W. Washington, 928/282-3034, www.azstateparks.com, hours vary seasonally, $10) is a natural water park in Oak Creek Canyon. A cool creek with a natural red-sandstone waterslide sits surrounded by huge rock formations. Three short hiking trails are available, but there is no camping. The rocks are slippery, so water-resistant shoes are recommended; if you are wearing light-colored clothing, the sediment from the rocks can cause stains.

The best seasons to enjoy this drive are late spring, summer, and early fall; however, the creek water is usually too cold in fall and winter. It gets extremely busy during the summer months, and there may be a long wait to enter the park. If the parking lot is full, enter via the southbound turn lane. If that lane reaches the highway, the park will be inaccessible until the road clears.

State Route 179

In Sedona, U.S. 89A splits to head west. Stay south on State Route 179 to revel in the area's spectacular scenery. From Sedona, State Route 179 winds 7.5 miles south through the Coconino National Forest along some of the most gorgeous red-rock sandstone and geological formations in the country. There are several places to pull off the road and stare at the grand and vibrant otherworldly landscape.

In about 3 miles, look for **Cathedral Rock** (6246 SR-179), the Empire State Building of Sedona's skyline. Back on

State Route 179, continue south and in less than 1 mile, turn east (left) onto Chapel Road and drive 1 mile to view the **Chapel of the Holy Cross** (www. chapeloftheholycross.com). Built in 1956, the pyramidal structure juts dramatically from the surrounding red rocks.

Return to State Route 179 and drive 3 miles south to the parking lot for **Bell Rock** (6246 SR-179). This distinctive, bell-shaped monolith sits surrounded by one of the four major vortexes in the area. (It's reported to have the strongest and most electrifying energy field, enough to strengthen one's psychic abilities.) There are two parking lots; the lot for Courthouse Vista is the closest to the base of the rock.

Sights

As you drive into Sedona, the majority of the restaurants and hotels are either on the route or within 0.25 mile of the highway. The town of Sedona is divided into four sections: The **Village of Oak Creek** (SR-179) has restaurants and hiking trails; **Upton** is full of tourist shops; **Oak Creek Canyon** has B&Bs and mountain biking trails; and **West Sedona** is more residential.

Sedona is the center for spirituality and peace. For a beautiful spot to rest, meditate, or just contemplate life's mysteries, visit **Amitabha Stupa and Peace Park** (2650 Pueblo Dr., 877/788-7229, dusk-dawn daily, free). The rare 36-foot stupa is a five-minute walk from Pueblo Drive along a well-marked trail.

Tlaquepaque (336 SR-179, 928/282-5820, www.tlaq.com, 10am-5pm daily)—pronounced Tla-keh-pah-keh—has been a Sedona landmark since the 1970s. This distinctive shopping experience is fashioned after a quaint Mexican village, complete with cobblestone walkways, vine-covered walls, and arched entryways situated on the banks of Oak Creek. There are more than 40 specialty shops, 19 galleries, and 5 restaurants

A Spa For You (30 Kayenta Ct. Ste 1,

Sedona red rocks

928/282-3895, www.aspaforyou.com, call for appointment, $60-310) offers signature massages, body wraps, and Japanese facial massages that restore and rejuvenate the spirit. To get there, drive west on U.S. 89A and turn right (north) on Navajo Drive. Continue two blocks and turn left (west) on Hopi Drive. Take your first right into the parking lot; the spa is straight ahead on the right.

Sedona is also a good place to realign your chakras. Try a Reiki session at **International I AM** (3190 W. State Route 89A, Suite 150, 928/451-6368, www.internationaliam.com, $50-200), where all types of psychic and spiritual healing services are available.

Hiking

Brins Mesa Trail (5 miles round-trip) is a diverse trek that travels through Sedona's stunning red-rock formations. From the trailhead, you'll pass by Devil's Sinkhole, a 100-foot wide and 50-foot deep active sinkhole that formed in the 1880s. The

trail winds through canyon arches and up to Soldier Pass.

To access the trailhead from downtown Sedona, drive west on U.S. 89A and turn right (north) on Soldiers Pass Road. Continue 1.5 miles before turning right (east) on Rim Shadows for 0.2 mile. Parking is available to the left.

The **Palatki Heritage Site** (10290 Forest Service Rd. 795, 928/282-3854, www.fs.usda.gov, 9:30am-3pm daily, $5), in the Coconino National Forest, was built by the Sinagua people. The site is nestled among ancient, red sandstone cliffs with rock art and pictographs. It is reachable via a short and easy 1-mile round-trip hike, but tour reservations are required.

From Sedona, take U.S. 89A west for 5 miles and turn right onto Forest Road 525. Continue north for 5 miles, then stay straight to continue north onto Forest Road 795. Drive 2 miles to the parking lot for the Palatki ruins.

Accommodations

Adobe Hacienda (10 Rojo Dr., 928/284-2020, www.adobe-hacienda.com, $189-300) is Sedona's only bed-and-breakfast on a golf course. Decor includes 100-year-old Oaxacan doors; rooms are spacious with cactus garden and red-rock views, kiva fireplaces, and bathrooms with southwestern features such as hand-painted Mexican sinks and punched tin mirrors.

Just a few steps from Tlaquepaque shopping area, the **El Portal Sedona Hotel** (95 Portal Ln., 800/313-0017, www.elportalsedona.com, $270-329) is a pet-friendly adobe inn with rustic river-rock fireplaces and elegant flagstone floors. Several rooms include outdoor fenced patios. They really do love dogs, and consider them just as special as their human guests.

Hilton Sedona Resort and Spa (10 Ridge Trail Dr., 928/284-6975, www.hiltonsedonaresort.com, $189-300) has stunning red-rock views and beautifully appointed rooms, with fireplaces, private balconies, flat-panel televisions and luxurious beds with down-filled comforters. There's also an 18-hole golf course on-site.

Las Posadas of Sedona (26 Avenida De Piedras, 888/284-5288, www.lasposadasofsedona.com, $199-259) is a boutique inn with stunning 650-square-foot suites, a double-sided fireplace, complimentary gourmet breakfast, and kitchenette. It's a great value set beautiful location tucked away in the Village of Oak Creek (about 8 miles from the center of Sedona). Pets are welcome.

The **Amara Resort & Spa** (100 Amara Ln., 855/324-1313, www.amararesort.com, $179-359) offers hip contemporary accommodations in Uptown Sedona away from tourist center. The property has an infinity-edge saltwater pool, daily yoga classes, and beds with posh pillow-top mattresses and headboards made from locally fallen trees. Pets are welcome.

Junipine Resort (8351 N. SR-89A, 928/282 3375, www.junipine.com, $255-429) has well-equipped creek-side condos with spacious accommodations (ranging 900-1,400 square feet) with spiral staircases, balconies, fully-furnished kitchens, redwood decks, free movies, and wood-burning fireplaces. The resort is nestled in a pine forest about 15 minutes outside Sedona.

Food

If you want to dine at **Elote Cafe** (Kings Ransom Sedona Hotel, 771 Hwy. 179, 928/203-0105, www.elotecafe.com, 5pm-9pm Tues.-Sat., $25), it's best to arrive one hour early because the wait will be at least that long. Order a drink and enjoy the complimentary popcorn until you can dive into the eclectic, authentic menu of gourmet Mexican dishes including smoked pork cheeks, short rib tacos, and big, tender chunks of lamb adobo.

For American and Italian favorites with a modern twist, try **The Golden Goose Cafe & Bistro** (2545 W. SR-89A, 928/282-1447, www.goldengoosecafe.com, 7am-8pm Mon.-Sat., 8am-8pm Sun., $20-25). The popular, family-owned restaurant offers a relaxing, fine dining experience at an affordable price. Dogs are welcome on the patio.

Even the kale is massaged at **Chocola Tree Organic Oasis** (1595 W State Route 89A, 928/282-2997, www.chocolatree.com, 9am-9pm daily, $20-25). The organic, locally sourced, and nutritious menu offers healthy and tasty options. For die-hard vegans, the green goddess salad and green mountain juice are pure nirvana. The on-site store sells herb tinctures, nut butters, pet products, and healthy snacks to go.

Sip champagne by the creek and watch the hummingbirds while you eat wild game, imported truffles, and artisan cheeses at **L'Auberge Restaurant on Oak Creek** (301 L'Auberge Ln., 855/905-5745, www.lauberge.com, 7am-10:30am, 11:30am-2:30pm, and 5:30pm-8pm Mon.-Sat., 9am-2pm and 5:30pm-8pm Sun., veranda bar 2:30pm-8:00pm daily, $70-85). Reservations are recommended at least two weeks in advance. It is pricey and the food is good, but the scenery makes it unforgettable.

Indian Gardens Oak Creek Market (3951 N. SR-89A, 928/282-7702, www.indiangardens.com, 7:30am-4pm daily, $10) is a charming café nestled in a relaxing atmosphere and serving a varied menu of delicious black bean stew, curry quinoa, and grass-fed beef. They also have delicious snacks to go. It's a perfect place to stop before taking a hike in the canyon.

Grab a sandwich to go from **Sedona Memories Bakery and Cafe** (321 Jordan Rd., 928/282-0032, 10am-2pm Mon.-Fri., $8-10 cash only). Sandwiches are huge with quality ingredients on thick soft and chewy slices of freshly baked bread. If you call ahead, you get a free cookie.

Eat breakfast with the locals at the

Coffee Pot (2050 SR-89A, 928/282-6626, www.coffeepotsedona.com, 6am-2pm daily, $10). Have it your way with 101 omelet choices; if that's too overwhelming, settle on chicken-fried steak and eggs or a fluffy and delicious waffle. It's a popular spot, so be prepared to wait.

For a steak house experience you can only have in the Southwest, go to the **Silver Saddle at the Cowboy Club** (241 N. SR-89A, 928/282-4200, www.cowboyclub.com, 11am-10pm daily, $15-30). Nosh on cactus fries, buffalo, and rattlesnake under wrought-iron antler chandeliers and gas lanterns.

For Mexican cuisine, locals love **Cafe Jose** (2370 W. SR-89A, 928/282-0299, www.sedonacafejose.com, 5:30am-9pm Mon.-Fri., 6:30am-9pm Sat., 6:30am-8pm Sun., $10-15). They dish out affordable, tasty, and freshly made meals, homemade soups, and American favorites such as prime rib and pot roast.

They take their beer seriously at the **Oak Creek Brewery & Grill** (336 SR-179, 928/282-3300, www.oakcreekpub.com, 11:30am-8:30pm daily, $15-20). The pub fare goes down easily with their award-winning lagers, porters, seasonal stouts and pale ales.

Sedona closes down early, but **Sound Bites Grill** (101 N. State Route 89A, 928/282-2713, www.soundbitesgrill.com, 11:30am-10pm Sun.-Thurs., 11:30pm-11pm Fri.-Sat. $12-40) serves good food with friendly service, red-rock canyon patio views, and evening entertainment. Performers include Grammy nominated artists, international jazz musicians, and retro rock and roll.

Parks

⊕ Route 66 through Parks
To drive the post-1940s alignment, from Flagstaff take I-40 west for 14 miles, past Bellement, and take Exit 178 to Parks. Turn north (right) and take the next left onto Old Route 66.

Sights
Between Flagstaff and Williams, Parks is a small community that was formerly a railroad depot and sawmill. It showcases an interesting facet of the power of the Mother Road. Sometimes Route 66 only moved a few feet or so; when the new alignment shifted one block, the **Parks in the Pines General Store and Post Office** (12963 Old Route 66, 928/635-4741, 8pm-7pm Mon.-Sat., 8am-6pm Sun.) changed its front door from the south side of the building to the north side to face the new road. Today, the General Store sells pizza, pastrami melts, and Philly cheesesteaks. The original 1926-1931 alignment is right behind the store.

⊕ Back on 66
Keep heading west on Old Route 66 (Wagon Wheel Rd.) for about 5 miles and then jump back onto I-40 West via Ponderosa Road (Exit 171). Drive 5.5 miles to Exit 165. Turn left (south) on Highway 64, cross under I-40 and continue to Williams on Historic Route 66.

Williams

This quaint mountainside town that was settled by sheepherders in 1874 sits at a 6,780-foot elevation in the heart of the Kaibab Forest. Soon after, it became a hub for ranching, lumber, and railroad workers and with them came the saloons, brothels, opium dens, and gambling parlors. Today it's more a hub for Grand Canyon tourists, but with many of the historic buildings still intact you can get a glimpse of the spirit that made this place special.

Williams has one of the most charming stretches of Route 66, and they are proud of their Route 66 heritage. This was the last town on Route 66 to be bypassed by I-40, and they fought to keep travelers coming through town until the bitter end, October 13, 1984, just nine months

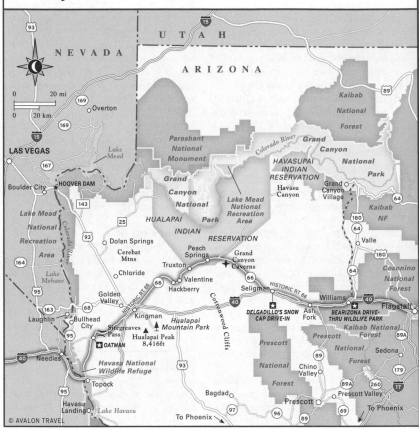

Flagstaff to Needles

before the official decommission of the Mother Road. In the end, the town let go with a bang-up celebration with a live performance by Bobby Troup singing his signature song that defined the American road trip.

Even though Williams was bypassed more than 30 years ago, it's still a fairly busy town and full of 19th-century character. They offer carriage rides, a zip line, museums and lots of restaurants, events and parades. Plan to spend at least an afternoon, and if you have the time, book a room in a historic brothel for the night.

◆ Route 66 through Williams

The 1926 alignment entered Williams in the north part of the town and made several turns before reaching downtown. We are going to take the **post-1940s alignment** that leads straight into downtown. From I-40, take Exit 165 and turn left. Drive under I-40 and follow Route 66 (Railroad Ave.). Railroad Avenue travels one-way through downtown Williams for six blocks. Once you reach the end of the Railroad Avenue (one block after 9th St.), turn left and double-back taking the road that is parallel heading east. From here to 2nd Street is the 1926 alignment.

(It may feel inefficient to double back, but this is the charming downtown area of Williams where even more shops and restaurants are located.)

Sights
Stop by the **Williams Visitor Center** (200 W. Railroad Ave., 800/863-0546, www. williamsaz.gov/visitors.html, 8am-5pm daily, free) and discover the quaint, historic district of Williams with a self-guided 40-minute walking tour map that covers six square blocks in downtown Williams. The visitors center can answer practically any question you have, and their website includes a comprehensive list of lodging and dining, things to do, and upcoming events in the area.

★ Bearizona Drive-Thru Wildlife Park
One of the safest ways to get up close and personal with a black bear is at **Bearizona Drive-Thru Wildlife Park** (1500 Historic Route 66, 928/635-2289, 9am-4pm daily but hours vary, $20). On a 2.5-mile drive through the 160-acre park, you'll see up to 16 other species including bison, badgers, bighorn sheep, burros, and wolves. After the drive, enjoy a nature walk through an area with baby animals, goats, pigs, and horses. And be sure to time your visit to coincide with one of the daily shows, such as Birds of Prey Show (11am, 1pm, 3pm), Otter feedings (11:40am), the live animal meet-n-greet (1:40pm). If you'd like to take a break from driving, Bearizona also has tour buses (allow at least 2 hours).

Grand Canyon Railway
If you'd rather not drive to the Grand Canyon, recapture the romance of riding the train on the **Grand Canyon Railway** (200 W. Railroad Ave., 800/843-8724, www.thetrain.com, from $86). The scenic five-hour round-trip journey to the South

top to bottom: Tlaquepaque, Sedona; Chocola Tree, Sedona; Williams, AZ

Rim of the Grand Canyon is on vintage diesel-powered trains. On-board entertainment and a knowledgeable staff make this a worthwhile tour. Be sure to arrive early to visit the gift shop and museum in the Williams Depot.

Williams Depot

Even if you're not taking the train, stop by the **Williams Depot** (200 W. Railroad Ave.), a former Harvey House, to experience a slice of history and see turn-of-the-20th-century locomotives, a coal car, and a 1923 Harriman coach. The depot also houses a **visitor center** (928/635-4061, 8am-5pm daily in summer), with a gift shop and some offbeat exhibits, such as a stuffed version of their local squirrel with huge tufted ears.

Pete's Gas Station Museum

Pete's Gas Station Museum (101 E. Rte. 66, 928/635-2675, 10am-8pm daily in summer, call to verify, free) is a restored gas station with tall glass cylinder gas pumps and a classic Ford sedan. It's part gift shop, part museum with an impressive a collection of gas station memorabilia, vintage oil cans, signage. It was built in 1949 and operated as a gas station until 1989.

Grand Canyon Deer Farm

For more intimate "hands-on" animal encounters, visit the **Grand Canyon Deer Farm** (6769 Deer Farm Rd., 928/635-4073, www.deerfarm.com, 10am-5pm daily Jan.-mid-Mar., 9am-6pm daily mid-Mar.-mid-Oct., 10am-5pm daily mid-Oct.-Dec., $6.75-11.50) to see elk, llamas, camels, reindeer, and other animals. It's fun for the kids.

Entertainment

South Rims Wine & Beer Garage (514 E. Rte. 66, 928/635-5902, www.southrims. com, 4pm-9pm Mon. and Thurs.-Fri., 11am-9pm Sat.-Sun.) has a tasting room and lounge featuring more than 20 wines and 12 specialty craft beers from local brewers and vintners.

Spenser's Pub (200 W. Railroad Ave., www.thetrain.com, 4pm-close for dinner) is a beautiful dark wood oak bar that dates to 1887. It's inside the historic Grand Canyon Railway, a former Harvey House, and has a laid-back atmosphere.

The World Famous Sultana Bar (301 W. Rte. 66, 928/635-2021, 10am-2am daily) is a crusty, local dive bar in an early 19th-century building teeming with history. The Sultana claims to have the longest operating liquor license in the state of Arizona; it once operated as a speakeasy during Prohibition. A wooden trapdoor leads to underground tunnels built by Chinese workers that housed an opium den and were used by bootleggers and outlaws. The Sultana also premiered the first "talkie" film in the area in 1930.

Another great dive bar is the **Canyon Club** (126 W. Railroad Ave., 928/635-2582, 10am-1am daily), with pool tables, DJs, shuffleboard tournaments, and karaoke on the weekends. An outside patio is perfect for those warm, slow nights in Williams.

The **Grand Canyon Brewery** (233 Historic Route 66, 11am-11pm daily Mar.-Dec.) serves epic handcrafted IPAs, oatmeal stouts, and seasonal lagers. If they're closed, check out the beer taps at **Cruiser's Route 66** (233 W. Rte. 66, 928/635-2445, www.cruisers66.com, 11am-10pm daily), located next door.

Shopping

Thunder Eagle Native Art (221 W. Rte. 66, 928/635-8889, 10am-9pm daily) has an excellent selection locally made Native American jewelry, pottery, and art.

Quilts on Route 66 (221 W. Railroad Ave., 928/635-5221, call for hours) carries more than 450 bolts of fabric, organic wools, yarn, MODA Fabrics, Lecien from Japan, and the entire collection of Cosmo Floss embroidery thread. They also have

Gas Pump History

In the early 1900s, gas was dispensed using a manual pump that drivers would pull back and forth to literally "pump" the gas out of the underground tank. You needed a great deal of arm strength to get the gas into the 8- to 10-foot-tall cylinder, then gravity would control the flow into the car. Five to ten gallons of gas would collect in the transparent glass-topped cylinder so that customers could determine the quality of the fuel based on the clarity and the color. Once the electric gas pump hit the market, people still wanted to see the gas through this **"sight glass."** (It was a marketing and advertising strategy that gave the customer a perceived position of choosing a superior product.) By the 1930s, the sight glass at the top of the cylinder was gone. Customers now chose their gas station due to the cleanliness of the restrooms and who supplied the best toys, games, and coloring books. In the 1940s, the shape of the pump changed again into the rectangular posts we have today. The rolling numbers—called calculator pumps—were also a new feature. In the 1950s, gas pumps became shorter and wider, then even squatter in the 1960s and 1970s. The most significant change in gas pumps since the 1970s has been the addition of digital displays and televisions.

quilts for sale, so you can take a little comfort from Route 66 back home.

To buy western wear in a real Old West town, go to **De Berge Saddlery & Western Wear** (213 W. Rte. 66, 928/635-2960, 9am-6pm daily). They sell quality saddles, hand-tooled holsters, knife sheaths, belts, purses, hats, and Stetson boots.

The **Double Eagle Trading Company** (526 U.S. 180, 928-635-5393, 9am-5pm daily) is a great place to pick up Grand Canyon and Route 66 souvenirs. They also have a good collection of pelts, hides, horns, and handmade Native American arts and crafts such as rugs, pottery jewelry, moccasins, and more.

The **Gunsmoke Giftshop** (238 W. Rte. 66, 928/635-5232, 9am-5pm daily) is a family-owned store that sells luggage, home decor, gifts, and Route 66 memorabilia.

The Gallery in Williams (145 W. Rte. 66, 928/635-3006, www.thegalleryinwilliams.com, 9am-9pm daily) is an artist cooperative that sells a dozen local artists' work including oil, acrylic, and watercolor paintings, woodwork, sculpture, fiber arts, and jewelry.

Get your gun and saddle cleaned at

Buck's Place (117 W. Rte. 66, Ste. 145, 928/856-1428, 5am-2pm daily) at Canyon Vista Mall. They also have fast-draw and bullwhip lessons.

The Grand Canyon Railway Gift Shop (233 N. Grand Canyon Blvd., 928/635-4010, 6:30am-9pm daily) is within the Grand Canyon Railway and sells a wide collection of clothing, books, toys, and unique train-related gifts.

The Grand Canyon Deer Farm (6769 Deer Farm Rd., 928/635-4073, 10am-5pm daily) has a 2,500-square-foot store packed reasonably priced toys, painted glass, tin signs, and antler and cedar wood items.

Recreation

Ride through Williams in a horse-drawn carriage with **Cowboy's Service Carriage Co.** (Grand Canyon Railway Depot, 233 N. Grand Canyon Blvd., 928/635-2152 or 602/679-3866, www.azcarriagecompany.com, 5pm-11pm daily weather permitting, no reservations required, $25-75) is a family-owned and operated business with a fleet of white and black carriages, well-trained Belgian draft horses, and drivers decked out in western wear.

If you've ever wanted to move mountains, dig giant holes, or operate life-size Tonka Toys, the **Big Toy Playground** (671 S. Garland Prairie Rd., 928/637-8808, 10am-4:30pm daily, $149-400) can make your dream come true. Standard sessions are 90 minutes. No experience required.

The **Elephant Rocks at Williams Golf Course** (2200 Golf Course Dr., 928/635-4935, closed in winter, $20-40) was designed in the 1920s. Today it's a city-owned 18-hole championship course named after the massive lava rocks on the property that resemble the shape of elephants.

Route 66 Zipline (200 N. Grand Canyon Blvd., 928/635-5358, http://ziplineroute66.com, 10am-7pm daily in winter, 9am-10pm daily in summer, $12-20) offers a high-flying adventure. Passengers are seated and strapped into a harness that zips across Grand Canyon Boulevard in downtown Williams at 30 miles per hour. The zip-line platform is fashioned to resemble a 1950s diner with Route 66 signage and a classic red Chevy. No climbing or hiking is required.

Accommodations

The ★ **Red Garter B & B Inn** (137 Railroad Ave., 800/328-1484, www.redgarter. com, $135-175) is a beautifully restored Victorian saloon and bordello from 1897. The rooms with period furniture and fixtures, tall ceilings, and balconies overlook the Grand Canyon Railway depot and are just steps away from art galleries and restaurants. It's teeming with history, and the delicious complimentary breakfast in the bakery makes this one of the best places to stay in Williams.

For a clean and cozy resting spot, **The Lodge on Route 66** (200 E. Rte. 66, 928/635-4534, www.redgarter.com, $80-190) is right in the heart of Williams and within walking distance to the historic district.

The **Mountain Ranch Resort** (6701 E. Mountain Ranch Rd., 866/687-2624, closed during winter, $115-195) is a

Desoto's Beauty and Barber Shop, Ash Fork

family-run property with the personal and unique touches, great prices, and stellar customer service that make you feel like family.

Sleep in a 1950 Pullman Railway Car at the **Canyon Motel and RV Park** (1900 Historic Route 66, 800/482-3955, call for rates). There is also an indoor pool, horseshoe pit, and laundry facilities, which can come in handy on a long road trip.

The **Grand Canyon Railway Hotel** (235 N. Grand Canyon Blvd., 303/843-8724, www.thetrain.com, $169-359) is right next to the Grand Canyon Railway and one block from downtown Williams. Designed to look like an early 20th-century historic hotel, the Grand Canyon Railway Hotel offers several types of rooms to choose from. Value and standard rooms are basic two-star property accommodations; however, the deluxe rooms feature nicer bedding, 37-inch flat-screen TVs, modern furniture, and Keurig coffeemakers.

Food

Pine Country Restaurant (107 N. Grand Canyon Blvd., 928/635-9718, 6:30am-9pm daily, $5-16) is a cute breakfast spot with checkered tablecloths, delicious food, and don't forget to leave room for their world-famous homemade pies. It's not just good, many say it the best they've ever had.

Rod's Steak House (301 E. Rte. 66, 928/635-2671, www.rods-steakhouse.com, 11am-9:30pm Mon.-Sat., $26-46) opened in 1946, during the heyday of Route 66. Owner Rod Graves raised Hereford cattle and organized the first rodeo in Williams in 1941, and soon after he and his wife Helen opened the restaurant. The menu is standard steak house fare with appetizers made from scratch. If you like red meat, this is their specialty.

Red Raven (135 W. Rte. 66, 928/635-4980, 11am-2pm, 5pm-9pm daily, $7-28) is a quaint and casual bistro with a varied menu of pasta, salads, and flavorful entrées such as cilantro pork, perfectly cooked steaks, lamb, and perfectly seasoned mashed potatoes.

For top-notch huevos rancheros topped with green-chile pork and other breakfast items, you can't go wrong at **Grand Canyon Coffee and Cafe** (125 W. Rte. 66, 928/635-4907, 6am-3pm Sun.-Wed., 6am-8pm Thurs.-Sat., $7-10). All sauces are made on-site and have been passed down for generations.

With so many steak houses in Williams that serve salads with iceberg lettuce, **Dara Thai** (145 W. Rte. 66, 928/635-2201, call for hours, $8-12) might be the best place for a vegetarian meal. It's got a small dining room so it's not a good option for large groups, but the service is fast and friendly so the tables turn quickly.

Goldie's Route 66 Diner (425 E. Rte. 66, 928/635-4466, 7am-9pm daily, $6-20) is a mid-century diner with a cantilevered counter and a dining room of stone and glass walls. It's nothing fancy—just a classic diner in a really cool space.

For a slick, souped-up neon-lit diner, **Cruiser's Route 66** (233 W. Rte. 66, 928/635-2445, www.cruisers66.com, 11am-10pm daily, $7-14) conjures the spirit of sock hops, poodle skirts, and Elvis. There's a Route 66 mural, gift shop, full bar, live outdoor music, and the milk shakes are delicious.

For yummy Mexican food and great margaritas go to **Pancho McGillicuddy's** (141 W. Railroad Ave., 928/635-4150, www.vivapanchos.com, 11am-10pm daily, $10-18). They also serve organic grass-fed burgers, ribs, and have live local entertainment.

◈ Back on 66

As you leave Williams, head west on Railroad Avenue (Rte. 66) to I-40. Drive about 20 miles west on I-40 and take Exit 146 (Hwy. 89 S). Turn right (north) on Highway 89 (also called Business I-40) and drive west into Ash Fork. Highway 89 (Business I-40) turns into Lewis Street, which is one-way.

Ash Fork

In 1960, the Santa Fe Railway moved the rail line north, and as a result, Ash Fork lost about half its population since the railway employed most residents. Today, Ash Fork has a large number of stone quarries and calls itself "The Flagstone Capital of the World."

Sights

Ash Fork had a large Harvey House called Escalante that was built in 1907 and closed in 1948. A scale model of Escalante can be found in the **Ash Fork Historical Society's Route 66 Museum** (901 W. Old Route 66, 928/637-0204, 8am-4pm Mon.-Fri.). To get there from I-40 Business/Lewis Ave., turn left at 8th Street and the museum will be on the right.

For a cool photo op go to **Desoto's Beauty and Barber Shop** (314 W. Lewis Ave.), a former 1958 Texaco station with a

Delgadillo's Snow Cap Drive-In, Seligman

Burma Shave

Keep an eye out for the fun Burma Shave sign series with entertaining messages spaced out over several small signs. Burma Shave sold brushless shaving cream and the signs were a popular advertising campaign that ran from 1927 to 1963. Most Burma Shave signs on Route 66 can be found between Ash Fork and Kingman.

THE ONE WHO DRIVES WHEN
HE'S BEEN DRINKING
DEPENDS ON YOU
TO DO HIS THINKING
BURMA SHAVE

1960 Desoto sitting on the roof with Elvis in the driver's seat.

Food
If you're hungry, **Lulu Belle's BBQ** (33 W. Lewis Ave., 928/637-9818, 7am-10pm daily, $15) serves reasonably priced barbecue, steaks, and twice baked potatoes with corn on the cob. There's also the **Ranch House Cafe** (111 W. Park Ave., 928/637-2710, 7am-8pm Mon.-Sat., 7am-4pm Sun., $10), with homemade green chile, biscuits and gravy, chicken-fried steak, and patty melts.

◈ Back on 66
As you leave Ash Fork on I-40 Business/Lewis Street, rejoin I-40 and drive 5 miles west to Exit 139. Turn right onto Crookton Road (Rte. 66) where you can finally ditch I-40 and begin 159 miles of pristine Route 66, the longest unbroken stretch of the Mother Road.

Seligman

Seligman is one of those places that leave a warm, fuzzy feeling deep down inside your heart as only a simple, unpretentious small town can do. It's more than just the nostalgia that has been blatantly packaged and marketed along Route 66. Seligman is the real deal—a place with good, honest values and a moral compass that is anchored in the locals like resident barber Angel Delgadillo. Delgadillo is one of the most famous personalities on Route 66; he's been interviewed about 300 times and has been featured in more than 70 magazines and television outlets. He says:

"Seligman is special. There's no comparison, because in the cities you're just a number. What's still America can be found in the small towns, hometown cafes and filling stations, and we're losing this, faster than we care to admit. Too many people in the big cities are just interested

in making a buck. At the fast-food chains you're just a number. Here in Seligman we take the time to talk to you."

Despite the efforts of local preservationists, including Delgadillo, who founded the Historic Route 66 Association, The Havasu, a former Harvey House, was demolished in 2008. It was a rare Prairie-style Harvey House with a red tile roof. The roof tiles were salvaged by Allan Affeldt, the owner of Winslow's La Posada Harvey House.

Sights

★ Delgadillo's Snow Cap Drive-In

Route 66, which is also called Chino Street, goes right through the heart of Seligman. Once you arrive, keep an eye out for **Delgadillo's Snow Cap Drive-In** (301 W. Rte. 66, 928/422-3291, daily 10am-6pm, opens Mar. 1, closed in winter, $10) on the left. Grab an ice-cream cone at the Snow Cap and then walk down one block west to **Angel &**

Vilma Delgadillo's Route 66 Gift Shop and Visitor Center (22265 W. Rte. 66, 928/422-3352, daily 9am-5pm). Ask for Angel. He is one of the warmest people you'll ever meet and a great storyteller with extensive knowledge about Route 66. His stories inspired John Lasseter, the producer of the Pixar classic *Cars*.

Accommodations and Food

If you're planning to stay in Seligman, the **Canyon Lodge** (114 AZ-66, 800/700-5054, www.route66canyonlodge.com, $70) has immaculate Route 66, Marilyn Monroe and Elvis-themed rooms with pictures and memorabilia on the wall.

The **Historical Route 66 Motel** (22750 W. Rte. 66, 928/422-3204, www.route-66seligmanarizona.com, $75) has spotless rooms with fun decorations and cool Route 66 bedspreads.

The **Aztec Motel & Gift Shop** (22200 Historic Route 66, 928/422-3055, $60) is a quirky, family-owned property with

Hackberry General Store

murals that make you want to "head out on the highway ... looking for adventure."

Westside Lilo's (415 Chino St., 928/422-5466, www.westsidelilos.com, 6am-9pm daily, $15) has great service, huge portions of fluffy pancakes, juicy steaks, and make sure you save room for carrot cake and cream pie.

Route 66 Roadrunner (22330 W. Old Highway 66, 928/232-2004, www. route66roadrunner.com, 9am-5pm daily, $5-12) is a gift shop, café, and espresso coffee bar located in a vintage building that was formerly a 1936 Chevy garage. They have Route 66 souvenirs and original handmade gifts from local artists.

Both locals and tourists love the buffalo burgers at the **Road Kill Café** (502 W. Hwy. 66, 928/422-3554, 7am-9pm daily, $8-20). They also serve yummy breakfasts with crispy hash browns and peanut butter French toast.

◈ Back on 66

As you leave Seligman, drive west on Route 66 for about 20 miles until you reach the Grand Canyon Caverns.

Grand Canyon Caverns

The **Grand Canyon Caverns** (Route 66 mile marker 115, Peach Springs, 928/422-4565, www.gccaverns.com, 9am-5pm daily, $16-70) are the largest dry caverns in the United States and range between 200-300 feet deep. There are four cave tours from 25 minutes to 2.5 hours in length. Also on-site are a classic gas station, a restaurant, and a gift shop.

Accommodations

The **Grand Canyon Caverns** (928/422-3223, www.gccaverns.com/rooms-packages) also provides multiple lodging options, including **The Caverns Inn** (seasonal hours vary Nov.-Mar., $100) motel, a three-bedroom **Bunkhouse** ($230), and **The Cavern Suite** ($800), a motel room located 22 stories underground. There is also an **RV and Campground** (first-come, first-served, 928/422-4565, $40) with 48 hookup sites for RVs and "open-air rooms" for campers, with flush toilets, showers, and a swimming pool.

◈ Back on 66

Drive 12 miles west on Historic Route 66 to Peach Springs.

Peach Springs

As you drive west on Route 66 you'll reach Peach Springs, the tribal headquarters for the Hualapai ("WALL-ah-pie" whose name means "people of the tall-pines") Indian Reservation. In the 1880s the peach trees in the area led folks to the water source that was eventually used to water steam engine trains. The **Hualapai Tribal Forestry**

(863 Hwy. 66) is on the north side of the road in an old stone building erected in 1928, which was formerly operated as the Peach Tree Trading Post where the Hualapai swapped craft items for food, clothing, and medicine. It was also a meeting place for Native and European Americans to discuss the local news and gossip. When Route 66 came through there were several cafés, businesses, motor courts, and a Fred Harvey restaurant that served travelers.

Food

Diamond Creek Restaurant (900 Rte. 66, 928/769-2800, 6:30am-8:30pm daily, $7-18) serves a blend of standard and Native American specialties such as fry bread, Hualapai stews, tacos, and homemade pizza.

◆ Back on 66
As you leave Peach Springs, head west on Route 66 and pass through the ghost town of Truxton.

find a home here and guided Safari Tours ($10 per person) are offered.

Just down the road from the wildlife sanctuary is the **Truxton Canyon Training School,** a boarding school that forced American Indians (mostly Hualapai) to assimilate into mainstream American culture. The school was in operation from 1903 to 1937, when the children were separated from their families and subjected to hard labor. The building stands as a reminder of a shameful chapter in U.S. history.

In the town of Valentine, turn right (northwest) on Music Mountain Circle. The Truxton Canyon Training School building is on the southeast side of the road.

◆ Back on 66
To return to Route 66, continue straight a few hundred feet until Music Mountain Circle dead-ends. Take a left (southeast) and drive 250 feet to Route 66 and turn right (west).

Truxton

The classic **Frontier Motel** (16118 E. Hwy. 66) opened in 1951 with a landmark sign that has been restored with the support of the Historic Route 66 Association of Arizona, the National Route 66 Corridor Preservation Program, and the National Park Service.

◆ Back on 66
Less than 10 miles west of Truxton is the town of Valentine.

Valentine

Keepers of the Wild (13441 E. Hwy. 66, 928/769-1800, 9am-5pm Wed.-Mon., $18) is a nonprofit sanctuary for abandoned, neglected, and retired wildlife. Lions, tigers, bears, primates, wolves, and coyotes

Hackberry

Just around the bend from Valentine is the once-thriving mining town of Hackberry, which dates back to 1874. When the railroad came through here in 1882, the town "moved" 4 miles from its original site and became the third major loading stop for cattle. A silver mine earned almost $3 million before closing in 1919. Soon after, Hackberry became a virtual ghost town.

When Route 66 came through in 1926, the **Hackberry General Store** (11255 E. Hwy. 66, 928/769-2605, 10am-6pm daily) became a major service stop. It helped revive Hackberry until I-40 bypassed the town and abandoned it again. According to the *Victoria Advocate*, Bob Waldmire, the late Route 66 artist and the owner of the General Store, was believed to be the sole resident of

Hackberry from 1992 to 1997. Today, the store is a living museum with vintage gas pumps, old signs, a bright red 1956 Corvette, and lots of souvenirs and Route 66 memorabilia.

Just 6 miles west of the Hackberry General Store, the kitsch continues with a 14-foot tall Tiki sculpture, the **Giganticus Headicus,** which looks like a partially buried Easter Island head. It can be found at the corner of Antares Road near the old Kozy Corner Trailer Court.

◈ Back on 66

From Hackberry, Route 66 heads north for 6 miles then dips southwest for 20 miles into Kingman.

Kingman

Kingman sits in the Hualapai Valley between the Hualapai and Cerbat mountain ranges. Founded in 1882 as a railroad town, Kingman became a major supply center for ranchers and miners. Approaching town on Route 66, the road becomes East Andy Devine Avenue, the name of a character actor often featured as a devoted, comic-relief sidekick in Westerns. (Devine was the wagon driver in John Ford's *Stagecoach*.)

◈ Pre-1940 Alignment

To drive the scenic paved pre-1940 alignment from Route 66 (Andy Devine Ave.), turn left (south) on 4th Street. After about 1,000 feet, follow the main road as it curves to the right (southwest) onto Old Trails Road. Soon after it passes under a railroad trestle, slow down as the road takes a sharp left and then narrows between boulders on a blind curve. Once the road veers away from the railroad tracks, turn around and drive back to the post-1940 alignment via 4th Street and take a left (west) on Andy Devine Avenue.

Sights
Powerhouse Visitors Center

The **Powerhouse Visitors Center** (120 W. Andy Devine Ave., 928/753-6106, 9am-5pm daily, $4) is also the headquarters of the **Route 66 Museum.** The museum features the historical evolution of Route 66 with murals, photos, an old Studebaker, dioramas of a Dust Bowl family and wall-size quotes from *The Grapes of Wrath*. The Powerhouse is housed in the former Desert Power & Light Company building that was built in two phases in 1907 and 1911. This light company supplied the power to build Hoover Dam. The center provides info on a walking tour with 27 places to explore in and around downtown Kingman including the Hotel Beale and Locomotive Park.

The entry fee includes admission to the nearby **Mohave Museum** (400 W. Beale St., 928/753-3195, www.mohavemuseum.org, 9am-5pm Mon.-Fri., 1pm-5pm Sat., $4), which has an extensive Hualapai culture display and a section dedicated to the actor Andy Devine.

Hualapai Mountain Park

If you want to hike, bike, camp, or sleep in the mountains, the **Hualapai Mountain Park** (6250 Hualapai Mountain Rd., www.mcparks.com, 877/757-0915, $35-100) has tepees and rustic cabins equipped with stoves, heaters, and refrigerators that house up to 12 people. There are 10 miles of hiking trails that offer magnificent views of the desert and mountain landscape.

To get there from Route 66, turn left (southeast) onto Hualapai Mountain Rd. (SR-147) and drive about 11 miles until you reach the ranger station on your right. If you use your GPS, it will take you past the station. If you reach the Hualapai Mountain Resort you've gone too far; the ranger station is about 1 mile back.

Camp Beale Springs

Camp Beale Springs (928/757-7919) is

Kingman

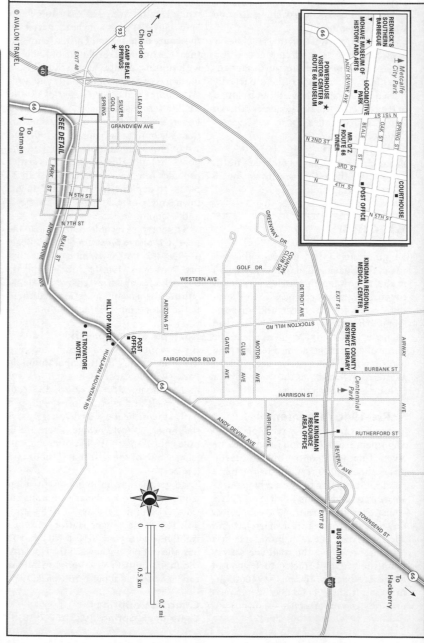

© AVALON TRAVEL

To Chloride

CAMP BEALE SPRINGS

To Oatman

SEE DETAIL

EXIT 48

LEAD ST
GOLD
SILVER
SPRING
GRANDVIEW AVE

PARK ST
N 5TH ST
N 7TH ST

BEALE ST

ANDY DEVINE AVE

GREENWAY DR
COUNTRY CLUB DR
GOLF DR
WESTERN AVE
DETROIT AVE
ARIZONA ST
STOCKTON HILL RD
GATES AVE
CLUB AVE
MOTOR AVE
FAIRGROUNDS BLVD
HARRISON ST
AIRFIELD AVE

HILLTOP MOTEL

EL TROVATORE MOTEL

HUALAPAI MOUNTAIN RD

POST OFFICE

EXIT 51
KINGMAN REGIONAL MEDICAL CENTER
MOHAVE COUNTY DISTRICT LIBRARY
AIRWAY
BURBANK ST
Centennial Park
BLM KINGMAN RESOURCE AREA OFFICE
RUTHERFORD ST
BEVERLY AVE
AVE

EXIT 53
TOWNSEND ST
BUS STATION
To Hackberry

0   0
0.5 km
0.5 mi

Detail inset

66
To Chloride
Metcalfe City Park
REDNECK'S SOUTHERN BARBEQUE
MOHAVE MUSEUM OF HISTORY AND ARTS
LOCOMOTIVE PARK
POWERHOUSE VISITOR CENTER & ROUTE 66 MUSEUM
ANDY DEVINE AVE
N 1ST ST
BEALE
OAK ST
SPRING ST
N 2ND ST
MR. D'Z ROUTE 66 DINER
3RD ST
4TH ST
COURTHOUSE
POST OFFICE
N 5TH ST

where the Hualapai were interned in 1871 in 20-foot barracks until the infamous forced walk of the Trail of Tears to the La Paz reservation. The reservoir is still partially standing today and the area is used for hiking and a picnic site. There is an historical marker at the site to pay homage to the Hualapai who suffered here.

Before heading to Camp Beale Springs, get a day pass (free) from the Powerhouse Visitor Center. Camp Beale Springs is on the northwest edge of Kingman. To get there from Route 66, turn right (north) on 1st Street and a quick left (west) onto West Beale Street. After about 1 mile, take a right (northeast) onto Fort Beal Drive. Camp Beal Springs is less than a mile west of the intersection of Fort Beale Drive and Wagon Trail Road.

Accommodations and Food

If you need a place to rest, Kingman has the usual suspects of two-star chain motels. For something with a little more flavor, **El Trovatore Motel** (1440 E. Andy Devine Ave., 928/753-6520, www.el-trovatoremotel.com, $60) is one of the few pre-WWII Kingman motels still standing. It was originally a service station built in 1937, and the tourist court was added in 1939. Today it's a Route 66-themed hotel celebrating its former guests Clark Gable, Marilyn Monroe, and James Dean.

Another old-fashioned motel is the **Hill Top** (1901 E. Andy Devine Ave., 928/753-2198, $50). Built in 1954 it has basic, inexpensive rooms, a pool, and a cool neon sign.

Roadrunner Café (401 W. Beale St., 928/718-2530, 7am-1pm Mon.-Fri., 8am-noon Sat., $12) offers a fresh home-cooked breakfast. **Redneck's Southern Pit BBQ** (420 E. Beale St., 928/757-8227, 11am-8pm Tues.-Sat., $15) smokes its meat with hickory wood and dishes out southern comfort with recipes that have been gathered over six generations across three families.

For creative pizzas and creamy shrimp alfredo, try **Vito's Italian Cuisine** (2775 E. Northern Ave., 928/757-7279, 11am-9pm Sun.-Thurs., 11am-10pm Fri.-Sat., $18). **Mr. D'z Route 66 Diner** (105 E. Andy Devine Ave., 928/718-0066, 7am-9pm daily, $12) is known for its Harley Dogs, a quarter-pound hot dog served on a hoagie with spicy sauce. The retro diner is decked out in turquoise and pink booths, a black-and-white checkered floor, and a blue 1954 Chevy parked outside.

◆ Back on 66

Make sure you get fuel in Kingman before you head to Oatman. Leaving Kingman via Route 66 (W. Andy Devine Ave.), follow signs to Oatman. You'll be driving next to I-40; keep an eye out for Exit 44. Turn right (west) on Shinarump Road and cross under I-40. Drive 0.3 mile and turn left (southwest) on Oatman Road.

If you're making the side trip to Chloride, take U.S. 93 north then backtrack to Kingman.

◆ Side Trip: U.S. 93 to Chloride

Getting There

From Kingman, take U.S. 93 (W. Beale St.) north for about 18 miles. Turn right (east) at the Chloride billboard at County Road 125. Chloride is 4 miles north up the road.

Sights

Just north of Kingman is the quirky living ghost town of Chloride, named after the silver chloride ore discovered here. Chloride was a busy town with more than 70 mines in operation. The **post office,** established in 1862, is the oldest continuously operating post office in the state of Arizona. Chloride also has an old general store with some original items, 30 vintage tractors, mock gunfights in the summer, gift shops, hiking trails, and what may possibly be the largest collection of homes with junkyard art you'll ever see.

Food

Digger Dave's Food & Spirits (4962 W. Tennessee Ave., 928/565-3283, 9am-8pm Tues.-Sat., 9am-6pm Sun., $8-15) is a fun stop with good barbecue, pulled pork sandwiches, and tuna melts. Owner Dave has great stories and will make you feel right at home.

Oatman Highway

The Oatman Highway snakes its way through the sharp switchbacks of Sitgreaves Pass and over the Black Mountains, dotted with ramshackle houses and tattered windmills until reaching Cool Springs. This scenic backcountry highway is highly recommended, but it is very steep—vehicles over 40 feet should not attempt it—and drivers must also watch for bighorn sheep and wild burros on the road. It's hard to believe this was a major thoroughfare on Route 66.

Cool Springs

The 1920s gas station in Cool Springs was in ruins before Ned Leuchtner, a real estate agent from Chicago, bought it in 2001 and restored it based on old photographs. After Route 66 bypassed the Oatman Highway in 1953, the station was abandoned within a decade. There used to be a café, bar, and cabins on the property, but today only a gas station remains, with museum-quality tall red Mobil gas pumps (not operational). What you will find are a cool souvenir and snack shop.

Chloride

★ Oatman

Heading west on Route 66, tight hairpin curves lead to Oatman, a mining town named after Olive Oatman. The legend states that, at the age of seven, **Olive Oatman** was kidnapped and enslaved by Apache—but it's more likely that she was taken by the Tolkepayas (Western Yavapai) tribe and sold to the Mojave, who then tattooed her chin. Some sources report that the chin tattoo was the mark of a slave; others believe that most of the women in this tribe received blue cactus chin tattoos as a way to identify them as Mojave in the afterlife. In 1857, when she was 19, authorities at Fort Yuma rescued Olive, trading her for blankets, beads, and a white horse.

Today Oatman is a gold rush town with plank sidewalks and wild burros roaming Route 66, blocking traffic and shaking down tourists for treats. (The burros are direct descendants of those the miners brought to the area in the late 1800s.) From 1908 to 1915, Oatman was a bustling town with 20 saloons within a three-block radius, more than 10,000 people, and two gold mines worth more than 25 million dollars. (By comparison, Kingman at that time had a population of about 300 people.) In 1941, gold-mining operations were halted by the U.S. government, as metals other than gold were needed for the war effort.

With the closing of the mines, Oatman's population dwindled from 10,000 to 200. As the railroad community also began to decline, a spring about 5 miles away ceased being used to water the trains. To avoid the tortuous hairpin curves along the mountain road, a new alignment of Route 66 was rerouted in 1952 via I-40. After the gas station shut down, the population dwindled to three people and remained that way for 30 years. It wasn't until the late 1970s, when a Route 66 organization promoted the original Route 66 alignment that the town came back to life.

General Store

As you approach Oatman, be mindful of the roaming wild burros. They are not shy and will approach the car looking for food. If you want to feed them, visit to the **General Store** (180 Main St., 928/768-9448, www.oatmangeneralstore.com, 10:30am-5pm daily), which sells burro pellets and carrots in addition to more than 100 kinds of hot sauce, Coca-Cola collectibles, and Oatman souvenirs. The **Ghost Rider Gunfighters** stage a gunfight in front of the store at 1:30pm and 3:15pm daily.

Food

The walls and ceiling of ★ **The Oatman Hotel & Restaurant** (181 Main St., 928/768-4408, 10:30am-6pm daily, $8-15) are covered in dollar bills, a reference to a time when miners started getting paid with paper rather than gold dust and coins. However, the mines were so

filthy that any paper money would be destroyed. Miners needed a safe place to keep their money, so they set up a system with their local bartender to put a dollar bill behind the bar with their name on it to cover their drinking tab. (In the early 1900s, a beer was about $0.05 and a shot of whiskey was about $0.10-0.15.) The oldest dollar bill is from 1923 and framed behind the bar. Today the walls are papered with more than 100,000 dollar bills and the tradition continues as tourists leave their own signed dollar bills wherever they can find a spot.

Though Carole Lombard and Clark Gable honeymooned upstairs, the hotel itself is no longer in operation. The restaurant, however, serves pulled pork sandwiches, buffalo burgers, and donkey ears (fries).

Judy's Saloon (260 Main St., 928/768-4463, 10am-10pm) is the place to shoot pool and catch up on the local gossip.

◈ Back on 66
Head west on Route 66 out of Oatman, following the Oatman-Topock Highway southwest for 3.5 miles. Turn left (southeast) on State Route 10 and continue following the Oatman-Topock Highway for 20 miles to the Arizona/California border.

◈ Side Trip: London Bridge

In 1968, Robert McCulloch bought **London Bridge** (yes, the one in London) for $2,460,000 and had it taken apart brick by brick and shipped across the Atlantic Ocean to the dusty, desert town of Lake Havasu. Don't be mistaken, this is not London's Victorian Gothic "Tower Bridge" that spans 800 feet with 200 foot towers. This is an elegant, and perhaps

top to bottom: Camp Beale Springs; Oatman burros; The Oatman Hotel & Restaurant

a bit understated 600-year-old medieval granite bridge with five semi-elliptical arches that gracefully frame Lake Havasu.

The **Lake Havasu City Visitor Center** (422 English Village, 928/855-5655, www.golakehavasu.com, 9am-5pm daily, $10) has a 90-minute walking tour of the bridge.

Getting There

From Oatman, head west on the Oatman-Topock Highway for 25 miles as it dips south toward I-40. Take I-40 east for 9 miles to Highway 95 (right); follow Highway 95 south for 19 miles. Turn right onto Palo Verde Boulevard South and take a quick left onto London Bridge Road.

California

From salt-crusted desert playas to towering mountain ranges and the stunning Pacific Ocean, California is a wonderland roadtrip.

© AVALON TRAVEL

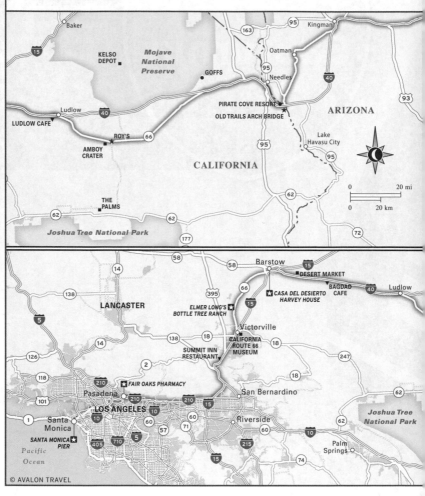

California

As Route 66 crosses the Arizona border into California, a parched, wind-swept desert awaits.

This is the same dry and barren landscape that greeted more than 200,000 Dust Bowl survivors in the 1930s. (When John Steinbeck's Joad family first set eyes on California in *The Grapes of Wrath*, they were afraid they had traded one barren homeland for another.) As they attempted to enter California, many faced up to 125 armed policemen who turned away "undesirables." About 40 percent of those immigrants who did make it across the state border picked cotton and grapes in the San Joaquin Valley, earning about $1 a day.

Highlights

★ **Casa del Desierto Harvey House, Barstow:** This beautiful 1910 Harvey House designed by Mary Colter has been fully restored with a Route 66 and Western Railroad museum (page 308).

★ **Elmer Long's Bottle Tree Ranch, Oro Grande:** Folk artist Elmer Long created a forest of glass and light in his front yard with nearly 200 installations of bottle trees (page 310).

★ **Fair Oaks Pharmacy, Pasadena:** This one-of-a-kind vintage soda fountain, pharmacy, and restaurant has been around since 1915 and is still going strong (page 314).

★ **Santa Monica Pier, Santa Monica:** Route 66's journey ends at this carnival pier floating over the Pacific Ocean (page 325).

This eerie, somewhat desolate intro-duction to the state lies far from the fa-mous sun-soaked beaches of Los Angeles and Santa Monica—the terminus of Route 66—yet the scattered tumbleweeds and bizarre Joshua Trees hold their own solitary beauty. Traveling west on Route 66, the creosote and cactus give way to lush pastures, swaying palms, and fruit trees of the Inland Empire. Upon arrival in Los Angeles, world-class museums, high-end shopping, and celebrity-filled nightlife offer cosmopolitan diversions before reaching Santa Monica and the breathtaking beauty of the Pacific Ocean. En route, set aside a couple of days for final side trips to Joshua Tree, a boulder-strewn national park surrounded by a vi-brant and eclectic arts community.

Planning Your Time

With approximately 315 miles of Route 66 still intact in California, there is a lot of ground to cover in your final **two days.** Needles marks the California state line and it's a remote and desolate 140 miles to the next service town of Barstow, an over-night option. Los Angeles is about a five-hour drive west of Needles, but if you stay true to Route 66, add at least a few hours to your travel time to account for inland traffic. Those with no time to spare can push on to Los Angeles (traffic willing), but a better option is to skip Barstow and stretch your journey another day with a side trip south to Joshua Tree instead.

Once you arrive in Los Angeles,

consider staying one night in downtown LA (the original terminus of Route 66) and one night in Santa Monica (the post-1930s terminus). After a long drive, this will make life easier when it comes to navigating one of the most gridlocked cities in the country.

Driving Considerations

Crossing the California border, make sure you have a full tank of **gas**; other-wise, gas up in Needles because you'll soon be driving through the Mojave Desert, and fuel is scarce. A worthwhile excursion is to spend a day or two in Joshua Tree, which involves a beautiful three-hour drive through one of the most desolate areas in the country. Make sure your car is gassed up and in good work-ing order, because there is no cell phone service for most of the drive. Spend the night in Twentynine Palms or head west on Route 62 to the town of Joshua Tree.

Getting There

Starting Points
Car
From the California border, Route 66 parallels I-40 east-to-west into Barstow. In between, a remote section of the alignment follows the National Trails Highway through Amboy; how-ever, the road is rough and subject to closure during heavy rains and flash floods. From Barstow, Route 66 turns south, still following the National Trails Highway and paralleling I-15 through

Best Accommodations

★ **Wigwam Motel, San Bernardino:** Spend the night in this kitschy roadside relic (page 312).

★ **Hotel Figueroa, Los Angeles:** This Moroccan-themed hotel is a fitting

place to end your Route 66 road trip (page 322).

★ **The Line, Los Angeles:** This slick, modern hotel sits right in the heart of one of LA's most vibrant, culturally diverse hoods (page 323).

Victorville into San Bernardino and the Inland Empire. A good stretch of Route 66 through the Inland Empire is along Foothill Boulevard, which at one time was flanked with fruit trees and is now lined with strip malls. From Foothill Boulevard west is where you will begin to encounter LA's infamous traffic, which will not ebb until you reach the shores of the Pacific.

Car Rental

Enterprise (8734 Bellanca Ave., 310/649-5400, www.enterprise.com) has good prices and a wide selection of cars at LAX (from baggage claim, walk outside to the center island and wait at the purple Rental Car Shuttles sign). **Budget** (2627 N. Hollywood Way, 818/841-0447, www.budget.com, 5:30am-11pm Mon.-Fri., 6am-11pm Sat.-Sun.) offers efficient and courteous customer service at Burbank Airport. **Hertz** (1426 Santa Monica Blvd., 310/394-2449, www.hertz.com, 7:30am-6pm Mon.-Fri., 9am-2pm Sat., 9am-1pm Sun.) is located right on Route 66 in Santa Monica. **Avis** (888 S. Figueroa St., 213/533-8400, www.avis.com, 7:30am-6pm Mon.-Fri., 8am-3pm Sat., 9am-2pm Sun.) has friendly service with a convenient location less than one mile from the original downtown terminus of Route 66.

Air

Route 66 is best driven westward, but if you must start the trip in Los Angeles, you have a couple of airports to choose from. **Los Angeles International Airport** (LAX, 1 World Way, Los Angeles, 424/646-5252, www.lawa.org) is the second-busiest airport in the country. Flying into **Burbank Bob Hope Airport** (BUR, 2627 N. Hollywood Way, Burbank, 818/840-8840, www.burbankairport.com) may be a better option—it's less crowded and easier to get in and out. Avoid flying into Ontario Airport in the Inland Empire; you will have to backtrack and drive west through LA traffic to begin the Route 66 road trip. For domestic flights, plan to be at the airport two hours before the departure; for international flights, arrive three hours early. The I-405 freeway is the main route to LAX, but if it's backed up, you can get off the freeway and take La Cienega Boulevard instead.

Train and Bus

Six of the seven commuter Metrolink rail lines run though **Union Station** (800 N. Alameda St., 800/371-5465, www.metrolinktrains.com) in downtown Los Angeles. Metrolink connects Los Angeles to San Bernardino, Riverside, Orange, San Diego, and Ventura counties. From Union Station, cabs (or the metro) offer service to downtown car rental companies.

While some Greyhound buses stop

Best Restaurants

★ **Red Lotus, Twentynine Palms:** Thai and Vietnamese dishes offer a change of pace from road food—and another reason to make the side trip to Joshua Tree National Park (page 305).

★ **Emma Jean's Holland Burger, Victorville:** Stop here for the classic Route 66 diner experience (page 311).

★ **Clifton's, Los Angeles:** Celebrate making it to the end of Route 66 at this fabulous, historic restaurant (page 323).

★ **Mo Better Burgers, Los Angeles:** This is fabulous food and service from folks who care (page 324).

★ **Sushi by H, Los Angeles:** Celebrate your arrival in LA with fresh, organic, and reasonably priced sushi (page 324).

at Union Station, the main depot for **Greyhound** (1716 E. 7th St., 213/629-8401, www.greyhound.com) operates in an industrial area just east of downtown Los Angeles. If you're in the middle of downtown, do not to walk to the Greyhound station, as you'll pass through some sketchy areas. It's best either to take a taxi or the metro; bus 60 Local or bus 760 Rapid will get you there.

Park Moabi

As I-40 heads west into California, take the Park Moabi Road exit (Exit 153) and turn right (north). Continue driving north, crossing railroad tracks in about 0.5 miles. Turn right (east) onto National Trails Highway/Route 66. In less than one mile, the road curves right to head south. The road then passes under I-40 in 0.2 miles. Continue south on National Trails Highway.

Sights
National Old Trails Arch Bridge
In about 200 feet, look for the **National Old Trails Arch Bridge,** an 800-foot span that carried cars across the Colorado River from 1916 to 1948—and was part of the original Route 66 alignment when the road opened in 1926. When built, the bridge was the longest and lightest of its kind, an engineering wonder thanks to a unique cantilevered construction system. (It was hoisted into place and supported with a ball-and-socket hinge in the center.) The bridge was featured in the 1940 film *The Grapes of Wrath* and became listed in the National Register of Historic Places in 1988. Though no longer drivable today, it remains a powerful reminder of the different kinds of travelers it carried and the relief they felt as they entered the promised land of California.

Pirate Cove Resort
At the intersection of Park Moabi Road

National Old Trails Arch Bridge over the Colorado River

and the National Trails Highway is the **Pirate Cove Resort** (100 Park Moabi Rd., Needles, 760/326-9000 or 877/301-3000, www.piratecoveresort.com), which sits on the banks of the Colorado River nestled among palm trees and white sandy beaches. It's that slice of paradise the Joad family hoped to find when they came to California. The riverfront resort offers boat rentals, yacht charter, waterfront cabins, and boat tours through the red rock canyon of Topock Gorge and the Havasu National Wildlife Refuge. Those looking for an off-road adventure can rent a 4WD vehicle to explore historic bridges and old mineshafts in the area.

If the price for **accommodations** ($200-369) is beyond your budget, you can enjoy a drink at the pirate beach bar or eat at the pirate-themed **restaurant** (11am-6pm daily, $10-15) while the kids play at the children's water park. Pets are welcome.

✪ Back on 66

Leave Pirate Cove Resort heading south on Park Moabi Road. In 400 feet, turn right (west) on National Trails Highway (Route 66).

Needles

The town of Needles, named after a rock formation on the Arizona border, is the gateway to Route 66 in California. Founded in 1883, Needles is one of the oldest towns in San Bernardino County. In the late 1880s, the town operated as a major hub for the Santa Fe Railroad and served as an icing station for fruits and vegetables that were shipped from inland valley farms in California. In the 1930s, Needles became a welcome haven for Dust Bowl and Depression-era transplants escaping poverty, signifying they had made it to the "land of opportunity."

But the town's most famous resident might be Charles Shultz, the creator of the *Peanuts* comic strip. Shultz lived in Needles from 1928 to 1930. His short stint here inspired the creation of Snoopy's brother Spike, a loner beagle who lived in the Mojave Desert. (Spike wore a trademark fedora and a long droopy mustache.) Several murals in Needles pay homage to one of Shultz's most offbeat characters.

✪ Route 66 through Needles

The original 1926-1947 alignment is not intact through Needles; it dead-ends into a sandy wash. However, the 1947-1966 alignment is drivable via Broadway Street.

1947-1966 Alignment

From I-40, take Exit 144 for U.S. 95 and make a slight right onto East Broadway Street (Historic Route 66). Broadway curves left past Quivera Street to become West Broadway Street as it continues through town. Turn left (west) onto

Business I-40/Needles Highway for food and lodging.

1926-1947 Alignment

To drive part of the original 1926-1947 alignment, continue straight past Quivera Street onto Front Street. Turn left (south) onto F Street, then right (west) onto Quinn Court. At G Street, turn right (north) and then make the next left (west) onto Front Street. The El Garces Harvey House will be on the north side of Front Street.

Sights
El Garces Harvey House

The **El Garces Harvey House** (950 Front St. at G St.) was built by Frances Wilson in 1908 to resemble a Greek temple; it operated as a freight and passenger depot with a hotel and restaurant. It was named after the Spanish Missionary and explorer Father Francisco Garcés. Fan palm trees surround the property with Tuscan columns, and El Garces was known as the "Crown Jewel" of Harvey Houses for its distinctive china, linens, silver, and quality service. The waitresses who worked there, called the Harvey Girls, said being assigned to work at the El Garces was like "going to Europe." The lunchroom served 140 people and had two horseshoe counters. The El Garces closed as a Harvey House in 1949. It was abandoned and under the threat of demolition until a group of local residents petitioned in 1993 to save it. In 2002, the National Park Service listed the El Garces on the National Register of Historic Places. It recently has undergone a $10 million restoration. Although, it's not yet open to the public, the exterior has been fully renovated to its former glory and is definitely worth seeing.

From I-40 west, take Exit 148 for Five Mile Road, which becomes East Broadway Street (Route 66). Stay on Broadway Street as it bears left through downtown. Turn right (north) onto

Needles

G Street and drive straight to Front Street. The El Garces Harvey House sits right alongside the Santa Fe Railroad tracks.

Havasu National Wildlife Refuge

Havasu National Wildlife Refuge (www. fws.gov/refuge/havasu, free) is a birding hotspot and nature utopia on the California/Arizona border. The refuge provides habitat for 318 species of birds and more than 25 types of dragonflies; desert bighorn sheep scale steep rock faces while coyotes, bobcats, and foxes forage for food. Entrances to the refuge vary, but the **park headquarters** (317 Mesquite Ave., Needles, 760/326-3853, 7am-3:30pm Mon.-Fri.) is located in Needles. This should be your first stop for maps and information.

From I-40 in Needles, take the J Street exit (Exit 142) and turn left (southwest). Continue 0.6 miles, then turn right at the refuge entrance sign. Follow the signs to the administrative office.

Accommodations and Food

If you need a place to stay, the **Rio Del Sol** (1111 Pashard St., 760/326-5660, www. riodelsolinn.com, $70) offers clean, well-appointed rooms at a good price. The award-winning **Juicy's River Café** (2411 W. Broadway St., 760/326-2233, www.juicysrivercafe.com, 5:30am-10pm Sun.-Thurs., 5:30am-10:30pm Fri.-Sat. spring-fall; 5:30am-9:30pm Sun.-Thurs. winter, $6-15) has delicious food at down-to-earth prices. The Baja chicken melt served on parmesan sourdough is amazing.

The menu at **The Wagon Wheel** (2420 Needles Hwy., 760/326-4305, www.wagonwheelneedles.com, 5:30am-10pm daily, $7-16) was designed by famed Route 66 artist Bob Waldmire. The pot roast is slow-roasted and served with real mashed potatoes in classic 1970s-era digs. There's also a gift shop on-site with Mother Road goodies.

✈ Back on 66

Route 66 from Needles to Barstow is notorious for temporary road closures due to fierce desert storms. Be safe and avoid driving over water on the road which could be a flash flood. (They happen in seconds and they are deadly.) Before venturing out, check **Cal Trans Road Closures** (http://www.sbcounty.gov) to make sure it's all clear. For areas that may be closed, take I-40 as an alternate route.

Follow Broadway through Needles, turning left (west) on Needles Highway (aka Historic Route 66, then W. Broadway St.). The road quickly changes names again, becoming River Road. Stay in the left lane to take National Trails Highway, which splits left after crossing over I-40. Turn left at West Park Road and take I-40 west for 6 miles Exit 133 onto U.S. 95 north (right). Follow Highway 95 north for 6 miles and turn left onto Goffs Road to follow the pre-1931 alignment.

Needles to Barstow

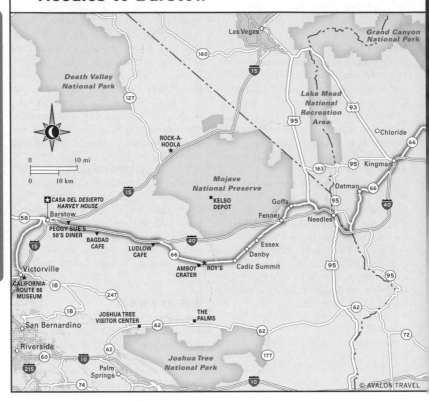

🔸 Side Trip: Las Vegas, Nevada

From the surface, Las Vegas appears to be Disneyland for grown-ups. But if you look a little deeper, there's a lot more to this shameless spectacle of excess.

Getting There

Las Vegas is about a two-hour drive from Needles and a three-hour drive from Barstow. From Needles, take I-40 west to U.S. 95 north and drive 80 miles north. At the US-95 N/ US-93 N ramp, continue onto US-93 N into Las Vegas. Follow I-515 N to I-215 W then to I-15 N, the main freeway through the center of

Las Vegas. If you're staying on the Strip, take I-215 W to I-15 N; if you're going, stay on I-515 and take Exit 75 for Las Vegas Boulevard.

Sights
South Strip

In front of the **Bellagio** (3600 Las Vegas Blvd. S., 702/796-9999, www.bellagio. com) intricate choreographed fountains dance to music. In the lobby, the **Conservatory and Botanical Gardens** exhibits flower-draped gazebos, bridges, and water features. This is also the home of **Cirque du Soleil's O** (7:30pm and 10pm Wed.-Sun.).

The Cosmopolitan (3708 Las Vegas Blvd. S. 702/698-7000, www.

cosmopolitanlasvegas.com) relives the glitz and glamour of classic Las Vegas at the **Chandelier Bar.**

Mandalay Bay (3950 Las Vegas Blvd. S., 702/632-4555, www.mandalaybay. com) has the **Shark Reef Aquarium** (10am-8pm Sun.-Thurs., 10am-10pm Fri.-Sat.), which holds 2,000 animals, including an eight-foot Komodo dragon.

Monte Carlo Casino (3770 Las Vegas Blvd. S., 702/730-7010, www.montecarlo. com) is the home of the **Blue Man Group,** a captivating show that has entertained more than 25 million people.

At **Paris Las Vegas** (3655 Las Vegas Blvd. S., 866/574-3851, www.caesars. com), *Jersey Boys* performs the story of Frankie Valli and the Four Seasons with an amazing cast of talented singers.

Vegas! The Show at **Planet Hollywood** (3667 Las Vegas Blvd. S., 702/463-0259, www.caesars.com) has a big band orchestra, shimmering showgirls and recreates some of the most spectacular entertainers in Vegas history including the Rat Pack and Elvis Presley.

Raiding the Rock Vault at the **Tropicana** (3801 Las Vegas Blvd. S., 800/829-9034) is a two-hour laser-filled live concert with rock anthems from Zeppelin, Queen, and Aerosmith.

Mid-Strip
The LINQ (3545 Las Vegas Blvd. S., 866/328-1888, www.caesars.com) is home to The **Auto Collection,** the world's largest classic car showroom, and **High Roller,** the world's tallest observation wheel. For live music, the **Brooklyn Bowl** is a mid-size music venue.

The **Mirage** (3400 Las Vegas Blvd. S., 702/791-7188, www.miragehabitat.com) is the famous home of Siegfried and Roy's **Secret Garden and Dolphin Habitat,** a lush tropical garden with dolphins, lions, tigers, and leopards.

The **Palazzo**'s (3325 Las Vegas Blvd S., 702/791-1818, www.palazzo.com) **LAVO** lounge feels like an avant-garde palace

with roman accents and lush embossed leather walls.

Mysètre at **Treasure Island Casino** (3300 Las Vegas Blvd. S., 702/894-7722, www.treasureisland.com) set the standard for Cirque du Soleil in Vegas. This powerful, high-energy performance is filled with the drama of Shakespeare and the surrealism of Salvador Dali.

Absinthe at **Caesars Palace** (3570 Las Vegas Blvd. S., 702/785-5395, www. caesars.com) is a provocative and uncensored circus-style act with raunchy burlesque performers, tightrope walkers, and aerialists.

At the **Venetian** (3355 Las Vegas Blvd. S., 866/641-7469, www.venetian. com), *Smokey Robinson Presents Human Nature: The Motown Show* offers a trip down memory lane.

XS at **Wynn Casino** (3131 S. Las Vegas Blvd, 702/770-7000, www.wynnlasvegas. com) is one of the hottest nightclubs in Vegas, with a large outdoor pool, a lavish dance area, and world-renowned DJ's. *La Rêve* at the **Wynn Theater** (7pm and 9:30pm Fri.-Thurs.) is an intimate dream-inspired fantasy production with fire, aquatic gymnasts and synchronized swimmers.

Downtown
The **National Atomic Testing Museum** (Mid-strip, 755 E. Flamingo Rd., 702/794-5151, www.nationalatomictestingmuseum.org, 10am-5pm Mon.-Sat., noon-5pm Sun., $22) features more than 12,000 thousand rare photographs, reports, videos, and artifacts chronicling the history of the Nevada Test Site and the Cold War.

Goodfellas and *Casino* fans shouldn't miss the **Mob Museum** (Downtown, 300 Stewart Ave., 702/229-2734, www. themobmuseum.org, 10am-7pm Sun.-Thurs., 10am-8pm Fri.-Sat., $20), a 41,000-square foot museum with four floors of exhibits, including Al Capone's personal items and a piece of the brick wall from the Valentine's Day Massacre.

The **Neon Museum**'s (Downtown, 770 Las Vegas Blvd N., 702/387-6366, www.neonmuseum.org, 9am-8pm daily, $18) Boneyard is a two-acre lot of more than 150 vintage signs from the 1930s through the 1990s.

Located in the center of the Las Vegas Arts district, **The Arts Factory** (Downtown, 107 E. Charleston Blvd., 702/383-3133, www.theartsfactory.com) is a collective of contemporary artists, photographers, and galleries. The space also hosts concerts, poetry readings, and theatrical performances.

Accommodations

Once owned by Bugsy Siegel, the **El Cortez** (600 E. Fremont St., 800/634-6703, www.elcortezhotelcasino.com) opened in 1941 and is the longest continually operating hotel in Vegas. Room styles range from 1950s glam to mobster chic.

Stratosphere Hotel and Casino (2000 Las Vegas Blvd S., 702/380-7777, www.stratospherehotel.com) towers 1,149 feet over the Strip. Rooms feature award-winning views of the Las Vegas skyline.

The Linq (3535 Las Vegas Blvd S., 800/634-6441, www.stratospherehotel.com) is a fresh, hip hotel with floor to ceiling windows and a cool television interactive system.

The D (301 Fremont St., 702/388-2400, www.thed.com) is housed in the classic 1970s Fitzgerald Casino. A $15-million dollar renovation showcases upscale decor and rock bottom prices.

The **Downtown Grand** (206 N. 3rd St., 702/953-4343, www.downtowngrand.com) is a cool, modern boutique hotel right in the heart of downtown Las Vegas, across the street from the Mob Museum.

At the **Aria Casino** (3730 Las Vegas Blvd. S., 702/590-7757, www.aria.com), every guest receives a well-appointed, corner room equipped with remote

top to bottom: downtown Las Vegas sights are larger than life; El Cortez Hotel, Las Vegas

control room temperature, lights, drapes, and sound systems.

Famed sushi chef Nobu Matsuhisa created **Nobu Hotel** (Caesars Palace, 3570 Las Vegas Blvd. S. 702/785-6677, www. nobucaesarspalace.com), a boutique property with Japanese-inspired decor and hot tea served in the rooms.

The Cosmopolitan (3708 Las Vegas Blvd. S., 702/698-7000, www.cosmopolitanlasvegas.com) is a modern, sophisticated, ultra-glam property with an eclectic blend of art, hot music and cool technology.

The Mandarin (3752 Las Vegas Blvd. S. 702/ 590-8888, www.mandarinoriental. com/lasvegas) offers the ultimate experience in comfort and serenity with beautiful accommodations and a two-story, 27,000 square-foot spa.

Platinum Hotel (211 E. Flamingo Rd., 702-365-5000, www.theplatinumhotel. com) is a non-gaming, smoke-free hotel one block from the Strip. Spacious rooms come with free Wi-Fi and no resort fees. Pets are welcome.

Vdara's (2600 W. Harmon Ave., 702/590-2111, www.vdara.com) is a sleek all-suite, non-gaming and smoke-free hotel with huge rooms and state-of-the-art kitchens. Dogs are welcome.

The **Artisan** (1501 W. Sahara Ave., 702/214-4000, www.artisanhotel.com) is an art deco-style hotel with a large collection of art on every wall, including the hallways and ceilings.

Oasis at Gold Spike (217 Las Vegas Blvd., 702/768-9823, www.oasisatgold-spike.com) is a boutique hotel for the urban, mid-century loving adventurer, with bike rentals, a library, and a turntable lounge to spin your favorite vinyl.

Food and Drinks
South Strip

America at **New York, New York Casino** (3790 Las Vegas Blvd. S., 702/740-6451, 24 hours, $15) is an affordable and perfect spot for a late night snack or breakfast.

Della's Kitchen (Delano Casino, 3940 Las Vegas Blvd. S., 702/632-9444, 6:30am-2pm daily, $18) is a farmhouse-chic restaurant that serves hormone- and antibiotic-free comfort food using locally sourced ingredients.

The **Peppermill Restaurant and Fireside Lounge** (2985 Las Vegas Blvd., 702/735-4177, www.peppermilllasvegas. com, 24 hours, $15) hasn't changed much since the 1970s, with low lighting, mirrored columns, and neon on the ceiling. They have a huge menu and even bigger portions.

Mid-Strip

Bobby Flay's award-winning **Mesa Grill** (Cesar's Palace, 3570 Las Vegas Blvd. S., 702/731-7731, 11am-2:30pm Mon.-Fri., 5pm-11pm daily, 10:30am-3pm Sat.-Sun., $40) serves vibrant, flavorful Southwestern food and signature dishes.

Trevi (Forum Shops at Caesar's Palace, 3500 Las Vegas Blvd. S., 702/735-4663, 11am-11pm Sun.-Thurs., 11am-midnight Fri.-Sat., $15), located at the Fountain of the Gods, serves up delicious and affordable Italian cuisine.

At **Lao Sze Chuan** (4321 W. Flamingo Rd., 866/942-6862, 11am-midnight, $15), Chicago chef Tony Hu serves Sze Chuan cuisine along with Mandarin, Hunan and Cantonese items in a stylish setting at the Palms Casino.

SUSHISAMBA (The Palazzo, 3327 Las Vegas Blvd., 702/607-0700, 11:30am-1am Sun.-Wed., 11:30am-2am Thurs.-Sat., $40) serves traditional and imaginative dishes that blend Japanese, Peruvian, and Brazilian cuisine.

Lotus of Siam (953 E. Sahara Ave., 702/753-3033, www.saipinchutima.com, 11:30am-2:30pm and 5:30pm-9:30pm Mon.-Thurs., 5:30pm-10pm Fri.-Sun., $15), east of the Strip, dishes out some of the best Thai food in Vegas. Make reservations or arrive early; waits can take up to an hour.

The **Earl of Sandwich** (Planet Hollywood, 3667 Las Vegas Blvd., 702/463-0259; and The Palms, 4321 W.

Flamingo Rd., 702/257-0067; both 24 hours, $8) serves a variety of hot sandwiches on artisan bread with salads and freshly baked desserts.

Downtown

Tacos El Gordo (1724 E. Charleston Blvd., 702/251-8226, 9am-2am Sun.-Thurs., 9am-4am Fri.-Sat., $7) dish out authentic Mexican tacos with a delightful selection of sauces.

Vegans will want to try the **Bronze Café** (401 S. Maryland Pkwy., 702/202-3100, 7am-10pm Mon.-Fri., 10am-8pm Sat.-Sun., $10). The Tree of Life pita is filled with roasted red peppers, avocado, and housemade vegan cashew "crema." Wash it down with a kale banana smoothie.

Grab a bite at the **Bar+Bistro** (107 E. Charleston Blvd., 702/202/6060, www.barbistroaf.com, 11am-10pm Mon.-Fri., 11am-midnight Fri.-Sat.) and browse the artist studios.

Relive the Prohibition era at the **Mob Bar** (206 N. 3rd St., 702/719-5100, http://mobbarlv.com), with intimate jazz performers, dueling pianos, and handcrafted cocktails.

Goffs and Fenner

Goffs Road travels 13.5 miles along the pre-1931 alignment of Route 66, which leads to the forgotten desert town of **Goffs.** It was a smidge higher in elevation than Needles, so residents would go to Goffs to beat the 120-degree heat in Needles—although it was still well over 100 degrees.

Goffs was home to employees of the Santa Fe Railroad, and was a popular stop on Route 66 until 1931, when the Mother Road was realigned to follow a more direct route from Needles to Essex. As you enter Goffs, look for the abandoned **General Store** on the north side of the highway. In better condition is the Spanish Mission-style **Goffs Schoolhouse**

Mojave desert

(37198 Lanfair Rd., 9am-4pm Sat.-Mon. Oct.-June, free), which was built in 1914 using stucco and steel mesh. By 1982 it was practically considered a ruin until the **Mojave Desert Heritage and Cultural Association** (760/733-4482, www.mdhca. org) restored it to its original condition.

From Goffs, continue west on Route 66 for 10 miles as it dips south to Fenner.

Fenner is one of many ghost towns sprinkled throughout the Mojave Desert. Established in 1883, the town operated primarily as a watering station for steam trains. Today, Fenner has gas and limited services along I-40. If you're low on **gas,** get it in here because the next service station is 55 miles away.

◆ Back on 66

Leave Fenner heading south on Route 66 for 4.5 miles, then join the National Trails Highway (Route 66) for 28 miles crossing Kelbaker Road. For the side trip to Mohave National Preserve (about 30 miles away), turn right (north) on

Kelbaker Road or continue heading west on Route 66.

◆ Side Trip: Mohave National Preserve

From I-40 at the junction to Amboy, turn north on Kelbaker Road to explore the **Mojave National Preserve** (90942 Kelso Cima Rd., www.nps.gov/moja, free). The road stretches through a desolate landscape composed of the remains of volcanic activity and desert dunes. In 22 miles along Kelbaker Road, you'll reach the **Kelso Depot,** a beautifully restored 1920s-era railroad depot. The Mission Revival and Spanish Colonial architecture was designed to resemble the Harvey Houses along the Santa Fe Railroad. Inside, a marvelous 1920s horseshoe counter with vintage stools has been re-purposed into the **visitors center** (Kelso Cima Rd., 760/252-6108, 9am-5pm daily), with exhibits, films, an art gallery, a bookstore, restrooms, and a picnic area. As you walk toward the depot from the parking lot, look for two tan cages in front of the railroad tracks. In the 1940s, this was the Kelso Jail, which housed unruly drunks from the nearby Kaiser mine and Union Pacific Railroad.

Kelbaker Road terminates at I-15 in 56 miles, passing cinder cones and lava beds that range from 10,000 to 7 million years old. This short stretch offers just a glimpse into the 1.6-million-acre park. Primitive campgrounds are available via a north turn on Essex Road, just west of Fenner.

Essex, Danby, and Cadiz Summit

The former railroad water stations and towns along this stretch of Route 66 were named in alphabetical order—Amboy, Bristol, Cadiz, Danby, Essex, Fenner, and Goffs. From I-40 near Fenner, head south on Route 66 for 6 miles to the practically non-existent town of **Essex**. This was once a busy town with cafes and garages to fill radiators and rescue stranded folks that underestimated the severity the desert weather. Today the post office is pretty much the only operational business.

Continue west on Route 66 for 9 miles to the abandoned town of **Danby** with dilapidated ruins and fenced-off buildings. About 12 miles west, the next "town" is Chambless, near the **Cadiz Summit**. After I-40 opened in 1973, Chambless became a ghost town, today marked by graffiti-covered rubble.

⬥ Back on 66
From Chambless, continue 11 miles west to Amboy.

Amboy

Route 66 helped put Amboy on the map. By the time Roys opened in 1938, the desolate desert town had a population of around 65 people.

Sights
Roy's Motel and Café
On the north side of the National Trails Highway (Route 66) is the dusty, deserted town of Amboy, home to the iconic **Roy's Motel and Café** (87520 National Trails Hwy., 760/733-1066, www.amboyroute66.com, 8am-6pm Mon.-Sat.). Though the motel is closed, gas is available out front and the café sells soft drinks. Restrooms are located outside in the back of the building. It's definitely worth a quick stop to see the classic atomic-age Googie signage.

In 2003, the entire town was on sale on eBay for $1.9 million, but the highest offer ($995,000) was not accepted. In 2005, Albert Okura, owner of the Juan Pollo restaurant chain, bought the town (all 490 acres) for $425,000. Okura is hoping to resuscitate the near-ghost town, but it's a venture that could easily cost more than $1 million.

Amboy Crater
About three miles west of Roy's, on the south side of National Trails Highway, is **Amboy Crater** (BLM Needles Field Office, 760/326-7000, www.blm.gov). The 250-foot crater formed about 6,000 years ago; a moderate hiking trail (1.7 miles) leads to the top. Hiking to the rim is not recommended during summer or in windy conditions. Avoid pathways where people tried to drive ATVs up to the crater; these are not trails and can be dangerous.

⬥ Back on 66
To stay on Route 66, continue heading west. To reach Joshua Tree, head west on National Trails Highway, turn left onto Amboy Road and continue 40 miles south.

⬥ Side Trip: Joshua Tree

Getting There
From Amboy and the National Trails Highway (Route 66), turn left (south) on Amboy Road. Drive 40 miles south, passing through the unincorporated town of **Wonder Valley,** where abandoned homestead cabins are slowly decomposing in the desert. At the junction with Godwin Road, turn left to reach Highway 62 in 2 miles. In **Twentynine Palms,** turn left (south) onto Utah Trail, which turns into Park Boulevard after crossing SR-62 (Twentynine Palms Hwy.). Park Boulevard continues south to the east entrance of Joshua Tree National Park.

Joshua Tree National Park
Joshua Tree National Park (760/367-5500, www.nps.gov/jotr, $20) is one of the most popular rock climbing parks in the state. The landscape twists and curves around tan boulders to flatten

Joshua Tree National Park

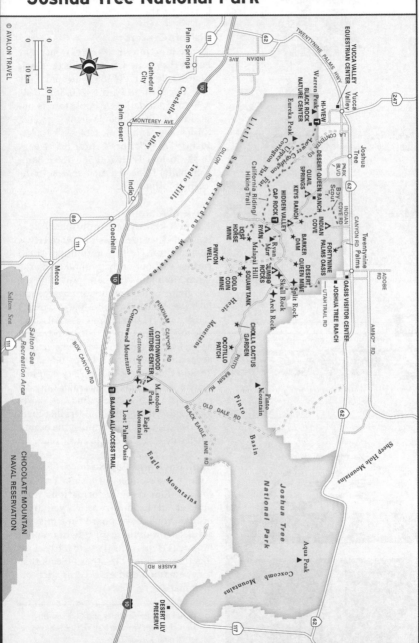

© AVALON TRAVEL

into seas of the namesake Joshua Tree, which is actually a flowering plant belonging to the agave family.

Visitors Centers
At the junction of SR-62 (Twentynine Palms Hwy.) and Utah Trail is the **Oasis Visitors Center** (74485 National Park Dr., Twentynine Palms, 760/367-5500, 8:30am-5pm daily). A bookstore is onsite and facilities include drinking water, flush toilets, and picnic tables. The larger **Joshua Tree Visitors Center** (6554 Park Blvd., Joshua Tree, 760/366-1855, 8am-5pm daily) is located farther west in the town of Joshua Tree.

Oasis of Mara
The best-known oasis in Joshua Tree is the well-developed **Oasis of Mara** (Hwy. 62 and Utah Trail). A number of small springs well out of the ground along the Pinto Mountain fault here, providing the life-giving water that supports a large and lush (well, lush for the Mojave Desert) ecosystem. Though the Oasis sits outside the park boundaries, it's still treated as part of the park. A lovely wheelchair-accessible nature trail loops 0.5 miles around the oasis with a variety of informative signs about the natural features of the oasis. You'll see the palm trees, hardy grasses, and huge light boulders that characterize the region and hint at the beauty you'll find elsewhere in Joshua Tree.

Skull Rock and Cap Rock
Among the wonders of Joshua Tree are the fabulous boulder formations scattered about the landscape. As you drive or hike, you'll have a hard time missing at least a few of these great light orange-tan rocks. Two rocks that are fairly close together so resemble other objects that they're named and marked as such on park maps.

top to bottom: Roy's Motel and Café, Amboy; the drive through Wonder Valley; sights along Route 62, near Joshua Tree

Take the east-west connecting road from Pinto Basin Road (the main north-south corridor) to Keys View and Hidden Valley. You'll first pass **Skull Rock** (Park Blvd., 7 miles east of Hidden Valley), one of the many giant stones that provide shade at the aptly named Jumbo Rocks campground. Just past the intersection toward Hidden Valley, **Cap Rock** and its buddies offer interesting geology, a small picnic area, and a good spot for rock climbers to dig in and start scrambling.

Hidden Valley

One of the centerpieces of Joshua Tree, the **Hidden Valley** (Park Blvd., 10 miles south of West Entrance) offers hikes, a nature trail, a campground, and a rare view of a tiny desert valley. Park in the day lot and follow the tourists off to the right to the sort-of trail onto and through the big tan boulders. You'll scramble up, getting a great up-close view of the surprising granite mineral content of the pale boulders on either side of you. Emerge from the rocky trail into a small rocky meadow-like area, which includes small signs describing the natural features.

Keys Ranch

William and Frances Keys were among the rugged settlers of the Mojave Desert. They ranched on the sparse desert grasses and raised five children on this patch that would become part of Joshua Tree National Park. Today, visitors see the weathered pine buildings that housed the original ranch house, the schoolhouse that educated the few local children, the local general store, and a workshop. The orchard and landscaping have been replanted and revived. A collection of mining and farm equipment sits in the dry desert air, and relics like the old well dot the property.

The only way to get a real look at **Keys Ranch** (760/367-5522, 6pm and 9am Sun. June-Sept., $10) is to take a docent-guided tour of the buildings and land.

Reservations are required; call between 9am and 4:30pm or purchase tickets on-site at one of the visitors centers. Tours cover 0.5 miles, last about 1.5 hours, and are limited to groups of 25 people.

Keys View

One of the best views in all of Joshua Tree is from **Keys View** (end of Keys View Rd., bear right off Park Blvd. past Cap Rock). On a clear day, the view redefines the concept of "panoramic," letting travelers see the whole of the Palm Springs urban sprawl, the Coachella Valley farmland, the notorious San Andreas Fault, and even the Salton Sea many miles to the southeast. You'll drive all the way to the end of the road out of the West Ranger Station, up to about 5,000 feet elevation and the sizeable parking lot. Get out of your car and climb a brief paved trail to the vantage point at the top of the ridge. The best time to catch a good view at Keys is the early morning.

Black Rock Canyon

Follow Park Boulevard west to exit the park at the Joshua Tree Visitors Center. West of the main entrance, and just south of the tiny town of Yucca Valley, is **Black Rock Canyon** (SR-247 at the northwest corner of the park) with a developed campground, nature and ranger center, and hiking trails surrounded by the famed Joshua trees, which begin the spring bloom late each February. Visitors often walk the **Hi-View Nature Trail** (1.3 miles), a lovely interpretive stroll that points out and describes the plants and other natural features that characterize the northern Mojave Desert region.

Hiking

There are 12 self-guided nature trails in the park. Before you take a hike—even a short two- or three-mile jaunt—be sure you're properly prepared. Joshua Tree is a harsh and unforgiving desert. Bring lots of water (at least one gallon per person), maps, first-aid, and sun protection.

Five miles from the Oasis Visitors Center, the trail to the **49 Palms Oasis** weaves 1.5 miles south to pools of water surrounded by fan palms. Look for the trailhead two miles south of SR-62 off Canyon Road.

Popular **Barker Dam Nature Trail** loops 1.3 miles around an early water tank built by cattle ranchers. Note that the tank may be empty in times of drought, but the walk is still an enjoyable entry into the desert environment. The trailhead is located near the parking area for Keys Ranch.

Located on Park Boulevard near Cap Rock, the strenuous trail to **Ryan Mountain** (2.8 miles round-trip) climbs to the 5,461 summit with views of the surrounding valleys below.

If you're looking to stretch your legs after the drive to Keys View, consider hiking the **Lost Horse Mine Loop** (6.2 miles round-trip), which passes by the site of an abandoned ten-stamp mill as the trail climbs above 5,000 feet.

Accommodations and Food

There are nine **campgrounds** in Joshua Tree National Park. Most sites are first-come, first-served year-round, however, many do not have water and are fairly primitive. Bring everything you think you'll need. Reservations are accepted for **Black Rock** and **Indian Cove Campgrounds** (www.recreation.gov, 877/444-6777, $15-20) and are recommended from October through May.

Twentynine Palms

Located east of the east entrance to Joshua Tree National Park is **The Palms** (83131 Amboy Rd., Twentynine Palms, 760/361-2810, 3pm-6pm Wed.-Thurs., 3pm-9pm Fri.-Sat., 9am-6pm Sun., $5-10), a restaurant, bar, and live music venue featuring everything from indie pop and bluegrass to experimental. The owners are the Sibleys, who perform on stage in back and are not to be missed. It's an odd place, way out in the middle of nowhere, with an eclectic mix of

Bonita Domes, Joshua Tree

locals, desert rats, and urbanites escaping normality. David Lynch would love it here.

Just 0.5 miles from the Oasis Visitors Center is the **29 Palms Inn** (73950 Inn Ave., Twentynine Palms, 760/367-3505, www.29palmsinn.com, $8-30), which sits on 70 acres in the 9,000-year-old Oasis of Mara. Choose from adobe bungalows and cabins that date from the 1920s, with private backyards and decks, all surrounded by palm trees. The on-site restaurant overlooks the pool and serves delicious meals with produce from the adjacent organic garden. (The chicken salad with organic greens and homemade dressing is superb.)

If you're in the mood for Thai or Vietnamese, the curry and pho dishes at ★ **Red Lotus** (73511 Twentynine Palms Hwy., 760/367-4080, 11am-9pm Tues.-Thurs., 11am-10pm Fri.-Sat., 11am-9pm Sun., $7-12) are out-of-this-world. Don't miss it.

Joshua Tree

Joshua Tree Mountain Vista Vacation Rentals (415/717-5595, www.joshuatreemv.com, $150-250) offers accommodations with great mid-century modern style. The house has two bedrooms and two bathrooms, with a detached studio space (with bedroom and bathroom.) A large living room with a vaulted wood-beam ceiling welcomes guests with a fireplace, two large sofas, and a daybed. If the house is booked, check their other rental, **Rabbit Run Retreat,** an 800-square foot house with two bedrooms that is set against a stunning desert mountain with thousands of acres to hike.

For people who love to camp, but want to try something completely different, reserve a "pod" at the **Bonita Domes** (www.bonitadomes.squarespace.com, $80). These sustainable geometric domes were built with Earthbag Technology; the 18-inch walls produce a thermal mass enabling the structures to maintain a comfortable temperature. The domes sleep one to two people and come with a shower, porta-potty, and a shaded outdoor kitchen.

In Joshua Tree, there are several places to eat. **Crossroads Café** (61715 Twentynine Palms Hwy., Joshua Tree, 760/366-5414, 7am-9pm Mon.-Sat., 7am-8pm Sun., $6-12) offers a good range of breakfast and lunch items for vegetarians and carnivores alike. For a quick slice, **Pie for the People** (61740 Twentynine Palms Hwy., Joshua Tree, 760/366-0400, 11am-9pm Mon.-Thurs., 11am-10pm Fri.-Sat., $5-10) dishes out thin-crust pizza with gourmet toppings and options for vegan and gluten-free customers.

For dinner, try **Royal Siam** (61599 Twentynine Palms Hwy., Joshua Tree, 760/366-2923, 11:30am-9pm Mon.-Thurs., 11am-10pm Fri.-Sat., $5-10) for tasty but spicy Thai dishes (on a scale of 1 to 5, with 5 being the hottest, a 5 in most places is a 3 here). If you're in the mood for Indian, stop at **Sam's Pizza** (61380 Twentynine Palms Hwy., Joshua Tree, 760/366-9511, 11am-9pm Mon.-Sat., 3pm-8pm Sun., $8-14), tucked away in a mini-mall on the north side of SR-62 next to Sam's Market. Yes, they serve pizza, but if you step inside, you'll find a full-service authentic Indian restaurant with delicious lamb, chicken, and Marsala dishes.

◈ Back on 66

To head back to Route 66, drive 16 miles east on Twentynine Palms Highway (Route 62). Turn left (north) on Utah Trail. In less than 2 miles, turn right (east) on Amboy Road. Follow Amboy Road for 17 miles until it curves north and climbs 28 miles; the road dead-ends into Route 66 (National Trail Hwy.). Turn left (west) and drive 5 miles to the silent, deserted town of **Bagdad.**

Bagdad was once a relatively busy place, considering it's in the middle of nowhere. After Route 66 was rerouted in 1973, the town dwindled to nothing. By 1991, the remaining buildings were razed leaving little more than rusted-out cars and creosote. The Bagdad Café, which inspired the Percy Adlon film, was originally located here, but the actual filming took place further west in Newberry Springs.

Continue west on National Trails Highway (Route 66) for 20 miles to the town of Ludlow.

Ludlow

In 1882, Ludlow was a regular water stop for the Atlantic and Pacific Railroad. It was also a prosperous mining town after ore was discovered in the nearby hills. In the 1940s, Ludlow had a motor court, cabins, and the lonely **Ludlow Café** (68315 National Trails Hwy., Ludlow, 760/733-4501, 6am-5:30pm daily, $5-10). Folks rave about the biscuits and gravy at this desert diner that serves breakfast all day.

Ludlow Café

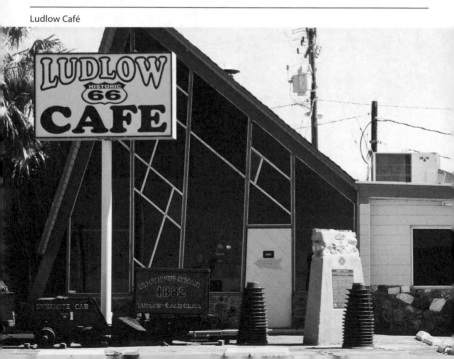

If you need **gas,** there is a Chevron station on the north side of National Trail Highway. A 76 station is found north of I-40 on Crucero Road.

◆ Back on 66
Continue driving west on Route 66 for 28 miles to Newberry Springs.

Newberry Springs

Although the original Bagdad Café was located in Bagdad about 50 miles east, today the **Bagdad Café** (46548 National Trails Hwy., Newberry Springs, 760/257-3101, 7am-7pm daily, $6-11) lives on in Newberry Springs. The cafe was used in the 1987 German film of the same name directed by Percy Adlon. The food is hit-or-miss, but the ambiance and its filmic history make it worth a pit stop for a cold drink on a 120-degree day in the desert.

◆ Back on 66
Keep heading west on Route 66 for 11 miles (National Trails Hwy) to Daggett.

◆ Side Trip: North to I-15

Rock-a-Hoola
About 20 minutes north of Bagdad Café and Newberry Springs is an abandoned water park. **Rock-a-Hoola** (Hacienda Rd.) is on private property, so enter at your own risk. For urban explorers who love this stuff, it's easy to access and worth a stop.

The park was originally a children's playground with a 273-acre artificial lake. Though it was quite popular in the 1970s, attendance dwindled in the 1980s and by 1990 the park had closed. After a renovation in 1998, an employee slid into a partially filled pool and was injured. The resulting lawsuit bankrupted the park, forcing it to close down again in 2004.

Today, rusted water towers, dying palm trees, empty graffiti-covered pools, and chunks of concrete are strewn throughout the park. Several murals remain painted on billboards (one is of a couple sitting in a 1950s convertible; framed above them is the phrase: "The Future is Blight"). The park was purchased again in 2013; the new owners are trying to bring it back to life, so it may not stay abandoned long.

Getting There
From Newberry Springs, take Newberry Road north for six miles, turning east as it becomes Palma Vista Road. In one mile, turn left (north) on Harvard Road. Follow Harvard Road north for 3 miles to I-15 and turn west onto Hacienda Road. Drive 2.5 miles west on Hacienda Road to the waterpark on the north side of the road.

⬥ Back on 66

Continue south on Hacienda Road for about 2.5 miles. Turn right onto Yermo Road and drive 5.5 miles west. At a T-junction, turn left (west) to continue on East Yermo Road and the town of Yermo.

Yermo

Peggy Sue's 50's Diner (35654 W Yermo Rd., Yermo, 760/254-3370, www.peggysuesdiner.com, 6am-10pm daily, $7-13) is a Hollywood version of the 1950s, with black-and-white checkered floors, pictures of Marilyn and Elvis on the walls, and a life-size sculpture of Betty Boop dressed as a waitress. Onsite is a gift shop with old-fashioned candy and classic movie memorabilia. The food is hit or miss, but you can't go wrong with old-fashioned cherry, strawberry, and chocolate milkshakes.

⬥ Back on 66

To return to Route 66, head west on Yermo Road and turn left (south) on Dagget-Yermo Road. In 2.5 miles, turn right (west) on National Trails Highway (Route 66).

Dagget

Daggett was named after California Lieutenant Governor John Daggett. In the late 1800s, the town was a supply center that accommodated the nearby silver mines in Calico; 20-mule teams hauled water and ore from Daggett to Calico. By 1902, Daggett was supported by three borax mines and more than $90 million worth of silver was removed from the Calico Hills. (Dagget was also the California inspection station mentioned in the Steinbeck's *Grapes of Wrath*.) Some of the buildings left standing date back more than 100 years.

If you want to stock up on sods, snacks, or overhear the latest gossip in a small desert town, stop by the **Desert Market** (35596 Santa Fe Ave., 760/254-2774,

8am-8pm Mon.-Sat., 9am-7pm Sun). Owner Joe Khawaldeh cashes checks for locals and gives credit when needed. Though it's not much more than a convenient store, it offers an interesting snapshot of Mojave desert life.

To get there from Route 66 (National Trails Hwy.). turn right (north) on Daggett-Yermo Road. Cross the tracks and take the first right (east) on Santa Fe Street. The market is two blocks on the north side, across the street from an old garage that used to repair mining equipment.

⬥ Back on 66

Drive west on National Trails Highway for 2.5 miles. Turn left (south) on Nebo Street and take the next right to join I-40 West. Continue 2.5 miles on I-40 to take Exit 2. Turn left, go under I-40, and then turn right to take the South Frontage Road for about one mile. Turn right (north) to follow E. Main Street into Barstow.

Barstow

As the mining boom busted in the nearby Calico and Daggett mines, Barstow became a busy railway hub and stopping point for emigrants entering California via Route 66. After rail travel diminished, car travel became more prevalent. In the 1950s, Barstow's main drag was a popular place to stop along Route 66. As you head west on Route 66, you'll enter Barstow, with motels, restaurants, and classic neon road signs.

Sights

★ Casa del Desierto Harvey House

The beautiful **Casa del Desierto Harvey House** (681 N. 1st Ave., www.barstowharveyhouse.com) was built in 1885 as a restaurant and hotel to serve Santa Fe Railroad passengers. After it burned down in 1908, it was rebuilt by architect Mary Colter in 1913. The building

Barstow to Pasadena

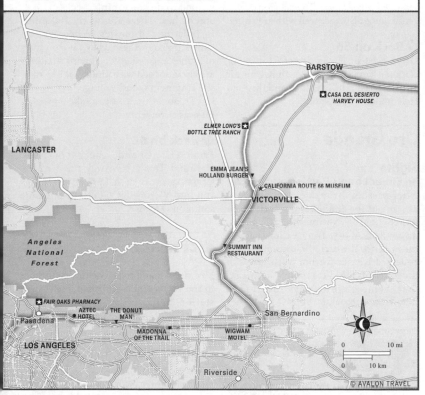

BARSTOW

CASA DEL DESIERTO
HARVEY HOUSE

ELMER LONG'S
BOTTLE TREE RANCH

LANCASTER

EMMA JEAN'S
HOLLAND BURGER

CALIFORNIA ROUTE 66 MUSEUM

VICTORVILLE

*Angeles
National
Forest*

SUMMIT INN
RESTAURANT

FAIR OAKS PHARMACY

AZTEC
HOTEL   THE DONUT
MAN

Pasadena

San Bernardino

MADONNA
OF THE TRAIL   WIGWAM
MOTEL

LOS ANGELES

Riverside

0   10 mi

0   10 km

© AVALON TRAVEL

effortlessly fuses 16th-century Spanish and Classical Revival architecture.

When Route 66 was created in 1926, rail travel was the most efficient cross-country pathway, so much of Route 66 was built to run parallel to the Santa Fe Railroad. Once Amtrak dominated the railway business, many Harvey Houses were torn down. Casa del Desierto sat abandoned for about 15 years until the city of Barstow spent significant funds to renovate and reopen it in 1999. Today it houses the **Western Railroad Museum** and the **Route 66 Museum** (760/255-1890, www.route66museum.org, 10am-4pm Fri.-Sat., 11am-4pm Sun., free).

From Route 66, turn right (north) onto 1st Avenue. Drive 0.4 mile and the road

will curve to the right (east). The Harvey House is on the right.

Accommodations and Food

Unfortunately, decent lodging and food options in Barstow are limited. The 1922 **Route 66 Motel** (195 W. Main St., 760/256-7866, www.route66motelbarstow.com, $50-60) offers a festive choice, with a neon sign of the shield of the Mother Road, vintage cars, and Route 66 memorabilia. Rooms are painted in cheerful colors and some even have round beds.

Lola's Kitchen (1244 E. Main St., 760/255-1007, 4:30am-7:30pm Mon.-Sat., $5-12) is tucked away in a strip mall, next to a pawn shop and a Vons grocery store.

It's easy to miss, but if you like Mexican food, make a point to try their perfectly seasoned carne asada. The delicious chili-verde sauce also goes well with anything.

◆ Back on 66

Drive west on Main Street (Route 66/National Trails Hwy.) through Bartow for 23 miles past Hinkley Road and through Helendale to Oro Grande.

Oro Grande

Sights

★ Elmer Long's Bottle Tree Ranch

After passing through Helendale, keep an eye out for **Elmer Long's Bottle Tree Ranch** (24266 National Trails Hwy., dawn-dusk daily, free) in less than 2 miles. Since the early 1950s Elmer Long collected treasures from trash heaps in the desert as a kid camping with his father. Some of the things they found dated back to the 1800s. His father

started collecting bottles, and after he died, Elmer inherited his collection. He wanted to do something special with it, and he has. There are nearly 200 mini-installations of bottles. When the sun shines through them, they take on hues of amber and emerald. The installations are also adorned with animal bones, missile fragments, and vintage toys. If you leave a donation, you can take a piece of glass as a souvenir.

◆ Back on 66

From Oro Grande, head south on National Trails Highway for 4 miles. Crossing under the I-15 overpass brings you into Victorville. Continue one mile south on D Street.

Victorville

Mormons made their way to Victorville in the 1860s and established a telegraph station here. When Route 66 came

Elmer Long's Bottle Tree Ranch, Oro Grande

through in 1926, it passed through the center of what is today considered "Old Town" Victorville. During the heyday of Route 66, Victorville's dude ranches and apple orchards were the perfect site for Hollywood to film several Hollywood B-films, including *It Came From Outer Space*. In 1940, Herman J. Mankiewicz penned the first two drafts of *Citizen Kane* at the Green Spot Motel on Route 66.

Sights
California Route 66 Museum
To see the Green Spot Motel's green neon sign, as well as other iconic Route 66 memorabilia, visit the **California Route 66 Museum** (16825 S. D St., 760/951-0436, http://califrt66museum.org, 10am-4pm Thurs.-Sat., 11am-3pm Sun., free but donations welcome). More than 4,500-square feet of information and memorabilia include antique radios, vintage photographs, artifacts from closed Route 66 businesses (such as the Trails Restaurant), lots of books on Route 66, a Model-T Ford, and a friendly, knowledgeable staff.

Food
★ **Emma Jean's Holland Burger** (17143 N. D St., 5am-3pm Mon.-Thurs., 6am-12:30pm Sat., cash only, $6-10) is the classic Route 66 diner experience. Emma Jean's specializes in thick towering milk shakes, crispy chicken-fried steak, and juicy burgers. The Brian Burger is a favorite, with Ortega chili and Swiss cheese nestled between thick parmesan-crusted garlic bread. The portions are huge, so split a sandwich or leave your diet outside where it belongs. (Emma Jean's was also the place Uma Thurman walked into after being buried alive in Tarantino's *Kill Bill 2*.)

Back on 66
Leaving Victorville, the southbound lanes of I-15 cover Route 66, so take I-15 south for about 20 miles through the Cajon Pass.

Cajon Pass

On I-15, take the Cleghorn Road (Exit 129) and turn right onto Cajon Boulevard to drive through the Cajon Pass. This mountain pass is between the San Bernardino and San Gabriel Mountains and was created by the shifting of the San Andreas Fault. Popular with train spotters, Cajon Pass is often photographed and featured in books and magazines.

The 1952 **Summit Inn** (5970 Mariposa Rd., 760/949-8688, 6am-7pm Mon.-Thurs., 6am-9pm Fri.-Sun., $5-13) got its name from the original Summit Inn (now closed) built in 1928 to serve Route 66 travelers. The restaurant interior is decked out with vintage gas company signs, including a 1939 Standard Oil sign with Mickey Mouse. The food is general diner fare, but the ostrich burger, ostrich omelets, and date shakes are popular.

A small gift shop sells Texaco-related memorabilia. (Legend has it Elvis kicked the jukebox, because none of his records were inside). The vintage building around the back of restaurant was once a Texaco station.

The Summit Inn is on the east side of the I-15. Traveling west on I-15, take Exit 138 and turn left (east) to cross the freeway. Take the first right (south) to the restaurant.

◈ Back on 66

From the Cajon Pass, the road begins to run parallel to I-15. In less than 2 miles, turn left on Kenwood Avenue and join I-15 South. Immediately after entering the freeway, get into the middle/left lanes toward Riverside/San Bernardino I-215. Bear left to follow I-215. Drive 3.5 miles to Exit 50 and turn right. In about 1,000 feet, cross the railroad tracks and take an immediate left (south) on Cajon Boulevard. Drive 4.5 miles to 21st Street. Make a right (west) and then an immediate left to follow N. Mt. Vernon Avenue as it heads south into San Bernardino. In 1.5 miles, turn right (west) on to W. 5th Street, which soon turns into Foothill Boulevard.

San Bernardino

The San Bernardino Valley is surrounded by stunning mountain ranges and recreation areas. However, driving through on Foothill Boulevard (Route 66), you'll see little more than a concrete slab of suburbia and a gateway to the sprawling metropolis of Los Angeles.

Sights
Santa Fe Depot
Built in 1918, the **Santa Fe Depot** (1170 W. 3rd St., 800/371-5465) is a historical landmark and former Harvey House that sports Mission Revival, Moorish Revival, and Spanish Colonial Revival features. The interior includes four domed towers, handcrafted high beam ceilings, and decorative columns. A former Harvey House, it is now listed on the National Register of Historic Places. Today, it functions as the San Bernardino Amtrak station.

To get here from the Cajon Pass, take I-15 south, keep left at the fork, and continue on I-215 south. Take the West 3rd Street/West 2nd Street exit and turn right onto West 5th Street, which is Route 66.

Original McDonalds Site and Museum
In San Bernardino, The **Original McDonalds Site and Museum** (1398 N. E St., west of I-215, 909/885-6324) was home to the first McDonald's restaurant. The original building was torn down in 1972 but the Juan Pollo chain features a collection of historical items such as hamburger boxes, Happy Meals, and toys that date back to the 1940s. There's a small Route 66 museum in the back with lots of road signs. To get here from I-215, take the West Baseline Road exit and turn left onto North E Street.

Madonna of the Trail
In Upland, at the corner of Euclid Avenue, the **Madonna of the Trail** statue on Foothill Boulevard is one of 12 monuments installed along the National Old Trails road to acknowledge the tenacity and strength of pioneer women.

Accommodations and Food
The ★ **Wigwam Motel** (2728 W. Foothill Blvd., 909/875-3005, www.wigwammotel. com, $73) is the epitome of the kitschy Americana roadside relic. These distinctive and historic concrete hotel rooms were built in 1949 in the shape of 20-foot-tall tepees. Operator Kumar Patel has spent more than $500,000 renovating the property, and it shows. The tepees are comfortable, cozy, and immaculate, with flat-screen TVs, free Wi-Fi, and mini-fridges. There is also a garden, a fire pit, palm trees, a swimming pool, classic cars, and a gift shop on-site.

The historic 1848 **Sycamore Inn** (8318 W Foothill Blvd., 909/982-1104, www. thesycamoreinn.com, 5pm-9pm Mon.-Thurs., 5pm-10pm Fri.-Sat., 4pm-8:30pm Sun., $18-50) opened almost 70 years before Route 66 came through. The restaurant serves traditional comfort food, like buttery prime rib, creamy mashed potatoes, and stuffed-mushrooms capped with blue cheese. Look outside for the sculpture of a bear, a reference to when the inn served as a stagecoach stop used by 18th-century Spanish visitors, who named the area Bear Gulch (Arroyo de los Osos).

The **Magic Lamp Inn** (8189 Foothill Blvd., Rancho Cucamonga, 909/981-8659, www.themagiclampinn.com, 11:30am-9pm Mon., 11:30pm-10pm Tues.-Thurs., 11:30am-4pm and 5pm-10:30pm Fri., 5pm-10:30pm Sat., 10am-2pm and 4:30pm-9pm Sun., $15-40) has been serving steaks, seafood, and classic cocktails since 1955. They also have more than 400 bottles of wine as well as live entertainment and karaoke. The Magic Lamp Inn is almost across the street from the Sycamore Inn.

⚐ Back on 66

If you're not pressed for time, continue west on Foothill Boulevard for 11 miles through Claremont, Pomona, Laverne, and San Dimas to Glendora. If time is an issue, turn north on Euclid Avenue and make a right (west) on West 16th Street. From here, you can jump on I-210 west (Foothill Freeway) and exit at South Lone Hill Avenue (Exit 44) in Glendora. Turn right (north) and after 0.25 mile make a left on East Route 66.

Glendora

As you cruise through Glendora, make a point to stop at **The Donut Man** (915 E Rte. 66, Glendora, 626/335-9111, www. thedonutmanca.com, 24 hours daily), where they have been dishing out delectable morsels of fried dough for 42 years. Folks line up around the corner for their peach- and strawberry-stuffed doughnuts.

⚐ Back on 66

As you head 10 miles west to Monrovia, Foothill Boulevard turns into Huntington Drive as you reach Duarte. In 3 miles, after Route 66 becomes Huntington Drive, turn right (north) on Shamrock Avenue to follow the 1926 alignment. After one mile, turn left (west) on E. Foothill Boulevard into Monrovia.

Monrovia and Duarte

The **Aztec Hotel** (305 W. Foothill Blvd., Monrovia, 626/358-3231, www.aztec-hotelmonrovia.com) is one of the few remaining examples of Mayan Revivalist architecture in America. In 1925, architect Robert Stacy-Judd merged art deco sensibilities with Mayan hieroglyphs in a Spanish Colonial style. This rare historical landmark has faced foreclosure and undergone renovations, but the domed windows, light fixtures, tile floor, and fireplace are all original.

Le Roy's The Original (523 W. Huntington Dr., Duarte, 626/357-5076, 5:30am-3pm Mon.-Fri., 6am-3pm Sat.-Sun., $5-11) is a landmark eatery that serves breakfast all day and classic home-cooked comfort food for locals and travelers alike.

⚐ Back on 66

Follow Huntington Drive west for about 10 miles through San Marino and Arcadia. Huntington Drive turns into East Colorado Boulevard in Pasadena. Turn north onto Fair Oaks Avenue to visit the Fair Oaks Pharmacy. Along the way, consider a side trip to the Huntington Library.

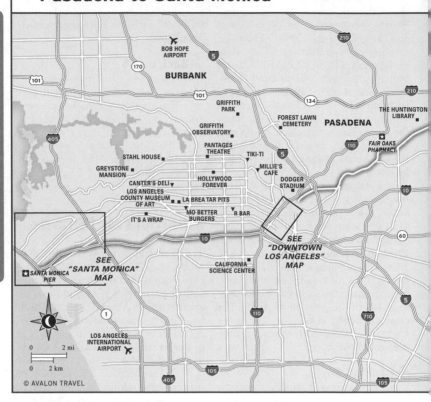

Pasadena to Santa Monica

BOB HOPE AIRPORT

BURBANK

GRIFFITH PARK

GRIFFITH OBSERVATORY

FOREST LAWN CEMETERY

PASADENA

THE HUNTINGTON LIBRARY

FAIR OAKS PHARMACY

PANTAGES THEATRE

TIKI-TI

STAHL HOUSE

MILLIE'S CAFE

DODGER STADIUM

GREYSTONE MANSION

CANTER'S DELI

HOLLYWOOD FOREVER

LOS ANGELES COUNTY MUSEUM OF ART

LA BREA TAR PITS

IT'S A WRAP

MO BETTER BURGERS

R BAR

SEE "DOWNTOWN LOS ANGELES" MAP

SEE "SANTA MONICA" MAP

SANTA MONICA PIER

CALIFORNIA SCIENCE CENTER

LOS ANGELES INTERNATIONAL AIRPORT

0   2 mi

0   2 km

© AVALON TRAVEL

⚑ Side Trip: Huntington Library

If the weather is nice and you have a couple of hours, make the side trip to visit the **Huntington Library, Art and Botanical Gardens** (1151 Oxford Rd., San Marino, 626/405-2100, www.huntington.org, noon-4:30pm Mon. and Wed.-Fri., 10:30am-4:30pm Sat.-Sun., $20-23). There are 120 acres of botanical gardens, including Japanese, English, desert, tropical, and Chinese. It's not on Route 66, but it's very close.

To get there from Huntington Drive, turn right on East California Boulevard and make a left on South Allen Avenue.

You'll make a second right on Orlando Road, then another right onto Oxford Road.

Pasadena

Sights
★ Fair Oaks Pharmacy

The **Fair Oaks Pharmacy** (1526 Mission St., South Pasadena, 626/799-1414, www.fairoakspharmacy.net, 9am-9pm Mon.-Sat., 10pm-7pm Sun.) is an old corner drug store where soda jerks have been pouring floats, phosphates, egg creams, and lime rickeys since 1915. In addition to the old-school soda fountain and restaurant, there's a fully functional pharmacy where you can consult with a clinical pharmacist about anything that ails you. It's the perfect place to pick up unique gifts, Route 66 memorabilia, greeting cards, bath and beauty products, retro toys, and rare vintage candies from Mary Jane's to Bit-O-Honey.

◆ Route 66: First End Point

To follow the original Route 66 from Pasadena into Los Angeles (and to avoid freeway traffic), drive south on Fair Oaks Avenue to where it dead-ends at Huntington Drive. Turn right (west) and drive 3.5 miles on Huntington Drive. Continue on North Mission Road for about 0.3 miles, then take a right (west) onto North Broadway. In 1.5 miles, stay right (don't follow Spring St.) to continue on Broadway. Drive 2.5 miles down Broadway to 7th Street, throw your arms in the air and celebrate. You did it—you've made it to the **first end point** of the original Route 66! But don't fret, it's not over just yet. Route 66 is the gift that keeps on giving.

There were actually *three endings* on Route 66 in Los Angeles. The first western terminus at 7th and Broadway Streets took place between 1926-1936. Later, the second terminus was extended further west to Santa Monica at the intersection of Olympic and Lincoln Boulevards. In 2009, the terminus was moved a third time to the Santa Monica Pier, where the Mother Road dead ends within view of the dramatic Pacific Ocean. Now in Hollywood-ease, that's an ending.

Los Angeles

Los Angeles is a huge metropolis of more than 10 million people living within 400 square miles. Apart from the traffic and the celebrities, the City of Angels is one of the most diverse places in the United States, with a multicultural synthesis of food, art, and architecture.

◆ Route 66 through Los Angeles

The major freeways into Los Angeles are I-405 and I-5, both of which run north-south, while the I-10 freeway, another major artery, runs east-west. Traffic is practically unavoidable in Los Angeles, but life will be easier if you stay off the freeways 7am-10am and 3pm-7pm Monday-Friday. We'll pick up Route 66 in downtown Los Angeles at the first terminus (S. Broadway and 7th Sts.).

Sights
Bradbury Building

The first Route 66 terminus is located in a historic theater district with beautiful old movie palaces that span about seven blocks along South Broadway, between 2nd Street and 9th Street. Take the time to check out the **Bradbury Building** (304 S. Broadway, Downtown, 213/626-1893). It may not look like much from the outside, but inside is a grand five-story cathedral of wrought iron, glass, and light. The Bradbury has been featured in numerous sci-fi and noir films, most notably in the climactic scene in *Blade Runner*.

Grand Central Market

Grand Central Market (317 S. Broadway, 213/624-2378, www.grandcentralmarket. com), located across the street from the Bradbury Building, is a Downtown landmark that celebrates the cultural cornucopia of Los Angeles. Open since 1917, it has 30,000 square feet of over 90 vendors, including grocers, butchers, baked goods, coffee, cheese, delis, and fishmongers.

El Pueblo de Los Angeles

El Pueblo de Los Angeles (125 Paseo de la Plaza and Cesar Chavez Blvd., Downtown) is a 44-acre district that celebrates the rich history, culture, and ethnicity that makes LA different from any other place on the planet. It's located in the oldest section of Los Angeles and consists of 27 historic buildings, including

the **Avila Adobe** (10 Olvera St.). The walls are almost three-feet thick, and it's the oldest surviving residence in Los Angeles. Also at the Pueblo are two outdoor plazas, museums, and a Mexican marketplace.

Union Station
The stunning and dramatic **Union Station** (800 N. Alameda St., near U.S. 101, Downtown, 213/485-6855) is the largest passenger terminal in the western United States and combines Dutch Colonial Revival, Mission Revival, and Streamline Moderne architecture. Walking through Union Station feels like stepping back into a noir film.

Velveteria
Tucked away on a side street in Chinatown is the quirky and surreal **Velveteria: The Museum of Velvet Art** (711 New High St., 503/309-9299, 11am-6pm Thurs.-Sun., $10). On exhibit are more than 400 awesomely weird velvet paintings, trinkets, and oddities of pop icons—from Elvis to TuPac. The Velveteria is just north of downtown. From Route 66 (Broadway St.), head east on Ord Street. After one block, take a left on New High Street.

Hollywood Forever Cemetery
Skip the throngs of tourists and panhandlers on the Hollywood Walk of Fame and celebrate the celebrities that have passed on at the **Hollywood Forever Cemetery** (6000 Santa Monica Blvd., Hollywood, 323/469-1181 www.hollywoodforever.com). Tour the 62 acres of manicured lawns, complete with peacocks and swans, and discover the final resting place of classic stars like Douglas Fairbanks and rockers like Johnny Ramone.

top to bottom: Grand Central Market, Los Angeles; The Last Bookstore, downtown Los Angeles; Fair Oaks Pharmacy, Pasadena

Downtown Los Angeles

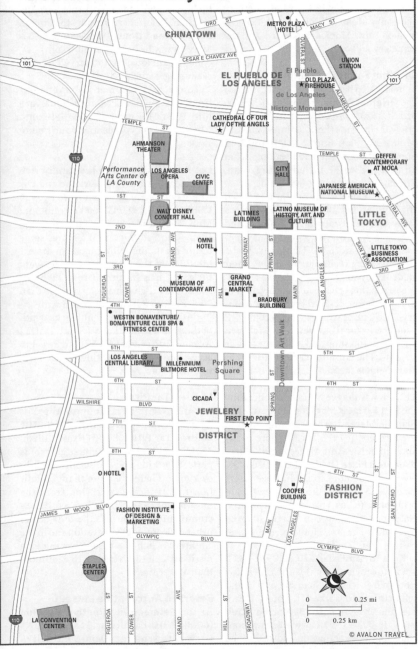

CHINATOWN

ORO ST

METRO PLAZA HOTEL

MACY ST

UNION STATION

OLVERA ST

CESAR E CHAVEZ AVE

EL PUEBLO DE LOS ANGELES

El Pueblo

OLD PLAZA
★ FIREHOUSE

de Los Angeles

Historic Monument

ALAMEDA ST

CATHEDRAL OF OUR
LADY OF THE ANGELS
★

TEMPLE ST

AHMANSON
THEATER

TEMPLE ST

GEFFEN
CONTEMPORARY
AT MOCA

Performance
Arts Center of
LA County

LOS ANGELES
OPERA

CIVIC
CENTER

CITY
HALL

JAPANESE AMERICAN
NATIONAL MUSEUM ★

1ST ST

WALT DISNEY
CONCERT HALL

LA TIMES
BUILDING

LATINO MUSEUM OF
HISTORY, ART, AND
CULTURE

LITTLE
TOKYO

CENTRAL AVE

2ND ST

GRAND AVE

OMNI
HOTEL

BROADWAY

SPRING ST

LITTLE TOKYO
BUSINESS
ASSOCIATION

SAN PEDRO ST

FIGUEROA ST

FLOWER ST

3RD ST

MUSEUM OF
CONTEMPORARY ART ★

HILL ST

GRAND
CENTRAL
MARKET

MAIN ST

LOS ANGELES ST

3RD ST

4TH ST

BRADBURY
BUILDING

4TH ST

WESTIN BONAVENTURE/
BONAVENTURE CLUB SPA &
FITNESS CENTER

Downtown Art Walk

5TH ST

LOS ANGELES
CENTRAL LIBRARY

MILLENNIUM
BILTMORE HOTEL

Pershing
Square

5TH ST

WILSHIRE BLVD

6TH ST

6TH ST

CICADA ▼

SPRING ST

JEWELERY

FIRST END POINT
★

7TH ST

7TH ST

DISTRICT

8TH ST

8TH ST

O HOTEL

8TH ST

WALL ST

SAN PEDRO ST

COOPER
BUILDING

FASHION
DISTRICT

JAMES M WOOD BLVD

9TH ST

FASHION INSTITUTE
OF DESIGN &
MARKETING

SPRING ST

LOS ANGELES ST

MAIN ST

OLYMPIC BLVD

OLYMPIC BLVD

STAPLES
CENTER

FIGUEROA ST

FLOWER ST

GRAND AVE

HILL ST

BROADWAY

0   0.25 mi

0   0.25 km

LA CONVENTION
CENTER

© AVALON TRAVEL

To reach Hollywood from downtown, hop on U.S. 101 north near Union Station and drive (or crawl) 4.5 miles north to the Santa Monica Boulevard exit. Head west on Santa Monica Boulevard, and the cemetery will be on the left.

Original Farmer's Market

To really step back in time, stroll through the **Original Farmer's Market** (6333 W. 3rd St., 323/933-9211 or 866/993-9211, www.farmersmarketla.com, 9am-9pm Mon.-Fri., 9am-8pm Sat., 10am-7pm Sun.), with more than 100 vendors from all over the world, including Brazilian, French, and Southern food stands.

In the 1880s, Arthur Gilmore settled the land at 3rd and Fairfax and ran a fairly successful dairy farm. Gilmore and his son struck oil in 1900 and his business, the Gilmore Oil Company, had a sly marketing technique of selling their trademark blue-green gas. By 1934, drilling regulations changed and they had to move. Gilmore decided to turn the property into a place where farmers could sell produce to local housewives. Eighteen farmers set up shop and it became a huge success. The Gilmore Family still owns and operates the market today.

Magee's Kitchen (stall 624, 323/938-4127, www.mageesnuts.com) became the first Farmers Market restaurant after Blanche Magee started serving lunch to the farmers in 1917. It's still here today and run by the same Magee family. **Patsy d'Amore's Pizza** (stall 448, 323/9384938, www.patsydamore.come) has been here for 66 years and was the first operation to bring pizza to Los Angeles. Frank Sinatra, Nat King Cole and Dean Martin all loved this place. The fresh tomato, garlic, and basil pizza is fabulous.

Kip's Toyland (stall 720, 323/939-8334, www.kipstoyland.com) is the oldest toy store in LA. It's been here since 1956 and sells vintage toys like Mr. Potato Head, Life, and Operation. **The Barbershop Club** (stall 116, 323/931-9916, www.barbershopclub.com) does things the old-fashioned

way. Owner Woody Lavell is a 3rd-generation barber and his staff is at the top of their craft, cutting in fades that look airbrushed. Before heading out stock up on **Bob's Coffee & Donuts** (stall 450, 323/933-8929, www.bobscoffeeanddoughnuts.com), a delicious, well-deserved treat in case you get stuck in traffic.

To reach the Farmer's Market, continue west on Santa Monica Boulevard into West Hollywood. Turn left onto North Fairfax Avenue and continue to West 3rd Street.

Los Angeles County Museum of Art

The locals call it LACMA, and the **Los Angeles County Museum of Art** (5905 Wilshire Blvd., 323/857-6000, 11am-5pm Mon.-Tues. and Thurs., 11am-8pm Fri., 10am-7pm Sat.-Sun., $15) features some of the most compelling modern art exhibitions in the country. Outside, walk through Chris Burden's Urban Light installation, which is made up of more than 200 cast iron antique street lamps.

LACMA is located eight blocks south of the Farmer's Market off South Fairfax Avenue. Turn right on West 6th Street to access the Pritzker parking garage ($12, free after 7pm).

La Brea Tar Pits

Located right next door to the Los Angeles County Museum of Art, **The La Brea Tar Pits** (5801 Wilshire Blvd., 323/857-6300, www.tarpits.org, free) is perfect for kids and the science geek in everyone. There are more than 5.5 million fossils in the collection from the most recent ice age, including a full skeleton of a mastodon. It's the only active urban paleontology excavation site in the country. Watch the excavators unearth fossils in a pit that's been active for more than 100 years.

Petersen Automotive Museum

At the **Petersen Automotive Museum** (6060 Wilshire Blvd., 323/930-2277, www.petersen.org, 10am-6pm daily), the history of the automobile is explored over four floors and more than 300,000 square feet of space. Historic and current examples of auto design and technology are features in rotating galleries and exhibits that display more than 150 rare and classic cars, trucks, race cars, concept cars, movie cars, and motorcycles.

To reach the museum, continue south on South Fairfax Avenue to Wilshire Boulevard.

Greystone Mansion

The **Greystone Mansion** (905 Loma Vista Dr., Beverly Hills, 310/550-4796, www.greystonemansion.org, 10am-5pm daily, free) is an elegant Tudor Revival mansion with 18 acres of lush, manicured English gardens. The mansion was built in 1927 by Edward L. Doheny, an oil tycoon, and has been featured in the films *The Big Lebowski, The Dark Knight, The Social Network, Ghostbusters,* and *There Will Be Blood.* Exteriors are open to the public via self-guided tours. The interiors can only be accessed by private tour (first Sat. Dec.-Apr, $15 per person, pre-registration required). No pets or picnicking is allowed.

Stahl House

Located high in the Hollywood hills, mid-century modern fanatics will love the **Stahl House** (1635 Woods Dr., Hollywood, 323/744-1635, $35-60), one of the most celebrated homes in the United States, made famous by Julius Shulman's photographs. The sleek modern marvel offers breathtaking views of Los Angeles. Viewings are available by reservation only and must be booked in advance. Parking restrictions apply.

Grammy Museum

Grammy Museum (800 W Olympic Blvd., 213/765-6800, www.grammymuseum.org) has dedicated four floors of exhibits that celebrate the best Grammy musicians and their contribution to American culture. It features vintage footage and interviews from a broad spectrum of artists who play everything from classical, pop, gospel, folk, country, hip-hop, Latin, jazz, and R&B.

From 7th Street and Broadway in downtown Los Angeles, drive southwest on Broadway for three blocks to Olympic. Turn right (northwest) and the Grammy Museum will be 0.5 mile near the corner of Figueroa Street.

California Science Center

California Science Center (700 Exposition Park Dr., 323/724-3623, 10am-5pm daily, http://californiasciencecenter.org, free) is one of the largest hands-on science museums on the West Coast. It features innovative, interactive exhibits, live demonstrations, and films in over 400,000 square feet of exhibitions that examine every type of life, from single-cell bacteria to the 100-trillion-cell human being. And the best part? Admission is free!

From downtown LA, head south on I-110. In less than 3 miles, take the Exposition Boulevard exit. Make a soft left at the bottom of the ramp onto Flower Street. Turn left (south) on Figueroa Street. The museum complex will be on the right.

Entertainment

The **Writer's Room** (6675 or 6685 Hollywood Blvd., Hollywood, 323/466-1900 or 323/491-4148, 10pm-2am Fri.-Sat.) is a former backroom speakeasy rumored to have served the famous writers who dined next door at Musso and Frank's Grill. It's not easy to find: From Cherokee Avenue, enter the parking lot behind Musso & Frank's Grill and head toward the parking attendant's booth; to the left is a double-door that leads to the Writer's Room. Once inside, ask nicely and they may make you the off-menu Blue Blazer, a flaming hot toddy.

The gothic **Chateau Marmont** (8171 Sunset Blvd., 323/656-1010, 6pm-2am daily), a castle that looms over Sunset Boulevard, is the perfect place to soak up the sinful atmosphere where troubled celebrities like John Belushi and badly behaved stars like Lindsay Lohan made national headlines.

Rainbow Bar (9015 Sunset Blvd., 310/278-4232, www.rainbowbarandgrill.com, 11am-2am daily) is one of LA's most famous rock bars. Alice Cooper, Led Zeppelin, Guns & Roses, Ringo Starr, John Lennon, and Keith Moon are rumored to have hung out upstairs. Slash's favorite booth is under his picture, and his guitar is on the wall.

R Bar (3331 W. 8th St., Koreatown, 213/387-7227, 7pm-2am daily) is a hip Koreatown dive with crazy karaoke nights, DJs, and special events. To get in, check their Facebook page (www.facebook.com/rbarktown) or twitter feed @ Rbarla for the password, which changes every two weeks.

Tiki Ti (4427 Sunset Blvd., Los Feliz, 323/669-9381 www.tiki-ti.com, 4pm-2am Wed.-Sat.) is a family-owned tiki-themed tavern and a Los Feliz favorite that's been serving almost 100 different kinds tropical drinks since 1961. The Blood and Sand cocktail, created for a Tyrone Power movie, is mixed with tequila, cherry, and orange juice. When ordered, a small motorized bull parades down the bar while locals chant, *"Toro! Toro! Olé! Olé!"*

The **Varnish** (118 E. 6th St., Downtown, 213/622-9999, 7pm-2am daily) is a 1920s speakeasy tucked away behind the legendary Coles restaurant. Classic drinks from the 1890s are served in frozen glassware, with blocked ice and fresh juices, while a standup bassist and pianist provide atmosphere. During prohibition, gangster Mikey Cohen is rumored to have held meetings in the back, where the Varnish is located now.

Good Times at Davey Wayne's (1611 N. El Centro Ave., Hollywood, 323/962-3804, www.goodtimesatdaveywaynes.com, 5pm-2am Mon.-Fri., 2pm-2am Sat.-Sun.) is the ultimate throwback to the 1970s. Cleverly hidden from plain view, a secret "refrigerator door" entrance is located in the back of a garage. Inside, drinks are named after '70s songs, Coors is served in coffee mugs, and liquor-spiked snow cones take you back to one of the coolest decades.

The Wiltern (3790 Wilshire Blvd., Koreatown, 213/388-1400, www.wiltern.com, parking $20) is a beautiful and intimate art deco theater with great acoustics. Everyone from Devo to Tony Bennett has played here. With fewer than 2,000 seats, tickets sell out quickly.

Chill Out at The Dime (442 N. Fairfax Ave., West Hollywood, 323/651-4421, www.thedimela.net, 7pm-1:30am Tues.-Sat., 6pm-1:30am Sun.-Mon.) spins down-to-earth, old-school hip-hop in a cool dive.

Hollywood Pantages Theater (6233 Hollywood Blvd., Hollywood, 323/468-1770) is a gorgeous art deco hall featuring the best Broadway productions, music, and live entertainment. This iconic venue has the timeless essence of Hollywood's glamour and is steeped in history.

See a movie at the restored 1922 **Grauman's Egyptian Theater** (6712 Hollywood Blvd., Hollywood, 323/461-2020, www.americancinemathequecalendar.com), an early example of a majestic movie theater located on Hollywood's Walk of Fame.

During the heyday of Route 66, **Barney's Beanery** (8447 Santa Monica Blvd., 323/654-2287, www.barneysbeanery.com, 11am-2pm Mon.-Fri., 9am-2am Sat.-Sun.) would take customers' license plates as collateral for food. Some returned, paid their bill, and got their license plate back—some didn't. The owner decorated the ceiling with the left license plates and they're still there today (some date back 80 years). Today, Barney's is primarily a sports bar with more than 200 beers, couches, bar seating, and pub fare.

Shopping

The Downtown **LA Fashion district** spans 90 blocks with more than 1,000 stores.

The Fashion district extends from 7th and Los Angeles Streets north, west from Broadway and Spring Streets, from I-10 south, and east from San Pedro Street north of 9th Street. The best day to go is on Saturday, when wholesale stores sell to the public. Samples go for 40-70 percent off retail. Stores marked "Solo Mayoreo" means they are not open to the public. For knockoff designer labels, go to **Santee Alley** (Olympic Blvd. between Santee St. and Maple Ave.). For a more traditional shopping experience, check out **Morrie's** (934 S. Maple Ave., 213/623-3083). Pico Boulevard between Main Street and Santee Street is like a discounted Rodeo Drive. It's still pricey, but the quality is sublime.

Olvera Street (125 Paseo de la Plaza, Downtown, 10am-7pm daily) is a world-renowned Mexican marketplace that has been in operation for more than 75 years. It's lined with historic buildings, authentic Mexican restaurants, and vendor stalls selling everything from leather goods to artwork, clothing, imported crafts, candles, traditional Mexican wares, and colorful souvenirs.

The Last Bookstore (453 S. Spring St., Downtown, 213/488-0599, 10am-10pm Mon.-Thurs., 10am-11pm Fri.-Sat., 10am-6pm Sun.) is a bibliophile's dream with more than 10,000 square feet of vintage books, new releases, and vinyl. Don't miss the Labyrinth, on the mezzanine level, with more than 100,000 books all priced at $1 each.

Bar Keeper (3910 W. Sunset Blvd., Silver Lake, 323/669-1675, www.barkeepersilverlake.com, 11am-6pm Sun.-Thurs., 11am-7pm Fri.-Sat.) has 2,700 bar tools, rare liquors, mid-century glassware, and more than 100 aromatic bitters. It's a candy store for boozehounds and a mecca for mixologists.

Comic book fans shouldn't miss **Secret Headquarters** (3817 W. Sunset Blvd., Silver Lake, www.thesecretheadquarters.com, 11am-9pm Mon.-Sat., noon-7pm Sun.). It's one of the coolest, classiest comic-book stores in the country with comfy leather chairs, art on the walls, and a great selection of graphic novels and indie comics displayed on beautiful dark wood shelving.

Wacko (4633 Hollywood Blvd., Los Feliz, 323/663-0122, 11am-7pm Mon.-Wed., 11am-9pm Thurs.-Sat., noon-7pm Sun.) is one of the coolest places to shop for gifts for the young, the old, and the inspired. They have hard-to-find toys, gag gifts, T-shirts, puzzles, books, and knickknacks. Don't forget to check out the **La Luz de Jesus Gallery** in the back.

It's a Wrap (1164 S. Robertson Blvd., Hollywood, 310/246-9727, 10am-8pm Mon.-Fri., 11am-6pm Sat.-Sun.) is technically a thrift shop, but that's in an "only in LA" kind of way. They sell clothing, furniture, props, and collectibles used in film and TV productions. It's pricier than Goodwill but unlike anything you'll find anywhere else.

The Grove (189 The Grove Dr., 323/900-8080, www.thegrovela.com, 10am-9pm Mon.-Thurs., 10am-10pm Fri.-Sat., 11am-8pm Sun.) adjoins the historic Farmers Market. This mid- to upscale outdoor mall has a trolley that takes passengers to 40 stores, 9 restaurants, and a 12-screen movie theater.

Recreation

Explore LA on foot and take a **Los Angeles Conservancy Walking Tour** (523 W. 6th St., Suite 826, 213/623-2489, www.laconservancy.org/walking-tours, $10). Tours cover LA's most-celebrated architectural marvels and reveal history from when the city was founded in 1781 to the present day.

Stretch your legs and lounge, picnic, and take a two-mile stroll around the **Silver Lake Reservoir** (1854 Silver Lake Blvd.), with great views, and see if you can spot a couple of Richard Neutra houses perched above the lake in the hills.

If you're a fan of Laurel and Hardy, the **Music Box Steps** (936 N. Vendome St., Silver Lake) are the actual staircase

Classic LA Drives

Mulholland Drive winds 24 miles through the Santa Monica Mountains along the crest of the Hollywood Hills with amazing views. Jack Nicholson and Warren Beatty live on this iconic, classic road, which inspired the 2001 David Lynch film of the same name. From U.S. 101, take the Cahuenga exit and follow the signs. Drive west until you get to I-405 (San Diego Freeway) and go south to head back to Los Angeles. Allow at least an hour for the drive.

The **Pacific Coast Highway** (locals call it PCH) is a signature LA drive that winds up and down the Pacific coastline with soul-stirring ocean views. Take Santa Monica Boulevard (Route 66) to Ocean Avenue, turn right (north), and merge left onto the Pacific Coast Highway (SR-1). If you're short on time, Malibu is a good place to stop for lunch and turn around.

where they attempt to carry a piano up a steep flight of steps. It's a secluded but public staircase with about 130 steps in the hills of Silver Lake.

After a hearty breakfast, take a hike in **Griffith Park** (4730 Crystal Springs Dr., 323/913-4688) to walk off those pancakes. Griffith Park is the second largest urban park in the country. The **Griffith Park Observatory** (2800 E. Observatory Rd., 213/473-0800) has public solar telescopes, a planetarium, a café, exhibits, a bookstore, and spectacular views of Los Angeles. Admission and parking are free.

Runyon Canyon (2000 N. Fuller Ave., Hollywood, 323/666-5046) is a 160-acre park with a variety of hiking trails that offer spectacular views of the Hollywood sign, the Griffith Observatory, and downtown Los Angeles. Parking is difficult, so you might want to leave extra time or plan to park farther away and walk to the canyon.

Accommodations

Elaines' Hollywood B&B (1616 N. Sierra Bonita Ave., Hollywood, 323/850-0766, www.elaineshollywoodbedandbreakfast. com, $100-200, cash only) is a renovated 1910 bungalow on a palm tree-lined street walking distance from the Hollywood Walk of Fame. Some rooms have a canopy bed and a private sundeck.

The **Ace Hotel** (929 S. Broadway, Downtown, 213/623-3233, www.acehotel.

com/losangeles, from $180-500) is a luxury boutique hotel in the historic 1927 United Artists building. Rooms have an industrial-chic vibe with exposed wood-beam ceilings, sleek low-slung beds, and custom Revo radios; some rooms have acoustic Martin guitars. Located downtown, it is walking distance to the original terminus of Route 66.

The **Magic Castle Hotel** (7025 Franklin Ave., Hollywood, 323/851-0800, www. magiccastlehotel.com, $190-350) offers apartment-style suites with kitchens. Rooms are spacious and modern, with crisp white walls, comfortable beds, and well-stocked kitchens. It's walking distance to grocery stores and includes lots of free stuff, such as movies, Wi-Fi, snacks, and continental breakfast.

★ **Hotel Figueroa** (939 S. Figueroa St., Downtown, 213/627-8971, $109-259) is a beautiful and historic Moroccan-themed hotel with eclectic accents, bold, rich colors, tile floors, unusual textiles, and ornate chandeliers. Rooms are swathed in bold jewel-tones and the romantic wrought-iron head boards evoke old-school glamour.

Farmer's Daughter (115 S. Fairfax Ave., 800/344-1658, www.farmersdaughterhotel.com, $206-369) is an adorable 1950s-inspired boutique motel. Rooms are decked out in denim fabric with hardwood floors, spacious desks, gingham curtains, paintings of barnyard animals, and country-style rugs. Some have rocking chairs and rain shower-heads. It's located right across the street from the Farmer's Market and the Grove shopping center.

The **Redbury Hollywood** (1717 Vine St., Hollywood, 877/613-0772, www. theredbury.com, $199-404) is a whimsical yet plush all-suite luxury hotel with well-stocked kitchenettes and a sophisticated lounge. Rooms feature heavily patterned textiles, deep-red walls, colorful couches, old record players, kitchens, and private balconies. Vine suites offer views of signature LA icons like the Capitol Building, the Hollywood Sign, and the Griffith Observatory.

★ **The Line** (3515 Wilshire Blvd., Koreatown, 213/381-7411, www.theline-hotel.com, $179-439) is a slickly modern hotel with concrete walls, plush textiles, original artwork, and rooms with views of the Hollywood Hills. On-site restaurants include the Commissary and Pot, both run by Roy Choi, a talented chef who reinvented the food truck movement. It's centrally located between downtown and Beverly Hills, right in the heart of Koreatown.

Food

★ **Clifton's** (648 Broadway, 213/627-1673, www.cliftonsla.com, 11am-2am Mon.-Fri., 10am-2pm Sat.-Sun., $10-25) is full of atmosphere, intrigue, taxidermy, and incredible history. This classic cafeteria-style restaurant opened in 1935, closed in 2011, and underwent a $10 million renovation to reopen in 2015. Owner Clifford Clinton followed what he called the "The Cafeteria Golden Rule." He never turned away anyone who was hungry, allowing customers to pay what they could afford. The large, unusual cafeteria covers five floors with a giant fake redwood tree rising through the center. Items include cafeteria comfort food, such as mac and cheese, peas and carrots, mashed potatoes, and throwback desserts like Jello.

In the evening, there's a full bar serving classic concoctions; a 250-pound meteorite sits on the bar.

Clifton's main branch (618 Olive St.) was listed in the Negro Motorist Green Book and served blacks during Jim Crow. It's located at 7th and Broadway, the original terminus of Route 66, making it the perfect place to celebrate the end to a long and wonderfully strange trip.

Philippe's (1001 N. Alameda St., Downtown, 213/628-3781, 6am-10pm daily, $5-10, cash only) is a classic cafeteria-style restaurant that has been dishing out French dip sandwiches, kosher pickles, hearty soups, tangy coleslaw, homemade spicy mustard, and pickled eggs since 1908. To place your order, jump in any of the 10 lines, and sit anywhere you like.

The front door at the **Original Pantry** (877 S. Figueroa St., Downtown, 213/972-9279, www.pantrycafe.com, open 24 hours daily, $5-28, cash only) has no key because this place hasn't closed since it opened in 1924. Twenty-four hours a day, seven days a week, this Los Angeles landmark has served perfectly crisp hash browns, bacon, and fluffy, perfectly griddled pancakes. Ask for the homemade salsa; it's a tasty compliment to the succulent sausage patties and thick-cut sourdough bread. There's usually a line on the weekends and at lunchtime. It's even busy at 2am, but it's worth the wait. Once you sit down, don't wait for a menu; everything you need to know is on the wall. There's a parking lot across the street for $2 with validation.

Millie's Café (3524 W. Sunset Blvd., Silver Lake, 323/664-0404, www.mil-liescafe.net, 7:30am-4pm daily, $7-12) opened in 1926, the same year Route 66 was born. The bread is baked fresh every day; they use real butter and hormone-free dairy and grind each pot of French-roast coffee to perfection. They take the time to make everything the old-fashioned way, from scratch, and it shows.

Sip sublime martinis with a juicy

steak while you soak in the history at **Musso & Frank Grill** (6667 Hollywood Blvd., Hollywood, 323/467-7788, www.mussoandfrank.com, 11am-11pm Tues.-Sat., $20-49). They have been serving Hollywood's A list since 1919. Chaplin, Garbo, Bogart, and Bacall lounged in red leather booths and hobnobbed with literary legends like F. Scott Fitzgerald and William Faulkner, who mixed his own mint juleps behind the mahogany bar. Today it's still a place to see and been seen. *Mad Men* filmed an episode onsite and also celebrated their premier party here.

In 1930, **Pinks Hot Dogs** (709 N. La Brea Ave., 323/931-7594, www.pinkshollywood.com, 9:30am-2am Sun.-Thurs., 9:30am-3am Fri.-Sat., $4-10) opened as a push-cart food stand back before food trucks were trendy. Today, people drive from all over southern California to eat one of the more than 30 different types of hot dogs to choose from (you can't go wrong with the chili cheese). It's busy day and night.

For a burger like no other, go to ★ **Mo Better Burgers** (901 S. La Brea Ave., 11:30am-5pm Wed. and Fri., noon-5pm Sat., $5-8). If you don't eat meat, try the delicious vegan tacos with creamy avocado, and have some patience—everything is cooked to order.

An impressive collection of **Food Trucks** lines up on Wilshire Boulevard near Fairfax Avenue, outside the Los Angeles County Museum of Art. From the Thai Fusion Arroy truck to Blazing Burgers and Vietnamese Banh Mi Sandwiches to Cool Haus ice cream, it's the most eclectic selection of food that can be found in one block. To find other food trucks in the city (like Koji, LA's best Korean taco truck), check www.roaminghunger.com for schedules and locations.

Huge pastrami and mouthwatering corned beef sandwiches can't be beat at **Canter's Deli** (419 N. Fairfax Ave., 213/651-2030, 24 hours daily, $7-25). This third-generation family owned business has attracted famous politicians, rock stars (Guns N' Roses used to hang out here), and regular folks since 1931. There is free parking with validation on the corner lot.

It's not hard to find good sushi these days, but with so many places to choose from, ★ **Sushi by H** (480 S. San Vicente Blvd., Beverly Hills, 323/782-0547, www.harusushicafe.com, 5:30pm-10pm Mon., 11:30am-2:30pm and 5:30pm-10pm Tues.-Fri., noon-2:30pm and 5:30pm-10pm Sat., $10-25) stands out as one of the best reasonably priced options. Head chef Iwata goes the extra mile by shopping for the freshest organic ingredients every day. The thinly sliced carpaccio specials are creative, flavorful, and unforgettable.

✇ Back on 66

While Santa Monica Boulevard technically follows Route 66, it's also one of the most congested roads in the city. From Los Angeles, I-10 is the quickest way to get to Santa Monica and the next terminus of Route 66. However, the rush hours of 7am-10am and 3pm-7pm Monday-Friday should be avoided. If your travel falls during these times, take Olympic Boulevard instead.

Take I-10 heading west. Cross under I-405 and in approximately 3 miles, turn right (northwest) onto 4th Street. Turn left (southwest) at the next street, which is Colorado Avenue. The entrance to the Santa Monica Pier is a few blocks straight ahead.

Santa Monica

✇ Route 66 Ends

The second "official" ending point of Route 66, at the corner of Lincoln Boulevard and Olympic Boulevard, isn't the most exciting place, but for purists who want to know where it ended, this is it.

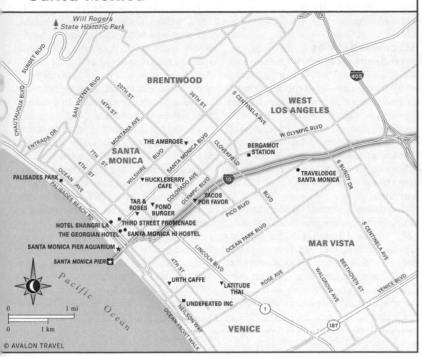

Santa Monica

Sights
★ Santa Monica Pier

Everything must come to an end—even Route 66—so it may as well be at a carnival floating above the Pacific Ocean. Walk the famed 1909 **Santa Monica Pier** (200 Santa Monica Pier, 310/458-8901, www.santamonicapier.org, open daily) to shop, people-watch, and breathe in the salty ocean air while you wait in line to ride the world's first solar-powered Ferris wheel. Free historic walking tours are offered on the weekend, and there is parking on the pier deck, accessible via the ramp at Ocean Avenue and Colorado Avenue.

Camera Obscura

The camera obscura is believed to date back to the ancient Greeks, and may have been used by Renaissance painters to project images onto their canvases as a guide. There are only a handful of public camera obscuras left in North America. This **Camera Obscura** (1450 Ocean Ave., 9am-2pm Mon.-Fri., 11am-4pm Sat., free) is hidden away in the Senior Recreation Center, near the Santa Monica Pier.

Bergamot Station

Bergamot Station (2525 Michigan Ave., 310/453-7535, 10am-6pm Tues.-Fri., 11am-5:30pm Sat., free) is the largest art gallery complex and cultural center in Southern California. The Santa Monica Museum of Art, several architecture and design firms, and a café are on-site.

Palisades Park

Get some fresh air at **Palisades Park** (Ocean Ave. and Washington Ave.). It's a great place grab a bite from a food truck and sit on a bench to people-watch—they're dancing, running, walking dogs—with the Pacific ocean as the perfect backdrop.

Accommodations

Hotel Shangri-La (1301 Ocean Ave., 310/394-2791, $350-500) is an architectural Streamline Moderne gem that is shaped like an enormous ocean liner. Rooms are tastefully decorated with plush, jewel-toned comforters, flat-panel televisions, and ocean-facing windows that let in the Pacific breeze. A pool, hot tub, spa, and rooftop bar with 180-degree views of the Pacific Ocean round out the amenities.

The **Georgian Hotel** (1415 Ocean Ave., 800/617-1529, www.georgianhotel.com, $289-389) is a timeless Santa Monica landmark that blends vintage glamour with modern amenities. Rooms are painted in warm neutral tones, with work desks and seating areas with ocean views. An evening turn-down service spoils guests, while a special treat, water bowl, or toy and treat will spoil your pet.

Ambrose (1255 20th St., 310/315-1555, $250) is a relaxing and elegant eco-boutique hotel. Rooms feature hardwood floors, vaulted ceilings with fans, spacious bathrooms, and balconies. Amenities include a complimentary organic continental breakfast, Intelligentsia coffee, and taxi service within a three-mile radius of the hotel.

Lodging is expensive in Santa Monica, so the **Santa Monica HI Hostel** (1436 2nd St., 310/393-9913, $50) is a godsend to those on a budget. Relatively spacious rooms are filled with natural sunlight; the bunk-bed mattresses are comfortable and the shared bathrooms are clean and well maintained. Modern and clean common areas offer movies and Internet access, with a kitchen, laundry, and breakfast available. Plus it's only two blocks from the beach.

The **Travelodge Santa Monica** (3102 Pico Blvd., 800/535-5440, $150) is an

Santa Monica Pier

affordable option, with comfortable beds, nice-size baths, and a friendly staff. Free Wi-Fi and parking are available.

Food

Flavorful soups and spicy stir-fries are popular at **Latitude Thai** (2906 Lincoln Blvd., 310/396-4726, 11am-9:30pm Mon. and Wed.-Fri., noon-9:30pm Sat.-Sun., $7-17). Creative dishes like garlic prawns with spinach noodles and pumpkin chicken curry with brown rice are local faves.

Pono Burger (829 Broadway, 310/584-7005, www.ponoburger.com, 11am-9pm Sun.-Thurs., 11am-10pm Fri.-Sat., $9-15) is one of the best burger joints in town. The surprisingly delicious salted caramel shake with bacon is unlike anything you'll find elsewhere. Free parking is available in an underground lot through the alley off Broadway between 8th and 9th Streets.

There's almost always a line at the beloved **Huckleberry Bakery and Cafe** (1014 Wilshire Blvd., 310/451-2311, 8am-8pm Mon.-Fri., 8am-5pm Sat.-Sun., $9-15), but the maple bacon biscuits and blueberry cornmeal pancakes are worth the wait.

Tacos Por Favor (1406 Olympic Blvd., 310/392-5768, 8am-8pm daily, $3-13) serves exquisite, authentic, and fresh Mexican food at rock-bottom prices. Excellent carne asada tacos, brilliant burritos, and the green sauce are all amazing.

Urth Caffé (2327 Main St., 310/314-7040, 6am-11pm Sun.-Thurs., 6am-midnight Fri.-Sat., $7-15) serves a good selection of fresh, healthy, organic options for breakfast and lunch, along with smoothies, coffee, and teas.

Tasty tapas and innovative seasonal specialties are all the rave at **Tar and Roses** (602 Santa Monica Blvd., 602/587-0700, www.tarandroses.com, 5:30pm-10:30pm Mon.-Sat., 5:30pm-9:30pm Sun., $22-60). Choose from oxtail dumplings, duck, or venison.

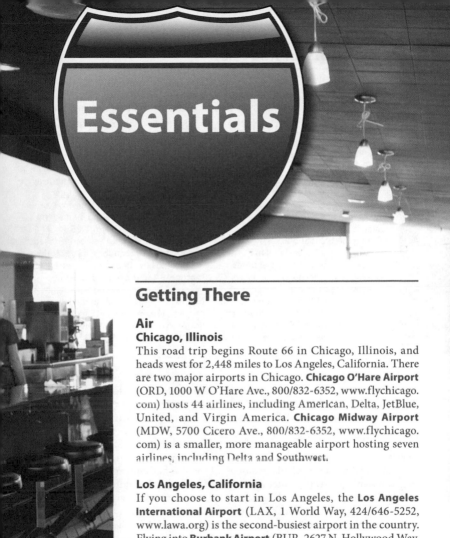

Getting There

Air
Chicago, Illinois
This road trip begins Route 66 in Chicago, Illinois, and heads west for 2,448 miles to Los Angeles, California. There are two major airports in Chicago. **Chicago O'Hare Airport** (ORD, 1000 W O'Hare Ave., 800/832-6352, www.flychicago. com) hosts 44 airlines, including American, Delta, JetBlue, United, and Virgin America. **Chicago Midway Airport** (MDW, 5700 Cicero Ave., 800/832-6352, www.flychicago. com) is a smaller, more manageable airport hosting seven airlines, including Delta and Southwest.

Los Angeles, California
If you choose to start in Los Angeles, the **Los Angeles International Airport** (LAX, 1 World Way, 424/646-5252, www.lawa.org) is the second-busiest airport in the country. Flying into **Burbank Airport** (BUR, 2627 N. Hollywood Way, Burbank, 818/840-8840), also called the Bob Hope Airport, may be a better option.

Las Vegas, Nevada
Las Vegas McCarran International Airport (LAS, 5757 Wayne Newton Blvd., 702/261-5211, www.mccarran.com) hosts American, British Airways, Delta, Edelweiss, JetBlue, Southwest, United, Virgin Atlantic, and 22 others. Las Vegas is about a two-hour drive north of Needles, California, and 103 miles west of Kingman, Arizona.

Albuquerque, New Mexico
Albuquerque International Sunport (ABQ, 2200 Sunport

The History of Route 66

Route 66 was born on November 11, 1926, right before the Great Depression and the Dust Bowl. At the time, only 800 miles of the 2,448-mile road was paved. The remaining 1,500 miles comprised gravel, bricks, graded dirt, and wood planks. It took 11 more years before the entire road was paved—and it couldn't happen quickly enough. In 1921, there were approximately 9 million cars on the road; by 1929, there were more than 26 million—an estimated one car for every four people in the United States.

During the 1920s and 1930s, Route 66 quicky became a "road of dreams" and symbolized a pathway to easier times. Gas stations, motor courts, and diners dished out hospitality to thousands of emigrants, and with few resources and a little hope they motored west in search of a better life. Route 66's diagonal trajectory across the country offered quick access to California, like a shortcut to freedom.

In the 1940s, the asphalt was thickened along parts of Route 66 in Illinois and Missouri to handle military convoys during World War II. During postwar times, vacationers cruised kitschy tepee motels, trading posts, and Wild West theme parks.

In 1959, Eisenhower's Federal Highway Act changed everything. The bigger, faster four-lane interstate highway system bypassed Route 66 and marked the beginning of its demise. In 1985, Route 66 was decommissioned. Businesses closed and towns were abandoned. The Mother Road could have become a forgotten footnote—but the spirit of Route 66 lives on. Life is percolating once again on this beloved highway as revitalization projects, like the National Park Service Route 66 Corridor Preservation Program, breathe new life into historic Route 66.

Blvd., 505/244-7700, www.abqsunport.com) is located just a few miles from Route 66, with nonstop service to 23 cities via Alaska, American, Delta, JetBlue, Southwest, and United Airlines.

Train

Since part of Route 66 was laid out alongside the Santa Fe train route, **Amtrak** (800/872-7245, www.amtrak.com) offers easy access to the Mother Road. **Chicago's Union Station** (210 S. Canal St., 5am-1am daily) is the third-busiest rail station in the U.S. and operates as a major hub for Amtrak with service to cities throughout country. Amtrak's California stations are located along Route 66 in **Needles** (900 Front St.), **Barstow** (685 N. 1st Ave.), **Victorville** (16858 S. D. St.), **San Bernardino** (1170 W. 3rd St.), and **Los Angeles** (800 N. Alameda St.).

The *Southwest Chief* route travels west from Chicago to Los Angeles with stops in Albuquerque (320 1st St. SW) and Gallup (201 E. Hwy. 66), New Mexico; through Winslow (303 E. 2nd St.), Flagstaff (1 E. Rte. 66), Williams (Railroad Ave. at Rte. 66), and Kingman (402 Andy Devine Ave.), Arizona; and ending at Union Station in Los Angeles.

The *Texas Eagle* route travels south from Chicago to St. Louis, Missouri, with stops in Joliet, Pontiac, Normal, Lincoln, and Springfield. Amtrak also offers a 14-day **Route 66 By Rail tour** (www.amtrakvacations.com, call for fares) that starts in Chicago with stops in St. Louis, Albuquerque, Williams, the Grand Canyon, and Los Angeles. The *Heartland Flyer* makes daily trips from Oklahoma City (100 S. E. K. Gaylord Blvd.), Oklahoma, to Fort Worth, Texas.

Other major stations located near Route 66 include downtown **St. Louis** (430 S. 15th St.), Missouri.

Bus

Greyhound Bus (www.greyhound.com) lines don't follow Route 66 entirely, but there are stations located along the way. The Greyhound station in **Chicago** (630 W. Harrison St., 800/231-2222) offers service to all major U.S. cities. California stations are located in **San Bernardino** (596 N. G St., 909/884-4796) and **Los Angeles** (1716 E. 7th St., 213/629-8401). Other stations include:

Oklahoma: Oklahoma City (1948 E. Reno Ave., 405/606-4382) and Tulsa (317 S. Detroit Ave., 918/584-4428)

New Mexico: Tucumcari (McDonalds, 2608 S. 1st. St., 575/461-1350), Albuquerque (320 1st St. SW, 505/247-0246), and Gallup (Route 66 Mini Mart, 3060 W. Hwy. 66, 505/863-9078)

Arizona: Holbrook (101 Mission Lane, 928/524-3832), Flagstaff (880 E. Butler Ave., 928/774-4573) and Kingman (953 W. Beale Ave., 928/753-1818)

Car Rental

Route 66 travels through many remote areas, so if renting a car, stick with these major chains, which have locations throughout the United States in case you need roadside assistance or have to switch cars.

Alamo (800/462-5266, www.alamo.com)

Avis (800/633-3469, www.avis.com)

Budget (800/218-7992, www.budget.com)

Dollar (800/800-4000, www.dollar.com)

Enterprise (800/261-7331, www.enterprise.com)

National (888/826-6890, www.nationalcar.com)

Hertz (800/654-3131, www.hertz.com)

Thrifty (800/334-1705, www.thrifty.com)

To rent a car, you must have a valid driver's license and be at least 21 years old. (Some companies add a surcharge for those ages 21-25). Multiple drivers may incur an additional charge of $5-7 per day. Airport locations usually have the largest fleet to choose from and often

top to bottom: Route 66 gas station, Illinois; Oatman Highway; railroad station in Kingman, Arizona

Desert Driving Tips

In an episode of *Peanuts*, Snoopy's brother Spike put his trademark Fedora into a time capsule but reconsidered after he nearly froze to death on a cold desert night. Let that be a lesson to you: The desert can be deadly, so come prepared.

* Use caution when driving on dirt roads and avoid driving on soft sand; it's very easy to get stuck.

* Watch and listen for flash floods and avoid driving through flooded areas.

* Do not rely on GPS in remote desert areas, as the directions are notoriously unreliable. It's always best to have a print map on hand as a guide.

* Always travel with plenty of water, gas, and layers of clothing (70°F days can drop to 20°F at night).

offer unlimited mileage. Most importantly, shop around for the best out-of-state drop-off rate, which can climb to a whopping $1,000.

Car rental fees may change drastically with seemingly no rhyme or reason. To save money, consider renting a hybrid vehicle, which can cut the gas bill in half. A 4WD vehicle is not needed for this road trip, and is not recommended due to high gas consumption.

Road Rules

Since there are so many alignments of Route 66, it is possible to drive practically any type of vehicle on it. People have driven RVs on Route 66 since the 1920s. However, with 15 percent of the road gone, many old alignments have been reduced to dirt and gravel. Jerry McClanahan's *EZ66 Guide for Travelers* offers helpful tips on taking some of the older dirt alignments.

Since Route 66 passes through cities and along tight winding roads, RVs are not recommended for the complete route, as motorhomes can make driving and parking more of an endurance test than a fun road trip. In addition, much of the fun of driving Route 66 includes eating in roadside diners and staying in quirky motels.

For experienced motorcyclists, driving Route 66 this can be a wonderful way

to see the United States. Thousands of motorcyclists have taken to the Mother Road, and there are several motorcycle tours that travel Route 66. A large community of bikers often meets up at points along the way. **Eagle Riders** (877/557-3541, www.eaglerider.com) offers 15-day tours and also rents Harleys, Indians, Hondas, and BMWs.

Adventure Cycling Association (www.adventurecycling.org, $15.75 per map) created one of the first comprehensive Route 66 bicycle maps. Six cartographers, four researchers, and cooperation from state tourism bureaus contributed to the waterproof map with turn-by-turn directions and essential lodging information, hardware stores, grocery stores, and libraries with free Internet access.

Driving and Highway Safety

When driving Route 66, be a courteous, considerate driver. There are many two-lane stretches on Route 66; when driving on highways, stay to the right and use the left lane for passing. Earlier alignments have tight turns and slower speed limits, and require more effort and attention to the road.

Take special care when driving on American Indian lands; each community has its own guidelines, rules, and judicial system. In addition, many people walk along roads in these communities, so drive carefully and pay close attention to the speed limits.

If driving your own car, have a mechanic examine the belts, lights, and turn signals; check all fluid levels, including oil, brakes, coolant (you'll need this driving through the desert), and power steering. Tires should have at least 2/32-inch tread, and check the tire pressure before and during your trip. Check the tire pressure when cold, as hot tires expand and can yield a false PSI reading.

If your car breaks down in a remote area, pull off to the right side of the road; if the car stalls on the road, put the car in neutral and coast or push it off to the right side of the highway. If you have cell service, contact **AAA** (800/222-4357, www.aaa.com) or the rental car company emergency number. Put on your hazard lights while waiting for help; if it's night, turn on the inside ceiling light and keep the car running to avoid draining the battery while you wait for help to arrive.

In the event that you are stranded, be prepared for any kind of weather. Always travel with water, blankets, a first-aid kit, and nonperishable food items such as protein bars or jerky.

Gas

When driving Route 66, don't let the gas tank dip below a half tank and fuel up in major towns whenever possible. Illinois, Missouri, and Oklahoma have several small towns with gas stations, but in Texas, New Mexico, Arizona, and California, there are long stretches of Route 66 with limited or no services. Keep an eye on the gas gauge.

Visas and Officialdom

Passports and Visas

Visitors from other countries must have a **valid passport** and a **visa.** Visitors with current passports from one of the following countries qualify for the **visa waivers:** Andorra, Australia, Austria, Belgium, Brunei, Chile, Czech Republic, Denmark, Estonia, Finland, France, Germany, Greece, Hungary, Iceland, Ireland, Italy, Japan, Latvia, Liechtenstein, Lithuania, Luxembourg, Malta, Monaco, the Netherlands, New Zealand, Norway, Portugal, San Marino, Singapore, Slovakia, Slovenia, South Korea, Spain, Sweden, Switzerland, Taiwan, and the United Kingdom. They must apply online with the Electronic System for Travel Authorization at www.cbp.gov and hold a **return plane ticket** to their home countries less than 90 days from the time of entry. Holders of **Canadian passports** don't need visas or waivers. In most countries, the local U.S. embassy can provide a **tourist visa.** Plan for at least two weeks for visa processing, longer during the busy summer season (June-Aug.). More information is available online at http://travel.state.gov.

If you lose your passport, visit the **U.S. Department of State** (www.usembassy.gov) to find an embassy from your home country to help.

When you drive across the state line into California, there is an agricultural checkpoint; do not bring any fresh fruit or plants into the state.

Customs

Foreigners and U.S. citizens age 21 or older may import (free of duty) the following: 1 liter of alcohol; 200 cigarettes (one carton); 50 cigars (non-Cuban); and $100 worth of gifts.

International travelers must declare amounts that exceed $10,000 in cash (U.S. or foreign), traveler's checks, or money orders. Meat products, fruits, and vegetables are prohibited due to health and safety regulations.

Drivers entering California stop at **Agricultural Inspection Stations.** They don't need to present a passport, visa, or even a driver's license, but should be prepared to present fruits and vegetables, even those purchased within neighboring states just over the border. If you've got produce, it could be infected by a known problem pest or disease; expect it to be confiscated on the spot.

International Drivers Licenses

International visitors need to secure an **International Driving Permit** from their home country before coming to the United States. They should also bring the government-issued driving permit from their home country. They are also expected to be familiar with the driving regulations of the states they will visit. More information is available online at www.usa.gov/Topics/Motor-Vehicles.shtml.

Travel Tips

Wi-Fi is available at lodging facilities, libraries, and visitors centers along Route 66. Cell phone service is widely available with the exception of remote areas in northern New Mexico and the Mojave Desert in California.

Budget

Traveling on Route 66 can be done on a budget, but if you have the means, there are many opportunities to splurge. The moderate traveler should plan $125 per night for lodging, and about $40 per day for modest meals. Fuel costs vary widely depending on your vehicle's mileage and the current prices. To save money, fill up your tank in large towns or cities, as prices in rural locations can be up to $1 more per gallon.

For folks on a budget, **Priceline**'s (www.priceline.com) "name your own price" option for discount hotels is a great deal. You may be able to book four- and three-star hotel rooms for the price of a budget motel. Priceline deals tend to be better in cities than small towns.

Accommodations that serve a continental breakfast, and dining at a restaurant only twice per day, can add up to a savings of at least $600 for a family of four on a two-week trip. Avoid larger museums or parks with high entrance

Goffs, California

fees; these places are not unique to Route 66, and the smaller, quirky museums generally charge less than $5 in entry fees. There are also loads of free things to do and see on Route 66, so if you can cover your gas, lodging, and food, you will have a wonderful time.

Time Zones

Route 66 passes through eight states and three time zones, so as you travel west, it is an hour earlier as you cross into each time zone. Illinois, Missouri, Kansas, Oklahoma, and Texas are in the central time zone. New Mexico and Arizona are in the mountain time zone, but Arizona does not observe daylight saving time, except in the Navajo Nation. California is in the Pacific time zone.

Access for Travelers with Disabilities

The Americans with Disabilities Act (ADA), enacted in 1990, requires public places to provide facilities to

accommodate disabled patrons. Most museums and restaurants are wheelchair accessible, but vintage mom-and-pop motels located in older properties were grandfathered and did not have to abide by the new laws. Chain motels generally have rooms with larger doors for wheelchair access, but it's best to call ahead and reserve the room you need.

Before you pay entrance fees to National Parks, U.S. citizens with permanent disabilities are eligible for a lifetime **Access Pass** (www.store.usgs.gov/pass/access.html) with free entry to 2,000 National Parks. You can obtain an Access Pass in person at any federal recreation site or by submitting a completed application (www.nps.gov/findapark/passes.htm, $10 processing fee may apply) by mail. The pass does not provide benefits for special recreation permits or concessionaire fees. Passes generally take 3-5 days to process and about one week to ship.

Traveling with Children

Route 66 is the perfect family trip. There are plenty of attractions with animals, like Bearizona Wildlife Park in Williams, Arizona, and the Rattlesnake Museum in Albuquerque. Interactive museums like the City Museum in St. Louis will entertain parents and kids alike. Since there are plenty of diners on the road, kids' meals are available on most menus, and motels equipped with pools are not hard to find. One of the best things about Route 66 is that each day there are so many different topographies and cultures to see. You'll drive through though farmland, city streets, natural wonders, urban neighborhoods, and rural housing, offering a surplus of subjects to discuss with your kids. Route 66 also has throngs of international tourists, which exposes kids to people and things they may never see in their hometowns.

Gay and Lesbian Travelers

Gay and lesbian travelers can feel comfortable in major cities along Route 66, such as Chicago, Flagstaff, and Los Angeles (surprisingly, Amarillo, Texas, has at least four gay bars). However, when driving through smaller rural towns, travelers should use well-honed safety instincts. Generally, the Route 66 folks are friendly, so the people you meet are likely to be welcoming.

Resources

Suggested Reading

No other road has captured the imagination and the essence of the American Dream. Route 66 inspired John Steinbeck's *The Grapes of Wrath,* Pixar's film *Cars,* and even the video game Grand Theft Auto.

Hinckley, Jim. *The Illustrated Route 66 Historical Atlas.* Minneapolis, MN: Voyager Press, 2014. A state-by-state illustrated guide exploring the history of Route 66.

Jakle, John A. and Keith A Sculle. *The Gas Station in America,* Baltimore, MD: The Johns Hopkins University Press, 1994. A comprehensive history of the gas station and its role in American roadside culture.

Krim, Arthur. *Route 66: Iconography of the American Highway.* George F Thompson Publishing, 2014. A meticulously researched cultural geography of the symbolism and history of Route 66.

Magnum, Richard K. and Sherry G. Mangum. *Route 66 Across Arizona: A Comprehensive Two-Way Guide for Touring Route 66.* Flagstaff, AZ: Hexagon Press, Inc., 2001. Illustrations, color maps, photos,

hikes, bike rides and tours along Route 66 in Arizona.

Mahar-Keplinger, Lisa. *American Signs: Form and Meaning on Route. 66.* The Monacelli Press, 2002. American Signs examines the history and iconography of roadside signage, offering a different way to see and think about Route 66.

Olsen, Russell A. *The Complete Route 66 Lost & Found,* Saint Paul, MN: MBI Publishing Company, 2008. Filled with 150 side-by-side photos of modern day and mid-century-era filling stations, street scenes, motor courts, cafes and truck stops on Route 66.

Steinbeck, John. *The Grapes of Wrath: 50th Anniversary Edition.* New York, NY: Viking, 1989. This seminal Pulitzer Prize-winning novel traces the Joad family fleeing the Dust Bowl during the Great Depression. Steinbeck was the first to call Route 66 the "Mother Road."

Taylor, Candacy A. *Counter Culture: The American Coffee Shop Waitress,* Ithaca, NY: Cornell University Press, 2009. This book documents a subculture of older women who have been waitressing their entire lives in roadside diners, some of which are on Route 66.

Wallis, Michael, *Route 66 The Mother Road 75th Anniversary Edition.* New York, NY: St. Martin's Griffin, 2001. A richly illustrated cultural history book, filled with compelling stories from people who have lived and worked on the Mother Road.

Internet Resources
National Historic Route 66 Federation
www.national66.org
A non-profit organization dedicated to documenting the cultural heritage, preserving the landmarks and revitalizing the economy along Route 66.

Route 66 Playlist

Route 66 is the only highway with its own soundtrack. Nat King Cole was the first to record the iconic theme song in 1946; it went on to become a hit on the both the R&B and pop charts. Since then, "(Get Your Kicks) Route 66" has been covered by more than 50 musicians—everyone from Aerosmith to Yo La Tengo.

Acoustix
Areosmith
Asleep at the Wheel
Chuck Berry
Patrick Burns
The Cheetah Girls
Natalie Cole
Chris Connor
The Cramps
The Lamont Cranston Band
Bing Crosby & the Andrew Sisters
The Dead Boys
Depeche Mode
The Doughboys
Dr. Feelgood
E-Type Jazz
Earth Quake
Four Freshman
Guitar Wolf
Half Japanese
Harry James
Wayne Hancock

Hot Zex
Jason & the Scorchers
Juggernaut Jug Band
The Jolt
The Legendary Tiger Man
Jerry Lee Lewis
George Maharis
The Manhattan Transfer
John Mayer
Eddie Meduza
The Outlaws
Brad Paisley
Pappo (Spanish version)
The Wes Paul Band
Tom Petty and the Heartbreakers
John Pizzarelli
Jane Powell
Louis Prima
The Replacements
Rockfour
The Rolling Stones
Scatman John
The Brian Setzer Orchestra
Nancy Sinatra
The Strypes
Hans Teeuwen
Them featuring Van Morrison
U.K Subs
Buckwheat Zydeco
Yo La Tengo

National Park Service
www.nps.gov/nr/travel/route66/index.html
A comprehensive website with essays detailed histories about sights along Route 66, including many that are listed on the National Historic Register.

National Park Service Route 66 Corridor Preservation Program
http://ncptt.nps.gov/rt66
This site features information about the preservation efforts taking place on Route 66 and the cost-share grants that are keeping historic businesses alive.

Illinois
www.illinoisroute66.org
A mile-by-mile exploration of Route 66 in Illinois.

Missouri
www.missouri66.org
A state resource featuring Route 66-related activities happening in Missouri.

Oklahoma
www.travelok.com/route_66
An excellent tourism guide on the cultural heritage of Oklahoma and Route 66.

New Mexico
www.rt66nm.org
A site dedicated to the promotion, preservation and education of Route 66 in New Mexico.

Arizona
ww.azrt66.com
A site outlining activities, sites and the history along 26 Route 66 counties in Arizona.

California
www.route66ca.org
A non-profit, volunteer run organization dedicated to preserving and promoting Route 66 including brief histories of the desert towns and communities along Route 66.

INDEX

IJ

K

L

LIST OF MAPS

MAP SYMBOLS

▬▬▬	Expressway	○	City/Town	✈	Airport	⛳	Golf Course
▬▬▬	Primary Road	◉	State Capital	✕	Airfield	🅿	Parking Area
▬▬▬	Secondary Road	⊛	National Capital	▲	Mountain	▰	Archaeological Site
-------	Unpaved Road	★	Point of Interest	✛	Unique Natural Feature	⛪	Church
——	Feature Trail	•	Accommodation			⛽	Gas Station
- - - -	Other Trail	▾	Restaurant/Bar	🌫	Waterfall		Glacier
··········	Ferry	■	Other Location	⚑	Park		Mangrove
▭▭▭	Pedestrian Walkway			ⓣ	Trailhead		Reef
▥▥▥	Stairs	▲	Campground	🎿	Skiing Area		Swamp

CONVERSION TABLES

$°C = (°F - 32) / 1.8$
$°F = (°C \times 1.8) + 32$
1 inch = 2.54 centimeters (cm)
1 foot = 0.304 meters (m)
1 yard = 0.914 meters
1 mile = 1.6093 kilometers (km)
1 km = 0.6214 miles
1 fathom = 1.8288 m
1 chain = 20.1168 m
1 furlong = 201.168 m
1 acre = 0.4047 hectares
1 sq km = 100 hectares
1 sq mile = 2.59 square km
1 ounce = 28.35 grams
1 pound = 0.4536 kilograms
1 short ton = 0.90718 metric ton
1 short ton = 2,000 pounds
1 long ton = 1.016 metric tons
1 long ton = 2,240 pounds
1 metric ton = 1,000 kilograms
1 quart = 0.94635 liters
1 US gallon = 3.7854 liters
1 Imperial gallon = 4.5459 liters
1 nautical mile = 1.852 km

°FAHRENHEIT	°CELSIUS	
230	110	
220		
210	100	WATER BOILS
200		
190	90	
180	80	
170		
160	70	
150		
140	60	
130		
120	50	
110		
100	40	
90	30	
80		
70	20	
60		
50	10	
40		
30	0	WATER FREEZES
20		
10	-10	
0		
-10	-20	
-20		
-30	-30	
-40	-40	

MOON ROUTE 66 ROAD TRIP
Avalon Travel
An imprint of Perseus Books
A Hachette Books Group company
1700 Fourth Street
Berkeley, CA 94710, USA
www.moon.com

Editor: Sabrina Young
Series Manager: Leah Gordon
Copy Editors: Ashley Benning, Christopher Church, Kristie Reilly
Production and Graphics Coordinator: Lucie Ericksen
Cover Design: Faceout Studios, Charles Brock
Moon Logo: Tim McGrath
Map Editor: Mike Morgenfeld
Cartographers: Brain Shotwell and Karin Dahl
Indexer: Rachel Kuhn

ISBN-13: 978-1-63121-071-6
ISSN: 2380-9620

Printing History
1st Edition — May 2016
5 4 3 2